WORLDCOMP'13
July 22-25, 2013
Las Vegas Nevada, USA
www.world-academy-of-science.org

PROCEEDINGS OF THE 2013 INTERNATIONAL CONFERENCE ON MODELING, SIMULATION & VISUALIZATION METHODS

MSV 2013

Editors

Hamid R. Arabnia
Leonidas Deligiannidis

Associate Editors

George Jandieri
Ashu M. G. Solo
Fernando G. Tinetti

FIREWALL MEDIA
(An Imprint of Laxmi Publications Pvt. Ltd.)
An ISO 9001:2008 Company

BENGALURU • CHENNAI • COCHIN • GUWAHATI • HYDERABAD
JALANDHAR • KOLKATA • LUCKNOW • MUMBAI • RANCHI • NEW DELHI
BOSTON (USA) • ACCRA (GHANA) • NAIROBI (KENYA)

This volume contains papers presented at The 2013 International Conference on Modeling, Simulation & Visualization Methods (MSV'13). Their inclusion in this publication does not necessarily constitute endorsements by editors or by the publisher.

Branches

Bengaluru	080-26 75 69 30	
Chennai	044-24 34 47 26,	24 35 95 07
Cochin	0484-237 70 04,	405 13 03
Guwahati	0361-254 36 69,	251 38 81
Hyderabad	040-27 55 53 83,	27 55 53 93
Jalandhar	0181-222 12 72	
Kolkata	033-22 27 43 84	
Lucknow	0522-220 99 16	
Mumbai	022-24 91 54 15,	24 92 78 69
Ranchi	0651-220 44 64	

Published in India by

FIREWALL MEDIA
(An Imprint of Laxmi Publications Pvt. Ltd.)

An ISO 9001:2008 Company
113, GOLDEN HOUSE, DARYAGANJ,
NEW DELHI - 110002, INDIA
Telephone : 91-11-4353 2500, 4353 2501
Fax : 91-11-2325 2572, 4353 2528
www.laxmipublications.com info@laxmipublications.com

C—

Printed at Repro Knowledgecast Limited, Thane

Foreword

It gives us great pleasure to introduce this collection of papers to be presented at the 2013 International Conference on Modeling, Simulation and Visualization Methods (MSV'13), July 22 through 25, 2013, at The New Tropicana Hotel, Las Vegas, USA.

An important mission of the World Congress in Computer Science, Computer Engineering, and Applied Computing (a federated congress to which this conference is affiliated with) includes *"Providing a unique platform for a diverse community of constituents composed of scholars, researchers, developers, educators, and practitioners. The Congress makes concerted effort to reach out to participants affiliated with diverse entities (such as: universities, institutions, corporations, government agencies, and research centers/labs) from all over the world. The congress also attempts to connect participants from institutions that have* ***teaching*** *as their main mission with those who are affiliated with institutions that have* ***research*** *as their main mission. The congress uses a quota system to achieve its institution and geography diversity objectives."* By any definition of diversity, this congress is among the most diverse scientific meeting in USA. We are proud to report that this federated congress has authors and participants from 82 different nations representing variety of personal and scientific experiences that arise from differences in culture and values. As can be seen (see below), the program committee of this conference as well as the program committee of all other tracks of the federated congress are as diverse as its authors and participants.

The program committee would like to thank all those who submitted papers for consideration. About 40% of the submissions were from outside the United States. Each submitted paper was peer-reviewed by two experts in the field for originality, significance, clarity, impact, and soundness. In cases of contradictory recommendations, a member of the conference program committee was charged to make the final decision; often, this involved seeking help from additional referees. In addition, papers whose authors included a member of the conference program committee were evaluated using the double-blinded review process. One exception to the above evaluation process was for papers that were submitted directly to chairs/organizers of pre-approved sessions/workshops; in these cases, the chairs/organizers were responsible for the evaluation of such submissions. The overall paper acceptance rate for regular papers was 28%; 9% of the remaining papers were accepted as poster papers (at the time of this writing, we had not yet received the acceptance rate for a few individual tracks.)

We are very grateful to the many colleagues who offered their services in organizing the conference. In particular, we would like to thank the members of the Program Committee of MSV'13, members of the congress Steering Committee, and members of the committees of federated congress tracks that have topics within the scope of MSV. Many individuals listed below, will be requested after the conference to provide their expertise and services for selecting papers for publication (extended versions) in journal special issues as well as for publication in a set of research books (to be prepared for publishers including: Springer, Elsevier, BMC, and others).

- *Dr. Selim Aissi (World Congress Steering Committee); formerly, Chief Strategist - Security, Intel Corp., USA; Senior Business Leader & Head of Global Enterprise Security Architecture, Visa Corporation, USA*
- *Prof. Babak Akhgar (World Congress Steering Committee); Fellow of the British Computer Society, CITP; Professor of Informatics; Co-Director of CENTRIC (Centre of Excellence in Terrorism, Resilience, Intelligence & organised Crime research), Sheffield Hallam University, Sheffield, UK*
- *Prof. Nizar Al-Holou (World Congress Steering Committee); Professor and Chair, ECE Department; Vice Chair, IEEE/SEM-Computer Chapter; University of Detroit Mercy, Detroit, Michigan, USA*
- *Prof. Hamid R. Arabnia (World Congress Steering Committee); Professor, Computer Science; Editor-in-Chief, The Journal of Supercomputing (Springer); Elected Fellow, Int'l Society of Intelligent Biological Medicine (ISIBM); The University of Georgia, Department of Computer Science, USA*
- *Peyman Arebi; Department of Computer Engineering, Technical and Vocational University, Bushehr, Iran*
- *Prof. Ezendu Ariwa (Publicity Vice-Chair); Chair, IEEE Consumer Electronics Chapter, UK&RI; Visiting Professor, Gulf University, Bahrain and University of Lagos and Kano State Polytechnic, Nigeria*
- *Prof. Juan Jose Martinez Castillo; Director of The Acantelys Research Group and Coordinator of the Computer Engineering Department, Universidad Gran Mariscal de Ayacucho, Venezuela*

- *Prof. Kevin Daimi (World Congress Steering Committee); Director, Computer Science and Software Engineering Programs; Department of Mathematics, Computer Science and Software Engineering; University of Detroit Mercy, Detroit, Michigan, USA*
- *Prof. Leonidas Deligiannidis; Professor, Computer Science, Wentworth Institute of Technology, MA, USA*
- *Prof. George A. Gravvanis; Democritus University of Thrace, Greece*
- *Prof. George Jandieri (World Congress Steering Committee); Georgian Technical University, Tbilisi, Georgia; Chief Scientist, The Institute of Cybernetics, Georgian Academy of Science, Georgia; Editorial Board Member: International Journal of Microwaves and Optical Technology, Georgia*
- *Prof. Dong Hwa Kim; Hanbat National University, Korea; Visiting Professor, Budapest University of Technology and Economic, Hungary; International Einstein awardee for Scientific achievement (2010)*
- *Prof. Dattatraya V. Kodavade (World Congress Steering Committee); Head of Computer Science and Engineering, D.K.T.E Society's Textile & Engineering Institute, Ichalkaranji, Maharashtra State, India*
- *Dr. Jong Kwan (Jake) Lee; Bowling Green State University, Ohio, USA*
- *Prof. Kun Chang Lee (World Congress Steering Committee); Professor of MIS and WCU Professor of Creativity Science, Business School and Department of Interaction Science, Sungkyunkwan University, Korea*
- *Dr. Bala Krishna Maddali (GCA); University School of IT, GGS Indraprastha University, New Delhi, India*
- *Muhammad Naufal Bin Mansor; University Malaysia Perlis, Kangar, Perlis, Malaysia*
- *Prof. George Markowsky (World Congress Steering Committee); Professor and Associate Director, School of Computing and Information Science; Chair International Advisory Board of IEEE IDAACS; Director 2013 Northeast Collegiate Cyber Defense Competition; Cooperating Professor Math and Statistics Department UMaine and School of Policy & International Affairs UMaine; University of Maine, Orono, Maine, USA*
- *Dr. Sara Moein; Editorial Board, International Journal of Science and Technology; Faculty of Engineering, MultiMedia University, Malaysia*
- *Dr. Ali Mostafaeipour; Industrial Engineering Department, Yazd University, Iran*
- *Dr. Saurabh Mukherjee; Banasthali University, Banasthali, Rajasthan, India*
- *Prof. Prashant R. Nair (FECS); Vice-Chairman, Information Technology & Accreditation; Faculty, AMRITA-TIFAC Centre of Excellence in Cyber Security; Amrita University, India*
- *Dr. Asoke Nath (EEE + FCS), St. Xavier's College, India*
- *Prof. G. N. Pandey (World Congress Steering Committee); Vice-Chancellor, Arunachal University of Studies, Arunachal Pradesh, India; Adjunct Professor, Indian Institute of Information Technology, Allahabad, India*
- *Prof. James J. (Jong Hyuk) Park (World Congress Steering Committee); Professor of Computer Science and Engineering, Seoul National University of Science and Technology (SeoulTech), Korea; President, KITCS; President, FTRA; Editor-in-Chiefs: HCIS, JoC and IJITCC Journals*
- *Prof. R. Ponalagusamy; National Institute of Technology, Tiruchirappalli, India*
- *Prof. Junfeng Qu; Clayton State University, Morrow, USA*
- *Prof. B. V. A. N. S. S. Prabhakar Rao (ICAI + SERP); VIT University, Chennai Campus, India*
- *Dr. Gerald Schaefer (Session Chair, IPCV); Loughborough University, United Kingdom*
- *Dr. Liang Shi; Senior Researcher, McAfee, USA*
- *Dr. Zhefu Shi; Microsoft Corporation, Redmond, Washington, USA*
- *Dr. Kok Swee Sim; Jalan Ayer Keroh Lama, Melaka, Malaysia*
- *Ashu M. G. Solo, (Publicity Chair); Fellow of British Computer Society, Principal/R&D Engineer, Maverick Technologies America Inc., USA*
- *Prof. Fernando G. Tinetti (World Congress Steering Committee); School of Computer Science, Universidad Nacional de La Plata, La Plata, Argentina; Co-editor, Journal of CS and Technology (JCS&T)*
- *Dr. Predrag Tosic (World Congress Steering Committee); Microsoft, Washington, USA*
- *Dr. Vinay Vaidya (IPCV); CTO and Vice President, Center for Research in EST, KPIT Cummins Infosystems Limited, India*
- *Prof. Vladimir Volkov (World Congress Steering Committee); The Bonch-Bruevich State University of Telecommunications, Saint-Petersburg, Russia*
- *Prof. Patrick Wang; Fellow of IAPR, ISIBM, WASE; Zijiang Chair Professor, ECNU, Shanghai and NTUST, Taipei, Taiwan; Founding President and CEO, Wang Teknowlogy Lab.; MIT Research Consultant; Harvard University, Adj. Faculty, USA; Northeastern University, Boston, MA, USA*
- *Dr. Wei Wei (GCA + ICOMP); Xi'an University of Technology, Xi'an, P. R. China*
- *Prof. Jane You; The Hong Kong Polytechnic University, Hong Kong*

As Sponsors-at-large, partners, and/or organizers each of the followings (separated by semicolons) provided help for at least one track of the World Congress: Aldebaran Robotics Inc., USA (http://www.aldebaran-robotics.com); Altera Corporation, USA (http://www.altera.com/); Computer

Science Research, Education, and Applications Press (CSREA); Impulse Accelerated Technologies, Inc., USA (http://www.impulseaccelerated.com/); NVIDIA Corporation, USA (http://www.nvidia.com/object/about-nvidia.html); Parallella Community, Supercomputing for Everyone, USA (http://forums.parallella.org/); Pico Computing, Inc., USA (http://picocomputing.com/); SemiWiki.com, The Semiconductor Wiki Project, USA (http://www.semiwiki.com/); Solarflare Communications, Inc., USA (http://www.solarflare.com/); Stream Computing, Performance Engineers, The Netherlands (http://streamcomputing.eu/); Taylor & Francis, UK (http://www.taylorandfrancis.com/); US Chapter of World Academy of Science (http://www.world-academy-of-science.org/) ; and WEBestSOL & Webest Solutions Ltd, UK (http://webestsol.com/). In addition, a number of university faculty members and their staff (names appear on the cover of the set of proceedings), several publishers of computer science and computer engineering books and journals, chapters and/or task forces of computer science associations/organizations from 5 countries, and developers of high-performance machines and systems provided significant help in organizing the conference as well as providing some resources. We are grateful to them all.

We express our gratitude to keynote, invited, and individual conference/tracks and tutorial speakers - the list of speakers appears on the conference web site. We would also like to thank the followings: UCMSS (Universal Conference Management Systems & Support, California, USA) for managing all aspects of the conference; Dr. Tim Field of APC for managing the printing of the proceedings; and the staff of the New Tropicana Hotel in Las Vegas for the professional service they provided. Last but not least, we would like to thank the Co-Editors and Associate Co-Editors of MSV'13: Prof. Hamid R. Arabnia, Prof. Leonidas Deligiannidis, Prof. George Jandieri, Ashu M. G. Solo, and Prof. Fernando G. Tinetti.

We present the proceedings of MSV'13.

Steering Committee, 2013
http://www.world-academy-of-science.org/

Contents

SESSION: SIMULATION AND NUMERICAL METHODS

SESSION: VISUALIZATION, GRAPHICAL USER INTERFACE, TOOLS AND TECHNIQUES

SESSION: MODELING

SESSION: VISUALIZATION, HCI, FUZZY LOGIC, MANET, AND APPLICATIONS

SESSION

SIMULATION AND NUMERICAL METHODS

Chair(s)

TBA

Anti-Symmetry and Logic Simulation

Peter M. Maurer
Dept. of Computer Science
Baylor University
Waco, Texas 76798-7356

Abstract – Like ordinary symmetries, anti-symmetries are defined by relations between function cofactors. For ordinary symmetries, two cofactors must be equal, for anti-symmetries two cofactors must be complements of one another. This paper shows that anti-symmetries can be used to improve simulation performance in the same manner as ordinary symmetries. Detailed detection, clustering and simulation algorithms are given along with a set of experimental results to demonstrate the effectiveness of the algorithms. These results show that anti-symmetries can be just as effective as ordinary symmetries in enhancing simulation performance. In fact, in some cases, anti-symmetries give better performance than ordinary symmetries.

1 Introduction

Detecting function symmetries has proven to be useful in many areas of electronic design automation [1-7]. Many symmetry detection algorithms have been created, and permutations are the basis of virtually all of these algorithms [8-10].

The most important types of symmetry are *total symmetry* and *partial symmetry*. The inputs of a totally symmetric function can be rearranged arbitrarily, while a partially symmetric function has subsets of inputs that can be rearranged arbitrarily. Examples of totally symmetric and partially symmetric functions are $abcd$ and $abc+d$ (where − represents OR and multiplication represents AND). There are many other types of permutation-based symmetries (see [9, 11]) which are often lumped together and called *weak symmetries*, But in this paper we will be concerned only with total and partial symmetry.

Total and partial symmetries are common in the circuits we encounter in practice, and can be detected by examining pairs of variables. Two variables constitute a *symmetric variable pair* if they can be exchanged without altering the output of the function. Symmetric variable pairs are transitive. Thus, if (a,b) and (b,c) are symmetric variable pairs, then so is (a,c). A function is totally symmetric if and only if every pair of input variables is a symmetric variable pair. A function is partially symmetric in the variables $x_1,\ldots,x_k$ if (x_i,x_j) is a symmetric variable pair for all i and j, $1 \le i < j \le k$.

The symmetric variable pairs of a function f can be detected using the cofactors of f. If f is an *n*-input Boolean function with input variables $x_1,\ldots,x_n$. The cofactors of f with respect to x_1 are the functions $f_{0x\ldots x}$ and $f_{1x\ldots x}$, which are computed by setting the variable x_1 to 0 and then to 1. The exact procedure for computing a cofactor depends on the representation of the function. Cofactors can be computed with respect to a single variable or with respect to a set of variables. When there is no opportunity for confusion, we omit the x's and simply place the 1's and 0's in the subscripts. In symmetry detection, it is common to compute cofactors with respect to pairs of variables. There are four such cofactors f_{00}, f_{01}, f_{10}, and f_{11}. Different relations between these cofactors can be used to define different types of symmetry [12, 13].

One of the latest developments in symmetry detection is matrix-based symmetry [7]. All permutations can be specified as non-singular matrices, but not all non-singular matrices can be specified as permutations. Thus matrix-based symmetry is an extension of permutation-based symmetry. Conjugate symmetry is one form of matrix-based symmetry, some forms of which can be detected using cofactor-relations.

The algorithms discussed in this paper are based on cofactor relations, the two most important of which are the classical relations and the anti-relations [14].

2 Classical Symmetry

The classical relations are defined in terms of the two-variable cofactors of a function, f_{00}, f_{01}, f_{10}, and f_{11}. There are six possible relations, each of which represents a certain type of symmetry. These relations are given in Figure 1, along with their respective symmetry types.

In a sense, the only relation that truly represents symmetry is $f_{01}=f_{10}$, ordinary symmetry. The other relations represent variable pairs that are *not* symmetric, but can be "corrected" to become symmetric. Our algorithm tests for all six relations to detect symmetric variable pairs. When a symmetric variable pair is detected, it is "corrected," if necessary, and combined into a single clustered variable. In fact, we test only for ordinary symmetry. The other five relations are detected by transforming the state space of the function, and then testing for ordinary symmetry. (See Section 4 for details on the state space transformations.) Our classical symmetry algorithms are described in [7], but for completeness, we repeat some of the details here.

Relation	Symmetry Type
$f_{01}=f_{10}$	Ordinary
$f_{00}=f_{11}$	Multi-Phase
$f_{01}=f_{11}$	Single-Variable A
$f_{10}=f_{11}$	Single-Variable B
$f_{10}=f_{00}$	Multi-Phase Single-Variable A
$f_{01}=f_{00}$	Multi-Phase Single-Variable B

Figure 1. Cofactor Relations.

The multi-phase relation, $f_{00}=f_{11}$, indicates that the function is symmetric, but one variable is inverted with respect to the other. It is possible to treat the multi-phase relation as ordinary symmetry after performing a state-space transformation and adding a NOT gate to one of the inputs.

The single-variable relations represent two types of conjugate symmetry. Not all conjugate symmetries manifest themselves as single-variable symmetries, but the mechanisms used to detect single-variable symmetries can be extended to detect most conjugate symmetries. As with multi-phase symmetries, it is possible to treat conjugate symmetries as if they were ordinary symmetries using a state-space transformation and a collection of XOR gates on the function inputs. The XOR gates compute a matrix transformation of the inputs prior to passing the inputs into the function. The input transformation is similar to the first layer of logic in some forms of three-level minimization [16, 17].

The multi-phase single-variable relations represent the combination of conjugate symmetry and multi-phase symmetry. These types of symmetry can be handled by combining the techniques for multi-phase and conjugate symmetry.

The result of symmetry detection is a multi-dimensional state machine which represents the state of a Boolean function. Each dimension of the state machine represents a cluster of symmetric variables. It is convenient to think of the multi-dimensional machine as an extended type of hypercube with several states along each dimension. For a simple, non-clustered input variable, the dimension will have two states representing input values of zero and one. For a cluster of n variables, the dimension will have $n+1$ states with the state representing the number of one-inputs in the cluster of n variables. Figure 2 illustrates a function with a simple variable A, and a clustered variable containing three simple variables, B, C, and D.

Another way to view the n-dimensions of a gate state-machine is as a collection of n input-ports. For ordinary and multi-phase symmetries, there is a one-to one mapping between input ports and clusters of function inputs. For conjugate symmetry, an event on an input can generate events on many different ports. This technique is used to compute the XOR functions on the inputs. We will explain this further in Section 4.

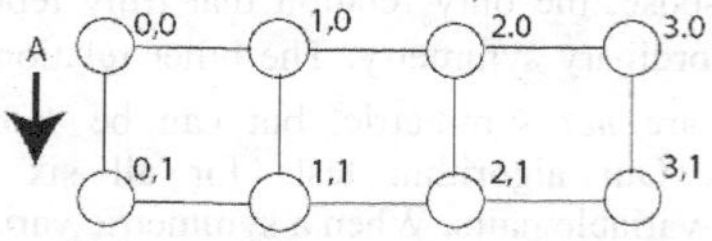

Figure 2. A Gate State-Machine.

3 Anti-Symmetry

Anti-symmetry is known by several other names, including *skew symmetry* and *negative symmetry*. Anti-symmetry is based on the observation that relations of the form $f_{01} = f_{10}$ can be written $f_{01} \oplus f_{10} = \overline{0}$, where $\oplus$ represents the XOR operation and $\overline{0}$ represents the constant zero function. If we reformulate our six relations and replace the constant zero with the constant one function, $\overline{1}$, we obtain the six anti-symmetry relations given in Figure 3. Note that if $f_{01} \oplus f_{10} = \overline{1}$, then f_{01} and f_{10} are inverses of one another.

As with multi-phase and conjugate symmetries, anti-symmetries can be transformed into ordinary symmetries using state-space transformations. These transformations are easier to visualize if we place the four cofactors f_{00}, f_{01}, f_{10} and f_{11} into a hyper-linear structure as shown in Figure 4. To convert the anti-symmetry into an ordinary symmetry, we invert one of the grayed cofactors.

There are several different state-space transformations that will transform an anti-symmetry into an ordinary symmetry, each one of which requires a different corrective action in the final function. The naïve transformation shown in Figure 4 results in a complex corrective action. Let us suppose that an ordinary anti-symmetry is found between the variables are a and b and that f_{01} has been complemented to transform the symmetry into a classical symmetry. This means that when the transformed function is evaluated, the output will be inverted whenever $a=0$ and $b=1$. The corrective function shown in Figure 5 is applied during the simulation process to produce the correct function output.

Relation	Anti-Symmetry Type
$f_{01} \oplus f_{10} = \overline{1}$	Ordinary
$f_{00} \oplus f_{11} = \overline{1}$	Multi-Phase
$f_{01} \oplus f_{11} = \overline{1}$	Single-Variable A
$f_{10} \oplus f_{11} = \overline{1}$	Single-Variable B
$f_{10} \oplus f_{00} = \overline{1}$	Multi-Phase Single-Variable A
$f_{01} \oplus f_{00} = \overline{1}$	Multi-Phase Single-Variable B

Figure 3. The Anti-Symmetry Relations.

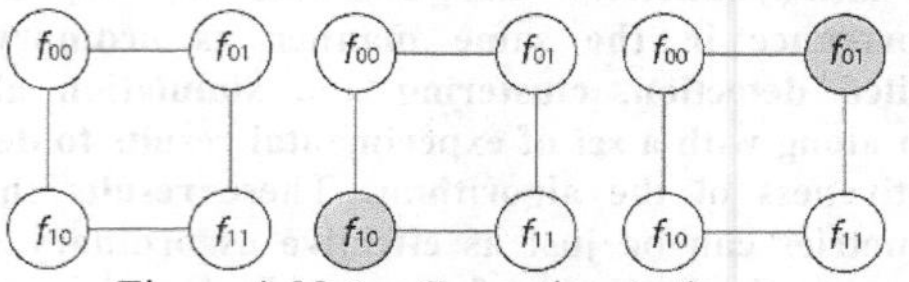

Figure 4. Naïve Corrective Actions.

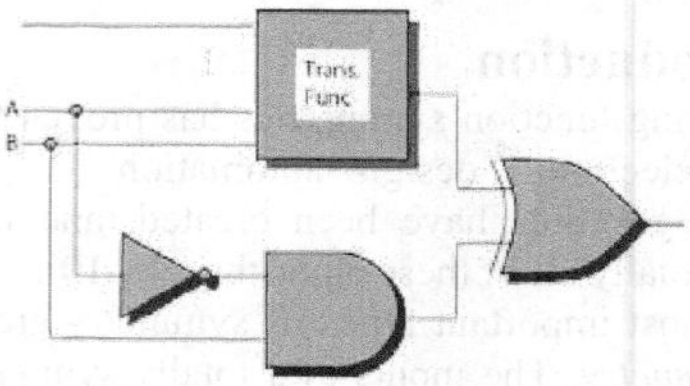

Figure 5. A Naïve Corrective Function.

To simplify the corrective procedure, we use an over-kill method when transforming the function. Instead of just complementing f_{01} (or f_{10}) we also complement f_{11}, as shown in Figure 6. This means that the output of the transformed function is inverted whenever $b=1$ (or $a=1$). This eliminates the AND and NOT gates, as shown in Figure 7. Regardless of how many anti-symmetric variable pairs are detected for a function, only a single XOR gate is required on the output. This XOR gate must have one input for each detected anti-symmetric pair. What is more, in Section 5 we will show how to get the XOR function for free.

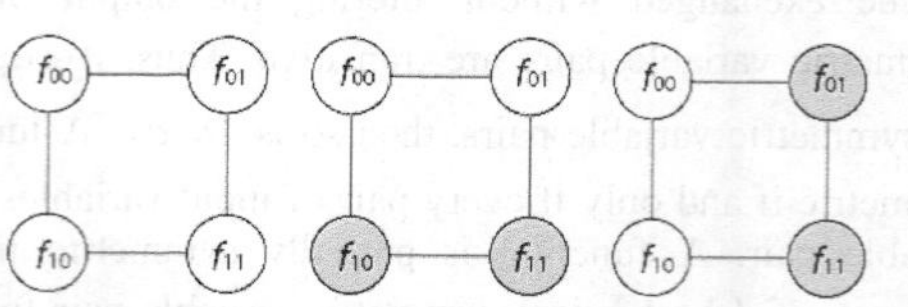

Figure 6. Sophisticated Corrective Actions.

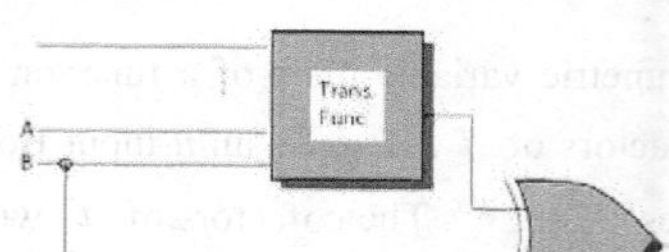

Figure 7. A Simple Corrective Function.

4 Symmetry Detection

There are several problems in determining the inputs of the corrective XOR gate. When combining anti-symmetry with conjugate symmetry, adding inputs to the correcting XOR becomes more complicated. We need to determine what should happen when a variable is added twice to the correcting XOR and we need to determine how to detect anti-symmetry with respect to clustered variables.

In hyperlinear structures ordinary symmetries can be detected by examining cofactors along the anti-diagonals. For there to be an ordinary symmetry in Figure 2, node (1,0) must equal (0,1), (2,0) must equal (1,1) and (3,0) must equal (2,1). If there are more than two dimensions, the diagonal tests must be repeated for each of the planes containing the two variables. There is no required relationship between separate diagonals or between separate planes.

Multi-phase symmetry can be detected by reversing the structure along one dimension and then testing for ordinary symmetry. Conjugate symmetry can be detected by reversing the odd numbered rows or the odd numbered columns, and then testing for ordinary symmetry. Combined multi-phase and conjugate symmetry is detected by reversing the even numbered rows and columns. The reversals can be done without altering the structure by indexing rows, columns, or the entire dimension in reverse order.

Consider the left-most state machine of Figure 8. This state machine represents a 4-input function with two clustered variables. Assume that the inputs to the function are a, b, c, and d. and have been clustered into two pairs (a,b) and (c,d). The horizontal dimension of the state machine represents the state of the pair (a,b), while the vertical dimension represents the state of the pair (c,d).

To detect symmetries between the clustered variables (a,b) and (c,d) it is necessary to examine the reverse diagonals. If the states with the same letter (L, F, and G) contain the same function, then the two clustered variables (a,b) and (c,d) are symmetric with one another.

When an anti-symmetry exists between any two variables in two different clustered pairs, then an anti-symmetry exists between every pair of variables in the two of clustered variables. This implies that a function must alternate with its complement along each back-diagonal. This condition is shown in the middle state-machine of Figure 8. (See [15] for more detail.)

To convert the anti-symmetry into an ordinary symmetry, we invert the functions in the odd-numbered rows or the odd-numbered columns, as shown in the third state machine of Figure 8, in which the center column is inverted. This column is where the XOR of the individual variables in the clustered variable takes the value 1. Thus to correct the inverted column of Figure 8, we must add the variables *a* and *b* to the corrective XOR gate as shown in Figure 9.

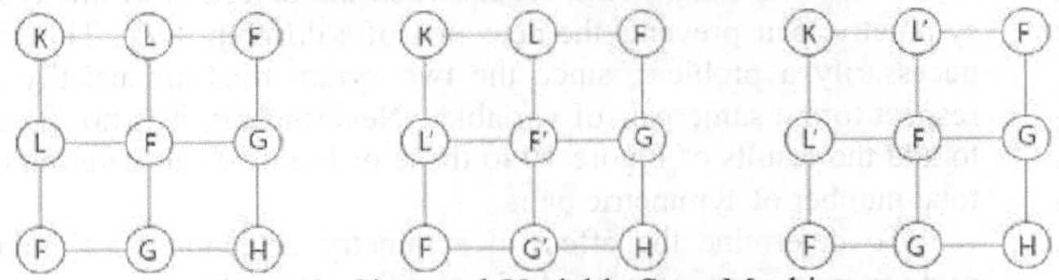

Figure 8. Clustered-Variable State Machine.

When the first anti-symmetry is detected, we add the XOR gate to the output of the function. We also create a list of the input variables that must be added to the inputs of the XOR gate. When new anti-symmetries are detected, new input variables are added to the list.

It is sometimes necessary to add the same input to the list twice. Since the two inputs are identical, the pair will have either the value (0,0) or the value (1,1). In both cases, the XOR of the two values is 0, which will not change the value computed from the other inputs, so both inputs can be removed. Thus, when we add an input to the list, we check to see whether it is currently on the list. If so, then we remove it instead of adding it.

When anti-symmetry is combined with conjugate symmetry we have an additional problem. The function has *n* inputs and the state-machine has *n* input ports, but with conjugate symmetry, the mapping between inputs and ports is not one-to-one. Several function inputs can be directed into a single port, and a single function input can be directed into several ports. Since symmetry detection is done with respect to ports, and correction is done with respect to function inputs, it is necessary to maintain a mapping between the two. The symmetry detection algorithm maintains a $n \times n$ matrix which shows the input-to-port mapping. When correction must be done with respect to a port, every function input directed into that port is added to (or removed from) the list of XOR inputs.

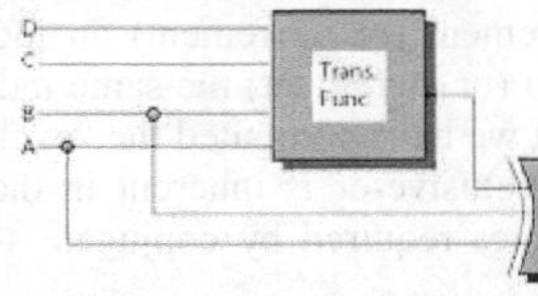

Figure 9. A Clustered Corrective Function.

To avoid conflicts with multi-phase and conjugate symmetry we take note of the reversing operations used during the detection process. To detect multi-phase symmetry it is necessary to reverse either all rows or all columns, but not both. If the rows have been reversed, then we transform the function by inverting the odd rows. If the columns have been reversed then we invert the odd columns. By placing the reversal and the inversion along the same dimension, we invert the same vertices that would have been inverted for an ordinary symmetry.

Conjugate symmetry is handled the same way. If the odd rows are reversed, we invert the odd rows. If the odd columns are reversed, we invert the odd columns. The algorithm for symmetry detection is given in section A1, Figure A1.

The algorithm for detecting symmetric variable pairs is virtually identical for ordinary symmetry and anti-symmetry. State-space transformations are used to combine ordinary and anti-symmetry with conjugate and multiphase symmetry. The basic algorithm is given in Section A1, Figure A2. This algorithm is executed twice, once for anti-symmetry and once for ordinary symmetry.

Checking the back diagonals is done by selecting each diagonal, and obtaining a comparator function from the first element of the diagonal. The comparator function is compared to the function contained in the other vertices along the diagonal. For anti-symmetry, two comparator functions are obtained. The first is taken from the first vertex of the diagonal and the second is obtained by inverting the first function. These functions are compared in alternating fashion along the diagonal. The two algorithms are given in Section A1, Figures A3 and A4.

5 Simulation Code

Detecting the various types of symmetry is beneficial because our simulator can operate faster with symmetric functions. It is possible for the corrective functions to negate the benefit of detecting symmetries, but as we will show in this section, we can either eliminate, or greatly reduce the cost of these functions.

Our simulator is a compiled simulator. Simulation detection is done during the code generation phase so that the cost of symmetry detection can be amortized over many simulations. When we report simulation times, these times do not include the cost of symmetry detection. Symmetry detection is extremely fast and takes less than a second for all but circuit c3540, which required 4 seconds.

At run time, each function is implemented as an *n*-dimensional state machine, with the current state represented as an *n*-element vector. A simple input can either increment or decrement a single index by 1. If $A = \{a_1, \ldots, a_k\}$ is a clustered variable, then each of the simple inputs, $a_1, \ldots, a_k$, operates on the same index. A separate index is used for each dimension.

The operations performed with respect to simple variables alternate with one another. If the current action increments the index, then the next action decrements it, and vice versa. It is not necessary to maintain the value of the input as long as we know which operation to perform next. The NOT gates required by multi-phase symmetry can be eliminated as long as the increment/decrement state of the input is initialized properly. Thus we get multi-phase symmetry for free.

Suppose we have two successive events for the same input. The first event will increment (or decrement) an index, and the second event will decrement (or increment) the same index, leaving the state unchanged. In effect we have computed the "exclusive or" of the two events. Since this exclusive-or is inherent in the state machine, we can get the XOR gates required by conjugate symmetry almost for free.

The state of each input port is recorded as 1 or -1, depending on whether the next operation is an increment or decrement. The data structure representing the event has an array of pointers to port states and port indices. When an event is executed, the port state is added to the port index and is then negated. The indices are used to determine whether the output of the function has changed. If the output changes then an event is queued. If an event is already queued for the output, the queued event is cancelled.

Surprisingly enough, we can get the anti-symmetry correction essentially for free. Since events are processed one at a time, we need only concentrate on the effect of one event. Referring back to Figure 7, suppose an event on input *B* causes the output of the transformed function to change. This change will propagate to the final XOR gate. The event on *B* will also propagate to the XOR gate, and the two events will cancel one another. Thus, if the output of the transformed function changes, no output event will be scheduled for the XOR gate.

Now suppose that an event occurs on input *B* , but the output of the transformed function *does not change*. Because the output does not change, no event propagates into the XOR gate from the function output. However, the event on *B* still propagates directly into the XOR gate, causing an event on the output of the XOR.

The correcting XOR gate causes the usual effect of an event to be reversed. Events propagate when the output of a function does not change, and no event propagates when the output changes. To take advantage of this, we generate two sets of run-time routines. The first set contains a comparison of the form "if Old = New then propagate" while the second contains a comparison of the form "if Old ≠ New then propagate". The first set is used for those inputs directed into the corrective XOR, the second is used for other inputs. These two routines are virtual functions that are called through function pointers determined at compile time. No run-time test is required to distinguish the two types of inputs. Effectively, the corrective XOR is obtained for free.

Figures A5 and A6 give the run-time code for processing an event. Our simulator does not require gate simulation code, so the algorithms of Figures A5 and A6 represent virtually the entire run-time code of our simulator.

6 Experimental Results

For our experimental results, we used the ISCAS 85 benchmarks [19]. Although these benchmarks are the *de facto* standard for determining simulation performance, they are specified at the gate level rather than at the Boolean function level. In this respect, they are not the most ideal vehicle for determining the effectiveness of our simulator, however they exhibit a wide variety of symmetries of all types.

The main problem with gate-level circuits is that one must attempt to reconstruct the Boolean functions from which the circuit was created. This is a decidedly non-trivial task. As an approximation to this we first identify the fanout-free networks in the circuit. These networks represent single-output functions, but are only an approximation of the original Boolean functions. About 50% of the gates in each circuit end up as isolated gates. We do not apply our algorithm to isolated gates, because their symmetries are already well-known.

A few circuits have very large fanout-free networks which represent several Boolean functions combined into a single network. To break these giant networks down into something resembling real Boolean functions we limit the number of inputs of a single network. We have experimented with different limits and have found that a limit of eight tends to expose the most symmetries. The limit is only approximate. It is possible for an individual partition to have more than eight inputs.

Our first experiment was to determine the number of anti-symmetries that appear in these circuits. Figure 10 gives the number of anti-symmetries found in each circuit when no other types of symmetries are detected. The numbers are counts of anti-symmetric variable pairs. These are further broken down into ordinary anti-symmetries (Ord.), multi-phase anti-symmetries (M.P.), conjugate anti-symmetries (Conj.), and combined multi-phase/conjugate symmetries (C.M.P). Every one of the ten benchmarks contains some anti-symmetries. The total ranges from a low of 10 for c432, to a high of 944 for c6288. This experiment verifies that anti-symmetries are indeed prevalent enough to be worth pursuing. If we examine the breakdown of sub-types, it is clear that it is necessary to combine anti-symmetry with multi-phase and conjugate symmetry. Note, for example, benchmark c499, which has no ordinary anti-symmetries, but has 104 symmetric pairs of other types.

To compare the prevalence of anti-symmetries with that of classical symmetries we determined the number of classical symmetries in each of the four categories. The results of this experiment are given in Figure 11. For most of the circuits there are significantly more classical symmetries than anti-symmetries, but there are two notable exceptions. Both c1355 and c6288, have more anti-symmetries than classical symmetries. Clearly we should detect anti-symmetries to handle these circuits effectively.

When combining the detection of anti-symmetries with that of classical symmetries, we encounter the phenomenon known as "symmetry masking." This occurs when the detection of one type of symmetric pair prevents the detection of a different type. This is not necessarily a problem, since the two symmetries are usually with respect to the same pair of variables. Nevertheless, it is not possible to add the results of Figure 10 to those of Figure 11 to determine the total number of symmetric pairs.

To determine the effect of symmetry detection on simulation performance, we compared four different simulations for each benchmark circuit. The four simulations are with no symmetry detection, with anti-symmetry alone, with classical symmetry alone, and with combined classical and anti-symmetry. Each simulation was performed on a dedicated 3.06 Ghz Xeon processor with 2GB of 233 Mhz memory. The results, which are shown in Figure 13, are in seconds of execution time for 500,000 input vectors.

The compile step, which includes all symmetry detection, took less than a second for each circuit, regardless of the types of symmetries detected. The run times given in Figure 13 do not include the time required to detect symmetry.

Ckt	Ord.	M.P.	Conj.	C.M.P.	Total
c432	10	0	0	0	10
c499	0	40	64	0	104
c880	5	12	18	2	37
c1355	104	104	0	0	208
c1908	14	2	99	0	115
c2670	14	11	72	2	99
c3540	173	11	52	9	245
c5315	29	46	139	22	236
c6288	480	464	0	0	944
c7552	53	126	310	44	533

Figure 10. Anti-Symmetries

Ckt	Ord.	M.P.	Conj.	C.M.P.	Total
c432	47	45	9	2	103
c499	110	24	40	0	174
c880	133	4	13	2	152
c1355	14	24	0	104	142
c1908	138	4	4	0	146
c2670	279	10	11	58	358
c3540	198	169	74	23	464
c5315	298	12	120	239	669
c6288	0	0	480	0	480
c7552	710	16	108	119	953

Figure 11. Classical Symmetries.

Ckt	Classical	Anti	Total
c432	103	0	103
c499	174	0	174
c880	152	19	171
c1355	142	104	246
c1908	146	0	146
c2670	357	34	357
c3540	463	5	468
c5315	664	32	696
c6288	480	464	944
c7552	951	99	1050

Figure 12. Classical and Anti-Symmetries

Ckt	None	Anti	Classical	Combined
c432	2.54	2.52	2.35	2.28
c499	3.75	3.43	3.20	3.20
c880	5.54	5.49	4.85	4.78
c1355	5.30	4.91	5.17	5.08
c1908	5.12	5.01	5.04	4.95
c2670	17.77	17.57	17.06	16.97
c3540	12.37	12.20	11.18	11.20
c5315	26.71	26.23	24.11	24.12
c6288	18.81	17.29	19.30	18.47
c7552	31.38	30.73	29.09	29.12

Figure 13. Running Times.

Several conclusions can be drawn from Figure 13. First, using either classical symmetries or anti-symmetries in isolation gives a substantial benefit. Second, combining the two gives improved performance in some cases, and roughly the same performance as Classical symmetries in other cases. When detecting symmetries, each variable pair can be assigned at most one type of symmetry. However for many variable pairs, there is a choice of which type of symmetry to assign. In this respect, the simulator is sensitive to the order in which symmetries are detected. For c6288, anti-symmetries give better performance than either classical symmetries or combined anti and classical symmetries. We corrected this problem by changing the order in which symmetries were detected. For Figure 13, for each pair of variables, we first detected classical symmetries and then anti-symmetries. We later changed the order to intersperse the detection of classical and anti-symmetries. This caused the anti-ordinary and anti-multiphase symmetries to be detected before the classical single-variable symmetries. This reduced the "combined" time for c6288 to roughly the same as that for anti-symmetries.

7 Conclusion

Detecting and using anti-symmetries can be of benefit for simulation performance. For all of our circuits, simulation detection was essentially instantaneous, even after adding the code for detecting anti-symmetries, so the cost of detecting anti-symmetries is worth the benefit. This is especially true because our simulator is a compiled simulator, and the cost of symmetry detection can be amortized over many hours of simulation. Furthermore, the ability to pick and choose among several different types of symmetry permits us to weigh several different detection options against one another and pick the best. Again, the cost of doing this can be amortized over many simulations. Even in a situation where the circuit is undergoing rapid changes, the cost of detecting symmetry is barely noticeable and will not substantially affect compilation time.

Because of these benefits, anti-symmetry detection is now a permanent part of our simulation engine.

8 References

1. C. E. Shannon, "The synthesis of two-terminal switching circuits," *Bell System Technical Journal,* Vol.28, *No.1,* pp. 59-98, 1949.
2. C. R. Edwards and S. L. Hurst, "A digital synthesis procedure under function symmetries and mapping methods," *IEEE Transactions on Computers,* Vol.27, *No.11,* pp. 985-997, 1978.
3. D. Moller, P. Molitor, R. Drechsler and J. W. G. U. Frankfurt, "Symmetry based variable ordering for ROBDDs," *IFIP Workshop on Logic and Architecture Synthesis,* pp. 47-53, 1994.
4. C. Scholl, D. Moller, P. Molitor and R. Drechsler, "BDD minimization using symmetries," *IEEE Transactions on Computer-Aided Design of Integrated Circuits and Systems,* Vol.18, *No.2,* pp. 81-100, 1999.
5. T. Sasao, "A new expansion of symmetric functions and their application to non-disjoint functional decompositions for LUT type FPGAs," *IEEE International Workshop on Logic Synthesis,* pp. 105-110, 2000.
6. V. N. Kravets and K. A. Sakallah, "Constructive library-aware synthesis using symmetries," *Design Automation and Test in Europe,* pp. 208-213, 2000.
7. P. M. Maurer, "Conjugate Symmetry," *Formal Methods Syst. Des.,* Vol.38, *No.3,* pp. 263-288, 2011.
8. V. N. Kravets and K. A. Sakallah, "Generalized symmetries in boolean functions," *IEEE International Conference on Computer Aided Design,* pp. 526-532, 2000.
9. J. Mohnke, P. Molitor and S. Malik, "Limits of using signatures for permutation independent Boolean comparison," *Formal Methods Syst. Des.,* Vol.21, *No.2,* pp. 167-191, 2002.
10. P. M. Maurer, "An application of group theory to the analysis of symmetric gates," Department of Computer Science, Baylor University, Waco, TX 76798, http://hdl.handle.net/2104/5438, 2009.
11. V. N. Kravets and K. A. Sakallah, "Generalized symmetries in boolean functions," Advanced Computer Architecture Laboratory Department of Electrical Engineering and Computer Science, The University of Michigan, Ann Arbor, MI 48109, http://web.eecs.umich.edu/techreports/cse/00/CSE-TR-420-00.pdf, 2002.

12. C. C. Tsai and M. Marek-Sadowska, "Generalized Reed-Muller forms as a tool to detect symmetries," *IEEE Transactions on Computers,* Vol.45, *No.1,* pp. 33-40, 1996.
13. M. Chrzanowska-Jeske, A. Mishchenko and J. R. Burch, "Linear Cofactor Relationships in Boolean Functions," *IEEE Transactions on Computer-Aided Design of Integrated Circuits and Systems,* Vol.25, *No.6,* pp. 1011-1023, 2006.
14. C. C. Tsai and M. Marek-Sadowska, "Boolean functions classification via fixed polarity Reed-Muller forms," *IEEE Transactions on Computers,* Vol.46, *No.2,* pp. 173-186, 1997.
15. P. M. Maurer, "Extending symmetric variable-pair transitivities using state-space transformations," Department of Computer Science, Baylor University, Waco, Texas 76798, http://hdl.handle.net/2104/8185, 2011.
16. F. Luccio and L. Pagli, "On a new Boolean function with applications," *IEEE Transactions on Computers,* Vol.48, *No.3,* pp. 296-310, 1999.
17. A. Bernasconi, V. Ciriani, F. Luccio and L. Pagli, "Synthesis of Autosymmetric Functions in a New Three-Level Form," *Theory of Computing Systems,* Vol.42, *No.4,* pp. 450-464, 2008.
18. P. M. Maurer. Efficient event-driven simulation by exploiting the output observability of gate clusters. *Computer-Aided Design of Integrated Circuits and Systems, IEEE Transactions on* Vol.22, *No.11,* pp. 1471-1486.
19. F. Brglez, P. Pownall and R. Hum. Accelerated ATPG and fault grading via testability analysis. Presented at Proceedings of IEEE Int. Symposium on Circuits and Systems.

A1. Appendix 1: Algorithms

Compute f_{00}, f_{01}, f_{10} and f_{11} and place them in a 2-dimensional hypercube structure.
Repeat Until No variables remain
  Test the back diagonals for ordinary symmetry
  Test the back diagonals for anti-symmetry
  If a symmetric variable pair is detected
    Collapse the structure by combining vertices along diagonals.
    Add any required corrective functions
  Endif
  If uneliminated variables remain
    Compute two new cofactors from each existing cofactor
    Double the size of the structure increasing dimensions by 1.
    Insert the new cofactors into the new structure
  Endif

Figure A1. Symmetry Detection.

Remove all State-Space transformations.
Check Back diagonals, stop if symmetry is detected.
Reverse Hyper Linear structure along one dimension
Check Back diagonals, stop if symmetry is detected.
Restore Hyper Linear Structure
Reverse Odd Rows
Check Back diagonals, stop if symmetry is detected.
Restore Hyper Linear Structure
Reverse Odd Columns
Check Back diagonals, stop if symmetry is detected.
Restore Hyper Linear Structure
Reverse Hyper Linear structure along one dimension
Reverse Odd Rows
Check Back diagonals, stop if symmetry is detected.
Restore Hyper Linear Structure
Reverse Hyper Linear structure along one dimension
Reverse Odd Columns
Check Back diagonals, stop if symmetry is detected.

Figure A2. General Symmetry Pair Detection.

For each plane containing the pair to be tested
  For each diagonal
    Comparator = HeadVertex.function;
    For V = each vertex after the head vertex
      If Comparator Not Equal V.function **Then**
        Report Failure
      Endif
    Endfor
  Endfor
Endfor
Report Success

Figure A3. Ordinary Symmetry Diagonal Check.

For each plane containing the pair to be tested
  For each diagonal
    Comparator = HeadVertex.function;
    AntiComparator = Negate(Comparator)
    Odd = 1;
    For V = each vertex after the head vertex
      If Odd = 1 **Then**
        If AntiComparator Not Equal V.function **Then**
          Report Failure
        Endif
        Odd = 0;
      Else
        If Comparator Not Equal V.function **Then**
          Report Failure
        Endif
        Odd = 1;
      EndIf
    Endfor
  Endfor
Endfor
Report Success

Figure A4. Anti-Symmetry Diagonal Check.

GateState[i] = GateState[i] + PortState;
PortState = -PortState;
// note the contents of the Then and Else sections
If Value[GateState] **Not Equal** OldGateState **Then**
  If EventQueued **Then**
    Dequeue Event
  Else
    Queue Event
  Endif
Else
  Do Nothing;
Endif
OldGateState = Value[GateState];
GoTo NextEvent

FigureA5. Ordinary Symmetry Event Processor.

```
GateState[i] = GateState[i] + PortState;
PortState = -PortState;
// note the contents of the Then and Else sections
If Value[GateState] Not Equal OldGateState Then
   Do Nothing;
Else
   If EventQueued Then
      Dequeue Event
   Else
      Queue Event
   Endif
Endif
OldGateState = Value[GateState];
GoTo NextEvent
```

Figure A6. Anti-Symmetry Event Processor.

Fire and Flame Simulation using Particle Systems and Graphical Processing Units

T.S. Lyes and K.A. Hawick
Computer Science, Massey University, North Shore 102-904, Auckland, New Zealand
email: { t.s.lyes, k.a.hawick }@massey.ac.nz
Tel: +64 9 414 0800 Fax: +64 9 441 8181

February 2013

ABSTRACT

Simulating fire, flames or other natural phenomena can be difficult because of the inherently complex systems used to model them, while also requiring an adequate amount of realism visually. Simulating such a system in real-time can also be a problem if the system is too large, so a parallel computing techniques can be used to good effect. Particle systems have been shown to simulate flames and fires particularly well at relatively low computational cost. We describe how a simple particle system approach can be used to simulate a fire or flame in real-time in conjunction with using data parallelization, achieving a substantial performance speed up on graphical processing units (GPUs). Using NVidia's Compute Unified Device Architecture (CUDA) and OpenGL interoperability functionality allows for further performance increases when rendering the simulation with GPUs. Additionally, different rendering techniques are used to investigate trade-offs between performance speed and visual realism.

KEY WORDS
fire; flames; visualisation; rendering; simulation; turbulence; GPU

1 Introduction

Fire and flame simulation is an interesting and important area of research in computer graphics [3]. As with most natural phenomena, it can be a challenging to simulate, particularly due to its complex, turbulent nature [12]. To simulate such a complex system in real time is difficult even by today's computing power standards. Sufficient realism is an important aspect of fire simulation as well, and thus many different rendering techniques have emerged to make the simulated fire look and behave as convincingly as possible. Fire simulation has applications in many industries, such as movie making special effects, video games and scientific visualization, as well as areas such as fire control and military emulation [19] [6].

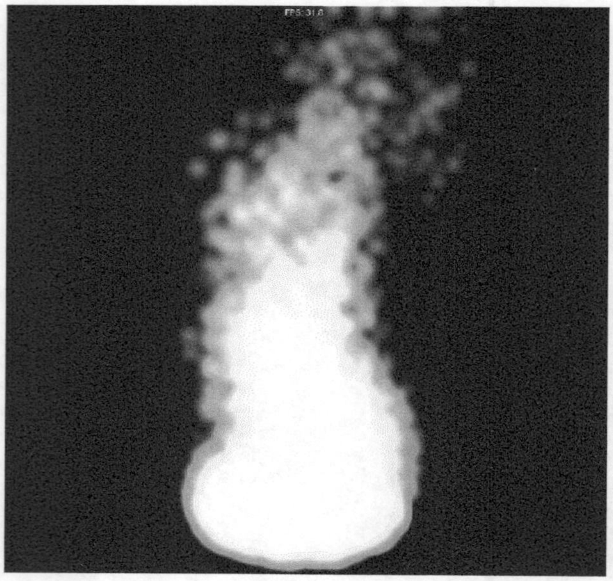

Figure 1: A fire particle system simulation

To date there have been many methods on simulating and rendering a fire or flame in real time. Some methods include using a spring-mass model to model flame kinematics [1] allowing external forces such as gravity and wind to be incorporated for added realism, or a method for rendering fire on the surface of a polygon mesh [2] by generating points on the surface of the polygon and using individual flame primitives to render the fire, or by simulating the fire as an "evolving front" of particles [9] moving across a polygonal mesh. Other methods combine simple particle systems and advanced rendering techniques [6] to generate highly detailed fire simulations at relatively low computational cost. Combustion models [17] [20] and hydrodynamics [18] have also been used to model fires.

There are many different rendering techniques to consider

when simulating a fire. One technique involves uses two dimensional sprites or "splats" [16] as textures to simulate the fire, giving the illusion of the fire being three-dimensional by using rendering techniques such as billboarding (rotating the image to always face the camera) and blending (colours in the background partially fade through to the foreground). Three dimensional techniques such as utilizing polygons or polygonal surfaces to model flames are far more complicated but can provide much more realistic results.

Particle systems are a simple but effective way of modeling a lot of complex systems, and is the core basis for many fire simulation methods [6] [9] [19]. A particle system consists of many particles sharing similar attributes such as position, velocity, and lifetime, all controlled by a specific set of rules or functions. Particles will be created and destroyed throughout the lifetime of the system. The size of the system can vary from just a few hundred particles to tens of thousands of particles, but realistic and real-time results will depend on the computing hardware used. Graphics Processing Units (GPUs) [10] can help with this limitation [13,14], and using GPU implementations allow simulations to be only limited by the particle data transfer between the processor and GPU [7] [8].

GPU's are designed to handle problems which can be expressed in parallel [15] such as particle systems [4]. Particles can be divided up into blocks and updated in parallel as each particle's update function will typically be the same for all particles in the system. Compute Unified Device Architecture (CUDA) [11] is an extension of the C programming language developed by NVidia specifically designed for usage on NVidia GPUs. Using CUDA we can take advantage of not only the data parallelism of the GPU, but also CUDA's built-in functionality to allow it to interact with the OpenGL rendering library [5] or the purpose of rendering directly on the GPU, resulting in even better performance from the program.

This paper focuses on using a simple particle system to simulate a fire or flame, as well as using CUDA and OpenGL to simulate and render the system using various simple rendering techniques. An example of a flame rendered using particles is shown in Figure 1. In Section 2 we describe the methods and functionality used, describing the core CUDA and OpenGL concepts behind simulating the fire. Section 3 shows some screen caps of the program in action highlighting the differences in the rendering techniques. Section 4 presents a discussion of the performance of the program using different rendering setups, and finally Section 5 lays forth some concluding remarks on the project as well as some future work suggestions.

2 Implementation Method

This fire particle system uses the following properties - particles are born in a random position inside of a circular area (based on the radius and angle specified by the kernel), with an upwards velocity and a slightly deviated acceleration along the x and z axes. Wind effects increase or decrease this deviation using according to a sine wave function. The fire is coloured using a randomly generated colour when it is born as well as a randomly generated colour when it dies. Throughout its lifetime the colour will not only transition from its start colour to its end colour, but also the alpha component will also decrease. All particles are born with an alpha component of 1.0 and die with an alpha component of 0.0 - in other words, particles will fade as they grow older until they completely disappear when the particle dies.

Algorithm 1 gives a general idea of how a particle system works.

Algorithm 1 the general layout of a particle system kernel

```
for all particles in system do
    update life
    if particle dies then
        destroy particle
        create new particle
        randomize particle values
    end if
    update positions, velocities
    update collisions, etc...
end for
```

CUDA has built in OpenGL interoperability functionality which can improve performance levels [11]. To take advantage of this, the general method is to use vertex buffer objects (VBOs) to store rendering data such as points and colours so that once the system has been updated, the particles can be rendered directly using the GPU rather than passing the values back to the CPU after the kernel has been executed. This takes slightly longer preparation as CUDA needs to map resources using the functions cudaGraphicsMapResources() and cudaGraphicsResourceGetMappedPointer() before executing the kernel. Additionally, OpenGL will use glBindBuffer() to bind an array buffer to the VBO needed. For this simulation, two VBOs were used - a vertex array for particle positions, and a colour array for particle colours.

Colours can be applied to the fire in two ways depending on the rendering method - when rendering on the CPU, colours can be applied using glColor4f, using four percentage floats to determine the red, green, blue and alpha components of the colour. The fire will always have a red component of 1.0f (100 percent red) while the green and blue components will be randomized to give a more orange or yellow colour to the fire. If the simulation is rendered on the GPU using CUDA-OpenGL interoperability, colours can be applied using a colour vertex buffer object (VBO) and using the functions glColorPointer() and glEnableClientState(GL COLOR ARRAY) to bind the colour VBO to OpenGL's

```
//Initialize the curand pseudo-random number generator for the device
__global__ void setup_kernel(curandState *state){
    //Each thread gets the same seed, but a different sequence number
    unsigned int x = threadIdx.x + blockIdx.x * blockDim.x;
    unsigned int y = threadIdx.y + blockIdx.y * blockDim.y;
    unsigned int id = x + y * blockDim.x * gridDim.x;
    curand_init(1234, id, 0, &state[id]);
}
```

Figure 2: Setup kernel for initializing the CURAND pseudo-random number generator

colour array buffer.

Pseudo-random numbers are sufficient to provide randomized data values when a new particle is created. However, conventional C pseudo-random number generators will not work when used in CUDA kernels. For this reason, NVidia recently developed the CURAND random number library for use of random numbers in parallel. CURAND random numbers can be generated either on the host or device. When generating on the device, curand_init must first be run to initialize a RNG state for each particle in the system. As shown in Figure 2 when using CURAND in parallel it is recommended to use the same random number seed and a different sequence number for each particle in the system.

In this case, 1234 was used as the seed for all particles, while each particle's id number was used as the sequence number. What results is an array of "curand states" which can be passed to the kernel similar to float arrays for position or colour. The kernel can then use this state to generate as many random numbers as needed, such as in Figure 2 when randomizing a particle's starting colour and decay rate. In this example, the function curand_uniform is used, which generates a uniformly distributed number between 0 and 1, however CURAND supports many other distributions as well.

The fire simulation was run on a single NVidia Quadro 4000 graphics card.

3 Visualisation Results

The particle system was tested using a range of system sizes (64x64, 128x128, 256x256, and 512x512), or from 4096 in the smallest system tested up to 262144 particles in the largest system tested. The frame rates were also monitored and displayed on screen in real-time. Additionally, a variety of rendering techniques were used to investigate their impact both visually and on the computational performance of the program.

Figure 3 shows the initial visualization of the system with a size of 128x128. Smaller systems (64x64) did not produce visually strong simulations so those screenshots were not used. This particular simulation used simple GL POINTS to represent each particle. While not the most visually interesting rendering method, GL POINTS did give the best frame rate performance of all the rendering methods. Note that the redness of the particles increases the further away from the center they get. This was intended to better simulate a flame, however it is not always apparent in other rendering methods seen later.

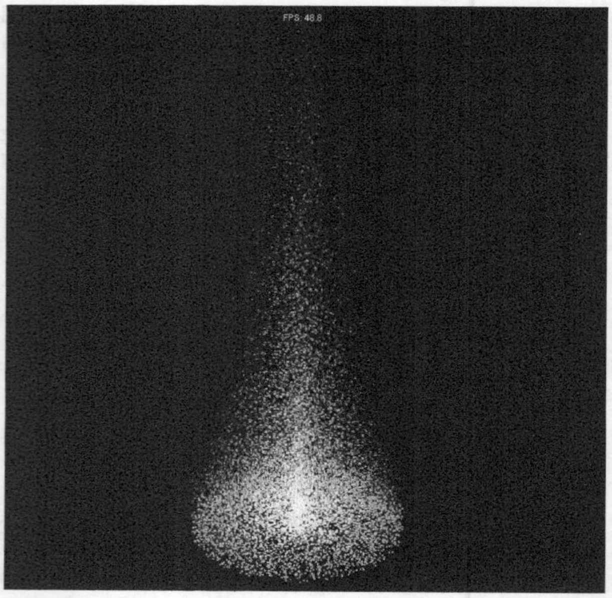

Figure 3: A simulation of the 128x128 fire particle system (16384 particles) rendered using simple GL POINTS

Figure 5 shows the same system size rendered using the CUDA-OpenGL interoperability functionality. A wind component has also been added. The simulation is almost identical to the non-VBO rendered simulation, however one big difference is that the frame rate has increased substantially.

Figure 6 uses GL LINES to render the fire instead of nor-

```
col[id].x = 1.0f;
//Make the red component of the colour more prominent towards the outside of the flame
col[id].y = 1.0f * ((0.5 + (0.8 - 0.5) * curand_uniform(&localState))* (1-(r)));
col[id].z = 1.0f * ((0.0 + (0.5 - 0.0) * curand_uniform(&localState))* (1-(r)));
col[id].w = 1.0f;

decay[id].x = (1.0f - col[id].x) / life[id];
decay[id].y = (0.4f * curand_uniform(&localState) - col[id].y) / life[id];
decay[id].z = (0.1f * curand_uniform(&localState) - col[id].z) / life[id];
```

Figure 4: Example of using CURAND to randomize the colour and decay rate of a created particle

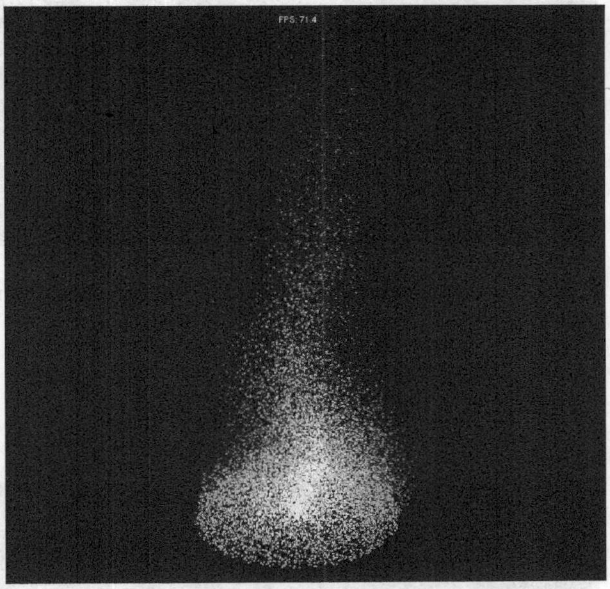

Figure 5: A simulation of the 128x128 fire particle system (16384 particles) rendered using CUDA-OpenGL interoperability (vertex and colour arrays)

mal points. This simulation was also rendered on the GPU using CUDA-OpenGL interoperability. In this simulation the flame appears to be slightly larger - this is due to the lines not taking into account the alpha component of the colour. The particles are showing up fully throughout their entire life when they should be fading away. The lines also accentuate the red colour a lot more as the outer red lines are drawn over the top of the inner yellow and white lines.

Figure 7 uses GL TRIANGLES instead of lines or points. While the colour progression looks much better than the lines or points, the shape of the flame is rather "pointy" (similar to Figure 6). Because this simulation is rendered using polygons, GL BLEND has been enabled, however this means that the red colour on the outer particles is almost lost as there are far more lighter particles on the inside of the fire which are blended through. It is also worth noting that this simulation suffered a significant frame rate drop when compared to Figure 3 and Figure 6.

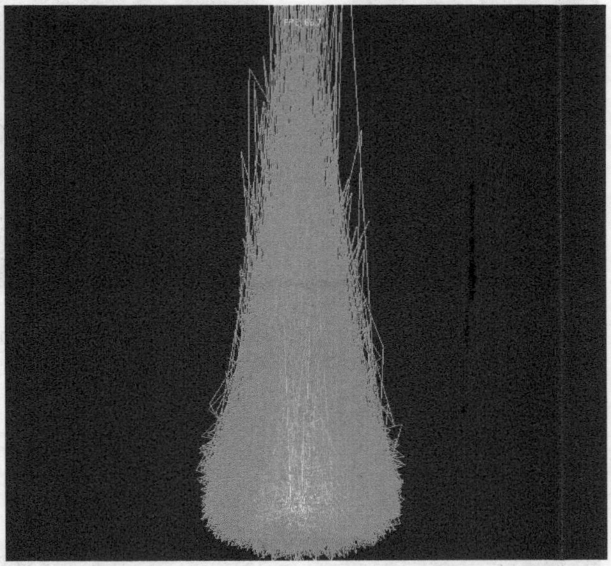

Figure 6: A simulation of the 128x128 fire particle system (16384 particles) rendered using VBOs and GL LINES

Figure 8 uses a texture mapped onto GL QUADS to represent each particle. This simulation produced the best visualization for a flame but at the cost of the lowest frame rate for all the 128x128 particle systems.

Figure 9 shows the simulation of the larger 256x256 particle system with added wind effect rendered using points. The system is much more dense which is good visually, but the system suffers from a dramatic frame rate drop when compared to the 128 x 128 system. Using more advanced rendering methods other than GL POINTS such as triangles or textures would reduce the frame rate to unmanageable levels.

Finally, Figure 10 shows the simulation of the largest system tested, 512x512 or 262144 particles. At this point, the frame rate is low enough to the point that it has started affecting the kernel executions. As a result, "fluctuations" occur in the flame as many more particles die in between exe-

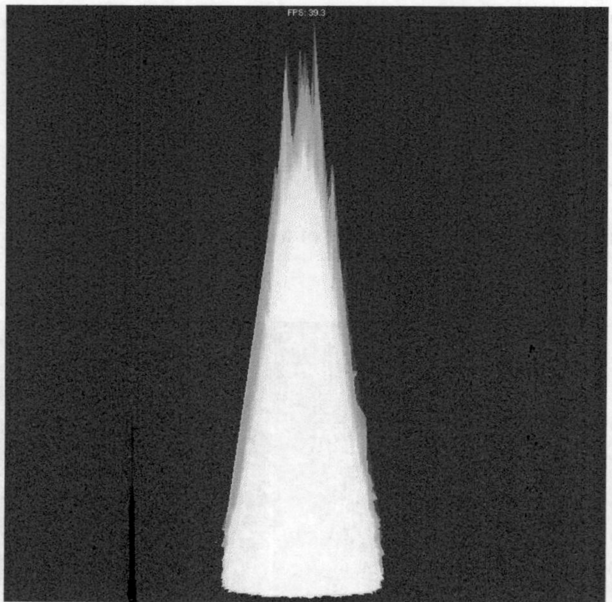

Figure 7: A simulation of the 128x128 fire particle system (16384 particles) rendered using VBOs and GL TRIANGLES

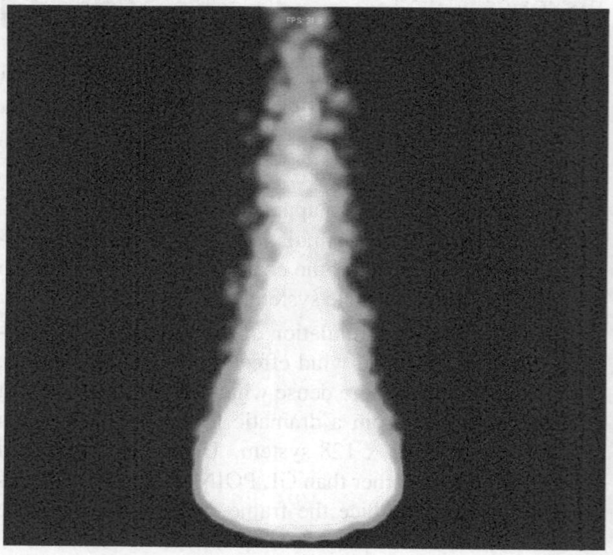

Figure 8: A simulation of the 128x128 fire particle system (16384 particles) rendered using texture maps

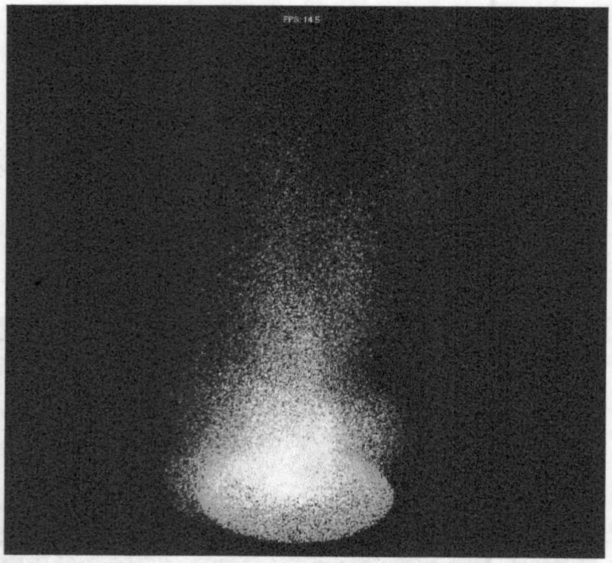

Figure 9: A simulation of the 256x256 fire particle system (65536 particles) rendered using GL POINTS

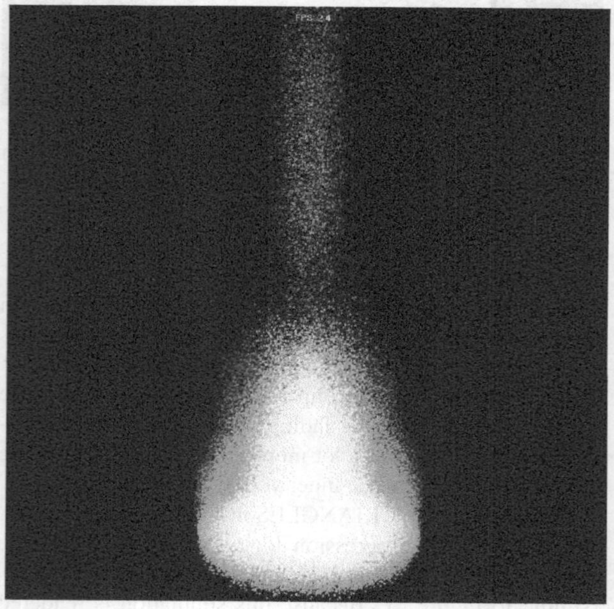

Figure 10: A simulation of the 512x512 fire particle system (262144 particles) rendered using GL POINTS

cutions of the kernel than would otherwise be expected.

4 Discussion

The performance of the system was monitored in various ways. Firstly, a comparison was made between the performance of sequential and parallel versions of the same update kernel. Performance was timed over 10,000 kernel executions and a mean kernel execution time was calculated. Secondly, performance was monitored for differences when using CUDA-OpenGL interoperability to render the simulation on the GPU. Additionally, the average frame rate of the simulation was also monitored and displayed in real-time above the fire rendering. As mentioned previously, the simulations were carried out a single NVidia Quadro 4000 graphics card.

No. of Particles	Seq. time seconds	Para. time seconds
64x64	0.0009	ca. 0.00001
128x128	0.0036	ca. 0.00001
256x256	0.0143	ca. 0.00001
512x512	0.0557	ca. 0.00002

Table 1: Performance results of a particle system of various sizes simulated sequentially and in parallel

Table 1 shows the performance results of a sequential kernel vs a parallel kernel execution. It is important to first note that the parallel execution speeds of the 64x64, 128x128 and 256x256 systems are not identical. The execution speeds of all three kernels were too fast for the precision used by the timer. This is mainly due to the simplicity of the particle code, which can be easily scaled and made far more complicated in future work. Nevertheless the parallel versions are clearly performing far better than their sequential counterparts.

An interesting point that was found was that if the parallel system synchronized its threads before the next kernel execution (using cudaThreadSynchronize) the parallel execution time was actually slower than the sequential time. This was not an issue with this simulation as thread synchronization was not needed, but in more complex systems which require it this might become a problem. Using VBOs and CUDA-OpenGL interoperability did not affect the execution time of the kernel whatsoever, simply because both methods used exactly the same kernel. However, there was a slight increase (0.0001 secs) in all update times when using the VBOs due to the graphics resource and pointer mapping and unmapping needed before and after the kernel execution. This extra time was negligible, however.

Table 2 compares the frame rates of both rendering methods on various particle system sizes. All renderings were done using OpenGL points. In all instances, rendering using VBOs and CUDA-OpenGL interoperability resulted in an improved frame rate of around ten percent. Considering there was no difference visually between the two methods, rendering using VBOs is clearly a better choice. It is important to note that NVidia Quadro cards can allow for even more performance improvements when used in a multi-GPU setup. A Quadro card performs OpenGL interoperability better than NVidia GeForce or Tesla cards. Therefore, in a multi-GPU set up it is preferential to use the Quadro card purely for rendering the simulation while using the other card or cards to perform the parallel computation parts of the program. Although this paper did not use a multi-GPU setup, it would be interesting to try this setup in the future.

No. of Particles	Avg. Norm FR frames / sec	Avg. VBO FR frames / sec
64x64	220.3	247.8
128x128	63.7	69.7
256x256	13.9	16.7
512x512	2.4	2.6

Table 2: Average frame rates of a particle system rendered normally vs using VBOs.

Render Method	Avg. Frame Rate seconds
Points	69.7
Lines	64.9
Triangles	39.3
Textures	31.0

Table 3: Average frame rates of a 128x128 particle system using different rendering methods.

Table 3 shows the average frame rates of each different rendering method using a 128x128 size particle system. In general, a more realistic looking rendering method resulted in a lower frame rate, which was to be expected. All methods resulted in an acceptable frame rate (anything below 20-25 frames per second becomes undesirable very quickly). A 128x128 sized particle system seems to be the optimal size at this point, because even using simple OpenGL points the frame rate drops to at most 16.7 frames per second and using a more complicated render method would lower this even further.

5 Conclusions

A simple particle system model was used to simulate a dynamical fire or flame, using OpenGL to visualize the simulation in real-time. Significant performance increases were observed when a CUDA parallel approach to the system was used, as opposed to a traditional sequential model. Several rendering techniques for the fire were investigated, each with certain trade-offs in performance and visual aspects. We have presented screenshots showing the major effects and tradeoffs that we found and explored.

Using simple points to represent particles resulted in fast frame rates, while using textures simulated a more visually appealing flame at the cost of a slower frame rate. Using CUDA-OpenGL interoperability increased the potential rendering performance across all rendering techniques by around 10 percent (measured in average frames per second). It was also found the ideal particle system size for the rendering techniques and kernels used was 128x128 or 16384 particles, as it provided the best trade-off between speed and visual appeal.

Future work in this area would be very interesting, having a look at other more complicated rendering techniques, as well as more complex kernels in order to simulate a more accurate and realistic fire or flame. As mentioned in Section 4, running this simulation on a multi-GPU set up to take advantage of the superior Quadro CUDA-OpenGL interoperability should also be possible in the near future. Other complex natural phenomena such as fluids have also simulated using particle systems, and this is also an area that could benefit from the techniques described here. Fountains or other structured particle model systems could be implemented using these techniques. More generally, visualising and modelling other plasma based systems is potentially of interest for both the gaming and movie industries where realistic physically based models of these complex systems can aid in attaining enhanced realism.

References

[1] Balci, M., Faroosh, H.: Real-time 3d fire simulation using a spring-mass model. In: Proc. 12th Int. Multi-Media Modelling Conference. pp. 108–115. Beijing, China (2006)

[2] Beaudoin, P., Paquet, S., Poulin, P.: Realistic and controllable fire simulation. In: Proc. Graphics Interface (GRIN'01). Toronto, Ontario, Canada (2001)

[3] Foley, J.D., van Dam, A., Feiner, S.K., Hughes, J.F.: Computer graphics: principles and practice (2nd ed.). Addison-Wesley Longman Publishing Co., Inc., Boston, MA, USA (1990)

[4] Hawick, K.A., Playne, D.P., Johnson, M.G.B.: Numerical precision and benchmarking very-high-order integration of particle dynamics on gpu accelerators. In: Proc. International Conference on Computer Design (CDES'11). pp. 83–89. No. CDE4469, CSREA, Las Vegas, USA (18-21 July 2011)

[5] Hearn, D., Baker, M.P.: Computer Graphics with OpenGL. No. ISBN 0-13-015390-7, Pearson Prentice Hall, third edition edn. (2004)

[6] Horvath, C., Geiger, W.: Directable, high-resolution simulation of fire on the gpu. ACM Trans. on Graphics 28(3), 41–1–8 (August 2009)

[7] Kolb, A., Latta, L., Rezk-Salama, C.: Hardware-based simulation and collision detection for large particle systems. In: Proc. Graphics Hardware (2004)

[8] Latta, L.: Building a million particle system. In: Game Developers Conference (2007)

[9] Lee, H., Kim, L., Meyer, M., Desbrun, M.: Meshes on fire. In: EG Workshop on Computer Animation and Simulation. pp. 75–84 (2001)

[10] Leist, A., Playne, D.P., Hawick, K.A.: Exploiting Graphical Processing Units for Data-Parallel Scientific Applications. Concurrency and Computation: Practice and Experience 21(18), 2400–2437 (25 December 2009), CSTN-065

[11] NVIDIA® Corporation: CUDA™ 3.1 Programming Guide (2010), `http://www.nvidia.com/`, last accessed September 2010

[12] Peyret, R., Taylor, T.D.: Computational Methods for Fluid Flow. Springer Series in Computational Physics, Springer-Verlag (1983)

[13] Playne, D.P., Hawick, K.A.: Classical mechanical hard-core particles simulated in a rigid enclosure using multi-gpu systems. In: Proc. Int. Conf. on Parallel and Distributed Processing Techniques and Applications (PDPTA'12). pp. 76–82. CSREA, Las Vegas, USA (16-19 July 2012)

[14] Playne, D.P., Johnson, M.G.B., Hawick, K.A.: Benchmarking GPU Devices with N-Body Simulations. In: Proc. 2009 International Conference on Computer Design (CDES 09) July, Las Vegas, USA. pp. 150–156. WorldComp, Las Vegas, USA (13-16 July 2009)

[15] Wei, W., Huang, Y.: Real-time flame rendering with gpu and cuda. Int. J. Info. Tech and Computer Science 1, 40–46 (2011)

[16] Wei, X., Li, W., Mueller, K., Kaufman, A.: Simulating fire with texture splats. In: Proc. IEEE Conf. on Visualization (VIS'02). Bostan, MA., USA (27 October - 1 November 2002)

[17] Xue, H., Ho, J.C., Cheng, Y.M.: Comparison of different combustion models in enclosure fire simulation. Fire Safety Journal 36, 37–54 (2001)

[18] Zhang, F., Hu, L., Wu, J., Shen, X.: A sph-based method for interactive fluids simulation on the multi-gpu. In: Proc. ACM SIGGRAPH Int. Conf on Virtual Teality Continuum and its applications in Industry (VRCAI'11). Hong Kong, China (11-12 December 2011)

[19] Zhaohui, W., Zhong, Z., Wei, W.: Realistic fire simulation: A survey. In: Proc. 12th Int. Conf. On Computer-Aided Design and Computer Graphics (CAD/Graphics 11). pp. 333–340. Jinan, China (September 2011)

[20] Zhou, J., Chang, Y., Wu, E.: Realistic, fast, and controllable simulation of solid combustion. Computer Animation and Virtual Worlds 22, 125–132 (2011)

Interactive Simulation and Visualisation of Falling Sand Pictures on Tablet Computers

B. Pearce and K.A. Hawick
Computer Science, Massey University, Albany, North Shore 102-904, Auckland, New Zealand
email: brad.pearce.nz@gmail.com, k.a.hawick@massey.ac.nz
Tel: +64 9 414 0800 Fax: +64 9 441 8181

February 2013

ABSTRACT

Sand pictures are made from a mix of coloured sands and water or oil sandwiched between two sheets of glass are a common desktop amusement. However, they also provide a good example of mixing and layering in materials science. We construct a lattice-based simulation of a sand picture based around the Kawasaki spin-exchange model with empirical couplings between cells. A Monte Carlo stochastic dynamic scheme is used to update pairs of neighboring cells using a Boltzmann like energy controlled probability process. The sand cells then diffuse around, with a preference parameter for sand to adhere to other sand cells of the same or different types. This model can be perturbed with a preferred directional gravitational force that leads to nearly correct physical phase separation of the coloured sands. The model provides a visually realistic simulation that can be rendered in real time. We implement this using Android and Java on tablet computers with inbuilt gyroscopic sensors that allow the simulated system to adapt to real gravity in interactive time. We describe the model and the implementation and software architecture for this App and the associated performance tradeoffs. We discuss possible future performance improvements using graphical processing units and other tablet specific features.

KEY WORDS
sand picture; App; tablet computer; gravity sensor; simulation.

1 Introduction

Sand pictures made from different grain sizes of sand suspended in oil or water and sandwiched between sheets of glass are common desktop toys. These complex fluid systems exhibit interesting layering and other turbulent patterns when they are inverted and the sand is allowed to fall in various ways.

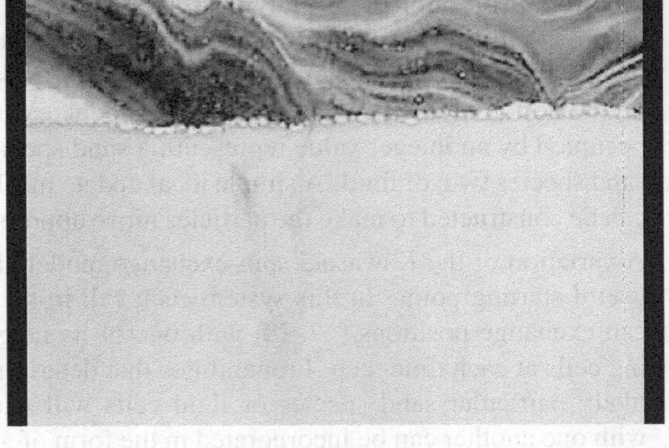

Figure 1: A Sand picture (Photographed real system.)

Figure 1 shows a photo of a real sand picture system - typically of dimensions around 20 cm across and with two or three different sand-species in the mixture, these models are often mounted on a rotatable frame so the picture can be inverted to create new swirling patterns until a new equilibrium is reached.

The picture is close to two dimensional in that the enclosing glass plates usually sandwich a very thin layer of sand and fluid - often less than 1mm. Sand grain sizes will typically range from 0.1 to 1 mm in diameter, and so there is enough room for a few grains of sand to flow past one another but this is not the dominant effect observed. It is sand weighing down on sand and sand displacing fluid that drives the layering and pattern generation.

A three-dimensional model can be built too of course, but since the opaque sand precludes seeing inside the system there is little artistic value in adding a full depth third dimension. It is in fact interesting to restrict the system to nearly two dimensions and a gradual increase of depth thickness introduces slip, shearing and other physical effects that it is interesting to control.

Sand and granular systems offer an experimental model that

can be observed in the laboratory, but there are industrial applications such as oil recovery from tar sands [9] where an understanding of the flow processes involved is important for achieving economically optimal extraction.

Other related applications where an understanding of sand flow is necessary include: dune modelling [2] and erosion studies [21]; use of sand in molding [18] for casting; sand conductivity problems [20]; sand slurry modelling [14]; and granular cohesion [11], fracturing [12] and layer shearing scenarios [1]. Sand avalanching has also provided a useful model platform for studying critical flow [5].

Models with downhill or gravitational granular flow effects [7] can be constructed in a number of ways. A molecular dynamical approach with many individual had disk or hard sphere particles that displace one another is one possibility. This approach is quite computationally intensive and to obtain a realistic number of individual sand particles, would require (x, y) directional floating-point positions and momenta values for each grain. A simpler approach is based on the notion of a lattice gas. In a lattice model, each cell is occupied by an integer value representing sand species one, sand species two, of fluid. A simple local update mechanism can be constructed to make the particles move appropriately.

A variation of the Kawasaki spin-exchange model [19] is a useful starting point. In this system each cell in the lattice can exchange positions [17, 28] with one of its neighbouring cells at each time-step. Probabilities that determine how likely particular sand species or fluid cells will exchange with one another can be incorporated in the form of a Boltzmann energy weighting factor and gravity can be applied by imposing a directional bias to these values. The total number of each species is conserved as only pair-wise swaps are executed.

The sand picture system is essentially a complex fluid - with a colloidal suspension of sand particles contained in water or oil. Modelling complex fluids is a challenging problem [3,22], particularly in situations with realistic geometric boundaries and barriers. One useful approach is the Invasion Percolation (IP) model [15] which has developed over many years [10, 29] and is a useful tool for experimenting with flow of immiscible fluids in model reservoir systems.

The IP model has a number of variations in its formulation and has been extensively researched in two and three dimensional configurations. It has been successfully used to model diverse applications ranging from drainage systems [23, 25, 27] to vascular network formation in tumours [4] as well as reservoir extraction and deposition processes where recent applications still find it useful [8].

We are interested in the somewhat simpler system of the sand picture in two dimensions. We believe it shares some dynamical growth properties in common with other systems and models that are also driven by an external force such as gravity. Although some research has been reported on the influence of gravity [6, 13, 24], it has not been thoroughly explored as a way of introducing a buoyancy parameter into the IP model.

Various heuristics and adjustments can be made to the model to make the sand falling behaviour look more realistic and in particular so that it forms layers [16] like a real sand picture. Typically a simple model would look "wrong" as there is no viscous drag component to make the fluid appear real, but this can be incorporated by adding a preference parameter for sand to adhere to other sand cells of the same or different types. This model can be perturbed with a preferred directional gravitational force that leads to nearly correct physical phase separation of the coloured sands. The model provides a visually realistic simulation that can be rendered in real time. We are implementing this using Android and Java on tablet computers with inbuilt gyroscopic sensors that allow the simulated system to adapt to real gravity in interactive time. We describe the model and the implementation and software architecture for this App and the associated performance tradeoffs. We discuss future performance improvements using graphical processing units and other tablet specific features.

Our article is structured as follows: In Section 2 we describe the rules for our sand picture simulation. We present selected results in Section 3 including some visual snapshots of the simulated system in Section 3.1 and also some computational performance analysis in Section 3.2. We discuss the implications of this sort of model in Section 4 and offer some conclusions and areas for further work in Section 5.

2 The Sand Picture Model

We have developed various simulation software for models like the Ising, Kawasaki, IP and sand picture system. In this work we are aiming to produce a graphical simulation model that runs effectively in real time so we can watch the complex fluidic behaviour and associated spatial patterns as they form.

The work shown here relates to the initial prototype Desktop PC implementation. Tablet computers with touch screen displays and built-in gyroscopic sensors allow both detailed user interaction and an automated sense of gravitational direction. We are experimenting with these devices [26] and are presently implementing an App version of the Sand picture simulation models which uses the Java and graphical support system available under the Android Operating system for mobile devices.

We base our sand model on a lattice of cells which contains a single variable that determines whether the cell is the suspending "water" or "oil" or contains a sand particle. We can further refine the model with multiple sand species or colours, which can be heavier or lighter.

We need to impose a dynamic scheme to determine how

sand and the suspending liquid move around. A useful starting point for this is the Ising model on a lattice. In the Ising model, a heat-bath algorithm is used to emulate thermal effects on atoms in a magnetic material arranged in a crystalline lattice. The Ising system consists of a micro crystalline array of single bit magnetic moments or "spins" which interacts with its nearest neighbours. At each time step of the simulation each spin is considered in turn and the energy and thermal probability of it "flipping" – reversing its direction are considered. The probability of flipping is different, depending upon the applied temperature.

Ising spins align with their neighbours when the system is cold, but thermally randomize when it is hot. The interesting feature about the Ising system in 2 (or 3) dimensions is that there is a definite Curie temperature that can be measured. In real magnets the Curie temperature is the temperature above which the material stops being a magnet, or an alternative viewpoint is that materials like iron spontaneously become magnetic below their Curie temperature. This is known as a phase transition and is very difficult to explain simply without a model to demonstrate.

In the sand system however we need to fix the number of sand and suspending liquid cells. A useful related model is therefore the Kawasaki exchange model which is constructed in a similar manner to the Ising system. In this case however we preserve a fixed ratio of the two microscopic species since instead of flipping or changing species, in the Kawasaki system we only allow them to swap positions with one of their (randomly chosen) neighbours. In this respect the Kawasaki system models diffusion and phase separation or "unmixing" of the two species. The rate and manner of unmixing is like the separation of two atomic species in a binary alloy. This sort of dynamical behaviour is of great importance in real materials. Without some separated granules an alloy typically lacks strength and other physical properties but if too much separation occurs it can break apart and cause catastrophic failure in for example fuel rods in a reactor. In the sand system, an exchange or cell-switching dynamical scheme similar to the Kawasaki model can be used.

We have already experimented with a variation of the Kawasaki model in 2-D and 3-D with a gravitational bias imposed [16]. It successfully exhibits complex layers with multiple phases. In this present work, we experiment with tuning the microscopic rules to try to obtain a more realistic set of behaviours for the sand picture.

Figure 2 shows a 2-dimensional mesh surrounding individual cells A (red), B (blue) and C (green). The colours show the surrounding neighbourhood "halos" for these cells. We can use nearest-neighbour or Moore neighbourhoods with 4 (1,2,3,4) or 8 (1,2,3,4,5,6,7,8) neighbouring cells respectively. For the exchange or switching dynamics, we consider the energy consequences of particle A switching with particle B or with particle C. In the case of A and B they are

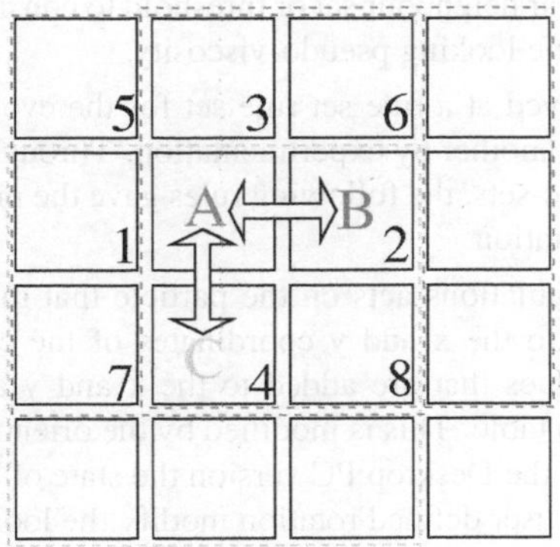

Figure 2: Mesh exchange dynamical schematic.

both at the same height and therefore gravity plays no part - unless the system is at a angular tilt as shown in the screenshots in column 3. The case of A and C will have gravitational consequences and there should be a bias so that the heavier of A and C prefers to move downwards.

To make the model behave realistically the Boltzmann approach allows a heavier particle to move upwards - but only with a very low probability. This stochastic dynamics emulates diffusion amongst the particles and also compensates for the rigidity of the mesh.

The simulation algorithm therefore consists of the following stages:

- Initialize a mesh of for example 1024 by 768 cells, that can be mapped to individual pixels on a display.
- Populate each cell randomly with either water or heavy sand or light sand.
- Iterate time steps of the model where each step consists of:
  - Consider each cell in random order
  - Look at the cell "below" the chosen cell
  - Follow the microscopic rules given in column 4 to determine whether to exchange or switch the contents of the two cells
  - Repeat

This model is essentially a variant of the Kawasaki Spin exchange model, where we have taken the Boltzmann energy probabilistic rate equation usually used in a Metropolis update scheme and made it more sophisticated by adding additional terms and effects to take account of gravity and a pseudo-viscosity within the complete fluid suspension.

There are a number of parameters that need to be investigated experimentally to tune the macroscopic behaviour of the system. The relative strength of gravity compared to the normal random diffusion of particles is one. Another is the particular neighbour set or threshold to consider to introduce a realistic looking pseudo-viscosity.

We arrived at a rule set rule set for the evolution from one state to another by experimentation. Through testing of various rule-sets, the following rules gave the most realistic implementation

The simulations acts on the particle that that is defined be adding to the x and y coordinates of the current position. The values that are added to the x and y are defined in a look-up table. This is modified by the orientation of the system, on the Desktop PC version the state of both the gravity and the user defined rotation modify the look-up table. This means the rules can be defined arbitrarily, it also means that the rules do not have to be heavily modified for the port to mobile devices which use a combination of Android/Java.

The rules make the use of random number generation for tie-breaks and for some of the stochastic conditions, and are as follows:

If the sand is white (lightest sand)

- if there are seven or more white sand particles around the white sand particle then do nothing
- if the same white sand particle or the heavier black sand is "below" then half the time look and see if there is water particles (lightest) to the bottom left and right otherwise do nothing
- if both are water to the left and right then coin toss to see which one we swap with. Otherwise fall into the one that as the water.
- if no water present then do nothing

If the sand is black (heaviest sand)

- if there are five or more black sand particles around the particle then do nothing
- if the same black sand is below then try to fall to the left or right of the if there is a light sand or water is on either side
- if the particle below is water then switch the particles
- if the particle below is white sand
  - 1/3 of the time swap the heaver sand for the lighter sand
  - 1/3 of the time see if there is water below left and right if there is then push the white sand left or right and let the black sand drop down
  - the final 1/3 of the time if there is a lighter particle below to the left or right then fall into its place (swap)

These rules conserve the amount of each particle to that which was first initialized in the system. This means we do not lose any particles from the simulation. In a real life sand picture the mounting case that holds the sands and water is sealed so it is also impossible to lose or change the proportion of particles present. Real life systems often leak air bubbles into the system and an area for future work is to explore how air bubbles might be suitably simulated.

Other areas for further investigation concern the dimensionality of the system. A real sand picture is almost two-dimensional, with a very thin region of colloidal fluid between the glass plates. It is an open question as to how this thickness in the third dimension will affect the complex fluid flow. A simulated system may be able to probe this issue.

3 Results

We illustrate the simulated system with a series of screen shots, with associated commentary, before discussion performance achievements in terms of frames per second on various platforms.

3.1 Simulated Snapshots

This series of screen-shots shows the simulated sand system rendered with the Desktop PC version and showing the orientation of the system with respect to the gravitational direction, on the right hand side. In each picture, the system consists of a suspending liquid (water or oil) represented by a blue particle species; a light yellow coloured sand species and a heavier black coloured sand species.

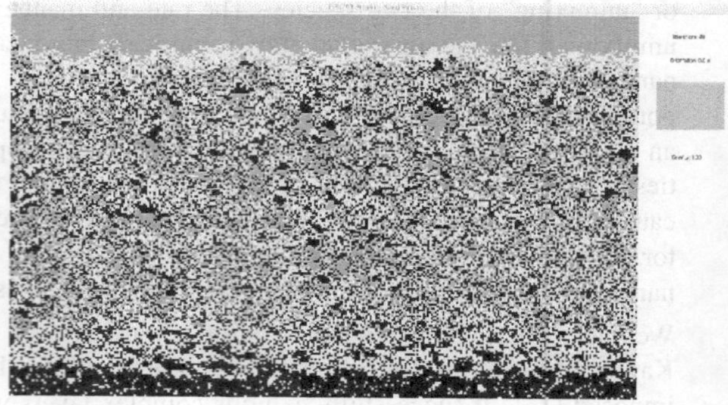

Figure 3: Sand starting to layer

Figure 3 shows the Desktop PC version of the sand simulation after 40 time steps. Following a random initialization, after only 40 time steps the black heavy particles are already starting to fall the fastest and are starting to accumulate at the bottom.

Figure 4 shows a simulation at its later stages when the particles have fallen into layers with pockets of lighter material spread throughout. This shows a similar layer behaviour to the actual sand picture.

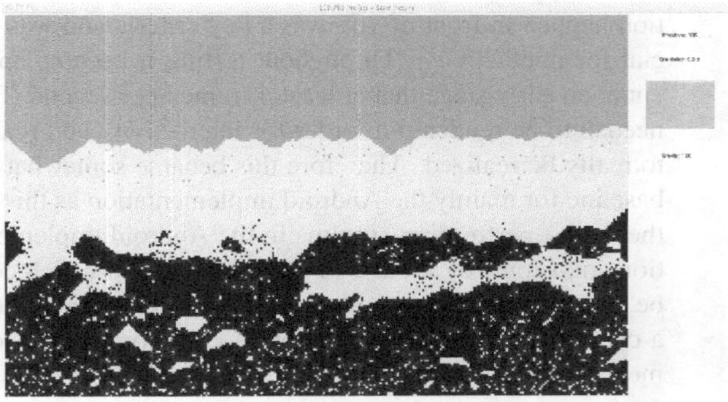

Figure 4: Layered sand simulation

Figure 5: Layered sand with rotation changed

Figure 5 demonstrates the ability to rotate the sand picture and the layering effects it has on the sand simulation.

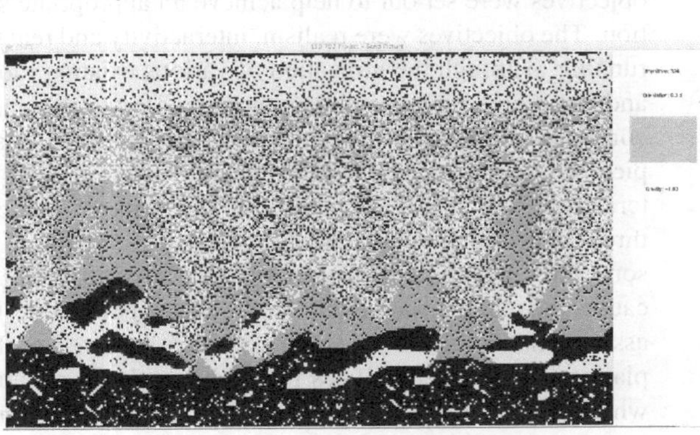

Figure 6: Relayering after change in gravity

Figure 6 shows the effect and re-layering after a gravity change in the sand simulation. As can be seen the lightest water particles are falling to the bottom and the heaviest black sand are moving to settle at the top of the screen.

Figure 7 shows a nearly steady-state of the sand simulation. This shows the effect that would happen in real life it the sand picture has been left for a few minutes for the particles to rearrange themselves.

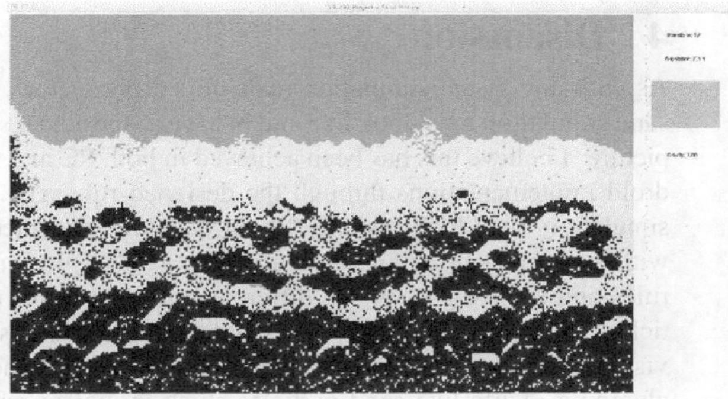

Figure 7: A near steady state of the simulation

3.2 Performance

It was determined empirically that a frame rate of at least four frames per second for the simulation to seem realistically similar to the flow seen on a real glass framed sand picture.

Two principle platforms were tested: a desktop PC running Ubuntu Linux 11.10 and with a Quad core 3.4GHz Intel processor with 8Gigabytes of memory and a high performance NVidia GTX 680 graphics card with its own graphics memory; and secondly a Google Nexus 7 tablet computer running Android 4.2.1 (Jellybean) and containing a quad core ARM processor running at 1.2GHz and with 1Gigabyte of available memory.

The desktop configuration obviously offers more choice of resolution and it was found that two interesting resolutions were firstly a 640×400 pixel resolution which yielded around 20 frames-per-second and used around 51 milliseconds to render each frame and approximately 45 milliseconds to execute the model computations. Secondly a full-screen resolution of 1280×800 pixel resolution yielded an adequate 5 frames-per-second and around 215 milliseconds to render with around 200 milliseconds used for computations.

The Nexus Android tablet implementation is obviously more interactive and "feels" more like a real sand picture. We obtained a frame rate of 5 frames per second when the resolution was lowered to 100×173 pixels. This gave around 100 milliseconds for rendering a frame but around 235 milliseconds for model computations.

The Nexus tablet is an attractive platform as it has accessible gravitational/gyroscopic sensors so it was possible to adapt the direction of simulated gravity to the orientation in which the tablet was held. This obviously carries an overhead however and the resolution had to be reduced to maintain a worthwhile frame rate.

4 Discussion

As with any visual simulation realism is a big factor. The sand simulation must look like and behave as the actual sand picture. I believe this has been achieved in both PC and Android implementations through the designed rule-set. The simulation does look visually like a real life sand picture with the sand layering appropriately due to the implemented rules and the weights of the different sand and water particles. The affect of pockets of white sand in black sand visually enhances the realism of the simulation. This shows clumping of life-like sand particles stuck in a state where they cannot move themselves free which could be due to being too tightly packed. This can be observed in a real sand picture and is a common phenomena. Complex rule-sets such as these can however be computationally expensive and this factor needed to be taken into account when considering interactivity and real time running. The main parameter of the system that affects realism is the resolution of the simulation. As sand particles are rather fine from about 0.0625 mm to 2 mm it is essential that the resolution is able to perform within or close to this range.

In both the PC and Android implementations the resolution is not extremely small and may not fall within this range, however it is fine enough to be a convincing simulation of sand. As the PC implementation has nearly twice the resolution as the Android implementation a visual difference can be seen, however, due to hardware performance limitations and the necessity for inter- activeness and real time running, a lower resolution was opted for as a tradeoff to achieve these other key factors. The resolution of the simulation is largely based on the speed and performance of the system it is implemented on. In this case the PC platform was far superior in performance and could perform.

As the real life sand picture can be rotated and flipped and is interactive, it was essential that the implemented simulations also had these features. The only way to measure this is to look at the simulations visually and see if can in fact be flipped and rotated. This unique interactivity gives both the sand picture and the implemented simulations a unique tactile feel. The implemented solutions can be manipulated this gives the affect of controlling the gravity in the simulations and determines how and in which direction the simulated sand particles fall in. Sensors were a key part in implementing this interactivity into the simulations. From simulated sensors in the PC version to the real gravity sensors in the Android version they both provided a fun and interactive interface that let the simulation be explored and played with. The raft of sensors available on the Android platform and through the range of devices made implementation of interactivity simple and easy to manage.

Finally for the implementations on both PC and Android the simulations needed to run in real time. This was needed for both the above realism and interactivity. Seeing the simulation happen in front of you was a key criteria and was crucial for interactivity. Throughout testing it became apparent at an early stage that at least 4 frames-per-second (FPS) needed to be rendered in order for interactivity and realism to really be realized. Therefore this became somewhat of a baseline for mainly the Android implementation as this was the lowest performing system. In the Android implementation an average of about 5 to 6 FPS is realized which could be better to enhance response time however realism required a certain resolution and therefore a compromise had to be met.

The PC implementation on a fast modern processor can perform in the range of 15 to 20 FPS and is visually faster. As can be seen from the above results and discussion all three factors of realism, interactivity and real time running all tie into each other. The common battle to balance the right mix of all three of these crucial aspects proved difficult throughout both development and testing of the simulation. The resulting systems on both PC and Android give realistic simulations of an actual sand picture.

5 Conclusion

The real life sand picture is an interesting desktop amusement that is interesting due to its interactive and visual aspects. The sand picture provided an excellent opportunity to simulate in a digital environment and take advantage of some of the latest technology available.

Simulation of the sand picture was not an easy task and clear objectives were set out to help achieve an appropriate solution. The objectives were realism, interactivity and real time running. Through the utilisation of various existing models and paradigms such as cellular automata, Boltzmann energy constants and Metropolis updates, a realistic looking sand picture was generated on both PC and mobile device. Interactivity was achieved on both PC and Android platforms through the use of both simulated and real gravitational sensors. This gave the sand picture the fun, interactive feel that causes the real life sand picture to be such a popular desktop assortment. Real time running was also achieved on both platforms however sacrifices had to be made on resolution which effected realism to achieve real time running. Performance was very much a factor on the Android platform and required a few tweaks to get the simulation to run as fast as possible.

In summary, a realistic algorithm was developed that produces realistic simulations of near physically sized sand grain on a desktop computer. It is likely that next generation tablet computers will have sufficiently powerful processors to enable similar realism. We There is also scope for a parallel partitioning of the problem amongst the multiple cores of the processor. We believe this will be worthwhile for 8-cored processing systems and higher.

References

[1] Alarcon, H., Geminard, J.C., Melo, F.: The effect of cohesion and shear modulus on the stability of a stretched granular layer. Phys. Rev. E 86, 061303–1–7 (2012)

[2] Araujo, A.D., Andrade, J.S., Maia, L.P., Herrmann, H.J.: Numerical simulation of particle flow in a sand trap. arXiv 0808.2649v1, Universidade Federal do Ceara, Ceara, Brazil (August 2008)

[3] Arratia, P.E.: Complex fluids at work. Physics 4(9), 1–3 (January 2011)

[4] Baish, J.W., Gazit, Y., Berk, D.A., Nozue, M., Baxter, L.T., Jain, R.K.: Role of tumor vascular architecture in nutrient and drug delivery: An invasion percolation-based network model. Microvascular Research 51, 327–346 (1996)

[5] Bak, P., Tang, C., Wiesenfeld, K.: Self-organized criticality: An explanation of 1/f noise. Phys. Rev. Lett. 59, 381–384 (1987)

[6] Birovljev, A., Furuberg, L., Feder, J., Jossang, T., Maloy, K.J., Aharony, A.: Gravity invasion percolation in two dimensions: Experiment and simulation. Phys. Rev. Lett. 67, 584–587 (1991)

[7] Borzsonyi, T., Ecke, R.E., McElwaine, J.N.: Patterns in flowing sand: Understanding the physics of granular flow. Phys. Rev. Lett. 103, 178302–1–4 (2009)

[8] Damron, M., Sapozhnikov, A.: Outlets of 2d invasion percolation and multiple-armed incipient infinite clusters. Probability Theory and Related Fields 150(1-2), 257–294 (2011)

[9] Doan, D.H., Delage, P., Nauroy, J.F., Tang, A.M., Youssef, S.: Microstructural characterization of a canadian oil sand. Can. Geotech J. 49, 1–9 (2012)

[10] Ebrahimi, F.: Invasion percolation: A computational algorithm for complex phenomena. Computing in Science and Engineering Mar/Apr, 84–93 (2010)

[11] Franklin, S.V.: Geometric cohesion in granular materials. Physics Today September, 70–71 (2012)

[12] Geminard, J.C., Champougny, L., Lidon, P., Melo, F.: Flexural fracturing of a cohesive granular layer. Phys. Rev. E 85, 012301–1–3 (2012)

[13] Glass, R.J., Conrad, S.H., Yarrington, L.: Gravity-destabilized nonwetting phase invasion in macroheterogeneousp orous media: Near-pore-scale macro modified invasion percolation simulation of experiments. Water Resources Research 37(5), 1197–1207 (May 2001)

[14] de Groot, M.B., Lindenberg, J., Mastbergen, D.R., den Ham, G.A.V.: Large scale sand liquefaction flow slide tests revisited. In: Proc. Eurofuge. pp. 1–22. Delft, The Netherlands (23-24 April 2012)

[15] Hawick, K.A.: Gravitational and barrier effects in d-dimensional invasion percolation reservoir models. In: Proc. Int. Conf. on Power and Energy Systems and Applications (PESA 2011). pp. 259–266. No. CSTN-134, IASTED, Pittsburgh, USA (7-9 November 2011)

[16] Hawick, K.: Visualising multi-phase lattice gas fluid layering simulations. In: Proc. International Conference on Modeling, Simulation and Visualization Methods (MSV'11). pp. 3–9. CSREA, Las Vegas, USA (18-21 July 2011)

[17] Hawick, K.A.: Domain Growth in Alloys. Ph.D. thesis, Edinburgh University (1991)

[18] Jakumeit, J., Jana, S., Waclawczyk, T., Mehdizadeh, A., Sadiki, A., Jouani, J.: Four-phase fully-coupled moldlling and solidi
cation simulation for gas porosity prediction in aluminum sand casting. IOP Conf. Series: Materials Science and Engineering 33, 012074 (2012)

[19] Kawasaki, K.: Diffusion constants near the critical point for time dependent Ising model I. Phys. Rev. 145(1), 224–230 (1966)

[20] Koch, K., Kemna, A., Irving, J., Holliger, K.: Impact of changes in grain size and pore space on the hydraulic conductivity and spectral induced polarization response of sand. Hydrology and Earth System Sciences 15, 1785–1794 (2011)

[21] Lammel, M., Rings, D., Kroy, K.: A two-species continuum model for aeolian sand transport. New Journal of Physics 14, 0930307–1–25 (2012)

[22] Martys, N., Cieplak, M., Robbins, M.O.: Critical phenomena in fluid invasion of porous media. Phys. Rev. Lett. 66(8), 1058–1061 (February 1991)

[23] Masek, J.G., Turcotte, D.L.: A diffusion-limited aggregation model for the evolution of drainage networks. Earth and Planetary Science Letters 119, 379–386 (1993)

[24] Meakin, P., Feder, J., Frette, V., Jossang, T.: Invasion percolation in a destabilizing gradient. Phys. Rev. A 46(6), 3357–3368 (September 1992)

[25] Prat, M.: Isothermal drying of non-hygroscopic capillary-porous materials as an invasion percolation process. Int. J. Multiphase Flow 21, 875–892 (1995)

[26] Preez, V.D., Pearce, B., Hawick, K.A., McMullen, T.H.: Software engineering a family of complex systems simulation model apps on android tablets. In: Proc. Int. Conf. on Software Engineering Research and Practice (SERP'12). pp. 215–221. SERP12-authors.pdf, CSREA, Las Vegas, USA (16-19 July 2012)

[27] Stark, C.P.: An invasion percolation model of drainage network evolution. Nature 352, 423–425 (1991)

[28] Wang, J.S., Binder, K., Lebowitz, J.L.: Computer simulation of driven diffusive systems with exchanges. J.Stat.Phys 56(5), 783–819 (1989)

[29] Wilkinson, D., Willemsen, J.F.: Invasion Percolation: a new form of percolation theory. J.Phys.A. 16, 3365–3376 (1983)

Modulo 10^M Calculator Increases Simulation Precision

Intelligence and Information Systems, Raytheon Company, Aurora, Colorado, USA

Scott Imhoff, 16800 E. CentreTech Parkway, Aurora, CO 80012
Scott_Imhoff@Raytheon.com, (720)-858-4287
Palak Thakkar, 16800 E. CentreTech Parkway, Aurora, CO 80012
Palak.P.Thakkar@Raytheon.com, (720)-858-4260
Contact Author - Kendy Hall, 16800 E. CentreTech Parkway, Aurora, CO 80012
Kendy.Hall@Raytheon.com, (720)-858-4535
Thomas Wang, 16800 E. CentreTech Parkway, Aurora, CO 80012
Thomas.K.Wang@Raytheon.com, (720)-858-4253

MSV'13

Abstract – *Many simulation software tools do not have arbitrary precision. This paper shows a way to increase the precision for multiplication of large numbers. This paper uses several tools from number theory together to provide a solution. The front part of the product (the most significant digits) is determined using a separate algorithm from the one used to determine the tail (the least significant digits). The least significant digits are determined by applying mod 10^M iteratively to the product of the tails of the two numbers input to the product. The most and the least significant bits are concatenated together to form the output product. Casting out nines is used to check the result.*

Keywords: Modular Arithmetic, Arbitrary Precision, Number Theory

1 Introduction

If we look at the last two digits of 7^n, we see that a repeating sequence occurs: 07, 49, 43, 01, 07, 49, 43, 01, 07, ... For example the last two digits of 7^{355} are 43. But if we use a popular software package used for simulation we see ...07, 49, 44, 0, ... for ...7^{17}, 7^{18}, 7^{19}, 7^{20},... In other words, we lose precision if the numbers become too large. Most simulation software tools do not have arbitrary precision. This paper shows a way to increase the precision for multiplication of large numbers.

This algorithm makes extensive use of the mod operator. The inputs to the mod operator are two numbers and the output is the remainder upon division of the first number by the second number. For example,

$2 \equiv 32 \bmod 5$

This is because 32 = 6*5 + 2. The symbol "≡" means "is congruent to."

A special case occurs when the number to the right of the mod operator is a multiple of 10. Consider the following:

$456 \bmod 100 \equiv 56$

This is because 456 = 4*100 + 56. Note that the result is the last two digits of the original number, 456. In general,

$x \bmod 10^M \equiv$ the last M digits of x

2 Increasing Precision

Our approach to gaining higher precision when multiplying is to break the problem into two algorithms, one to determine the least significant bits (the tail) and one to determine the most significant bits (the head). A third algorithm uses casting out nines to check the work of the first two algorithms.

Thus the overall algorithm for calculating z = x y consisting of three parts: A, B, and C.

All three algorithms start with a determination of the number of significant figures:

$$N = Ceiling(\log_{10} x + \log_{10} y)$$

The algorithms work together to determine a vector $\bar{b} = (b_1, b_2, ..., b_N)$ whose components can be concatenated together to form the final output number z, the product of x and y. M is the number of digits in the tail and N – M is the number of digits in the head. Thus:

$$\vec{b} = (b_1, b_2, \dots, b_N)$$
$$= concatenate[(b_1, b_2, \dots, b_{N-M}), (b_{N-M+1}, b_{N-M+2}, \dots, b_N)]$$

3 Algorithm A, for Determining the Least Significant Bits

Step 1: Determine the tails t_x and t_y of the input numbers x and y:

$$t_x \leftarrow x(mod\ 10^M)$$

$$t_y \leftarrow y(mod\ 10^M)$$

The algorithm finds the M least significant digits of the product z = x y by finding the M least significant digits of the product t_x, t_y of the tails.

Algorithm A input: $\{\{t_x, t_y\}, \{M, N\}\}$

Algorithm B output: $(b_{N-M+1}, b_{N-M+2}, \dots, b_N)$

Step 2: Find the least significant bit of the product of the tails:

$$b_N \leftarrow t_x t_y (mod\ 10)$$

Step 3: Find the next least significant bit by advancing the power of the modulus when finding what the product of the tails is congruent to. Then subtract off the previously determined bit and divide by one tenth of the modulus. Repeat until all of the M least significant bits are determine:

$for\ k = 1\ to\ M - 1$
$\quad b_{N-k} \leftarrow t_x t_y (mod\ 10^{k+1})$
$\quad for\ m = 1\ to\ k$
$\quad\quad b_{N-k} \leftarrow b_{N-k} - 10^{m-1} b_{N+1-m}$
$\quad end$
$\quad b_{N-k} \leftarrow {b_{N-k}}/{10^k}$
end

End Algorithm A.

4 Algorithm B, for Determining the Most Significant Bits

This algorithm determines the N-M most significant digits of the product z = x y.

Algorithm input: $\{\{x, y\}, \{M, N\}\}$

Algorithm output: $(b_1, b_2, \dots, b_{N-M})$

Step 1: Truncate off the least significant bits:

$$z_{most} \leftarrow floor\left(\frac{x\,y}{10^{M-1}}\right)$$

Step 2: Parse to determine the individual bits:

$for\ k = M\ to\ N - 1$
$\quad z_{most} \leftarrow floor\left(\frac{z_{most}}{10}\right)$
$\quad b_{N-k} \leftarrow z_{most}(mod\ 10)$
end

End Algorithm B.

The results of A and B can now be concatenated and the result is the input to algorithm C.

$$\vec{b} = (b_1, b_2, \dots, b_N)$$
$$= concatenate[(b_1, b_2, \dots, b_{N-M}), (b_{N-M+1}, b_{N-M+2}, \dots, b_N)]$$

5 Algorithm C, Check the Digits of the Product

This algorithm uses casting out nines to check the digits of the product.

Algorithm input: $\{\{x, y\}, \vec{b}\}$

Algorithm output: $\{\tau_1, \tau_2\}$

Theorem: *An integer is congruent, modulo 9, to the sum of its digits.*

Step 1: Calculate the sum of the elements of $\vec{b}$ modulo 9.

$$\tau_1 \leftarrow \left(\sum_{k=1}^{N} b_k\right)(mod\ 9)$$

Step 2: Find out what the product x y is congruent to mod 9 without actually calculating the product:

$c_x \leftarrow x(mod\ 9)$
$c_y \leftarrow y(mod\ 9)$
$\tau_2 \leftarrow c_x c_y (mod\ 9)$

Step 3: Compare τ_1 and τ_2.

End Algorithm C.

If: $\tau_1 \neq \tau_2$ advance M and start over A and B from the beginning.

Else: $\vec{z} \leftarrow \vec{b}$

End

6 Conclusion and Additional Notes

High precision cannot be assumed when building simulations with many of today's simulation tools. Simple number theory tricks can be used to increase precision for multiplies.

The modern approach to modular arithmetic was developed by Carl Friedrich Gauss when he was 21 and published in Latin in the number theory textbook *Disquisitiones Arithmeticae* in 1801. Congruences of the first and second Degree and the residues of powers are discussed in the first four sections of the textbook.

Abjectio novenaria (casting out nines) was known to Roman bishop Hippolytos in the third century A.D. Gottfried Leibniz used the method extensively in the 17th century.

Any two large integers, a and b, expressed in any smaller modulus μ as α and β have the same sum, difference or product as the originals modulo μ.

If $a \equiv \alpha(\mathrm{mod}\ \mu)$ and $b \equiv \beta(\mathrm{mod}\ \mu)$, then

$a + b \equiv \alpha + \beta\ (\mathrm{mod}\ \mu)$

$a - b \equiv \alpha - \beta\ (\mathrm{mod}\ \mu)$

$a \times b \equiv \alpha \times \beta\ (\mathrm{mod}\ \mu)$

What is special about $\mu = 9$ is that these are also true for the "digit sum." If a has digits $(a_1,a_2,\ldots,a_\nu)$ and b has digits $(b_1,b_2,\ldots,b_\xi)$, we have:

$a + b \equiv (a_1+a_2+\ldots+a_\nu) + (b_1+b_2+\ldots+b_\xi)\ (\mathrm{mod}\ 9)$

$a - b \equiv (a_1+a_2+\ldots+a_\nu) - (b_1+b_2+\ldots+b_\xi)\ (\mathrm{mod}\ 9)$

$a \times b \equiv (a_1+a_2+\ldots+a_\nu) \times (b_1+b_2+\ldots+b_\xi)\ (\mathrm{mod}\ 9)$

7 References

Dudley, Underwood, *Elementary Number Theory*, 2nd Ed., W. H. Freeman and Company, 1978.

Disquisitiones Arithmeticae at Yale University Press, 1965.

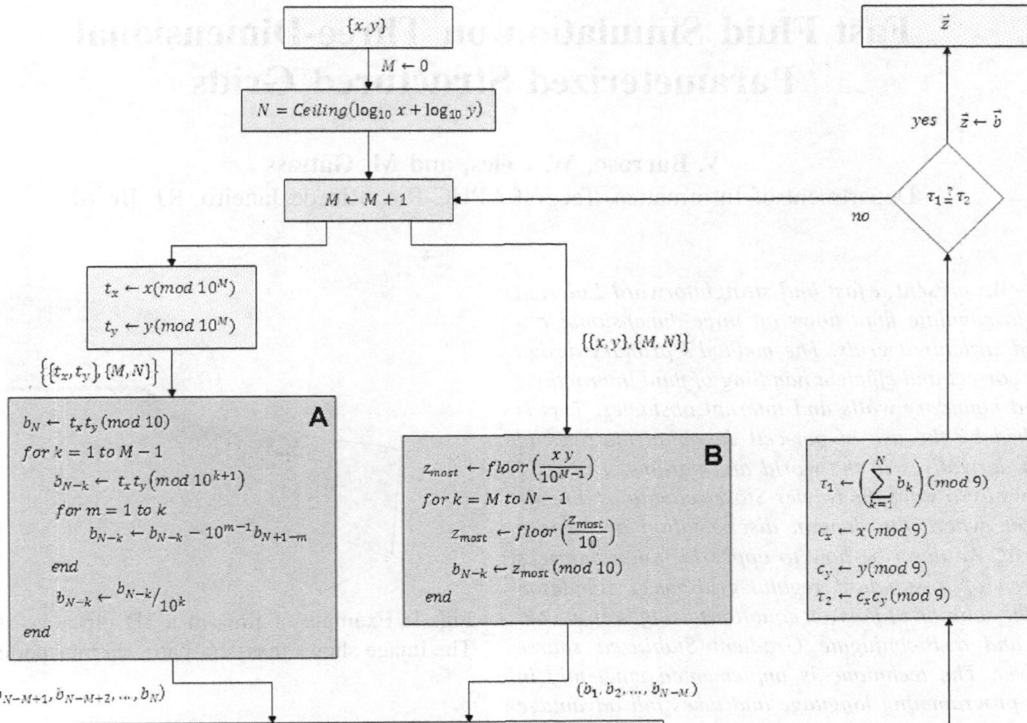

Figure 1: Summary of Algorithm

Fast Fluid Simulation on Three-Dimensional Parameterized Structured Grids

V. Barroso, W. Celes, and M. Gattass
Department of Informatics, Tecgraf / PUC-Rio, Rio de Janeiro, RJ, Brazil

Abstract— *We present a fast and straightforward Eulerian technique to simulate fluid flows on three-dimensional parameterized structured grids. The method's primary design goal is the correct and efficient handling of fluid interactions with curved boundary walls and internal obstacles. This is accomplished by the use of per-cell Jacobian matrices to relate field derivatives in the world and parameter spaces, which allows us to solve the Navier-Stokes equations directly in the latter, where the domain discretization becomes a uniform grid. We describe how to apply Jacobian matrices to each step of a standard regular-grid-based simulator, including the solution of Poisson equations using both Jacobi iterations and a Biconjugate Gradient Stabilized sparse matrix solver. The technique is implemented efficiently in the CUDA programming language and takes full advantage of the massively parallel architecture of graphics cards.*

Keywords: Computational fluid dynamics; eulerian fluid; domain parameterization; coordinate transformation; parallel computing

1. Introduction

Fluids play a fundamental role in many important natural phenomena. Understanding their behavior is of great importance to many areas of research, such as the study of wind passing by airplane wings, blood flowing through arteries, water and oil traveling through pipes, and the formation of hurricanes and tidal waves. Because of this broad range of applications, a lot of research effort has been put into the modeling, simulation, and visualization of fluid motion.

The dynamic behavior of a fluid is modeled by the Navier-Stokes partial differential equations, whose accurate and precise numerical solution turns out to be remarkably difficult and computationally expensive. Because of that, the development of fast and robust integration techniques has been an active research topic for many years. A common technique is to use efficient implementations of simplified physical models in order to generate fast approximate flow simulations. This is especially useful for rapid testing and for interactive scientific visualization applications.

The scope of this paper is limited to Eulerian fluid simulation. This approach samples the properties of a fluid on each element of a stationary space subdivision and integrates these properties over time to generate an implicit motion. We focus on generating good approximations of fluid behavior for scientific and interactive applications.

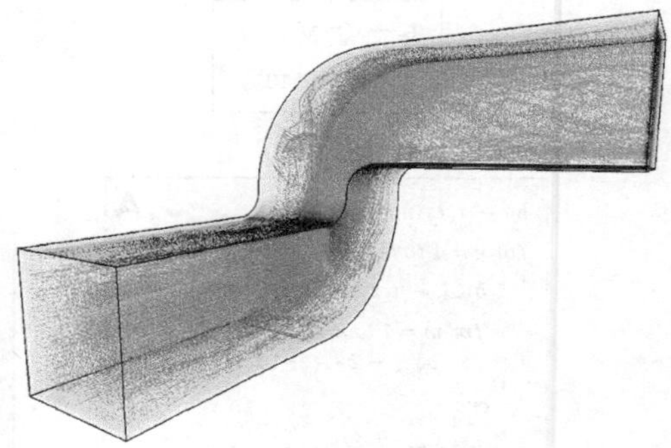

Fig. 1: Example of flow in a 3D pipe-like structured grid. The image shows massless particles transported by the flow.

Our goal is to efficiently simulate fluid flows on three-dimensional parameterized structured grids with arbitrarily-shaped boundaries, such as the tubular path in Fig. 1. We achieve high performance by employing a simplified physical model and a well-designed implementation which takes advantage of the parallel processing power available in graphics hardware. We simplify and accelerate the simulation by working on an underlying uniform grid in parameter space, whose coordinate derivatives are related to the world space ones by means of Jacobian matrices.

The foundation of our research is the seminal work on Stable Fluids by Stam [1], who achieved a very efficient and unconditionally stable Eulerian fluid simulation. In his approach, the Navier-Stokes equations are integrated in several sequential steps, each one using the partial results obtained in the previous one. In order to ensure stability, the advection phase is performed by an implicit semi-Lagrangian scheme, while the diffusion and pressure terms are integrated by solving implicit Poisson equations. This technique, which was implemented on the GPU by Harris [2], has become the basis for most modern high-performance algorithms today.

The simplest approach to represent boundaries and obstacles in regular grids is to voxelize them and flag the corresponding cells [3]. Unfortunately, this requires the grid to be discretized with a very fine resolution in order to accurately capture curved and complex shapes. Moreover, even with a fine discretization, the resulting behavior suffers from visible artifacts whenever an object's orientation does not exactly match the grid's [4]. In an attempt to deal with these issues, some methods account for object geometries explicitly by modifying the calculations in boundary cells [5], [6], but they cannot completely eliminate the artifacts. Other methods try to capture fine fluid motion detail only where needed by using octrees [7], [8] or tall grid cells [9]. However, although valuable as acceleration methods, they are still tied to a blocky representation. Another approach is to use simplicial meshes with explicit topological information [10], [11], but the overhead is usually too high for interactive applications.

In addition to these methods, some works generalize the domain representation to 3D surfaces with arbitrary topology [12], [13]. However, they require either a triangle mesh discretization [13] or an implementation of Catmull-Clark subdivision surfaces and their exact evaluation at arbitrary parameter values [12], [14]. Both depend on knowledge about the mesh topology. Moreover, the subdivision surface approach cannot be easily extended to volumetric domains, and it has to deal with overlapping surface patches.

In contrast to the previous techniques, our proposed method can handle planar surfaces and general volumes represented by regular grids with arbitrary geometry. We require no explicit topological information. All we need are the positions of the grid nodes in world space, from which we compute Jacobian matrices that relate field derivatives in the grid and world coordinate systems. This allows us to efficiently integrate the reduced Navier-Stokes equations directly in the parameter space, accounting for curves and deformations in a natural way. As a result, we avoid the overhead of working with simplicial meshes or refining the grid near curved boundaries, and thus we are able to produce faster simulations with a high level of parallelism. Also, internal obstacles can be voxelized into cells that approximate their shape a lot better than a regular grid.

2. Method

2.1 Navier-Stokes equations

A 3D fluid can be described by a velocity vector field $\vec{u} = [u, v, w]^T$ and a pressure scalar field p. We can also consider properties like density (ρ), kinematic viscosity (ν), and external forces ($\vec{F}$), constant or not, along the fluid.

The evolution of the velocity and pressure fields is given by the reduced Navier-Stokes equations for incompressible fluids [15], [16]:

$$\nabla\cdot \vec{u} = 0 \quad (1)$$

$$\frac{\partial \vec{u}}{\partial t} = -\left(\vec{u}\cdot\nabla\right)\vec{u} - \frac{1}{\rho}\nabla p + \nu\nabla^2\vec{u} + \frac{1}{\rho}\vec{F} \quad (2)$$

In the simplest Eulerian approach, a fluid is described by sampling its properties in a regular grid. Each cell is identified by an $[i, j, k]^T$ index and has the same size $[\delta_x, \delta_y, \delta_z]^T$. We can find an approximate expression for $\partial\vec{u}/\partial t$ by taking samples on each cell center $\vec{x} = [x, y, z]^T$ and applying finite differences to discretize the derivatives.

Unfortunately, explicit integration of (2) is quite unstable [3]. It also requires the solution of a large system with at least as many unknowns as grid cells, which can be very computationally expensive. As a result, the development of fast and robust solvers is still a challenging problem.

Note that velocity samples can be taken in a staggered MAC grid pattern, in which each component is stored in the grid face orthogonal to it [17]. Although the technique proposed in the next sections can also be applied to this kind of grid, we focus on the simpler collocated grid, which yields a good approximation while avoiding extra interpolations.

2.2 Jacobian matrix

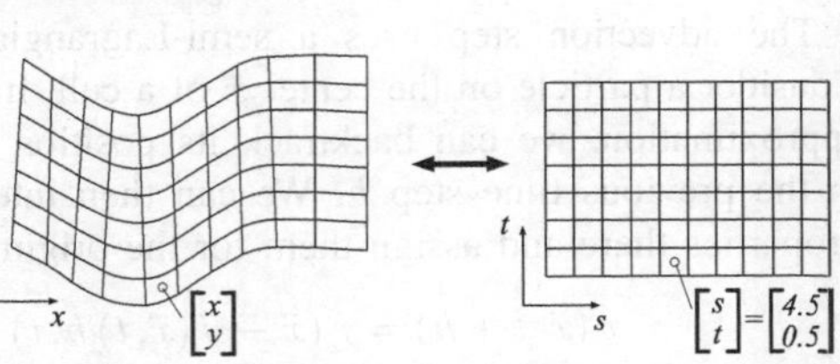

Fig. 2: Relating world (x, y) and grid (s, t) coordinates.

Our ultimate goal is to simulate flows on parameterized structured grids with arbitrary shape. This kind of discretization is interesting because, as illustrated in Fig. 2 for two dimensions, any such grid in the (x, y, z) world space can be associated with a uniform grid in the (s, t, p) parameter space. This suggests that the integration of the Navier-Stokes equations can be performed directly in parameter space, where the computations should be greatly simplified.

Looking back to (1) and (2), we note that the behavior of the fluid is described only in terms of velocities and other field derivatives, not depending directly on any positional information. Therefore, in order to transform the equations from world to parameter space, all we need is to relate these derivatives in the two coordinate systems. This can be done using Jacobian matrices J as below, where f_x denotes the derivative of field f in the x direction and $f_{(s,t,p)}$ denotes the value of f in the (s, t, p) coordinate space:

$$\nabla f_{(s,t,p)} = J\nabla f_{(x,y,z)} \qquad \vec{u}_{(s,t,p)} = (J^{-1})^T\vec{u}_{(x,y,z)} \quad (3)$$

$$\nabla f_{(x,y,z)} = J^{-1}\nabla f_{(s,t,p)} \qquad \vec{u}_{(x,y,z)} = J^T\vec{u}_{(s,t,p)} \quad (4)$$

$$J = \begin{pmatrix} x_s & y_s & z_s \\ x_t & y_t & z_t \\ x_p & y_p & z_p \end{pmatrix} \qquad J^{-1} = \begin{pmatrix} s_x & t_x & p_x \\ s_y & t_y & p_y \\ s_z & t_z & p_z \end{pmatrix} \quad (5)$$

The Jacobian and its inverse can be precomputed by the fluid solver. The nine terms of J (four in 2D) are calculated for each cell by finite differences with the positions of neighboring cell centers, and then stored like any other scalar fluid property. Second-order terms needed in Section 2.4.2 can also be precomputed in this fashion. It is important to note that, since the Jacobian is not constant over each cell, it must be interpolated when needed away from cell centers.

2.3 Stable Fluids

The inherent difficulty in the explicit integration of (2) led to the development of Stable Fluids [1], a fast and unconditionally stable method to evolve the velocity of a fluid in a regular grid. The technique solves the Navier-Stokes equations by sequentially applying four operators: external force (F), advection (A), diffusion (D), and projection (P). Each step uses the velocities computed by the previous one:

$$\vec{u}_{i,j,k}^{n+1} = P \circ D \circ A \circ F\left(\vec{u}_{i,j,k}^{n}\right) \quad (6)$$

The first step, force, does not present any instability problems, so an explicit Euler integration can be used.

The advection step uses a semi-Lagrangian approach. Consider a particle on the center $\vec{x}$ of a cell. In a first-order approximation, we can backtrack its position to $(\vec{x} - \vec{u}h)$ in the previous time step h. We can then interpolate fluid properties there and assign them for the original cell:

$$r\left(\vec{x}, t+h\right) = r\left(\vec{x} - \vec{u}\left(\vec{x}, t\right) h, t\right) \quad (7)$$

The stable diffusion step uses an implicit formulation:

$$\left(I - \nu h \nabla^2\right) \vec{u}_{i,j,k}^{n+1} = \vec{u}_{i,j,k}^{n} \quad (8)$$

In (8), we have a Poisson equation, where each velocity component represents a symmetric sparse linear system with one unknown per grid cell. Such a system can be efficiently solved by methods such as the preconditioned Conjugate Gradient [1], [16], [18]. In order to establish a performance baseline, we also consider a simple Jacobi iteration method [2], which is easily parallelizeable but has poor convergence.

Finally, on the projection step, we calculate the velocity divergence and use it to find the pressure gradient [1]:

$$\nabla \cdot \vec{u} = \nabla^2 p \quad (9)$$

Once again, we have a Poisson equation, for which we can use the same methods as before. Once the pressure is found, we project the velocities into a divergence-free field:

$$\vec{u}' = \vec{u} - \nabla p \quad (10)$$

After the velocities are integrated, we can also advect and evolve particle positions and scalar quantities such as temperature and density [1].

2.4 Simulation in the parameter space

2.4.1 Advection step

In the advection step, we first query the world-space flow velocity at the center of each grid cell. We then use (3) to transform it to grid coordinates, where the advection is to be performed. The backtracking of the Lagrangian particle can be done by an integrator of any desired order. After reaching the final location, the value of the advected field can be interpolated and copied back to the original cell.

If the time step allows the particle to traverse several grid cells at once, a large variation of the Jacobian can make the particle end up in a completely unexpected position. This can be a problem around tight corners, for example. In Fig. 3, the solid trajectory (A) is the desired result of a first-order world-space integration. However, the procedure above would inaccurately result in the dashed trajectory (B). It is possible to deal with this issue by tracking the particle as it traverses grid cells: whenever it crosses the boundary between two cells, we can resample the Jacobian and reconvert the remainder of the world-space step to grid space, which results in the dotted trajectory (C). Alternatively, a more interesting approach is the usage of an adaptive substep: simply resample the Jacobian whenever the particle travels some fixed distance (e.g. one unit) in parameter space. This avoids unnecessary resamplings when the particle crosses boundaries in two or three directions at once, while retaining the nice property of automatically adapting to the local grid cell size, since resampling is made more often when traversing small cells.

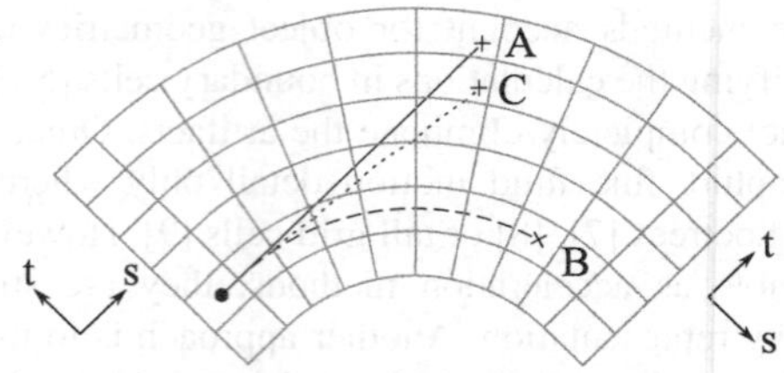

Fig. 3: Advecting a particle with a velocity in the s direction. A) Solid: desired trajectory. B) Dashed: using a large step in grid space. C) Dotted line: using Jacobian substeps.

When using higher-order integrators, the Jacobian resampling techniques above could be used for obtaining each intermediary velocity value in world space, but that could become very costly. An easier and more efficient approach is to completely ignore the effect shown in Fig. 3 and work entirely with grid-space velocities. This means intermediary velocities should be calculated in grid-space using the local Jacobian in their sampling point, and the final velocity should be a weighted sum of those grid-space velocities. This allows the integrator to effectively take into account variations in both velocities and Jacobians, which results in quite good approximations for small to medium time steps.

2.4.2 Diffusion step

The discretized equation for the diffusion step in parameter space must be derived from scratch. Our starting point is (8), the implicit Poisson equation from the Stable Fluids method [1]. The expression can be rewritten as follows, where $\vec{u}'$ represents the next value of $\vec{u}$ at the end of the current time step:

$$\frac{\vec{u}' - \vec{u}}{\nu h} = \left(\vec{u}'_{xx} + \vec{u}'_{yy} + \vec{u}'_{zz}\right) \quad (11)$$

By using (3) and (4) and the chain rule, this equation can be converted to a form that uses velocity derivatives in parameter space instead of world space. Then, approximating the result by finite differences in the underlying uniform grid, we can find the following iteration rule for $\vec{u}$:

$$\begin{aligned}
&\vec{u}'_{i,j,k}\left[\beta + 2\left(k_s + k_t + k_p\right)\right] = \alpha f + \\
&\left(\vec{u}'_{i+1,j,k} + \vec{u}'_{i-1,j,k}\right) k_s + \left(\vec{u}'_{i+1,j,k} - \vec{u}'_{i-1,j,k}\right) k_{ss} + \\
&\left(\vec{u}'_{i,j+1,k} + \vec{u}'_{i,j-1,k}\right) k_t + \left(\vec{u}'_{i,j+1,k} - \vec{u}'_{i,j-1,k}\right) k_{tt} + \\
&\left(\vec{u}'_{i,j,k+1} + \vec{u}'_{i,j,k-1}\right) k_p + \left(\vec{u}'_{i,j,k+1} - \vec{u}'_{i,j,k-1}\right) k_{pp} + \\
&\left(\vec{u}'_{i+1,j+1,k} + \vec{u}'_{i-1,j-1,k} - \vec{u}'_{i+1,j-1,k} - \vec{u}'_{i-1,j+1,k}\right) k_{st} + \\
&\left(\vec{u}'_{i,j+1,k+1} + \vec{u}'_{i,j-1,k-1} - \vec{u}'_{i,j+1,k-1} - \vec{u}'_{i,j-1,k+1}\right) k_{tp} + \\
&\left(\vec{u}'_{i+1,j,k+1} + \vec{u}'_{i-1,j,k-1} - \vec{u}'_{i-1,j,k+1} - \vec{u}'_{i+1,j,k-1}\right) k_{ps}
\end{aligned} \tag{12}$$

where:

$$\begin{aligned}
k_s &= s_x^2 + s_y^2 + s_z^2 & 2k_{st} &= s_x t_x + s_y t_y + s_z t_z \\
k_t &= t_x^2 + t_y^2 + t_z^2 & 2k_{tp} &= t_x p_x + t_y p_y + t_z p_z \\
k_p &= p_x^2 + p_y^2 + p_z^2 & 2k_{ps} &= p_x s_x + p_y s_y + p_z s_z \\
2k_{ss} &= s_{xx} + s_{yy} + s_{zz} & \alpha &= 1/\nu h \\
2k_{tt} &= t_{xx} + t_{yy} + t_{zz} & \beta &= 1/\nu h \\
2k_{pp} &= p_{xx} + p_{yy} + p_{zz} & f &= \vec{u}_{i,j,k}
\end{aligned}$$

The k_* terms (9 in 3D, 5 in 2D) can all be precalculated. However, the system matrix now has several super and subdiagonals, and the value of each unknown is dependent on no less than eighteen neighbors (8 in 2D). The system is also no longer symmetric, so we must use a more complex iterative solver, such as the Biconjugate Gradient Stabilized method with Algebraic Multigrid preconditioner.

Once again, we would like to use Jacobi iterations for performance comparisons. The update rule can be obtained from (12) by simply replacing every unknown velocity value $\vec{u}'$, with the exception of the central (i, j, k) sample, by the corresponding known value from the previous iteration.

2.4.3 Projection step

The projection step starts by using Equation (4) to calculate the divergence of the velocity field in grid space, which can then be used in Equation (9). The resulting sparse pressure matrix is analogous to (12), where we can simply replace $\vec{u}$ and $\vec{u}'$ by p and p', respectively, and use the following parameter values:

$$\alpha = -1,\ \beta = 0,\ f = \left(\nabla \cdot \vec{u}\right)_{i,j,k} \tag{13}$$

2.4.4 Transport step

The transport of particles by the fluid flow is achieved by integrating their positions forward in time. This process follows the same rules and adaptations described for the backtracking during advection.

An important remark is that we must store particle locations directly in grid coordinates, since converting a position from world to parameter space would require solving a nonlinear system. When rendering the particles, the world space positions can be easily approximated by interpolating grid node positions at the particle coordinates.

2.4.5 Boundary conditions

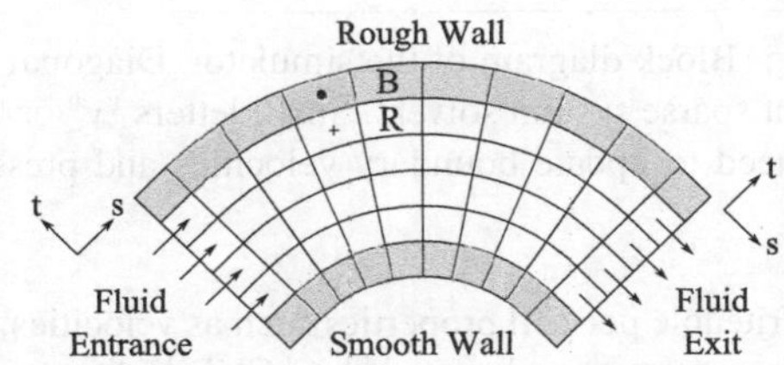

Fig. 4: Boundary conditions for the fluid velocity.

Since the calculation of derivatives for a cell requires accessing its neighbors, we need an extra layer of cells around the domain to impose some boundary conditions [3], [16]. Fig. 4 illustrates some examples.

In order to assign values for the pressure p_B and velocity v_B of the boundary cell B in Fig. 4, we must first find its internal reference neighbor R, which can be done by adding offsets to B's grid coordinates. Once we have R, we can compute the boundary conditions as follows, where $\|$ and $\perp$ refer to components parallel and orthogonal to the boundary.

$$p_B = p_R, \quad v_{B\|} = s_\| \cdot v_{R\|}, \quad v_{B\perp} = s_\perp \cdot v_{R\perp} + o_\perp \tag{14}$$

In (14), s and o are arbitrary scale and offset values. Table 1 shows how they can be used to achieve the different fluid behaviors shown in Fig. 4 at the boundaries.

Notice that the velocity components defined in (14) are always aligned with the grid coordinates. Therefore, the Jacobian matrix must be used both ways: we convert velocities and orthogonal offsets to grid space, apply the boundary conditions, and store the results back in world space.

Table 1: Boundary values for the fluid velocity.

Effect	$s_\|$	$s_\perp$	$o_\perp$
Rough wall	-1	-1	0
Smooth wall	1	-1	0
Fluid entrance	0	0	u
Fluid exit	0	0	u

3. Implementation

We have implemented our solver in standard C++ and CUDA [19]. We have also implemented basic visualization algorithms in GLSL to validate the results.

The domain geometry is specified as an array of node coordinates in world space, which are used to find the cell centers. Afterwards, we compute the Jacobian matrices and their inverses according to (5), as well as every k_* constant in (12). These properties are stored in read-only CUDA Arrays for fast access with 3D hardware interpolation.

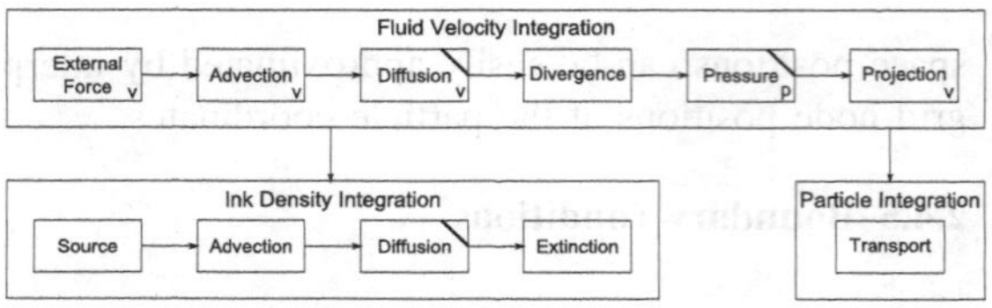

Fig. 5: Block diagram of the simulator. Diagonal stripes represent sparse system solvers. Small letters "v" or "p" indicate the need to update boundary velocities and pressures.

Writeable per-cell properties such as velocities, divergence and pressures are also stored in CUDA Arrays, but can be written to by CUDA Surfaces. If a property must be read and updated by a single kernel, we need to use two different memory areas and switch their pointers after each iteration.

Data arrays required by the visualization are stored as OpenGL resources (PBOs, VBOs or textures). As an example, the grid-space position of massless particles is kept in a VBO and accessed through a cudaGraphicsResource pointer.

External influences (forces and ink sources) and boundary conditions (reference offset, tangential and orthogonal scale and offsets) are also stored per-cell in 3D CUDA Arrays. If any change is required, a page-locked staging memory area is used to transfer the new data asynchronously without compromising the overall simulation performance.

Fig. 5 presents a block diagram showing every high-level operation performed by our simulator. The top row contains the steps responsible for the actual integration of the fluid velocities, while the bottom row shows the advection of ink densities and the transport of massless particles performed to allow a meaningful visualization of the results.

Each simulation step is associated with a specialized CUDA Kernel. The implementation is quite straightforward: there is no need to make use of the device's shared memory, since all global memory reads are either naturally coalesced or show good spatial locality for texture or surface access. Kernel launches use blocks of $(32 \times 2 \times 2)$ or $(32 \times 4 \times 4)$ threads, depending on register usage limitations.

The most expensive step of the algorithm is the solution of the Poisson equations (marked by diagonal stripes in Fig. 5), especially the unavoidable pressure solve. We investigated two different techniques for dealing with this problem: the simple Jacobi iterations and the fast-converging Biconjugate Gradient Stabilized method with an Algebraic Multigrid preconditioner. The former was implemented by calling a simple kernel inside an iterative loop. For the latter, however, we used a very efficient routine provided by the CUSP library [20]. Remember that the basic Conjugate Gradient solver cannot be employed here, since the system's matrix is not symmetric when we are using Jacobians.

Finally, for the visualization of the results, the ink densities and massless particles advected along the fluid are rendered using simple GLSL shaders.

4. Results and Discussion

In this section, we present example grids, describe validation experiments, and discuss the correctness and performance of our results. All fluids were simulated as flowing through a pipe from left to right. Except where explicitly noted, the simulations were performed with a time step of 0.05s, a density of 1.0, rough boundaries, fourth order Runge-Kutta advection and transport, 100 Jacobi pressure iterations, and no viscosity.

4.1 Regular grid

As an initial validation experiment, we applied our solver to a three-dimensional regular grid with cell size $[\delta_x, \delta_y, \delta_z]^T$, where the equations in Section 2 are reduced to their original versions. The resulting fluid behavior was verified to be identical to the one generated by the standard Stable Fluids algorithm.

4.2 Double elbow path

The path shown in Fig. 1 was designed to test the fluid's behavior while cornering and flowing along each direction.

Looking back at the figure, we note that the fluid responds correctly to each of the turns in the pipe, with the formation of vortices around each corner. This indicates the Jacobians are being correctly applied, otherwise the fluid would flow as if in a completely straight segment.

The detail in Fig. 6 shows an inside view from the last corner of the pipe to the end where the fluid exits the domain. After both turns, the fluid naturally begins to spin in the pipe in a spiral pattern, which is intuitively expected.

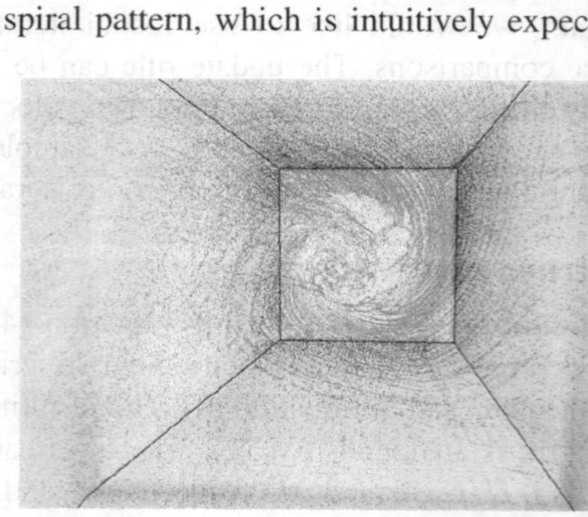

Fig. 6: Massless particles in the double elbow path with $(256 \times 32 \times 32)$ cells.

4.3 Constricted path

The path in Fig. 7 was designed to test the correctness of the fluid's behavior when flowing through a constriction.

For a laminar incompressible flow (with smooth boundaries and a viscosity of $0.1 Pa \cdot s$), the velocity inside the constricted region should be higher than elsewhere in order to keep the mass flow per area constant. This can be verified in Fig. 8, which shows the average flow velocity in the x

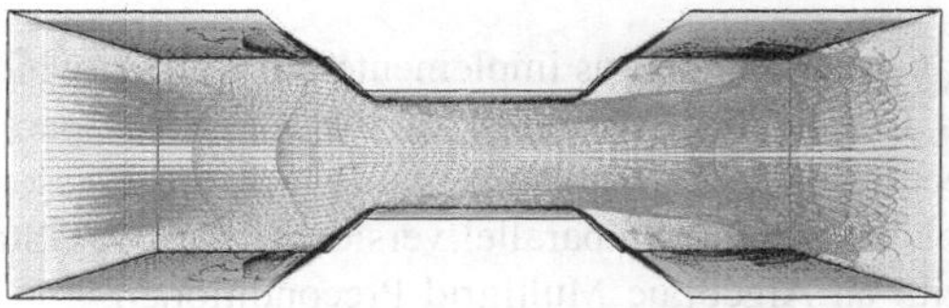

Fig. 7: Massless particles in the constricted path with $(256 \times 32 \times 32)$ cells.

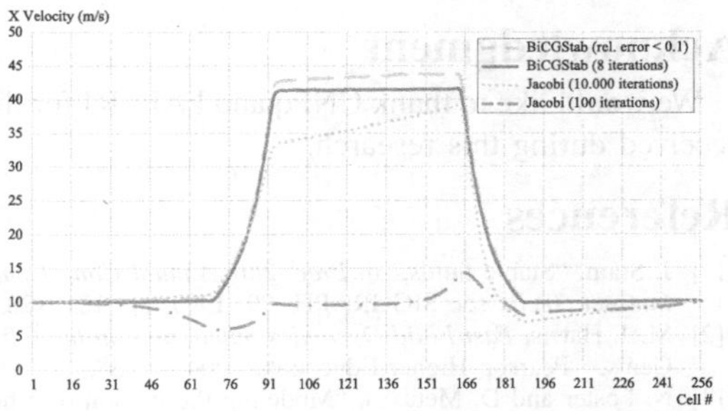

Fig. 8: Average flow velocity in the x direction through orthogonal sections taken at cells with increasing i index along the constricted path.

direction along the path, considering a constricted region with one fourth the normal section area. The plot shows that, as we increase the precision of the pressure solve, the velocity inside the constricted region tends to stabilize at four times the velocity elsewhere, as expected.

On the other hand, Fig. 7 shows a different behavior. With rough boundaries and zero viscosity, the fluid tends to generate large vortices when leaving the constriction.

4.4 Smooth curved path with internal obstacle

The example shown in Fig. 9 illustrates a smoothly curved path with an internal obstacle. While our model does not support actual holes in the grid topology, we can use a region whose cells approximate the shape of the intended obstacle. Smooth models such as this are particularly well suited to our technique, since there are no sudden variations in the Jacobian.

The effect of the obstacle in the flow can be identified clearly in Fig. 9. Vortices are formed above and below the obstacle, creating a turbulent zone behind it, as expected.

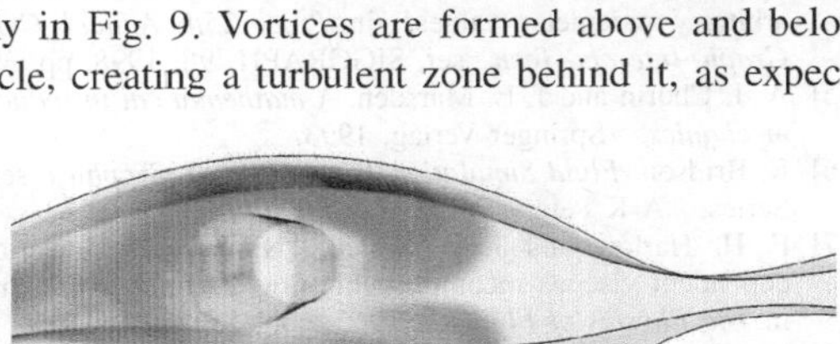

Fig. 9: Blue ink flowing through the smooth curved path with $(256 \times 32 \times 32)$ cells and an internal obstacle.

4.5 Performance and Stability

In order to evaluate the performance and stability of our algorithm, we performed a series of timed tests on a machine with an Intel Core i5 750 2.67GHz processor, 4GB of RAM and a GeForce GTX 550 Ti graphics card.

The most computationally intensive step of any Eulerian fluid solver is the solution of the Poisson equations, especially the pressure computation, which imposes a bound on the algorithm's efficiency. Because of that, we first investigated the performance and stability of two Poisson equation solvers: the simple and easily parallelizeable Jacobi iterations, and the fast-converging Biconjugate Gradient Stabilized (BiCGStab) with Algebraic Multigrid preconditioner.

Table 2 shows the time taken by a small number of BiCGStab iterations, as well as the number of Jacobi iterations that can be performed in the same period. The latter are clearly more lightweight, but our experiments showed that they did not achieve comparable results in quality. This can be verified by observing the decrease in the relative residual error of the solvers, i.e., how the length of the right-hand-side of the system with each successive iterative solution compares to its original value. The last row in Table 2 reveals that even 200 Jacobi iterations are not capable of reaching a relative residual error as small as the one obtained after only 3 BiCGStab iterations. The difference in the convergence of the methods can also be clearly seen in Fig. 8, which shows how even ten thousand Jacobi iterations do not generate a behavior as accurate as a few BiCGStab iterations.

Table 2: Number of iterations until a time limit is reached or the residual error becomes smaller than a threshold.

Stop Condition	BiCGStab Iterations	Jacobi Iterations
t = 23 ms	1	40
t = 37 ms	2	65
t = 51 ms	3	90
relative error < 0.1	3	>200

Despite the performance advantage of the BiCGStab method, we noticed that its stability was not optimal, for sometimes it did not converge to an appropriate solution, leading to somewhat awkward fluid behavior. Jacobi iterations, on the other hand, delivered more consistent results and never failed to converge, so we still found it useful for cross-checking simulation results.

Another important point to consider is the initial guess used for the pressure in the solvers. We found that using the previous solution as an initial guess tends to converge quite faster than starting from zero. The downside is that the integration constants arising from several consecutive solves (due to the fact that our boundary conditions apply to the derivative of the pressure, not the pressure itself) might accumulate over time. Because of that, we reset the initial guess back to zero after a fixed number of solves.

Table 3: Performance comparison between Stable Fluids and our proposed method in a $(64 \times 64 \times 32)$ grid

Pressure Iterations	Full Simulation		No Diffusion	
	Stable Fluids	Proposed Method	Stable Fluids	Proposed Method
1 BiCGStab	18 ms	45 ms	11 ms	16 ms
2 BiCGStab	22 ms	53 ms	15 ms	25 ms
3 BiCGStab	26 ms	63 ms	19 ms	33 ms
50 Jacobi	14 ms	48 ms	07 ms	18 ms
75 Jacobi	16 ms	53 ms	10 ms	25 ms
100 Jacobi	19 ms	59 ms	12 ms	31 ms

In the following tests, we compared our performance with that of a standard Stable Fluids solver. Table 3 shows the simulation times achieved for fluids in three-dimensional regular grids using the original Stable Fluids solver and our method. The first pair of timings in each row considers the full simulation of the fluid, including the advection of ink densities and massless particles, using a fixed 20 Jacobi iterations for the viscosity and diffusion steps. For the second pair, the viscosity and diffusion steps are skipped. The timings do not consider any rendering.

As can be seen in Table 3, our method doubled to tripled the computational cost of the original Stable Fluids solver. However, the parameterization can prevent artifacts and eliminate the need to oversample the fluid domain near its boundaries. Therefore, if the total number of cells required by the parameterized grid is less than a third of that needed for an equivalent regular grid, we can achieve much better performance and quality than the standard algorithm.

5. Conclusion

In this paper, we proposed a fast method based on a simplified physical model to simulate fluids in three-dimensional domains with arbitrarily-shaped boundaries. We employed a uniform grid to drive the simulation of a structured discretization of these domains in parameter space. In order to accomplish this, the Jacobian matrices that relate world and parameter spaces were derived using finite differences, and every step of Stam's Stable Fluids integrator [1] was modified accordingly. As a result, our approach was able to generate efficient flow simulations on complex domains, as demonstrated in the presented examples of three-dimensional paths with curves, constrictions, and internal obstacles.

Despite having a higher cost per-cell than the original Stable Fluids, our proposed method can produce convincing results for curved-boundary domains even with a relatively small number of cells, which greatly compensates the extra cost and allows for quite fast simulations. Moreover, our approach completely avoids artifacts caused by misaligned boundaries, which are difficult to eliminate using only regular grids, even with a large number of cells or adaptive refinement schemes.

Our simulator was implemented in CUDA, which allowed us to take full advantage of the massively parallel architecture of today's graphics cards. For the Poisson equation solvers, we used a parallel version of the BiCGStab method with an Algebraic Multigrid Preconditioner.

As future work, we plan to implement our method on a MAC grid. We will also add gravity and track the fluid's free surface to simulate ocean waves and other phenomena.

Acknowledgment

We would like to thank CNPq and FAPERJ for the funding received during this research.

References

[1] J. Stam, "Stable fluids," in *Proc. 26th Annual Conf. Comput. Graph. Interact. Tech.*, ser. SIGGRAPH '99, 1999, pp. 121–128.

[2] M. J. Harris, *Fast Fluid Dynamics Simulation on the GPU*, ser. GPU Gems. Pearson Higher Education, 2004, ch. 38.

[3] N. Foster and D. Metaxas, "Modeling the motion of a hot, turbulent gas," in *Proc. 24th Annual Conf. Comput. Graph. Interact. Tech.*, ser. SIGGRAPH '97, 1997, pp. 181–188.

[4] C. Batty, F. Bertails, and R. Bridson, "A fast variational framework for accurate solid-fluid coupling," in *ACM SIGGRAPH 2007 Pap.*, ser. SIGGRAPH '07. ACM, 2007.

[5] N. Foster and R. Fedkiw, "Practical animation of liquids," in *Proc. 28th Annual Conf. Comput. Graph. Interact. Tech.*, ser. SIGGRAPH '01. ACM, 2001, pp. 23–30.

[6] D. Roble, N. bin Zafar, and H. Falt, "Cartesian grid fluid simulation with irregular boundary voxels," in *ACM SIGGRAPH 2005 Sketches*, ser. SIGGRAPH '05. ACM, 2005.

[7] L. Shi and Y. Yu, "Visual smoke simulation with adaptive octree refinement," University of Illinois, Tech. Rep., 2002.

[8] F. Losasso, F. Gibou, and R. Fedkiw, "Simulating water and smoke with an octree data structure," in *ACM SIGGRAPH 2004 Pap.*, ser. SIGGRAPH '04. ACM, 2004, pp. 457–462.

[9] N. Chentanez and M. Müller, "Real-time eulerian water simulation using a restricted tall cell grid," in *ACM SIGGRAPH 2011 Pap.*, ser. SIGGRAPH '11. New York, NY, USA: ACM, 2011, pp. 82:1–82:10.

[10] N. Chentanez, B. E. Feldman, F. Labelle, J. F. O'Brien, and J. R. Shewchuk, "Liquid simulation on lattice-based tetrahedral meshes," in *Proc. 2007 ACM SIGGRAPH/Eurographics Symp. Comput. Animat.*, ser. SCA '07. Eurographics Association, 2007, pp. 219–228.

[11] P. Mullen, K. Crane, D. Pavlov, Y. Tong, and M. Desbrun, "Energy-preserving integrators for fluid animation," in *ACM SIGGRAPH 2009 Pap.*, ser. SIGGRAPH '09. ACM, 2009, pp. 38:1–38:8.

[12] J. Stam, "Flows on surfaces of arbitrary topology," in *ACM SIGGRAPH 2003 Pap.*, ser. SIGGRAPH '03, 2003, pp. 724–731.

[13] L. Shi and Y. Yu, "Inviscid and incompressible fluid simulation on triangle meshes," *Comput. Animat. Virtual Worlds*, vol. 15, no. 3-4, pp. 173–181, 2004.

[14] J. Stam, "Exact evaluation of catmull-clark subdivision surfaces at arbitrary parameter values," in *Proc. 25th Annual Conf. Comput. Graph. Interact. Tech.*, ser. SIGGRAPH '98, 1998, pp. 395–404.

[15] A. J. Chorin and J. E. Marsden, *A mathematical introduction to fluid mechanics*. Springer-Verlag, 1993.

[16] R. Bridson, *Fluid Simulation For Computer Graphics*, ser. Ak Peters Series. A K Peters, 2008.

[17] F. H. Harlow and J. E. Welch, "Numerical calculation of time-dependent viscous incompressible flow of fluid with a free surface," in *The Physics of Fluids 8*, 1965, pp. 2182–Ű2189.

[18] W. Hackbusch, *Multi-grid methods and applications*, ser. Springer series in computational mathematics. Springer, 1985.

[19] NVIDIA Corporation, *NVIDIA CUDA C Programming Guide Version 4.2*. NVIDIA Corporation, 2012.

[20] N. Bell and M. Garland, "Cusp: Generic parallel algorithms for sparse matrix and graph computations," 2012, version 0.3.0. [Online]. Available: http://cusp-library.googlecode.com

Integration of Numerical Simulation Data with Immersive 3D Visualization

Dong Fu[1], John Moreland[1], Litao Shen[1,2], Bin Wu[1], Chenn Zhou[1,3]
[1]Center for Innovation through Visualization and Simulation
[2]Electrical and Computer Engineering
[3]Mechancial Engineering
Purdue University Calumet
Hammond, IN, USA

Abstract - *The numerical simulation such as Computational Fluid Dynamics (CFD) and Finite Element Analysis (FEA) have been used in engineering design, optimization and troubleshooting. The visualization of numerical simulation results, however, is normally limited to 2D screens. Work has already been accomplished to integrate CFD results with 3D Virtual Reality (VR) visualization. This paper discusses how these previous efforts are being combined into a user-friendly software package named Center for Innovation through Visualization (CIVS) 3D-Immersive Data Visualization (3D-IDV) that simplifies the process of combining and interacting numerical results, scientific rendering, and photorealistic rendering in a virtual environment. The simulation results are intuitive to experts and non-experts by using the 3D-IDV software package. The 3D-IDV software package significantly enhanced the post possessing and the accessibility of simulation results.*

Keywords: 3D, Virtual Reality, Data Visualization, Simulation, CFD, FEA

1 Introduction

Numerical simulations for industrial processes have become increasingly sophisticated since solutions are often three dimensional, multi-phase, as well as time dependent [1]. With increasingly complex CFD/FEA capable of simulating and analyzing ever-larger amounts of data, interpolating and presenting the numerical data in a meaningful fashion is a key to effective communication between simulation experts and non-simulation experts. Traditionally, post processing of the simulation data involves 2D views and animation. However, the 2D pictures and limited 3D views may be limited and insufficient [2].

The integration of simulation with VR can significantly reduce the design and troubleshooting cycle. It also enable a collaborative environment among people with different background. In the effort to integrate VR visualization with simulation , VE-Suite [3] was developed at at Iowa State University's Virtual Reality Applications Center. It allows users to examine fluid flow characteristics using immersive visualization and three-dimensional user interaction. However, it provides limited interface customization and user function development.

A methodology to visualize the numerical simulation data has been described previously [4-6]. The post-processed data is converted as Virtual Reality Modeling Language (VRML) and Open Scene Graph (OSG) model for visualization. The 3D-IDV software package has been developed to incorporate the visualization and interaction of the simulation data in an immersive 3D environment. The current efforts has been made for the development of the user friendly menu system and streamlining the conversion process.

2 CIVS 3D-Immersive Data Visualization (3D-IDV) Software Package

2.1 Overview of the CIVS 3D-IDV

The 3D-IDV software package has developed to streamline the process of visualization and interaction with simulation data in the 3D immersive environment.

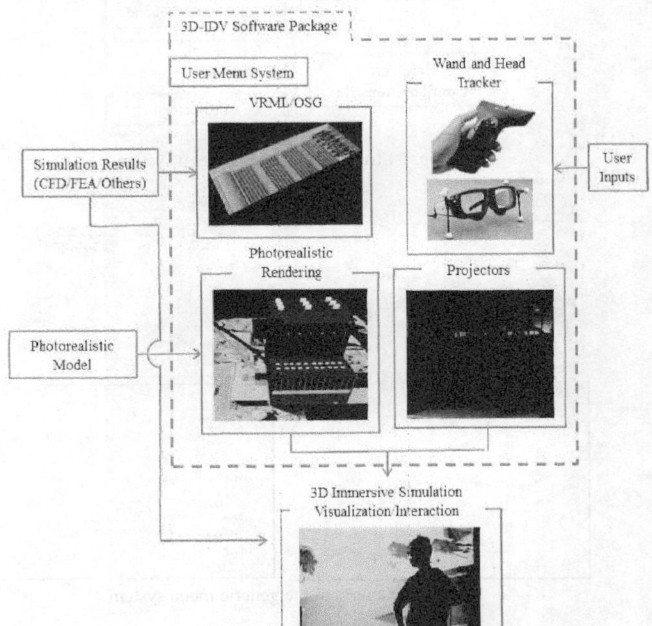

Fig. 1 Schematic of the 3D-IDV package

The schematic of the 3D-IDV software package is shown in Fig. 1. The CFD/FEA simulation results are processed by other software such as PARAVIEW [7] and ANSYS CFD-Post [8] to generate the VRML or OSG [9] 3D model. The photorealistic model form 3D Max [10] or other commercial 3D software can be intergraded with the simulation results 3D model to make the surrounding of the immersive environment more realistic. The 3D-IDV software package is integrated with VR Juggler [11] to configure the communication with the inputs hardware (wand and head tracker) and outputs hardware (3D projectors). The simulation results are also directly feed into the visualization scene to enable the interaction of real time retrieving the data at desired location in the 3D environment. Therefore, the 3D-IDV software package enables the immersive visualization and interaction with simulation data.

2.2 User Menu System

The user menu system is the a user friendly interface of the 3D-IDV software package. The user can configure the visualization of the simulation data. As illustrated in Fig. 2. The input file locations for the photorealistic model, simulation results and hardware configuration will be specified by the user. The user can save current status of the configuration or load from a previous setting.

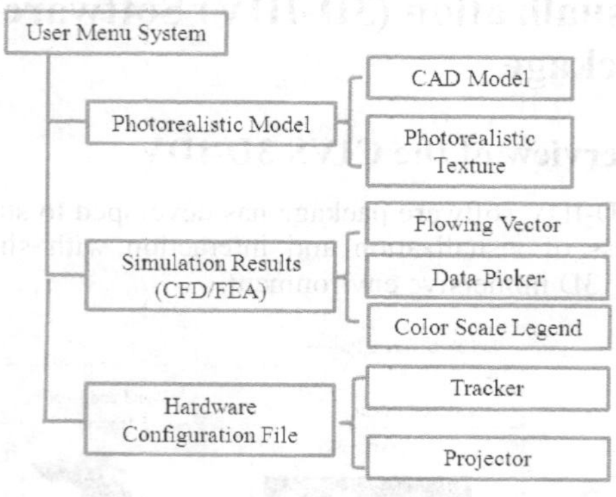

Fig. 2 Structure of the user menu system

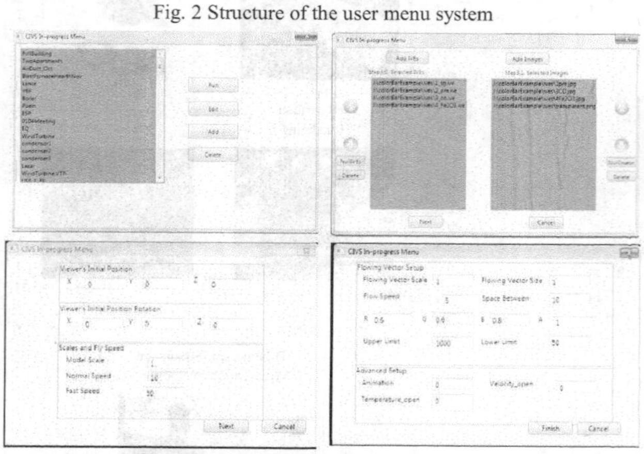

Fig. 3 Example of the generic menu system

The generic menu system is shown in Fig. 3. The user can create, modify and save the file list for the inputs of the 3D models and configurations. The configuration for each model includes the scaling, color legend, initial position and other functions. The menu system can also be customized for specific application. Fig. 4 shows an example for the customized menu system. Different icons and descriptions can be added for each 3D model.

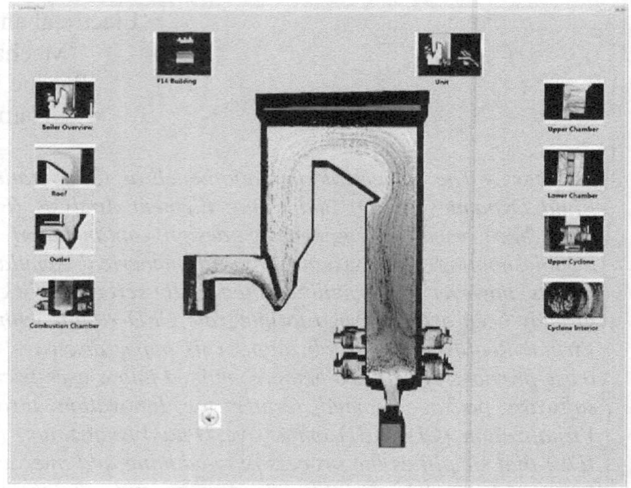

Fig. 4 Example of the customized menu system

2.3 Flowing vector

The flow visualization function includes in the 3D-IDV is the flowing vector. The flowing vector is a way to outline the flow patterns. As shown in Fig. 5, the flowing vector displays a trail of arrows that trace a path following the flow. The algorithm to calculate the position and directions of the path of the vector may involves a number of neighboring points depending on the accuracy. This provides an alternative to visualizing the flow as static arrows. The flowing vector can also applied to any vector filed visualization such as heat flux vector filed and magnetic vector field. An example of the flowing vector application for visualization the gas flow filed for a blast furnace CFD simulation is provided in Fig. 6.

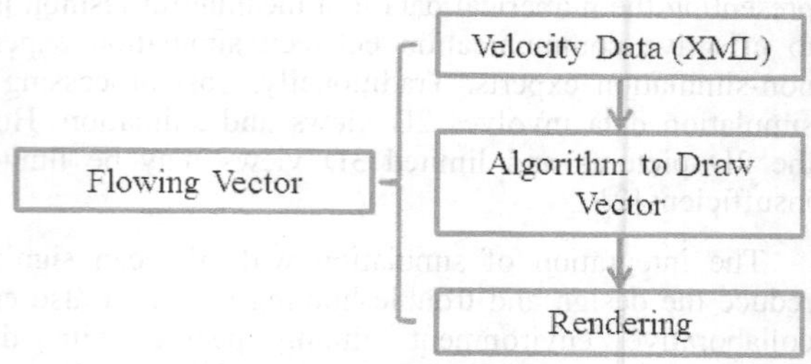

Fig. 5 Custom function of flowing vector

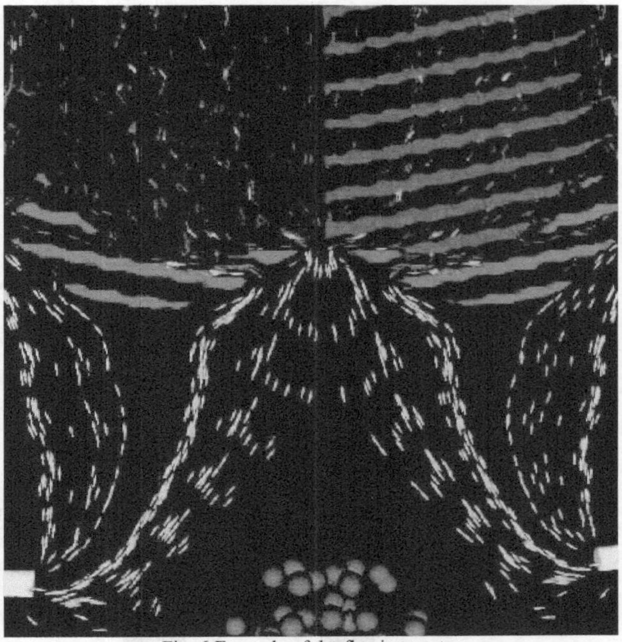

Fig. 6 Example of the flowing vector

2.4 User Interaction

The data picker function in the 3D-IDV software package is interactive data retrieval in the immersive system. It reads the quantitative data at a given location when the users visualize the simulation results. Fig. 7 shows the diagrams of the data retrieval processes described as follows.

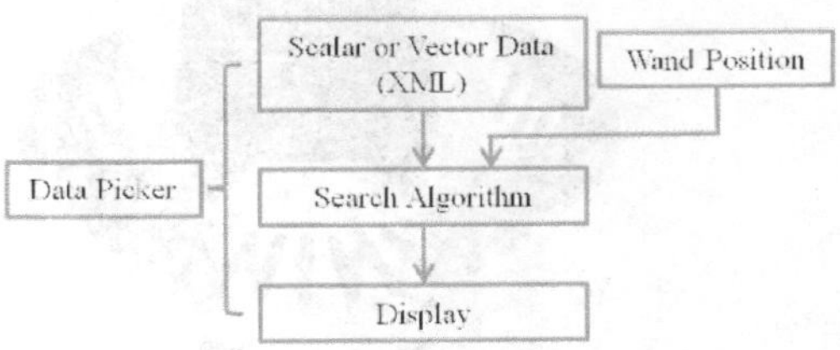

Fig. 7 Custom function of data picker

First, the program receives the wand position when a specific button is pressed, then compares the wand position coordinates with the simulation grid coordinates, finding the closest point in the grid coordinates. Once the grid index of the closest point is obtained, the corresponding scalar values are available for output to display in the immersive environment. The search algorithm may be optimized depending on the natural of the simulation data arrangement.

In this manner, the user can inspect the quantitative temperature, velocity and pressure in every corner of the blast furnace. Moreover, in order to show the location the wand is pointing at, the program would display a sphere in that position for convenience. One example of the data picker is illustrated Fig. 8. The user can control the location of the virtual probe and the CFD results at the corresponding location will be displayed in the screen.

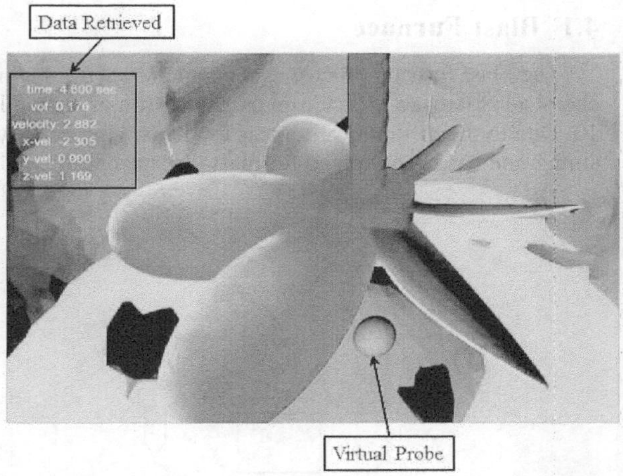

Fig. 8 Example of data picker

3 Facility

The 3D-IDV software package has been implemented in CIVS immersive theater. The Immersive Theater is a 70-seat theater featuring a large-scale 3-D virtual reality (VR) system known as the "Flex" that allows visitors to explore virtual worlds as shown in Fig. 9. The Flex consists of four projection screens (three walls and one floor) that can transform from a 30-foot wide display for large audiences, to a 12' x 9' 3D room for researchers and team collaborations. The system uses an optical tracking system that lets users interact with virtual environments.

Fig. 9 Photo of the CIVS immersive theater

4 Applications of the CIVS 3D-IDV Software Package

The 3D-IDV software package has been utilized for process and design simulation data visualization while contributing to more efficient, cost-effective solutions for industries, resulting in savings of over $30 million for companies. A few examples have been outlined in the following sections.

4.1 Blast Furnace

The blast furnace process is a counter-current moving-bed chemical reactor to reduce iron oxides to iron as shown in Fig. 10. Due to the difficulties in measurements, high fidelity CFD simulation has been utilized for blast furnace optimization.

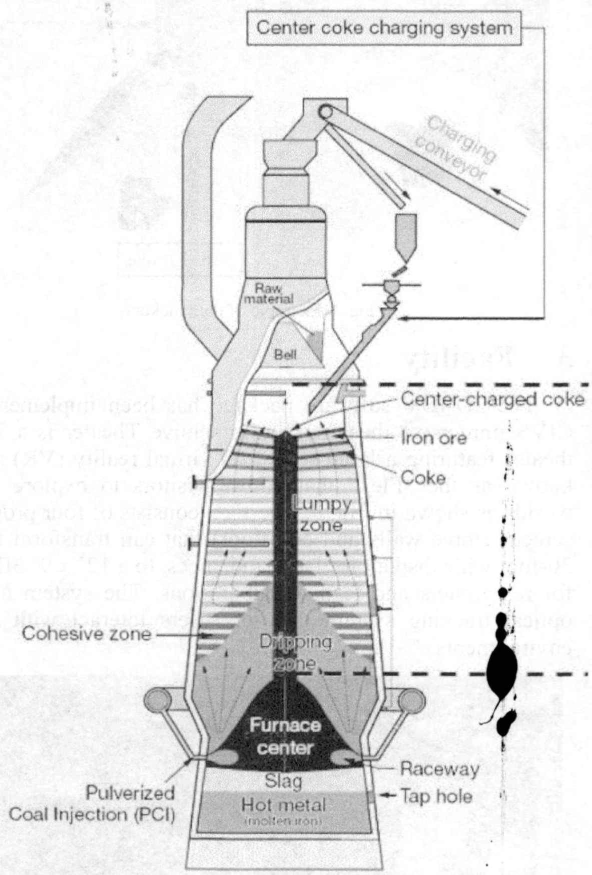

Fig. 10 Schematic of a Blast Furnace [12]

The traditional post processing for blast furnace process CFD simulation is shown in Fig. 11. With the application of 3D-IDV software package, a virtual blast as shown in Fig. 12 has been developed. The virtual blast furnace includes charging process, burden descending and gas distribution, coke and coal combustion, bottom hearth inner profile. In this application, Fig. 13 shows that advanced CFD simulation provided detailed flow characteristics while VR visualization offered a powerful way to present complex CFD data in an immersive 3D environment. This enabled researchers and collaborators to observe the facility operation in a virtual world from first-person perspective. It significantly reduced the time and effort needed for the evaluation, troubleshooting and optimization processes.

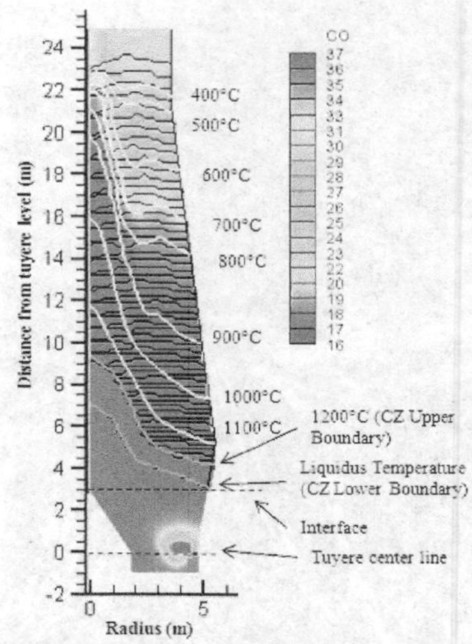

Fig. 11 Traditional post processing for blast furnace process CFD simulation [13]

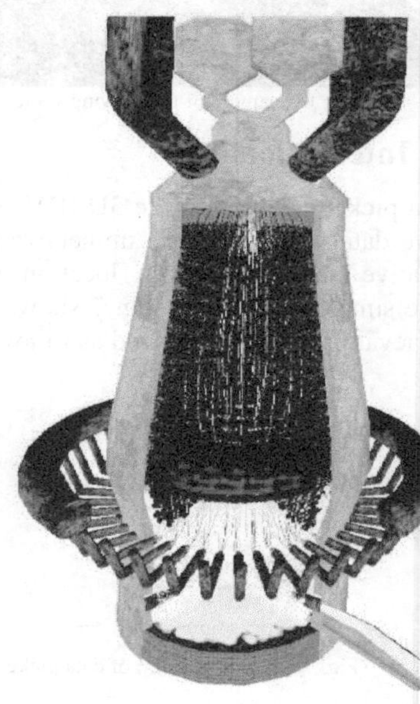

Fig. 12 Virtual blast furnace [14]

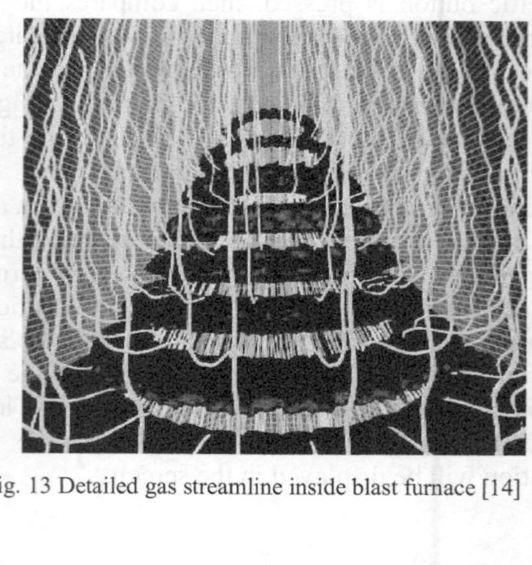

Fig. 13 Detailed gas streamline inside blast furnace [14]

In a blast furnace, natural gas co-injection with pulverized coal is primarily used as an alternative fuel source to partially replace coke. Fig. 14 shows a Schematic of the blast furnace injection system. Oxygen enriched air is supplied at the inlet of the blowpipe. A co-annular injection with pulverized coal carried by air in the inner lance and oxygen in the outer lance enters at an angle to the blowpipe. A natural gas lance also enters at an angle to the main blast air flow.

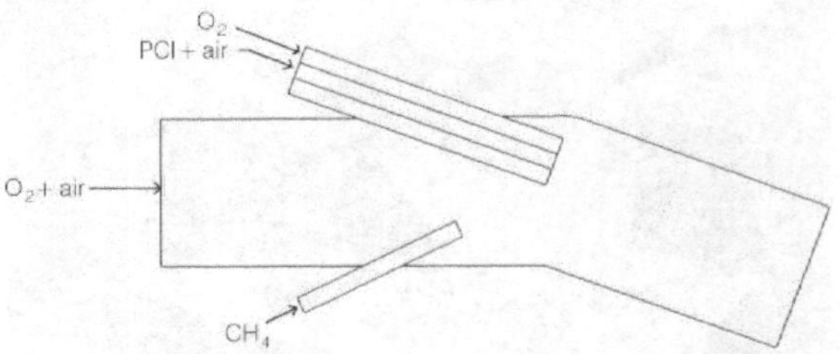

Fig. 14 Schematic of the injection system [15]

The multiphase reacting flow CFD model has been used to understand the cause of lance failure [15]. Fig. 15 shows that the visualization of the CFD results in VR immersive environment. It is obvious that the arrangement of the far back natural gas lance had caused the high surface temperature of the coal lance in the front. The VR system provides insights on the solution of the problem and optimization strategies.

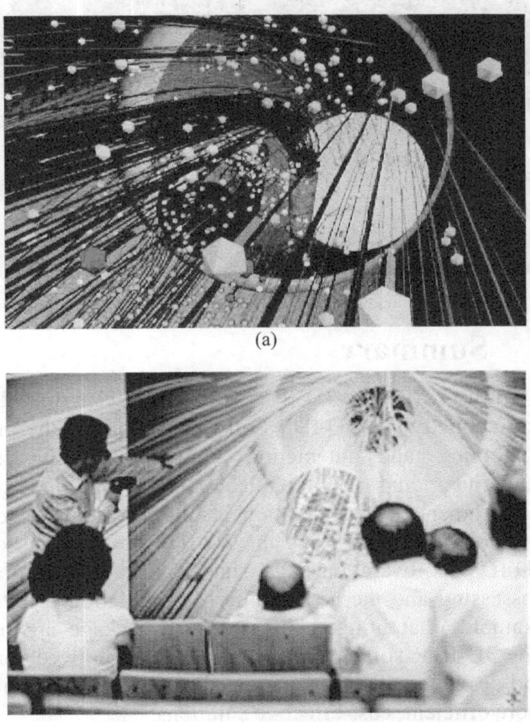

(a)

(b)

Fig. 15 VR visualization of the CFD simulation of blast furnace lances

4.2 Air Duct

One power company had an issue with a coal fired boiler. After completing the installation of pollution control equipment, the exhaust air ducts, through which exhaust gas from coal combustion is discharged to pollution control units, one of the two boilers was only able to operate at just 85 to 90 percent of maximum capacity. The reduced operating capacity diminishes overall energy production and revenue. The exhaust air duct of the joint section is heighted in the Google satellite image [16] as shown in Fig. 16.

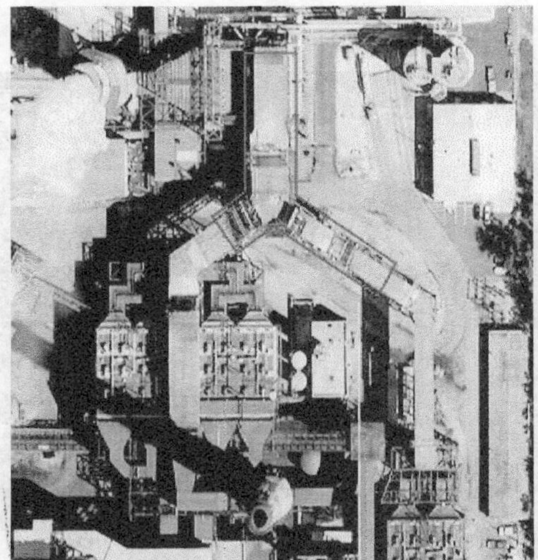

Fig. 16 Satellite Image of the Y joint facility at a power company [16]

Integration of VR Visualization with CFD simulation has been used in this study using the 3D-IDV software package.

Fig. 17 shows the streamline of the exhaust gas in the VR system. It is found a low velocity recirculation zone in the left side of the duct exit as shown in the blue color region. The user can "fly" into the region to examine the detailed flow pattern as shown in Fig. 18. Numerous cases with different turning vanes are compared in the VR system using the 3D-IDV software package. The optimized design shown in Fig. 19 was adopted by the company and both of the boilers are able to operate at maximum performance.

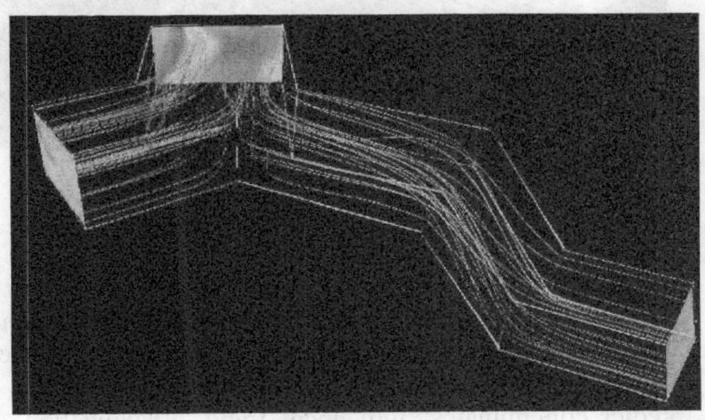

Fig. 17 VR visualization of the CFD simulation to identify the cause of flow restriction issue

(a)

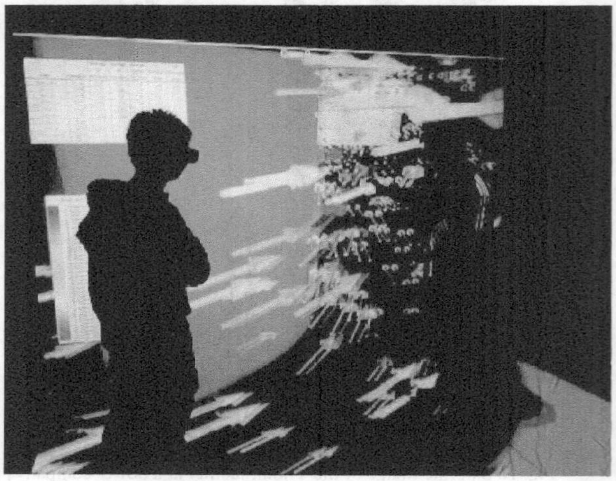

(b)

Fig. 18 VR visualization of the CFD simulation of gas flow inside duct [17]

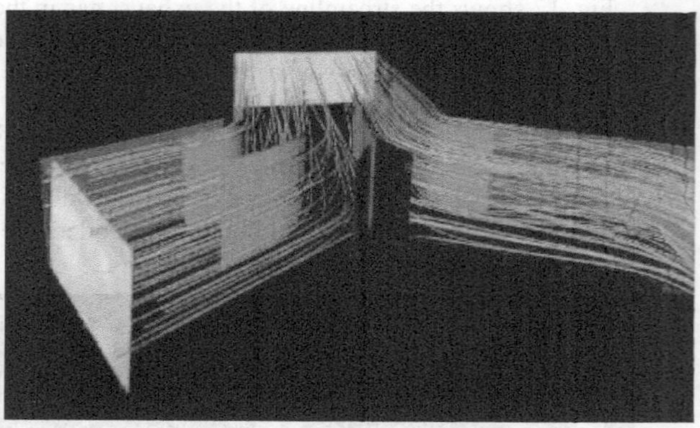

Fig. 19 Optimized turning vane design

4.3 Groundwater

Groundwater, as the major contributor to the fresh water resource, has been contaminated by agricultural and industrial activities in recent years. However, it is extremely difficult to obtain data to assess the current pollution situation or to predict contaminates' movement trend. Visualization of the simulation data of the diffusion of underground contaminates is important for both research and teaching aspects.

The 3D-IDV software package has been successfully used for visually observing the effects of contaminates diffusion on groundwater in the VR system. Fig. 20 shows the groundwater 3D model in the immersive system and Fig. 21 demonstrated the application of the virtual probe for monitoring transient change of the contaminate concentration.

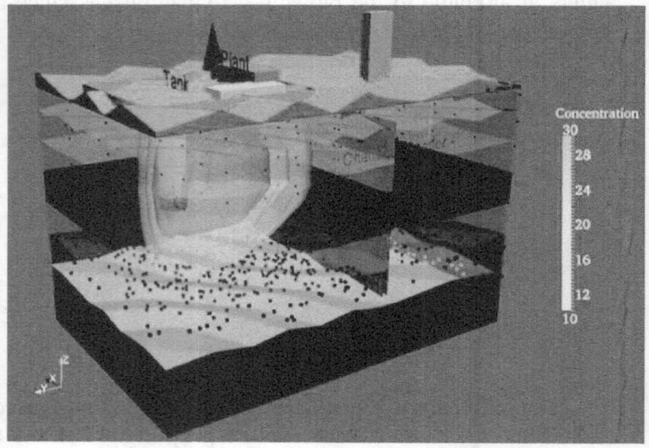

Fig. 20 VR visualization of groundwater simulation [18]

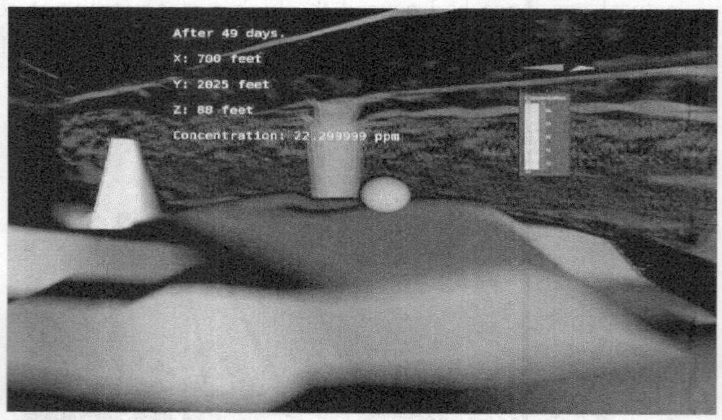

Fig. 21 Application of virtual probe in groundwater simulation [18]

5 Summary

A user-friendly 3D-IDV software package is developed and applied. The 3D-IDV software simplifies the process of combining and interacting numerical results, scientific rendering, and photorealistic rendering in a virtual environment. The simulation results are intuitive to experts and non-experts by using the 3D-IDV software package. The 3D-IDV software package significantly enhanced the post possessing and the accessibility of simulation results. A few examples that utilized this software package are presented. The 3D-IDV software package has been utilized for process and design simulation data visualization while contributing to more efficient, cost-effective solutions.

6 Acknowledgment

The authors would like to thank the all the students and staffs in CIVS at Purdue University Calumet for their contributions to this project. Special thanks go to Dr. Armin K Silaen for reviewing the manuscript.

This research was conducted with partial support from U.S. Department of Energy Grant DE-NA000741 under the administration of the National Nuclear Security Administration.

7 References

[1] Bakker, A., Haidari, A., and Oshinowo, L., 2001, "Realize Greater Benefits From CFD," Chem. Eng. Prog., 97(3), pp. 45–53.

[2] Duncan, J. T., and Vance M. J., 2007, "Development of a Virtual Environment for Interactive Interrogation of Computational Mixing Data", Trans. of the ASME J. of Mechanical Design, 129, pp. 361-367.

[3] Huang, G., and Bryden, K. M., 2005, "Introducing Virtual Engineering Technology Into Interactive Design Process With High-Fidelity Models", Winter Simulation Conference

[4] Chen, G., Moreland, J., Ratko, D., Jin, L., Shen, H., Wu, B., and Zhou, C. Q., 2010, "Virtual Reality for Engineering Applications", Proceedings of ASME World Conference on Innovative Virtual Reality, Ames, Iowa, United States, WINVR2010-3757, pp. 127-135.

[5] Fu, D., Wu, B., Chen, G., Moreland, J., Tian, F., Hu, Y., and Zhou, C. Q., 2010, "Virtual Reality Visualization of CFD Simulation For Iron/Steelmaking Processes", 2010 14th International Heat Transfer Conference (IHTC14), Washington, DC, USA, pp. 761-768.

[6] Fu, D., Wu, B., Moreland, J., Chen, G., and Zhou, C. Q., 2009, "CFD Simulations and VR Visualization for Process Design and Optimization", Proceedings of the Inaugural US-EU-China Thermophysics Conference, Beijing, China, UECTC-RE '09, UECTC-RE T5-S6-0298, (7 pages).

[7] Ahrens, J., Geveci, B., & Law, C. (2005). Paraview: An end-user tool for large data visualization. *The Visualization Handbook*, *717*, 731.

[8] CFD Post. (2011). 13.0. ANSYS. *Inc., Canonsburg, PA, USA*. http://www.ansys.com

[9] Osfield, R., & Burns, D. (2004). Open scene graph. 2005-08-15)[2007-10-08]. http://www.openscenegraph. org

[10] 3dsMax. (2013). Autodesk Inc. http://www.autodesk.com

[11] Bierbaum, A., Just, C., Hartling, P., Meinert, K., Baker, A., & Cruz-Neira, C. (2001, March). VR Juggler: A virtual platform for virtual reality application development. In Virtual Reality, 2001. Proceedings. IEEE (pp. 89-96). IEEE.

[12] http://www.kobelco.co.jp

[13] Fu D., Chen, Y., Rahman, Md.T., Zhao, Y., D'Alessio, J., Ferron, K. J., and Zhou, C. Q., 2012, "Validation of the numerical model for blast furnace shaft process", AISTech 2012, Atlanta, Georgia, USA, (11 pages)

[14] Wu, B., Ratko, D., Ren, R., Hu, Y., Jin, L., and Zhou, C. Q., 2010, "Development of a Virtual Reality Blast Furnace Package Using CFD", AISTech 2010, Pittsburgh, PA, USA, Vol. 1, pp. 617-628.

[15] Walker, W., Gu, M., Selvarasu, N. K. C., D'Alessio, J., Macfadyen, N., and Zhou, C. Q., 2007, "Numerical Study of Pulverized Coal Injection with Natural Gas Co-Injection in a Blast Furnace", AISTech 2007 - Proceedings of the Iron and Steel Technology Conference, Indianapolis, IN, USA, Vol. 1, pp. 453-462.

[16] maps.google.com

[17] Wu, B., Huang, D., Ratko, D., and Zhou, C. Q., 2010, "CFD and VR Application in Coal Fired Power Generation Components", IDMME - Proceedings of IDMME – Virtual Concept 2010, Bordeaux, France, (3 pages).

[18] Viswanathan, C., Moreland, J., Guo, S., and Zhou, C. Q., 2011, "Usefulness of Virtual 3D Modeling to Visualize the Effect of Uncertain Data In Groundwater Solute Transport", Proceedings of the ASME 2011 World Conference on Innovative Virtual Reality, WINVR2011, Milan, Italy, (5 pages).

Robust synchronization of a uncertain complex dynamical network with Markovian jumping topology via pinning sampled-data control

J.H. Park[1], T.H. Lee[1], H.Y. Jung[1], S.M. Lee[2]
[1]Department of EE/ICE, Yeungnam University, Kyongsan 712-749, Republic of Korea.
[2]Department of Electronic Engineering, Daegu University, Kyongsan 712-714, Republic of Korea.
Corresponding author: moony@daegu.ac.kr (S.M. Lee)

Abstract—*In this paper, the robust synchronization problem of a uncertain complex dynamical network with Markovian jumping topology via pinning sampled-data control is investigated. In order to make full use of the sawtooth structure characteristic of the sampling input delay, a discontinuous Lyapunov functional is used based on the Extended Wirtinger Inequality. By utilizing Finsler's lemma, a new stability condition is obtained in terms of linear matrix inequalities (LMIs) for the synchronization.*

Keywords: Complex network, Synchronization, Markovian jumping, Robust control, Sampled-data control, Pinning method.

1. Introduction

During the last decade, complex dynamical networks, which are a set of interconnected nodes with specific dynamics, have attracted increasing attention in various fields such as physics, biology, chemistry and computer science [1]-[2]. As science and society develop, our everyday lives have been closed to complex networks, for instance, transportation networks, World Wide Web, coupled biological and chemical engineering systems, neural networks, social networks, electrical power grids and global economic markets. Recently, one of the significant and interesting phenomena in complex dynamical network is the synchronization. Therefore, some attention of the problem, how to achieve the synchronization of asynchronous complex dynamical networks, has been increasing rapidly. Until now, in order to treat the synchronization problem for complex dynamical networks, several control schemes are applied. For example, the impulsive control scheme has been applied to achieve the projective synchronization of a complex dynamical network in [3]. In [4], a state observer-based control scheme has been proposed. In [5], an adaptive control scheme has been adopted to carry through the synchronization of a complex dynamical network, whereas in [6], the adaptive control for the synchronization between two complex dynamical networks has been investigated. Recently, the pinning-controllability and the method of choosing pinning nodes for the synchronization of a complex dynamical network are suggested in [7]. In addition, the synchronization of the complex dynamical network with linearly and nonlinearly coupling terms via pinning control has been studied in [8].

Recently, systems with Marvokian jumps have been attracting increasing research attention. This class of systems are the hybrid systems with two components in the state. The first one refers to the mode, which is described by a continuous-time finite-state Markovian process, and the second one refers to the state which is represented by a system of differential equations. The Markovian jump systems have the advantage of modeling the complex dynamical networks subject to abrupt variation in their communication topologies, such as component failures or repairs, sudden environmental disturbance, changing subsystem interconnections, and operating in different points of a nonlinear plant. However, just a few papers consider the complex network with Markovian jumping topology [9].

In many practical situations, the complex dynamical networks are usually subjected to parameter uncertainties, which are considered as one of the main source leading to undesirable behaviors [10]. Dynamic systems often have uncertainties due to parameter aging, saturation, modeling error and so on. Also, a real network system is usually influenced by external perturbations in communication between nodes. Therefore, the necessity of further investigation of robust synchronization schemes for an uncertain complex dynamical network is strongly raised.

On the other hand, because of the rapid growth of the digital hardware technologies, the sampled-data control method, whose control signals are kept constant during the sampling period and are allowed to change only at the sampling instant, has been more important than other control approaches. These discontinuous control signals which have stepwise form cause big trouble to control or analyze the system. In order to effectively deal with sampled-data control, Mikheev, Sobolev, and Fridman [11] and Astrom and Wittenmark [12] introduced a concept that discontinuous sampled control inputs treat time-varying delayed continuous signals, although applied actual control signals are discontinuous. Since the works of [11], [12], many types of the sampled-data control scheme by using the concept in [11]-[12] have been proposed. For instance, in [13], the robust $\mathcal{H}_\infty$ sampled-data control has been proposed. In [14], the sampled-data fuzzy controller has been proposed as well. Moreover, many researchers have adopted the sampled-data control scheme to solve control problems in various systems such as chaotic system [15], fuzzy system [16], neural networks [17] and so on. However, there are only a few papers for complex dynamical networks using the sampled-data control approach [18]. Besides, to the best of our knowledge, the pinning sampled-data control method has never been tackled. Therefore, it is very worth to consider the pinning sampled-data control method for complex dynamical networks.

From motivation mentioned above, this paper proposes a discontinuous Lyapunov functional approach to achieve robust synchronization of a uncertain complex dynamical network with Markovian jumping topology via pinning sampled-data control. The discontinuous Lyapunov functional makes full use of the sawtooth structure characteristic of sampling input delays. A convex representation of the nonlinearity in system dynamics is introduced, and then a sector-bounded constraint of the nonlinearity is represented to an equality constraint. By utilizing Finsler's lemma, the sufficient condition for the stability is formulated in terms of LMIs that is easily solvable using various numerical convex optimization algorithms.

Notation: $\mathbb{R}^n$ is the n-dimensional Euclidean space, $\mathbb{R}^{m\times n}$ denotes the set of $m\times n$ real matrix. $\mathbf{C}_{n,d} = \mathbf{C}([-d,0],\mathbb{R}^n)$ denotes the Banach space of continuous functions mapping the interval $[-d,0]$ into $\mathbb{R}^n$, with the topology of uniform convergence. $X > 0$ (respectively, $X \geq 0$) means that the matrix X is a real symmetric positive definite matrix (respectively, positive semi-definite). I denotes the identity matrix. $0_{n\times m}$ denotes the $n\times m$ zero matrix. $diag\{\cdots\}$ denotes block diagonal matrix. $\star$ in a matrix represents the elements below the main diagonal of a symmetric matrix. $\|\cdot\|$ refers to the Euclidean vector norm and the induced matrix norm. $\otimes$ stands for the notation of Kronecker product. Co denotes the convex hull. For a given matrix $X \in \mathbb{R}^{n\times m}$ with $rank(X) = r$, we define $X^{\perp} \in \mathbb{R}^{n\times(n-r)}$ as the right orthogonal complement of X; i.e., $XX^{\perp} = 0$.

2. Problem formulation

Given a complete probability space $(\Omega, \mathfrak{F}, P)$ where Ω is the sample space, $\mathfrak{F}$ is the algebra of events, P is the probability measure defined on $\mathfrak{F}$, $\rho(t)$ is a finite state Markovian jump process representing the system mode; that is, $\rho(t)$ takes values in a given finite set $\mathcal{S} = \{1,\ldots,L\}$ with generator $\Pi = \{\pi_{lg}\}$. The transition probability can be described as

$$Pr\{\rho(t+\delta) = g|\rho(t) = l\} = \begin{cases} \pi_{lg}\delta + o(\delta), & g \neq l, \\ 1 + \pi_{ll}\delta + o(\delta), & g = l, \end{cases} \quad (1)$$

where $\lim_{\delta\to 0^+}(o(\delta)/\delta) = 0$ and the transition probability rates satisfy $\pi_{lg} \geq 0$ for $l, g \in \mathcal{S}$, $l \neq g$ and $\pi_{ll} = -\sum_{l\neq g}\pi_{lg}$.

Consider a Markovian jumping complex dynamical network consisting of N linearly coupled identical nodes as follows:

$$\begin{aligned} \dot{x}_i(t) &= Ax_i(t) + Bf(x_i(t)) + \sum_{j=1}^{N} c_{ij}(\rho(t))x_j(t) \\ &\quad +u_i(t) \qquad i = 1,\ldots,N \end{aligned} \quad (2)$$

where $x_i = (x_{i1}, x_{i2},\ldots,x_{in})^T \in \mathbb{R}^n$ is the state vector of the ith node, $A \in \mathbb{R}^{n\times n}$, $B \in \mathbb{R}^{n\times n}$ are constant matrices, $f:\mathbb{R}^n \to \mathbb{R}^n$ is a smooth nonlinear vector field and $u_i(t)$ is the control input of ith node, $C(\rho(t)) = (c_{ij}(\rho(t)))_{N\times N}$ is the coupling matrix function of the random jumping process, where the coupling configuration parameter, $c_{ij}(\rho(t))$, is defined as follows: if there is a connection from node i to node $j (i \neq j)$ then $c_{ij}(\rho(t)) = 1$; otherwise $c_{ij}(\rho(t)) = 0$ $(i \neq j)$, and the diagonal elements of matrix $C(\rho(t))$ are assumed by

$$c_{ii}(\rho(t)) = -\sum_{j=1,j\neq i}^{N} c_{ij}(\rho(t)) = -\sum_{j=1,j\neq i}^{N} c_{ji}(\rho(t)), \quad i = 1,\ldots,N.$$

Throughout this paper, the following assumption is used.

Assumption 1. The smooth nonlinear function $f(\cdot)$ is satisfied the following sector and slop bound conditions:

$$\begin{aligned} b_k &\leq \frac{f_k(x_{ik}(t))}{x_{ik}(t)} \leq a_k, \\ \beta_k &\leq \frac{df_k(x_{ik}(t))}{dx_{ik}(t)} \leq \alpha_k, \quad k = 1,\ldots,n \end{aligned} \quad (3)$$

where b_k, a_k are lower and upper sector bounds, and β_k, α_k are lower and upper slope bounds, respectively.

Our objective of the paper is to achieve synchronization between all nodes of a complex dynamical network and a target node via controllers $u_i(t)$ which is denoted by the following definition.

Definition 1. A complex dynamical network is said to achieve the asymptotical inner synchronization, if

$$x_1(t) = x_2(t) = \cdots = x_N(t) = s(t) \quad \text{as } t \to \infty,$$

where $s(t) \in \mathbb{R}^n$ is a solution of a target node, satisfying

$$\dot{s}(t) = Ax(t) + Bf(s(t)). \quad (4)$$

For our synchronization scheme, let us define the error vectors as follows :

$$e_i(t) = x_i(t) - s(t). \quad (5)$$

From Eq. (5), the error dynamics is given to

$$\begin{aligned}\dot{e}_i(t) &= Ae_i(t) + B\big(f(x_i(t)) - f(s(t))\big) \\ &\quad + \sum_{j=1}^{N} c_{ij}(\rho(t))e_j(t) + u_i(t) \\ &= Ae_i(t) + B\bar{f}_i(t) + \sum_{j=i}^{N} c_{ij}(\rho(t))e_j(t) \\ &\quad + u_i(t),\ i = 1, \ldots, N \end{aligned} \tag{6}$$

where $\bar{f}_i(t) = f(x_i(t)) - f(s(t))$.

By the well-known mean value theorem, there exists a constant $\nu \in (x_{ik}(t), s_{ik}(t))$ such that

$$f_k(x_{ik}(t)) - f_k(s_k(t)) = \frac{df_k(\nu)}{d\nu}(x_{ik}(t) - s_k(t)). \tag{7}$$

From the slope bounds given in Assumption 1, we have

$$\beta_k \leq \frac{df_k(\nu)}{d\nu} \leq \alpha_k. \tag{8}$$

By Eqs. (7), (8) and $e_i(t) = x_i(t) - s(t)$, we have

$$\beta_k e_{ik}(t) \leq \bar{f}_{ik}(e_{ik}(t)) \leq \alpha_k e_{ik}(t). \tag{9}$$

Therefore, Eq. (9) can be represented the following equality condition by properties of the convex hull:

$$\bar{f}_i(e_i(t)) = \Delta_i e_i(t), \tag{10}$$

where Δ_i is an element of a convex hull $Co\{\alpha,\ \beta\}$.

Remark 1. The slope bound of nonlinear function, $f(\cdot)$, becomes new sector bound of the nonlinear function $\bar{f}(e_i(t)) = f(s(t)) - f(x_i(t))$. And this condition can be represented by a convex combination of the sector bounds α_k and β_k. This method was proposed in [19]. In general, most of nonlinear functions which consist of nonlinear system such as Chua's circuit [20] and so on, satisfy this condition. Also, this condition includes Lipschitz condition as a special case.

On the other hand, in order to design the pinning controller using the sampled-data signal, the concept of the time-varying delayed control input which is proposed in [11]-[12], is adopted in this paper. For this, the following pinning state feedback controller is considered

$$\begin{aligned} u_i(t) &= K_i e_i(t_k),\ t_k \leq t < t_{k+1}, \quad i = 1, \ldots, h \\ u_i(t) &= 0 \qquad\qquad\qquad\qquad\quad i = h+1, \ldots, N \end{aligned} \tag{11}$$

where K_i is the gain matrix of feedback controller to be determined and h is the number of pinning nodes.

Denote by t_k the updating instant time of the Zero-Order-Hold (ZOH), we assume that the sampling intervals satisfy

$$t_{k+1} - t_k = d_k \leq d, \tag{12}$$

for any integer $k \geq 0$, where d is a positive scalar and represents the largest sampling interval.

Thus, by defining $d(t) = t - t_k,\ \ t_k \leq t < t_{k+1}$, the controller (11) can be represented as following:

$$\begin{aligned} u_i(t) &= K_i e_i(t_k) \qquad\quad t_k \leq t \leq t_{k+1} \\ &= K_i e_i(t - d(t)) \quad i = 1, \ldots, h. \end{aligned} \tag{13}$$

From (12), we can find that $d(t) < t_{k+1} - t_k \leq d$ and $\dot{d}(t) = 1$ for $t \neq t_k$. Now, substituting (13) into (6) and considering system uncertainties gives

$$\begin{aligned} \dot{e}_i(t) &= Ae_i(t) + B\bar{f}_i(e_i(t)) + \sum_{j=i}^{N} c_{ij}(\rho(t))e_j(t) \\ &\quad + K_i e_i(t - d(t)), \\ &\quad t_k \leq t < t_{k+1},\ i = 1, \ldots, N. \end{aligned} \tag{14}$$

where $K_i = 0 (i = h+1, \ldots, N)$. Then Eq. (14) can be rewritten as a vector-matrix form

$$\begin{aligned} \dot{e}(t) &= A_N e(t) + B_N F(e(t)) + C_N(\rho(t))e(t) \\ &\quad + Ke(t - d(t)), \end{aligned} \tag{15}$$

where $e(t) = [e_1^T(t), \ldots, e_N^T(t)]^T$, $F(t) = [\bar{f}^T(e_1(t)), \ldots, \bar{f}^T(e_N(t))]^T$, $A_N = I_N \otimes A$, $B_N = I_N \otimes B$ and $C_N = C \otimes I_n$, $K = diag\{\underbrace{K_1, \ldots, K_h}_{h}, \underbrace{0, \ldots, 0}_{N-h}\}$.

In this paper, we consider system uncertainties as follows:

$$\begin{aligned} \dot{e}(t) &= (A_N + \Delta A(t))e(t) + (B_N + \Delta B(t))F(e(t)) \\ &\quad + (C_N(\rho(t)) + \Delta C(\rho(t)))e(t) \\ &\quad + Ke(t - d(t)), \end{aligned} \tag{16}$$

where $\Delta A(t)$, $\Delta B(t)$ and $\Delta C(\rho(t))$ are the uncertainties of system matrices of the form

$$\begin{aligned} &\left[\ \Delta A(t) \quad \Delta B(t) \quad \Delta C(\rho(t))\ \right] = \\ &DF(t)\left[\ E_a \quad E_b \quad E_c(\rho(t))\ \right] \end{aligned} \tag{17}$$

in which D, E_a, E_b are known constant matrices, $E_c(\rho(t))$ is known function of random jumping process $\{\rho(t)\}$ and the time-varying nonlinear function $F(t)$ satisfies

$$F^T(t)F(t) \leq I, \forall t \geq 0. \tag{18}$$

So, Eq. (16) can be rewritten as

$$\begin{aligned} \dot{e}(t) &= (A_N + C_N(\rho(t))e(t) + B_N F(e(t)) \\ &\quad + Ke(t - d(t)) + Dp(t), \\ p(t) &= F(t)q(t), \\ q(t) &= (E_a + E_c(\rho(t))e(t) + E_b f(e(t)) \end{aligned} \tag{19}$$

For simplicity of notations, in this paper, we denote the matrices associated with the lth mode $(\rho(t) = l)$ by $C_N^l = C_N(\rho(t))$, $E_c^l = E_c(\rho(t))$, where C_N^l and E_c^l are known constant matrices of appropriate dimensions.

In order to investigate the stochastic stability analysis for Markovian jumping complex dynamical network (19), we introduce the following definition and lemmas.

Definition 2. [21] The system (19) is said to be stochastically stable, if for any finite $\phi(s) \in \mathbf{C}_{n,d}$, and the initial condition of the mode $\rho_0 \in \mathcal{S}$ the following condition if satisfied

$$\lim_{t\to\infty} \mathbb{E}\left\{\int_0^t e^T(s)e(s)ds|\phi,\rho_0\right\} < \infty. \tag{20}$$

Remark 2. Many systems such as the continuous-time systems with the digital control, the networked control systems and so on, can be modelled by sampled-data systems. Now days, most of controllers are the digital controller or networked to the system, so the sampled-data control approach is eligible to receive much attention.

3. Main results

In this section, a design problem of the pinning sampled-data feedback controller for the synchronization of a complex dynamical network with Markovian jumping topology will be investigated via a discontinuous Lyapunov functional approach. Before proceeding further, the following notations of several matrices are given.

$$\begin{aligned}
\zeta(t) &= \left[e^T(t)\ e^T(t-d(t))\ e^T(t-d)\ F^T(t)\right. \\
&\quad \left.\dot{e}^T(t)\ p(t)\right]^T, \\
\Delta &= diag\{\Delta_1,\ldots,\Delta_N\} \\
\gamma &= \frac{\pi^2}{4} \\
\Phi^l &= \left[\ E_a+E_c^l\ \ 0\ \ 0\ \ E_b\ \ 0\ \ 0\ \right] \\
\Psi^l &= \left[\ A_N+C_N^l\ \ K\ \ 0\ \ B_N\ \ -I\ \ D\ \right] \\
\Gamma_{11}^l &= \sum_{g=1}^{L}\pi_{lg}P^g+Q-R-\gamma Z+\Delta N_1^T+N_1\Delta, \\
\Gamma_{12} &= R-S+\gamma Z,\ \Gamma_{14}=-N_1+\Delta N_2^T, \\
\Gamma_{22} &= -2R+S+S^T-\gamma Z, \\
\Gamma_{23} &= R-S,\ \Gamma_{33}=-Q-R, \\
\Gamma_{44} &= -N_2-N_2^T,\ \Gamma_{55}=d^2(R+Z), \\
\Gamma_{66} &= -\epsilon I, \\
\Gamma^l &= \begin{bmatrix}
\Gamma_{11}^l & \Gamma_{12} & S & \Gamma_{14} & P^l & 0 \\
\star & \Gamma_{22} & \Gamma_{23} & 0 & 0 & 0 \\
\star & \star & \Gamma_{33} & 0 & 0 & 0 \\
\star & \star & \star & \Gamma_{44} & 0 & 0 \\
\star & \star & \star & \star & \Gamma_{55} & 0 \\
\star & \star & \star & \star & \star & \Gamma_{66}
\end{bmatrix}, \\
\Upsilon^l &= \Gamma^l+\epsilon\Phi^{l^T}\Phi^l.
\end{aligned} \tag{21}$$

Now, the main result is given by the following theorem.
Theorem 1. For given matrix K and a positive scalar d, system (19) is stochastically stable for the conditions, if there exist positive definite matrices P^l $(l=1,\ldots,L)$, Q, R, Z $\in \mathbb{R}^{nN\times nN}$, matrices N_1, N_2, $S \in \mathbb{R}^{nN\times nN}$ and a positive scalar ϵ satisfying the following LMIs:

$$(\Psi^{l^\perp})^T\Upsilon^l(\Psi^{l^\perp}) < 0, \tag{22}$$

$$\begin{bmatrix} R & S \\ \star & R \end{bmatrix} \geq 0, \tag{23}$$

where $\Psi^{l^\perp}$ is the right orthogonal complement of Ψ^l.

Proof. Consider the following discontinuous Lyapunov functional for error system (14)

$$V(t) = V_1(t)+V_2(t)+V_3(t),\quad t\in[t_k,\ t_{k+1}). \tag{24}$$

where

$$\begin{aligned}
V_1(t) &= e^T(t)P^le(t), \\
V_2(t) &= \int_{t-d}^{t} e^T(s)Qe(s)ds \\
&\quad +d\int_{-d}^{0}\int_{t+\theta}^{t}\dot{e}^T(s)R\dot{e}(s)dsd\theta, \\
V_3(t) &= d^2\int_{t_k}^{t}\dot{e}^T(s)Z\dot{e}(s)ds \\
&\quad -\frac{\pi^2}{4}\int_{t_k}^{t}(e(s)-e(t_k))^T \\
&\quad \times Z(e(s)-e(t_k))ds.
\end{aligned}$$

It is noted that $V_3(t)$ which is first proposed by Fridman [23], can be rewritten as

$$V_3(t) = d^2\int_{t-d}^{t}\dot{e}^T(s)Z\dot{e}(s)ds+\hat{V}_4(t) \tag{25}$$

where

$$\begin{aligned}
\hat{V}_3(t) &= d^2\int_{t_k}^{t}\dot{e}^T(s)Z\dot{e}(s)ds \\
&\quad -\frac{\pi^2}{4}\int_{t_k}^{t}(e(s)-e(t_k))^TZ(e(s)-e(t_k))ds.
\end{aligned}$$

According to Extended Wirtinger Inequality [22], it is easy to find that $\hat{V}_3(t) \geq 0$. In addition, it is correct that $\lim_{t\to t_k^-} V(t) \geq V(t_k)$, because $\hat{V}_3(t)$ will disappear at $t=t_k$.

In [24], it is known that the random process $\{e(t),\rho(t),t\geq 0\}$ is a $\mathbf{C}_{n,d}\times\mathcal{S}$-valued Markovian jump process with initial state $(\phi(\cdot),\rho(t))$.

Applying on $V(e(t),l):\mathbf{C}_{n,d}\times\mathcal{S}\times\mathbb{R}^+\to\mathbb{R}$, its weak infinitesimal operator $\mathbb{L}$ is defined by

$$\begin{aligned}
\mathbb{L}V(e(t),l) &= \lim_{\delta\to 0_+}\frac{1}{\delta}[\mathbb{E}\{V(e(t+\delta),\rho(t+\delta))| \\
&\quad e(t),\rho(t)=l\}-V(e(t),\rho(t)=l)]
\end{aligned} \tag{26}$$

Then, for each $i \in \mathcal{S}$, we obtain

$$\mathbb{L}V_1(t) = 2e^T(t)P^l\dot{e}(t) + e^T(t)\left(\sum_{l=1}^{N} \pi_{lg}P^l\right)e(t), \quad (27)$$

$$\begin{aligned} \mathbb{L}V_2(t) &= e^T(t)Qe(t) - e^T(t-d)Qe(t-d) \\ &\quad + d^2\dot{e}^T(t)R\dot{e}(t) - d\int_{t-d(t)}^{t} \dot{e}^T(s)R\dot{e}(s)ds \\ &\quad - d\int_{t-d}^{t-d(t)} \dot{e}^T(s)R\dot{e}(s)ds, \end{aligned} \quad (28)$$

$$\begin{aligned} \mathbb{L}V_3(t) &= d^2\dot{e}^T(t)Z\dot{e}(t) - \frac{\pi^2}{4}\begin{bmatrix} e(t) \\ e(t-d(t)) \end{bmatrix}^T \\ &\quad \times \begin{bmatrix} Z & -Z \\ \star & Z \end{bmatrix}\begin{bmatrix} e(t) \\ e(t-d(t)) \end{bmatrix}. \end{aligned} \quad (29)$$

By Jensen ineqality and Theorem 1 in [25], the integral terms of the $\mathbb{L}V_2(t)$ can be bounded as

$$\begin{aligned} & -d\int_{t-d(t)}^{t} \dot{e}^T(t)R\dot{e}(s)ds - d\int_{t-d}^{t-d(t)} \dot{e}^T(s)R\dot{e}(s)ds \\ & \leq -\begin{bmatrix} \eta_1(t) \\ \eta_2(t) \end{bmatrix}^T \begin{bmatrix} \frac{d}{d(t)}R & 0 \\ \star & \frac{d}{d-d(t)}R \end{bmatrix}\begin{bmatrix} \eta_1(t) \\ \eta_2(t) \end{bmatrix} \\ & \leq -\begin{bmatrix} \eta_1(t) \\ \eta_2(t) \end{bmatrix}^T \begin{bmatrix} R & S \\ \star & R \end{bmatrix}\begin{bmatrix} \eta_1(t) \\ \eta_2(t) \end{bmatrix} \end{aligned} \quad (30)$$

where $\eta_1(t) = \int_{t-d(t)}^{t} \dot{e}(s)ds$, $\eta_2(t) = \int_{t-d}^{t-d(t)} \dot{e}(s)ds$.

From the convex representation (10), we can obtain the following equation:

$$F(t) = \Delta e(t). \quad (31)$$

The constraint (31) is rewritten as

$$\begin{bmatrix} \Delta & -I \end{bmatrix}\begin{bmatrix} e(t) \\ F(t) \end{bmatrix} = 0. \quad (32)$$

For matrices N_1 and N_2, the following equality is always satisfied:

$$2\begin{bmatrix} e(t) \\ F(t) \end{bmatrix}^T \begin{bmatrix} N_1 \\ N_2 \end{bmatrix}\begin{bmatrix} \Delta & -I \end{bmatrix}\begin{bmatrix} e(t) \\ F(t) \end{bmatrix} = 0. \quad (33)$$

Eq. (17) and (18) give

$$p^T(t)p(t) \leq q^T(t)q(t). \quad (34)$$

So, there exists a positive constant, ϵ, satisfying the following equation

$$\epsilon\left[\zeta^T(t)\Phi^{l^T}\Phi^l\zeta(t) - p^T(t)p(t)\right] \geq 0 \quad (35)$$

where $\zeta(t)$ and Φ^l are defined in (21).

From (27)-(30), (33) and (35), the $\mathbb{L}V$ has a new upper bound as

$$\mathbb{L}V(e(t), l) \leq \zeta^T(t)\Upsilon^l\zeta(t) \quad (36)$$

Also, the system (19) with the augmented vector $\zeta(t)$ and each $l \in \mathcal{S}$ can be rewritten as

$$\Psi^l\zeta(t) = 0 \quad (37)$$

where Ψ^l is defined in Theorem 1. Therefore, a delay-dependent stability condition for system (19) can be

$$\zeta^T(t)\Upsilon^l\zeta(t) < 0, \;\text{ subject to }\; \Psi^l\zeta(t) = 0. \quad (38)$$

From Finsler's lemma, the inequality (38) is equivalent to

$$(\Psi^{l^\perp})^T\Upsilon^l(\Psi^{l^\perp}) < 0, \quad (39)$$

Therefore if the LMI(22) satisfies, then the condition (38) holds. This completes proof. ■

4. Numerical examples

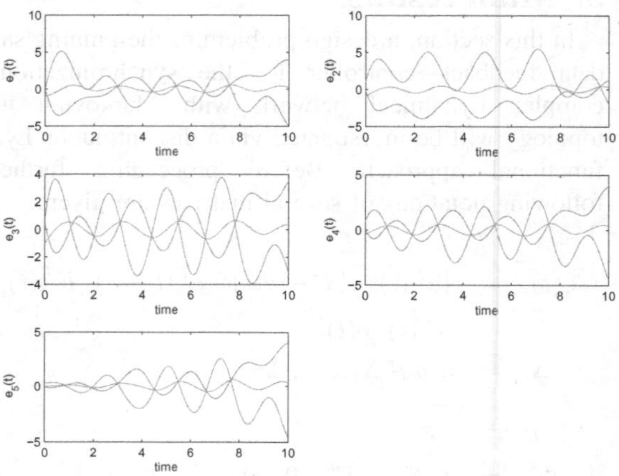

Fig. 1: The error signals of the uncontrolled system (19).

In this example, MATLAB YALMIP 3.0 and SeDuMi 1.1 are used to solve LMI problem. In order to show pinning controllability of a complex dynamical network with Markovian jumping topology using the sampled-data, we consider a set of five linearly coupled Chua's chaotic circuit [20] which is typical benchmark three dimensional chaotic systems. The parameters of Chua's circuit are given by

$$a = 9, b = 14.28, c = 1, m_0 = -1/7, m_1 = 2/7$$

$$A = \begin{bmatrix} -am_1 & a & 0 \\ 1 & -1 & 1 \\ 0 & -b & 0 \end{bmatrix},$$

$$B = \begin{bmatrix} -a(m_0 - m_1) & 0 & 0 \\ 0 & 0 & 0 \\ 0 & 0 & 0 \end{bmatrix},$$

$$f(x_{ik}(t)) = \frac{1}{2}(|x_{ik}(t) + c| - |x_{ik}(t) - c|), \quad k = 1, \ldots, n$$

where the nonlinear function $f(\cdot)$ belongs to sector $[0,\ 1]$ and slope $[0,\ 1]$. Chua's circuit is also chosen as a target

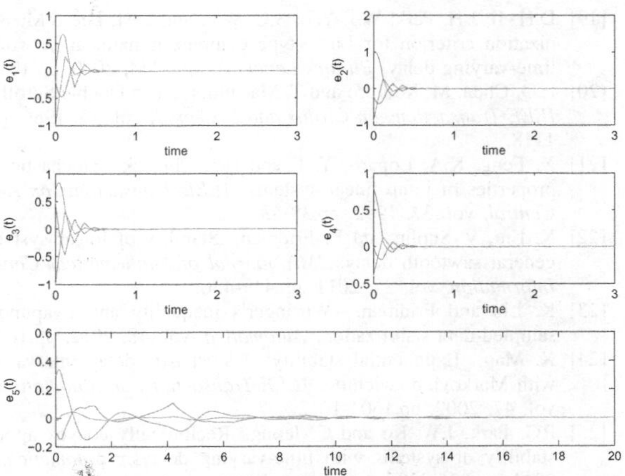

Fig. 2: The error signals of the controlled system (19).

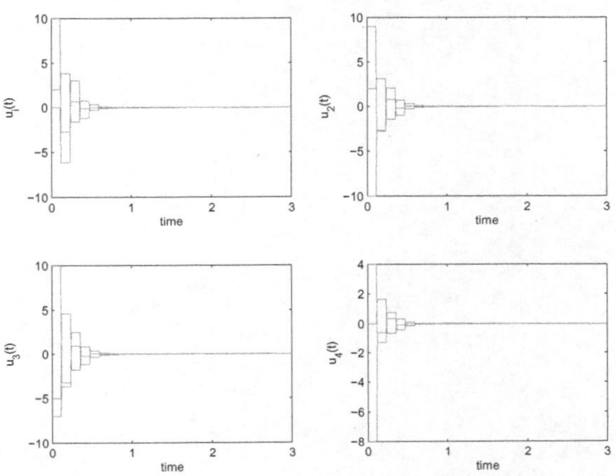

Fig. 3: The control input signals of Example.

node, $s(t)$ as well. The Markovian jumping coupling matrix, C^l, is given by

$$
\begin{aligned}
C^1 &= 0.9 \times \begin{bmatrix} -4 & 1 & 1 & 1 & 1 \\ 1 & -3 & 0 & 1 & 1 \\ 1 & 0 & -2 & 1 & 0 \\ 1 & 1 & 1 & -4 & 1 \\ 1 & 1 & 0 & 1 & -3 \end{bmatrix}, \\
C^2 &= 0.8 \times \begin{bmatrix} -4 & 1 & 1 & 1 & 1 \\ 1 & -4 & 1 & 1 & 1 \\ 1 & 1 & -4 & 1 & 1 \\ 1 & 1 & 1 & -4 & 1 \\ 1 & 1 & 1 & 1 & -4 \end{bmatrix}. \qquad (40)
\end{aligned}
$$

The number of pinning nodes, h, is chosen four, and control gain matrices are also chosen

$$
\begin{aligned}
K &= diag\{K_1, K_2, K_3, K_4, 0_{n\times n}\} \\
&= -10(diag\{I_n, I_n, I_n, I_n, 0_{n\times n}\}) \qquad (41)
\end{aligned}
$$

The parameters associated with system uncertainty are given

$$
\begin{aligned}
D = 0.1I_{nN},\ E_a = 0.4I_{nN},\ E_b = 0.2I_{nN}, \\
E_c^1 = 0.1 * I_{nN},\ E_c^2 = 0.2I_{nN}, \\
F(t) = 0.5\sin t \qquad (42)
\end{aligned}
$$

Under the above parameter settings, we can obtain the

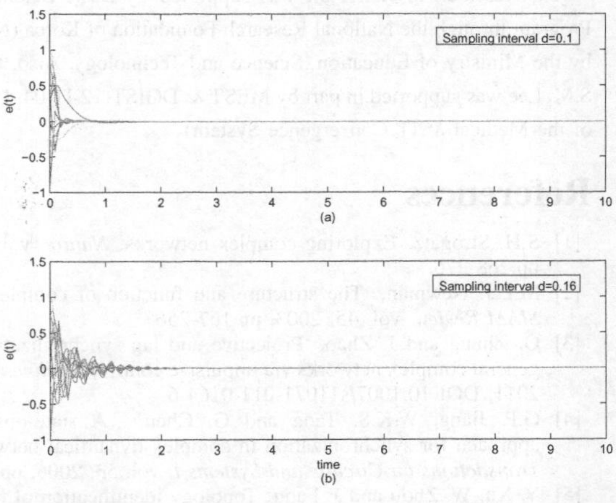

Fig. 4: The error signals of the controlled system (19) with (a) $d = 0.1$ (b) $d = 0.16$

maximum sampling interval $d = 0.16$ by Theorem 1.

In this example, initial conditions of each nodes are chosen: $x_1(0) = [-0.1\ -0.5\ -0.7]$, $x_2(0) = [-0.1\ -0.4\ 0.3]$, $x_3(0) = [0.6\ -1.5\ 0]$, $x_4(0) = [0.1\ 0.1\ 0.1]$, $x_5(0) = [0\ 0.5\ -0.4]$ and $s(0) = [0.1\ 0.5\ -0.7]$.

In order to show effectiveness of the controller, the error signals of the uncontrolled system (19) are depicted in Fig. 2. Under the given control gain, K, and sampling interval $d = 0.12$, the simulation result of the controlled system (19) and the sampled control inputs are presented in Fig. 3 and Fig. 4, respectively. As seen in Fig. 3, the trajectories of error systems are indeed well stabilized. It means that all states are synchronized up to the states of the target node by control inputs which are seen in Fig. 4. In order to show the effectiveness of the different sampling intervals, Fig. 5 is presented. Fig. 5 (a) and (b) show the error signals of the system (19) with sampling interval $d = 0.1$ and $d = 0.16$, respectively. From this figure, it is clear that short sampling interval time is more effective to control the system.

5. Conclusions

In this paper, the pinning sampled-data control for the robust synchronization of a uncertain complex dynamical network with Markovian jumping topology has been discussed. Based on Extended Wirtinger Inequality, a discontinuous Lyapunov functional which gives full information of sawtooth structure characteristic of the sampling delay has been used. Then the stability criterion of the controller has been derived in terms of LMIs which are based on Lyapunov stability theory, Finsler's lemma and the sector-slope restricted nonlinearity conditions. A numerical example has shown the effectiveness and good performance of the proposed method.

Acknowledgements

This research of J.H. Park was supported by Basic Science Research Program through the National Research Foundation of Korea (NRF) funded by the Ministry of Education, Science and Technology. Also, this work of S.M. Lee was supported in part by MEST & DGIST(12-IT-04, Development of the Medical & IT Convergence System)

References

[1] S.H. Strogatz, Exploring complex networks, *Nature,* vol. 410, 2001, pp.268-276.

[2] M.E.J. Newman, The structure and function of complex networks, *SIAM Review,* vol. 45, 2003, pp.167-256.

[3] Q. Zhang and J. Zhao, Projective and lag synchronization between general complex networks via impulsive control, *Nonlinear Dynamics,* 2011, DOI 10.1007/s11071-011-0164-6.

[4] G.P. Jiang, W.K.S. Tang and G. Chen, A state-observer-based approach for synchronization in complex dynamical networks, *IEEE Transactions on Circuits and Systems I,* vol. 53, 2006, pp.2739-2745.

[5] Y. Xu, W. Zhou and J. Fang, Topology identification of the modified complex dynamical network with non-delayed and delayed coupling, *Nonlinear Dynamics,* 2011, DOI 10.1007/s11071-011-0217-x.

[6] D.H. Ji, S.C. Jeong, J.H. Park, S.M. Lee and S.C. Won, Adaptive lag synchronization for uncertain complex dynamical network with delayed coupling, *Applied Mathematics and Conputation,* vol. 218, 2012, pp.4872-4880.

[7] P. Maurizio and B. Mario, Criteria for global pinning-contollability of complex networks, *Automatica,* vol. 44, 2008, pp.3100-3106.

[8] J. Feng, S. Sun, C. Xu, Y. Zhao and J. Wang, The synchronization of general complex dynamical network via pinning control, *Nonlinear Dynamics,* vol. 67, 2012, pp.1623-1633.

[9] J. Yu and G. Sun, Robust stabilization of stochastic Markovian jumping dynamical networks with mixed delays, *Neurocomputing,* 2012, doi:10.1016/j.neucom.2012.01.021.

[10] J.G. Barajas-Ramirez, Robust synchronization of a class of uncertain complex networks via discontinuous control, *Computers and Mathematics with Applications,* 2012, doi:10.1016/j.camwa.2012.01.08.

[11] Y. Mikheev, V. Sobolev and E. Fridman, Asymptotic analysis of digital control systems, *Automation and Remote Control,* vol. 49, 1988, pp.1175-1180.

[12] K.J. Astrom and B. Wittenmark, *Adaptive control,* Addison-Wesley, Reading, MA; 1989.

[13] E. Fridman, U. Shaked and V. Suplin, Input/output delay approach to robust sampled-data $\mathcal{H}_\infty$ control, *Systems and Control Letters,* vol. 54, 2005, pp.271-282.

[14] H.K. Lam and W.K. Ling, Sampled-data fuzzy controller for continuous nonlinear systems, *IET Control Theory Applications,* vol. 2, 2008, pp.32-39.

[15] J.G. Lu, Chaotic behavior in sampled-data control systems with saturating control, *Chaos, Solitons and Fractals,* vol. 30, 2006, pp.147-155.

[16] C. Peng, Q.L. Han, D. Yue and E.Tian, Sampled-data robust $\mathcal{H}_\infty$ control for T-S fuzzy systems with time delay and uncertainties, *Fuzzy Sets and Systems,* vol. 179, 2011, pp.20-33.

[17] C.K. Zhang, Y. He and M. Wu, Exponential synchronization of neural networks with time-varying mixed delays and sampled-data, *Neurocomputing,* vol. 74, 2010, pp.265-273.

[18] N. Li, Y. Zhang, J. Hu and Z. Nie, Synchronization for general complex dynamical networks with sampled-data, *Neurocomputing,* vol. 74, 2011, pp.805-811.

[19] D.H. Ji, J.H. Park, W.J. Yoo, S.C. Won and S.M. Lee S.M, Synchronization criterion for Lur'e type complex dynamical networks with time-varying delay, *Physics Letters A,* vol. 374, 2010, pp.1218-1227.

[20] L.O. Chua, M. Komuro and T. Matsumoto, The Double Scroll Family, *IEEE Transactions on Cirtuis and Systems I,* vol. 33, 1986, pp.1072-1118.

[21] X. Feng, K.A. Loparo, Y. Ji and H.J. Chizeck, Stochastic stability properties of jump linear systems, *IEEE Transactions on Automatic Control,* vol. 37, 1992, pp.38-53.

[22] K. Liu, V. Suplin and E. Fridman, Stability of linear systems with general sawtooth delay, *IMA Journal of Mathematical Control and Information,* vol. 27, 2011, pp.419-436.

[23] K. Liu and Fridman, Wirtinger's inequality and Lyapunov-based sampled-data stabilization, *Automatica,* vol. 48, 2012, pp.102-108.

[24] X. Mao, Exponential stability of stochastic delay interval systems with Markovian swiching, *IEEE Transactions on Automatic Control,* vol. 47, 2002, pp.1604-1612.

[25] P.G. Park, J.W. Ko and C. Jeong, Reciprocally convex approach to stability of systems with time-varying delays, *Autometica,* vol. 7, 2011, pp.235-238.

EpiViz: A Visual Simulation of an Epidemic Model using a Cellular Automaton

Matthew J. Farmer* and Tina V. Johnson
Department of Computer Science
Midwestern State University
Wichita Falls, TX 76308
matthew.farmer@mwsu.edu, tina.johnson@mwsu.edu

***Abstract*— Cellular Automata (CAs) are often used to simulate complex systems. One such application of a CA is to simulate the spread of disease through a susceptible population. This paper describes EpiViz, a CA-based epidemic simulator which uses a variety of input parameters, such as probability of infection, infectious period, vaccination rate, mode of infection, and probability of recovery to influence the resulting state of each entity in a CA over the course of a simulated disease outbreak. EpiViz then produces an animated representation of the outbreak. EpiViz allows a user to set disease related parameters prior to running a simulation to enable experimentation with various disease factors and to observe the effects on a susceptible population. Incorporating the traditional Susceptible-Infected-Removed (SIR) disease model, EpiViz is able to visually display an outbreak on a day-to-day basis.**

Keywords—cellular automata, computational epidemiology, SIR model, disease simulation

Submitted to: MSV '13

I. INTRODUCTION

Cellular automata (CAs) are powerful models for simulating discrete systems. John von Neumann is credited with defining a CA as a self-reproducing system in which each cell can be in one of several distinct states and the state of each cell as time progresses is dependent upon its own state and the states of its neighbors at the previous time-step [1]. Although CAs are simplistic in design, they have proven to successfully model diverse, complex systems, including power consumption [2], pedestrian flow [3], wildfire spread [4], and areas in applied physics [5] [6].

CAs are particularly well-suited for modeling epidemic behavior since the disease state of an individual (susceptible, infected, etc.) is dependent upon its own state as well as the state of its neighbors. Several researchers have developed CA models to investigate disease propagation [7] [8] [9] [10]. This paper presents an epidemiological CA model, EpiViz, which allows variation of disease parameters and visual animation of a simulated outbreak.

II. MODEL DESCRIPTION

EpiViz is a CA that was developed using the Susceptible-Infected-Removed (SIR) paradigm. SIR is a widely accepted mathematical model for simulating disease spread [11] [12]. In the basic SIR model, all individuals in a closed population belong in one of three states: Susceptible (S), Infected (I), or Removed (R). Individuals may move from S to I based on a transmission probability and from I to R based on a removal rate. Other states may be added to the basic SIR model to more accurately represent disease dynamics.

EpiViz was created in C++ based on the following considerations and rules:

- The grid is a two-dimensional array with a dimension of *n* x *n* entities.
- Each cell represents a single entity which is capable of being in one of the following five states:
  - Susceptible: The default state of all entities; vulnerable to infection. Depending on the disease, it may be possible for an infected individual to return to the susceptible population if immunity is disallowed.

*Contact Author

- Infected: The entity is harboring the disease and is able to infect other entities. After the infectious period has elapsed, the entity will either become immune, return to the susceptible population (if immunity is not possible), or die. Infected is a temporary state.
- Immune: The entity was once infected but is no longer infectious and cannot die, receive vaccinations, or be infected again. Immune is a permanent state.
- Deceased: The entity was once infected, but has died and is no longer able to infect others or be infected. Deceased is a permanent state.
- Vaccinated: The entity is immune to infection permanently; only susceptible entities may be vaccinated. Vaccinated is a permanent state.

• Contacts are established using the Moore Neighborhood, which includes top, bottom, left, right and diagonal neighbors. Only infected and vaccinated entities may affect the state of nearby entities.

• Each infected or vaccinated entity has a probability of changing the state of individuals within its Moore neighborhood. An entity in either of the aforementioned states will have the opportunity to cause anywhere from 0 to 8 entities to change states in a given day. Therefore, the likelihood of a state change occurring is greater if more of the surrounding entities are either infected or vaccinated.

• If entities are capable of traveling, each infected entity has an additional opportunity per day to infect a random entity anywhere in the grid. Vaccinated entities are not capable of travel.

• When an entity becomes newly infected, the entity is not infectious until the following day. The same applies for newly vaccinated entities.

• The grid allows wrapping; entities on the borders of the grid may affect entities on the opposite side of the grid. In this way, the grid is less like a flat square and more like a sphere.

• The simulation ends when either no entities are infected or two hundred days have elapsed.

When an EpiViz simulation begins, the user is greeted with a menu that allows selection from a predefined list of diseases to simulate. Each disease has the following characteristics: disease name, length of infection, probability of infecting other entities, probability of killing an infected entity, probability of an infected person traveling, whether immunity is allowed, and which day of the simulation vaccines are made available to the population. In addition, the user may create a custom disease to simulate by supplying the various characteristic values.

Once a disease has been selected, EpiViz will show the user all of the characteristics associated with the chosen disease and will ask for confirmation to begin the simulation. EpiViz provides the ability to conduct multiple simulations on the same data set to average the results. Once the animation is complete, a CSV file with average population data for the various states by day is produced. The user is returned to the main menu from which another simulation may begin.

Initially, a single entity is randomly chosen to be the first infected. The infected entity has the opportunity to infect others, and the day is concluded. Each day, the infected entities have the opportunity to infect other entities. Some diseases may have a day in which vaccinations are made available. On the predetermined vaccination day, four random susceptible entities are selected for vaccination. From each day forward, all vaccinated entities have the opportunity to vaccinate susceptible entities within the Moore Neighborhood (vaccinated entities may not travel). Vaccinations cannot cure an infected entity. Only on the first available day of vaccine availability are four random entities chosen for vaccination.

The grid consists of entities that are capable of knowing their current state and how long they have been infected, if applicable. Once the infection period has fully lapsed, the entity must change to one of three states: susceptible (only if immunity is not allowed), immune, or deceased.

At the conclusion of each day within the simulation, a new frame of the animation is rendered which consists of *n* x *n* cells. Each cell is filled with a color that represents the current state of a given entity within the grid (see Table 1). The animation visually demonstrates how the disease spreads each day. The CSV file contains the average state population data for each day of the user-specified number of simulations. The CSV data is used to create the SIR Graph.

A spreadsheet program, such as Microsoft Excel or Apple Numbers, can open the CSV file to produce a table of values and create a line graph similar to the one shown in Section IV.

III. Algorithm Overview

Initially, a two dimensional array is allocated and initialized with an entity object at each index. Each entity object consists of attributes used for storing its current state and length of time in the infected state. Next, an entity within the array is randomly chosen to enter the infected state, and is placed in a first-in first-out (FIFO) infected queue. For each day of the simulation, each entity in the infected queue has the opportunity to infect eight neighboring individuals and one distant individual, if traveling is allowed. After an entity has had an opportunity to infect others, its days-infected count is incremented by one, and the next individual in the queue is allowed to attempt infecting others using the same method.

If an infected entity successfully spreads the infection, the newly infected individual is placed in the FIFO queue reserved for recently infected entities, but not in the infected queue. Two queues are necessary because newly infected individuals must not be allowed to spread their infection the same day their infection occurs, else the entire population may succumb to infection within one simulated day. After all infected entities have completed their attempts to infect others, the recently infected entities are merged at the tail end of the infected queue. A simulation day concludes once the two queues are merged, a new frame of an animated grid is generated based upon the current status of each entity in the array, and population totals for each possible state are recorded. The process then repeats until no entities are in the infected queue or two hundred simulation days have been processed.

Given that the infected state is temporary, the user-defined days in which an entity may be in the infected state dictates how long an individual remains in the infected queue. After an entity has attempted to infect all other entities within reach, its days-infected counter is incremented, indicating that the time an entity stays in the infected state is limited. When the infection counter has reached its limit, the entity must enter either a removed or susceptible state depending upon the parameters specified for the disease

Table 1: Color/status Association

	Status (Color)
	Susceptible (yellow)
	Infected (green)
	Immune (blue)
+	Vaccinated (red)
	Dead (black)

by the user. When transitioning to the removed state, entities which were once infected enter either the immune or deceased state. In the event both death and immunity are allowed by the simulation, a random number is generated to determine which of the two removed states an entity enters based upon probability parameters for both states provided by the user.

IV. Example Simulation

For the example simulation, a custom disease was created to demonstrate parameter specification and user interaction with EpiViz. Selecting the custom disease option menu allowed the user to choose the parameters shown in Fig 1.

The animation created by this example run of EpiViz reveals that the disease spread slowly at first, but quickly began to infect the entire susceptible population. Because vaccinations were not made available until day 25, the disease had already spread too far for the vaccination stations to be created. Four of the thirty-three tables are shown in Fig 2. The graphical table for the last day of the simulation indicates that all entities were either immune or deceased.

The CSV file was used to generate the SIR curve as shown in Fig 3. The line graph shows a pattern that is characteristic of an SIR curve. The susceptible population begins high, and then begins to drop as the removed population begins to increase. The infected population starts low, peaks midway, and dies out at the point which the population of

```
+----------------------------------+
|                  Name: Silly_Pox
|         Days Infected: 6
|  Immune After Removed: 1
| Infection Probability: 20%
|       Death Probility: 5%
|    Travel Probability: 10%
|   Vaccinations Allowed: 1
|Day Vaccinations Begin: 25
|    Vaccine Probability: 0.3
+----------------------------------+
```

Fig. 1. Parameter selection of a custom disease

immune entities exceeds the population of susceptible entities. The graph does not explicitly show the removed population, but instead shows the immune, deceased, and vaccinated entities from which the removed population is composed.

V. Future Work

EpiViz was created to provide a CA model for epidemic simulation in a manner that provides a visual representation of an outbreak, input parameter customization, and outbreak data collection. While EpiViz meets that goal, there are areas for improvement. The following ideas have been identified for future enhancements of EpiViz:

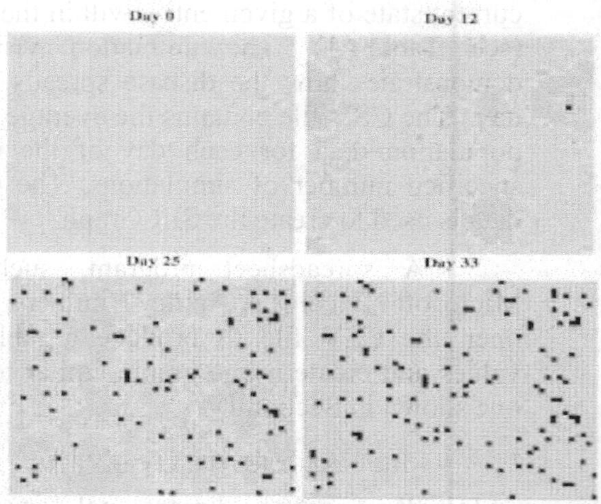

Fig. 2. Sample screenshots from an EpiViz simulation.

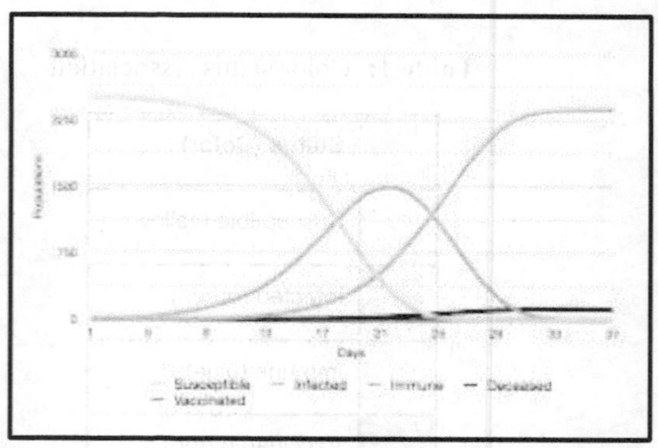

Fig. 3. Outbreak curve from an EpiViz simulation.

- Modify the artificial intelligence of the vaccinated entities to better combat the spread of diseases.
- Allow some cells in the grid to represent flora, structures, water, or other objects that are not affected by infections but instead, provide natural barriers that can alter the spread of a disease.
- Include a latent period to enable SLIR Model data collection.

VI. Conclusion

The SIR mathematical disease model can be effectively implemented using a CA approach. EpiViz is an epidemic simulator that allows a user to specify several disease related parameters and then models an outbreak using a set of rules for each entity in the CA. The simulation begins with one individual in the infected state and all others in the susceptible state. The outbreak proceeds as infected entities probabilistically infect susceptible neighbors. The simulation continues for two hundred days or until there are no longer any entities in the infected state. The primary benefit to EpiViz is the ability to visualize the day-to-day statistics along with data collection.

VII. References

[1] C. E. Shannon, "Von Neumann's contributions to automata theory," *Bull. Amer. Math. Soc.*, vol. 64, no. 3, pp. 123-129, 1958.

[2] G. C. Sirakoulis and I. Karafyllidis, "Cellular Automata and Power Consumption," *Journal of Cellular Automata,* vol. 7, pp. 67-80, 2012.

[3] P. Zhang, X.-X. Jian, S. C. Wong and K. Choi, "Potential field cellular automata model for pedestrian flow," *Phys. Rev. E,* vol. 85, no. 2, Feb 2012.

[4] G. A. Trunfio, D. D'ambrosio, R. Rongo, W. Spataro and S. Di Gregorio, "A New Algorithm for Simulating Wildfire Spread through Cellular Automata," *ACM Transactions on Modeling and Computer Simulation,* vol. 22, pp. 1-26, Dec 2011.

[5] I. Amlani and A. O. Orlov, "Digital logic gate using quantum-dot cellular automata," *Science,* vol. 284, no. 5412, p. 289, 1999.

[6] P. D. Tougaw and C. S. Lent, "Dynamic behavior of quantum cellular automata," *Journal of Applied Physics,* vol. 80, no. 8, 1996.

[7] A. R. Mikler, V. Sangeeta and K. Abbas, "Modeling infectious diseases using global stochastic cellular automata," *Journal of Biological Systems,* vol. 13, no. 4, pp. 421-439, 2005.

[8] S. C. Fu and M. George, "Epidemic modelling using cellular automata," *Proceedings of the Australian Conference on Artificial Life,* 2003.

[9] H. F. Gagliardi and D. Alves, "Small-world effect in epidemics using cellular automata," *Mathematical Population Studies,* vol. 17, no. 2, pp. 79-90, 2010.

[10] K. M. Bohannon and T. V. Johnson, "Cellular Automaton as an Epidemiological Model: A New Twist on Old Ideas," *In Proceedings of CAINE,* pp. 127-131, 2010.

[11] E. Allman and R. J., Mathematical models in biology, an introduction, New York, NY: Cambridge University Press, 2004.

[12] R. M. Anderson and R. M. May, Infectious diseases of humans, Oxford, NY: Oxford University Press, 2006.

Simulation and Monitoring of a University Network for Bandwidth Efficiency Utilization

Samuel N. John[1], Charles Ndujuiba[2], Robert Okonigene[3], Ndeche Kenechukwu[4]
[1,2,4]Department of Electrical and Information Engineering, Covenant University, Ota, Ogun State, Nigeria.
[3]Department of Electrical and Electronics Engineering, Ambrose Alli University, Ekpoma, Edo State, Nigeria.
[1]samuel.john@covenantuniversity.edu.ng, [2]charles.ndujiuba@covenantuniversity.edu.ng,
[3]robokonigene@yahoo.com, [4]kene.ndeche@gmail.com

Abstract - *As organization networks grow, it is essential that network administrators have knowledge of the different types of traffic traversing their networks and the methods of monitoring such traffic. Traffic monitoring and analysis is essential in order to troubleshoot and resolve issues as they occur in order not to bring the network to a total collapse. There are numerous tools and methods available for network traffic monitoring and analysis, no administrator can effectively carry out such activities without in-depth knowledge of the traffic on the network. The inefficient management of the network traffic may result into network collapse or degradation and these may negatively affect the network performance of the Corporate or University networks. This paper therefore, proposed a developed network topology and simulation to monitor the network performance. Therefore, achieving an effective management and controlling of the increase traffic flows in the network. The result obtained shows a better network performance in the bandwidth usage and utilization of the University network.*

Keywords: Network Monitoring, Simulation, Performance, Utilization, Efficiency.

1. Introduction

In today's IT-driven world, network administrators are tasked with the challenge of coping with increasingly expanding networks and providing excellent network performance around the clock in order to reduce down time to the barest minimum and thereby increasing business process with high productivity and maintaining or increasing revenue.

"Networking" is the buzz word of our times, networks are all around us. Networks are the key to
our life – virtually anything is connected with something other: Persons, corporations and their shareholders, our private and public life. Any structure that emerges from the mutual ties of its components may be conceived as a network [1, 2]. Network Monitoring is an active network communications practice for diagnosing problems and gathering statistics for administration and fine tuning, resulting in efficient bandwidth utilization and increasing the efficiency of data exchange in the network [3, 4]. Network monitoring for a corporate network is a critical IT function that can save money in network performance, employee productivity and infrastructure cost overruns. A network monitoring system monitors an internal network for problems. It can find and help resolve snail-paced webpage downloads, lost-in-space e-mail, questionable user activity and file delivery caused by overloaded, crashed servers, dicey network connections or other devices [5, 6].

Network monitoring can be achieved using various types of software or a combination of plug-and-play hardware and software appliance solutions. Virtually any kind of network can be monitored. It doesn't matter whether it's wireless or wired, a corporate LAN, VPN or service provider WAN. Devices on different operating systems with a multitude of functions, ranging from BlackBerrys and cell phones, to servers, routers and switches can be monitored. These systems can help in identifying specific activities and performance metrics, producing results that enable a business to address various and sundry needs, including meeting compliance requirements, stomping out internal security threats and providing more operational visibility [7, 8].

Network simulation, on the other hand, is a technique where a program models the behavior of a network either by calculating the interaction between the different network entities (hosts/routers, data links, packets, etc). using mathematical formulas, or actually capturing and playing back observations from a production network. The behavior of the network and the various applications and services it supports can then be observed in a test laboratory; various attributes of the environment can also be modified in a controlled manner to assess how the network would behave under different conditions [10, 12, 14].

Network simulators attempt to model real world networks. The idea being that if a system can be modeled, then features of the model can be changed and the results analyzed. As the process of model modification is relatively cheap and where a wide variety of scenarios can be analyzed at low cost (relative to making changes to a real network) [9, 11].

This project covers an investigation and recommendation of a network monitoring system for Covenant University. During the course of this project, research was conducted into the systems used by other organizations and the attitude and practices of both users and administrators on the network.

Since making changes to the networks are expensive and mistakes can cost a lot of money to rectify, Covenant University (CU) has a need for information regarding its network and this project aims at solving the challenges arising from the services provided by the Network Operating Center (NOC). By its nature the CU network contains a large number of computers connected wired and wireless which are not under direct control of the NOC. Also, a small percentage of the users on the network engage in illegal practices and do not adhere to the rules and regulations of the university network policy. It is known that, a good percentage of the students' downloaded files (often large files such as movies, videos and games) not only slowing the network but putting the institution at risk of prosecution from the legitimate/copyright owners of such files. Hence, the creation of a network monitoring system controlled by and created specifically for the academic needs of the institution cannot be overemphasized for an effective and efficient usage of bandwidth.

2. Specification of the Network Parameters

In performing this task, the following specifications/requirements were set for the proposed network:

- Traffic graphs,
- Details of data packet generation per time including packet flow and size,
- Graphic warning of any possible packet collisions observed,
- Details of traffic on critical ports or channels,
- Details of other dubious traffic or odd traffic patterns.

In order to generate a detailed report on the network performance it is imperative to have knowledge of the following performance metrics: Latency, Packet Size, Bandwidth, Throughput etc [7, 8].

3. Methodology

The processes involved with the implementation of this work were outlined and the different segments presented. Details regarding the technologies and tools utilized in developing the system, particularly the software implementation are also discussed with an overview of reports generated from the monitoring system.

The model follows a real topology of a section of Covenant University network and the performance characteristics of the model were to be ascertained. To determine this, server applications were modeled over the internet and local intranet and their performances evaluated.

Network simulation software was used in the simulation of the network and measurement of device performance and management applications in a virtual, scalable network environment [13]. This simulation package runs under Windows environment and it comprises a set of decision supporting tools, providing a comprehensive development environment for specification, simulation and performance analysis of communication networks, computer systems and applications.

4. Current Covenant University Network Layout

The Covenant University network is an enterprise class network with several network segments and hierarchies. Internet is provisioned on the network through two radio links terminated at two different service provider ports. The first service provider 21st Cenury GUAP-SAT1 (Google) provides 25Mbps of download traffic to the staff segment of the network while the second is eTranzact (MainOne) which provides a bandwidth of 60Mbps to the student segment as shown in Figure 1. The network has a 4-layer hierarchy which is broken down into the student segment and the staff segment. Dedicated elements are used in each segment not beyond the distribution switch. The network itself is based on a cascaded topology and all remote buildings are linked up to a central office as shown in Figure 2. As a campus there are central buildings and switches installed per building. Thus the switches can be seen as the connection point and an identity for each building.

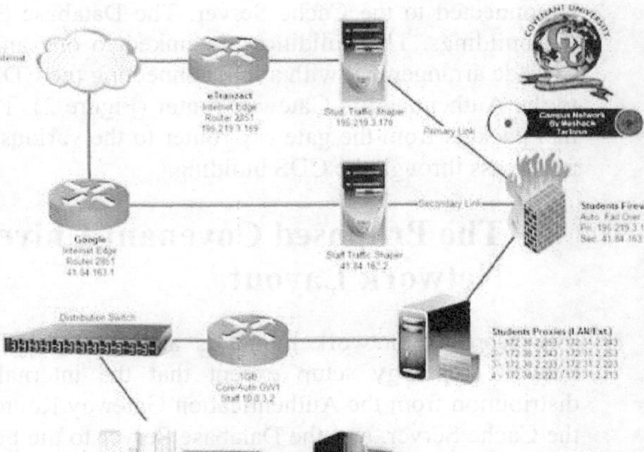

Figure 1. The Core Topology of the Covenant University Network

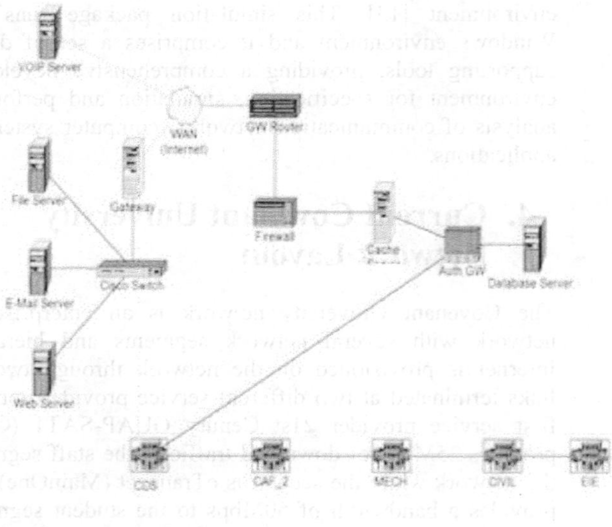

Figure 2. Current Covenant University Cascaded Network Topology

The current model is divided into 2 sections at the Gateway (GW) Router: the outside internet and the University network. The outside internet is represented by the VoIP, Web, Email and File servers (Figure 1). The University internet has a firewall which is designed to filter packets coming into the network. The Authentication Gateway router is connected to the Cache Server, The Database Server and the buildings. The buildings are linked to one another in a cascade arrangement with a link connecting the CDS building to the Authentication Gateway router (Figure 2). This means that packets from the gateway router to the various buildings must pass through the CDS building.

5. The Proposed Covenant University Network Layout

The proposed network model is analogous to the current network topology setup except that the internal network distribution from the Authentication Gateway Router through the Cache Server, and the Database Server to the buildings is in star topology as shown in Figure 3. The buildings therefore, are now connected directly to the Authentication gateway router which means that packets from the gateway are transmitted directly to the various buildings of the University.

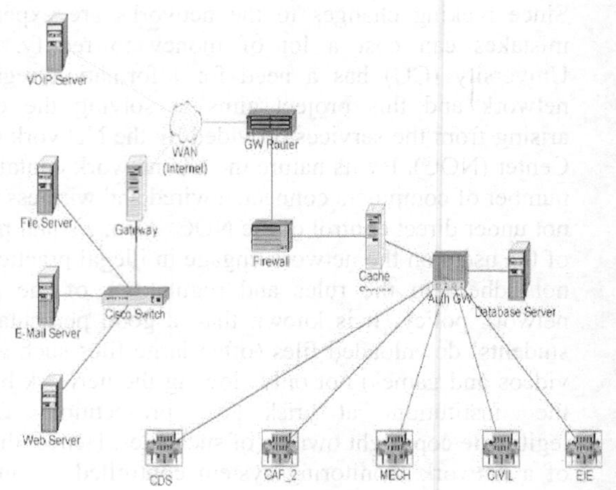

Figure 3. Diagram of the Proposed Covenant University Star Network Topology

6. Implementation and Testing

Each building network is composed of 19 systems distributed across 3 switches out of which one is selected for the report statistics. The applications modeled were VoIP Server, File Server, Email Server and Web Server. Two models were simulated, the current Covenant University network model showing critical areas of the network and an improved model based on the current model correcting bottlenecks and increasing efficiency on the network as shown in Figure 4.

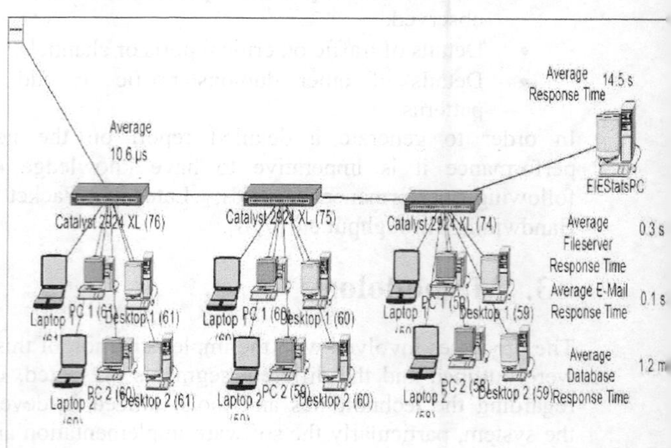

Figure 4. Average Response Time of a Sample Building System Distribution for the Current Network

The average response time on the EIE Stats PC is 14.5s while the average response time for file server, Email and Database applications are 0.3seconds, 0.1 seconds and 1.2 minutes respectively. Also, the average response time on the CDS Stats PC is 12.5s while the average response time for file server, Email and Database applications are 343.9

milliseconds, 51.4 milliseconds and 70.8 seconds respectively. Figure 5, shows the result and average response time of sample system distribution for the proposed network topology.

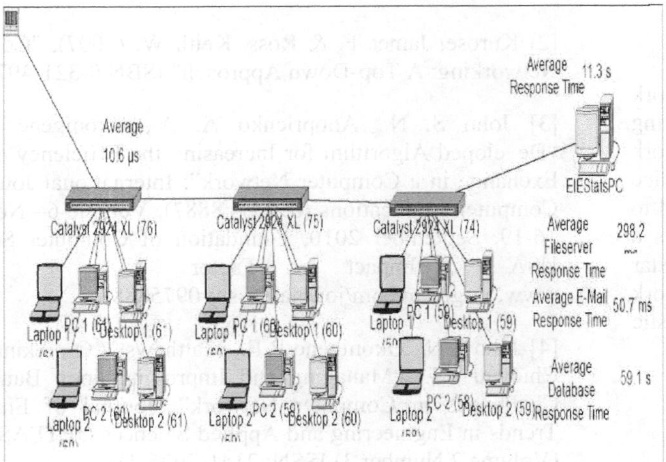

Figure 5. Average Response Time of a Sample Building System Distribution for the proposed Network

7. Results and Analysis

The results measured at the Authentication Gateway for the Networks are shown in Table 1, Table 2 and Table 3 shows the comparison between the application response times of EIE building and CDS building.

Table 1. Metrics Measurement Results at the Authentication Gateway for Current Network.

Packet Size (Kbytes)	Average Delay (µs)	No. of Packets	Throughput (Mbps)
10	23.1	3691	4.1
30	41.3	5035	3.4
40	53.7	4881	2.8
50	66.9	4339	2.6
60	75.9	5271	2.5

Table 2. Metrics Measurement Results at the Authentication Gateway for Proposed Network.

Packet Size (Kbytes)	Average Delay (µs)	No. of Packets	Throughput (Mbps)
10	12.5	4160	1
20	13	4116	1
30	12.5	4587	1.1
40	13.1	4707	1.1
50	12.4	5385	1.1
60	12.2	5257	1.2

Table 3. Comparison between the Application Response Times of EIE Building and CDS Building.

Metrics	Current Model	Improved Model
Average Response Time (EIE)	14.5 s	11.3 s
Average File Server Response Time (EIE)	300 ms	289.2 ms
Average Email Server Response Time (EIE)	100 ms	50.7 ms
Average Database Server Response Time (EIE)	72 s	59.1 s
Average Response Time (CDS)	12.5 s	11.1 s
Average File Server Response Time (CDS)	343.9 ms	290.8 ms
Average Email Server Response Time (CDS)	51.4 ms	50.8 ms
Average Database Server Response Time (CDS)	70.8 s	59.6 s

Figure 6 shows the measurement of throughput against packet size for current and proposed networks of the University. This result indicates that as the packets sizes increases, the throughput for the current network decreases while the throughput for the proposed network increases. This trend shows a better bandwidth utilization and efficiency in the proposed star network than in the current cascaded network topology.

In Figure 7, the average delay of the proposed network topology is relatively constant with an optimized characteristic while the average delay of the current network topology increases as the packet sizes increase. This will result into a better bandwidth utilization and network performance of the proposed network than the current network.

8. Conclusion

For network operators and administrators, network monitoring and analysis provides the means of being proactive (i.e. ability to detect faults prior to a network experiencing downtime). It also allows them manage service level contracts, to be assured of day-to-day operations and to validate system changes. The result of this work shows a highly improved network performance in the proposed star network topology than in the current cascaded network topology. This is an evidence of an optimized characteristic shown by the proposed star network topology

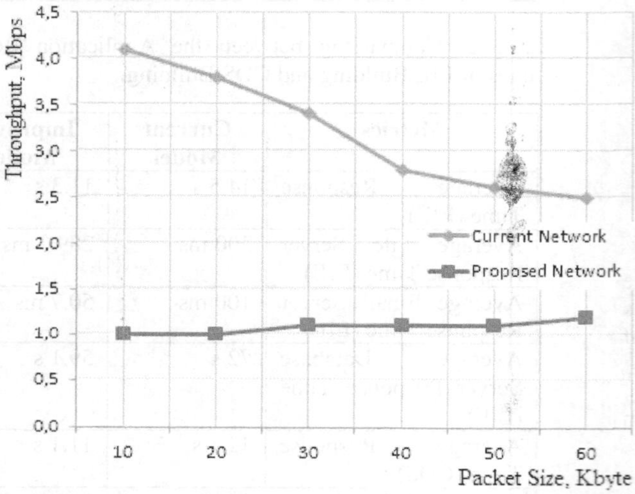

Figure 6. Measurement of Throughput against Packet size for Current and proposed Networks

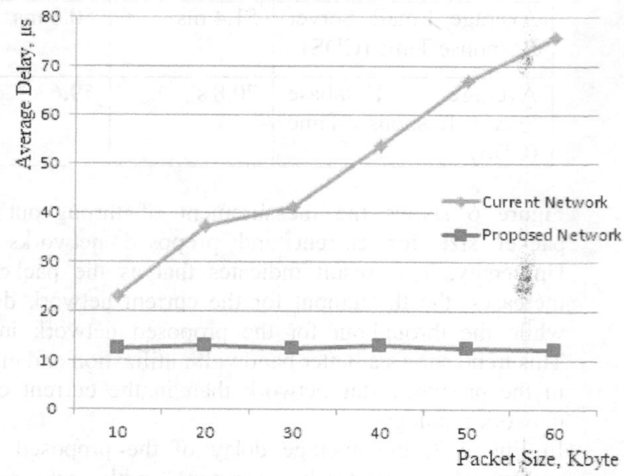

Figure 7. Measurement of Average Delay against Packet size for Current and proposed Networks

9. References

[1] Douglas Comer, Computer Networks and Internets , page 99 ff, Prentice Hall 2008.

[2] Kurose, James F. & Ross, Keith W. (2007), "Computer Networking: A Top-Down Approach" ISBN 0-321-49770-8.

[3] John S. N., Anoprienko A. A., Okonigene R. E.: "Developed Algorithm for Increasing the Efficiency of Data Exchange in a Computer Network": International Journal of Computer Applications (0975 – 8887), Volume 6– No.9, pp. 16-19, September 2010, Foundation of Computer Science, USA Impact Factor = 0.835: www.ourglocal.com/journal/?issn=09758887.

[4] John S.N., Okonigene R.E., Matthews V.O., Akinade B., Chukwu I.S.: "Managing and Improving upon Bandwidth Challenges in Computer Network", Journal of Emerging Trends in Engineering and Applied Sciences (JETEAS 2011) (Volume 2 Number 3) ISSN: 2141-7016, UK.

[5]http://www.masswerk.at/netmonitor2/netmonitor_1_en_help/intro.html., "An Introduction to Networks". *Masswerk Website.* [Online] 2011. [Cited: December 20, 2011].

[6] Fred Halsall, Introduction to data communications and computer networks, page 108, Addison-Wesley, 1985.

[7] S.N. John, F.A. Ibikunle, A.A. Adewale: "Performance Improvement of Wireless Network Based on Effective Data Transmission", The International Conference on Wireless, Mobile and Multimedia Networks organized by IET, 11-12 January 2008, IEEE Xplore Digital Library Journal: ISSN 0537-9989, pp.134-137, @ IEEE Xplore Digital Library, 2008, USA.

[8] John S.N., Akinade B.A., Chukwu I.S.: Wide Area Network Efficiency Through Optimization of Key Performance Indices: Proceedings: International Conference NIGERCON 2010, June 17 -19, 2010, pp., Rockview Hotel, Abuja.

[9] Penttinen A., Chapter 9 – Simulation, Lecture Notes: S-38.145 - Introduction to Teletraffic Theory, Helsinki University of Technology, Fall, 1999.

[10] Kennedy I. G., Traffic Simulation, School of Electrical and Information Engineering, University of the Witwatersrand, 2003.

[11] John S.N., Atayero A. A.: "Simulation of the Effect of Data Exchange Mode Analysis on Network Throughput», European Journal of Scientific Research ISSN 1450-216X,

Vol.24 No.2 (2008), pp.244-252, © EuroJournals Publishing, Inc. 2008.

[12] Anoprienko A.Y., John S.N.: "Basic Approaches to Simulation and Research of Network Infrastructure", Proceedings: "3rd International Scientific Technical Conference", (Integrated Computer Technology in Machine Construction), IKTM): Kharkov National Aeronautic University, Kharkov, Ukraine, Nov. 24th-27th, pp. 98, 2003.

[13] Netcraker Professional 4.1, http://www.netcracker.com/en/services/overview/ 2013.

[14] Flood, J.E. Telecommunications Switching, Traffic and Networks, Chapter 4: Telecommunications Traffic, New York: Prentice-Hall, 1998.

Numeric simulation tool of the weaving process

J. Vilfayeau[1, 2], F. Boussu[1, 3], D. Crépin[1, 3], D. Soulat[1, 3], P. Boisse[2]
[1]GEMTEX, ENSAIT, F-59100 Roubaix, France
[2]LAMCOS, UMR CNRS 5514, INSA Lyon, F-69621 Villeurbanne Cedex, France
[3]Univ. Lille Nord de France, F-59000 Lille, France

Abstract - *This project is directly attached to the challenge in the aerospace industry to meet the new environmental requirements as the Kyoto Protocol [1]. One of the potential axis being explored through various national and European programs is the global reduction of the structure's mass when economic conditions are met. One of the mass reduction's solution can be provided by the introduction of composite materials. To achieve substantial gains in the design of new materials based fibrous reinforcements, it is necessary to have numerical models of textile structures accurate and reliable. Currently, this modeling process is time consuming, random and can be costly.*

To answer this, the NUMTISS project proposes to model the main weaving motions during the manufacturing to obtain the geometry of the textile structure while incorporating its damage effect occurring during the production. Modeling and numerical simulation of the manufacturing process coupled with the understanding of the laws materials at different scales lead to an accurate answer of the actual geometry of the textile structure. This approach has been applied both on the modeling and simulation of 2D E-glass fabrics.

Keywords: Visualization tools and systems for simulation and modeling, Multi-level modeling, Simulation in industry, Finite element methods, Tools and applications

1 Introduction

The used modeling process to obtain a precise geometrical model for a 2D textile dry structure, to be implemented into a numerical computation system in order to predict its mechanical behavior, can be resumed in main four steps: the geometrical modeling of the textile structure, its real production, a geometrical characterization and an homogenization step. This current modeling process is time consuming and leads to several problems, as described in Figure 1.

The first problem is linked to the un-accurate geometry of the 2D textile structure provided by the different existing softwares which lead to broad assumptions on the yarn structure and, sometimes, don't manage the contact between yarns in the two directions which lead to interpenetration of material.

The second problem is linked to the weaving process of the 2D textile structure which takes a long time of preparation and induces many defects on the final structure due to the important uncertainty of the weaving production process. Most of the time, yarns damages occurring during the weaving process are not measured and thus can't be integrated as a key parameter of the predicted mechanical behavior of the final structure.

The third problem is due to the 3D tomography process which requires to fit the scale level of the textile structure representation while keeping the accuracy of the fibrous geometry. Additionally, the identification and selection of the representative unit cell may lead to a long time process of interpretations and discussions.

The fourth problem is mainly oriented on the images analysis process which needs to use a powerful data processing method in order to avoid huge time of human interpretations and decisions.

By the end, the last problem lies in the difficult integration of the accurate geometric modeling highlighting the residual mechanical properties of the 2D textile structure. No understanding of the internal stress caused by the weaving process which mainly influence the internal properties of the composite material is done.

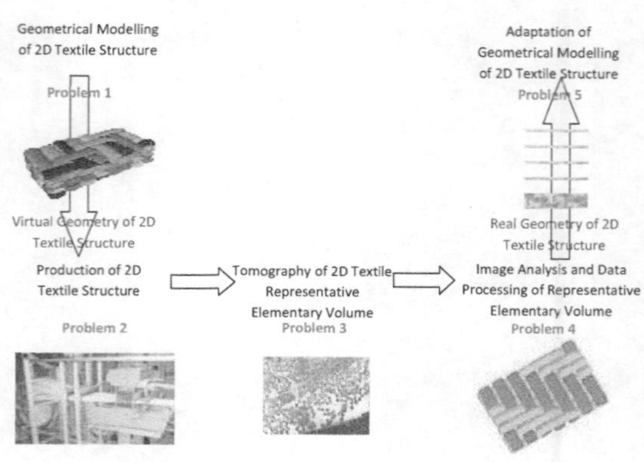

Figure 1. Existing problems linked with the 2D textile structure modeling

The complexity of 2D textile structures, especially for 3D warp interlock fabric, used as fibrous reinforcements for composites in structural applications, pushes us to simulate only the representative elementary cell (noted REC) [2][3][4][5][6][7]. Several specific studies have revealed significant difference (up to 30%) between the stiffness obtained by the REC behavior resulting from models and real experiments [8][9][10].

Such differences are mainly due to un-precised geometrical descriptions of these elementary cells from which a finite element meshing is performed [11]. These geometrical parameters include, in a non-exhaustive manner, the interlacing path of yarns and the choice of cross sections (shape, ratio aspect) [12]. A special attention must be paid to a bad description of reinforcements orientation as it affects material directions and therefore the material basis used to described the orthotropic behavior [13][14].

To refine geometrical description of models, many authors use the cross sections of yarns extracted from tomographic images performed on resin coated reinforcements [15][16][17]. Some studies describe more precisely the yarn geometry used inside woven reinforcements using 3D beam elements taking into account transverse deformations under compaction [18].

However, yarns are subjected to significant load during the weaving process which modify their positions inside the fabric, but also their transversal properties due to contacts with mechanical parts of the weaving loom and friction with other yarns. Contrary to studies conducted in braiding [19] or knitting [20] structures, so few numerical tools are focusing on simulating the weaving process. The objective of the present study is then to develop a simulation tool that mimics the weaving process to obtain more realistic textile samples. The proposed software architecture needs several input data, both geometric parameters of the textile fabrics and weaving process parameters, in order to provide a more realistic geometric modeling as described in Figure 2.

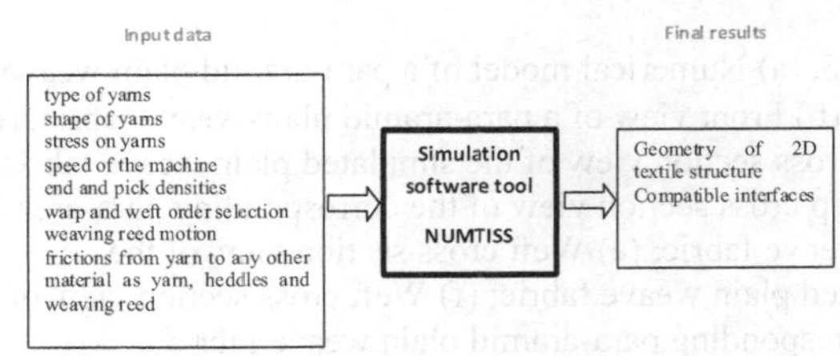

Figure 2. Proposed architecture of the NUMTISS simulation software tool.

In order to take into account the kinematic motions of the different weaving loom parts, a description of the step by step weaving process is briefly exposed in Figure 3.

2 Basic kinematic motions of the weaving process

The weaving of two orthogonal yarns, respectively warp and weft, occurs in a precise area of the loom allowing the shed motion, the filling insertion and the reed beat up.

The kinematic of the fabric forming zone (see Figure 3 (a)) can be described by these three main steps :

- Step 1 : Selection of each heddles involving the motion of warp yarns into two positions (up or down) (see Figure 3(b)). The obtained angle between these two warp yarns plans gives the shed value.

- Step 2 : Insertion of the weft yarn (filling) between the two warp yarns plans (see Figure 3(c)).

- Step 3 : Beat up of the weft yarn on the fabric by the use of the weaving reed (see Figure 3(d)).

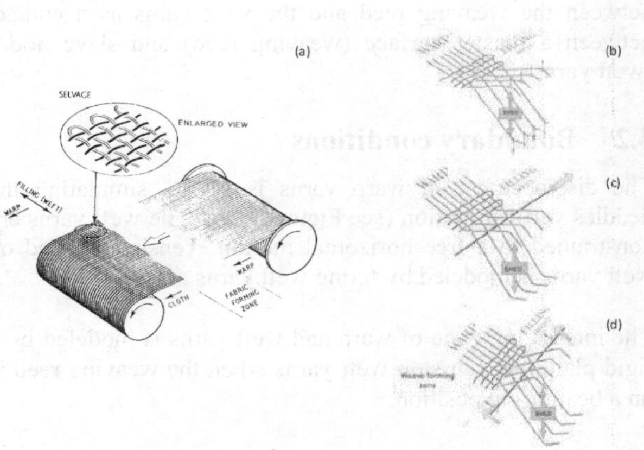

Figure 3. (a) Scheme of the fabric forming zone on a simplified weaving loom ; (b) Shed motion ; (c) Insertion of the weft yarn ; (d) Beat up of the weft yarn.

Taking into account these three main steps of the shed motion of the weaving process, a wider view of the weaving loom helps to locate the different parts in motion or in contact with the warp and weft yarns. The proposed simulation tool tends to reproduce all these main production steps in order to simulate the complete behavior of warp and weft yarns during the weaving process.

3 Simulation software tool of the weaving process

As the process is a time dependant problem, simulations are conducted with an explicit solver Radioss [25]. One of the objective of the intended numerical tool is to simulate warp yarns interlacing with few weft yarns. In order to control the computation time of simulation, the weaving reed is modeled as a rigid body. The heddles motions are transcribed via kinematic stresses imposed to yarns.

3.1 Description of the numerical model

Separately, yarns and their in-contact moving weaving components have been differently modeled with respect to their raw material characteristics. Yarns are considered deformable with a transverse isotropic elastic law. For the meshing, 8-nodes of hexahedra solid elements are used (see Figure 4 (c)). Existing and checked material law of para-aramid yarn has been used. Yarn to yarn friction is given by a coulomb's law with a coefficient equal to 0.3.

The weaving reed has been modeled by a steel plate composed of 4 quadrilateral elements for which an horizontal displacement has been imposed (see Figure 4 (b))

Contacts between warp and weft yarns have been represented like contacts between deformable surface, and contact between the weaving reed and the weft yarns as a contact between a master surface (weaving reed) and slave nodes (weft yarns) [21].

3.2 Boundary conditions

The displacement of warp yarns is set by simulating the heddles vertical motion (see Figure 4 (a)). The weft yarns are constrained to a free horizontal motion. Tension applied on weft yarns is modeled by fixing weft yarns at edges.

The interlacing zone of warp and weft yarns is modeled by a rigid plate that can stop weft yarns when the weaving reed is on a beating-up position.

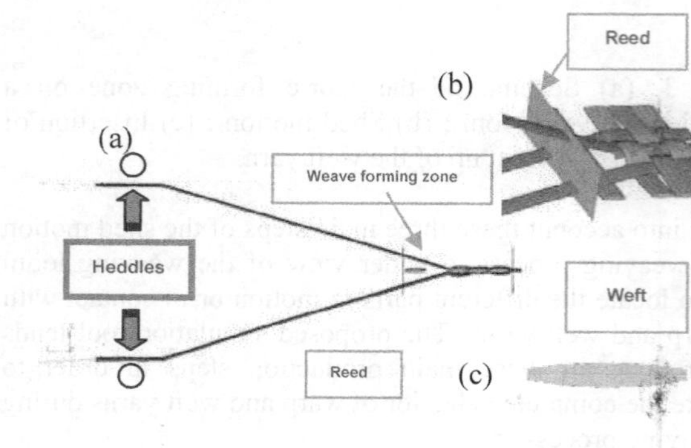

Figure 4. (a) Configuration of the kinematic conditions to produce a 2D plain weave fabric; (b) Configuration of the interlacing zone of warp and weft yarns; (c) the meshing of yarn section with solid elements.

In order to decrease the computation time, an acceleration of the weaving kinematic has been applied. The weaving cycle which lasts 600 ms for a weaving speed of 100 rounds per meter has been accelerated to 1.6 ms for our model where the material behavior's law is independent of strain rates. The required computing time was approximately 4 hours (on Personal computer equipped with 4 CPUs) to model the production of a 2D plain weave fabric made with 3 warp yarns and 4 weft yarns.

4 2D plain weave fabric simulation results

The Figure 5 (a) depicts the results of numerical simulation of a plain weave elementary cell including 8 warp yarns and 4 weft yarns. The modeling with 8 warp yarns was a good compromise between a reasonable computation time and a good representation of the edge effects occurring during the beating-up of the weaving reed. Numerical model from Figure 5 (a-c-e) reveals a good correlation with the experimental results of the para-aramid fabric produced on the weaving loom (Figure 5 (b-d-f)). Indeed, first numerical results have provided more realistic geometries than existing softwares, particularly concerning the warp and weft interlacing and the yarn deformations close to the contact zones of warp and weft yarns.

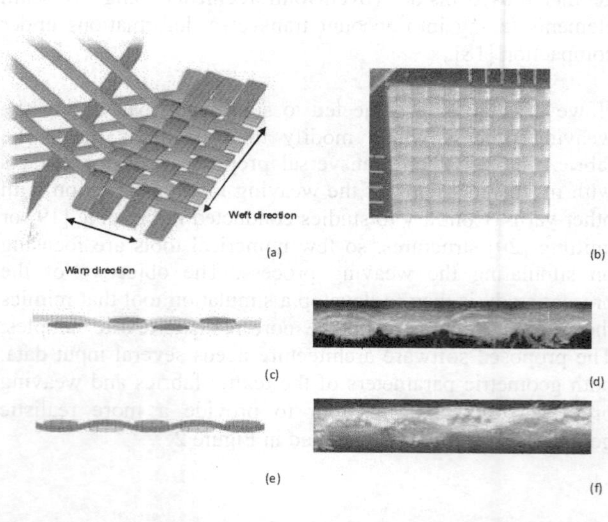

Figure 5. (a) Numerical model of a para-aramid plain weave fabric; (b) Front view of a para-aramid plain weave fabric; (c) Warp cross section view of the simulated plain weave fabric; (d) Warp cross section view of the corresponding para-aramid plain weave fabric; (e) Weft cross section view of the simulated plain weave fabric; (f) Weft cross section view of the corresponding para-aramid plain weave fabric

5 Conclusions

A numerical model has been designed to integrate weaving process conditions to act on the final geometric model of the 3D textile structure. The sequencing of the weaving process has been optimized in the model to fit with the weaving process of an industrial loom. By comparing the real and simulated geometries of the 2D plain weave fabric, a good correlation has been revealed which highlights the interest of introducing both weaving and geometrical parameters in the numerical model.

In the work in progress, the current model will be refined soon taking into account the circular geometry of an E-glass cross section yarn and real mechanical parameters obtained on yarns directly picked on the warps plan of the weaving loom.

6 Acknowledgement

This study has received support from the French National Agency of Research (ANR) with the project reference: ANR-09-MAPR-0018.

7 References

[1] ACARE, "Addendum to the Strategic Research Agenda," 2008.

[2] P. Boisse, A. Gasser, B. Hagege and J. Billoet, "Analysis of the mechanical behavior of woven fibrous material using virtual tests at the unit level," Journal of Material Science, vol. 40, no. 22, pp. 5955 - 5962, 2005.

[3] M. Khan, T. Mabrouki, E. Vidal-Sallé and P. Boisse, "Numerical and experimental analyses of woven composite reinforcement forming a hypoelastic behaviour. application to the double dome benchmark," Journal of Material, Process and Technology, vol. 2, pp. 378 - 388, 2010.

[4] P. Boisse, B. Zouari and A. Gasser, "A mesoscopic approach for the simulation of the woven fibre composite forming," Composite Science and Technology, vol. 65, no. 3 - 4, pp. 429 - 436, 2005.

[5] E. De Luycker, F. Morestin, P. Boisse and D. Marsal, "Simulation of 3D interlock composite preforming," Composite structure, vol. 88, no. 4, pp. 615 - 623, 2009.

[6] X. Peng and J. Cao, "A dual homogenization and finite element approach for material characterization of textile composites," Composites part B, vol. 33, no. 1, pp. 45 - 56, 2002.

[7] S. Lomov and I. Verpoest, "Model of shear of woven fabric and parametric description of shear resistance of glass woven reinforcements," Composite Science and Technology, vol. 66, no. 7 - 8, pp. 919 - 933, 2006.

[8] Z. Wu, "Three dimensional exact modeling of geometric and mechanical properties of woven composites," Acta Mechanica Solida Sinica, vol. 22, pp. 479 - 486, 2009.

[9] D. Li, D. Fang, N. Jiang and Y. Xuefeng, "Finite element modeling of mechanical properties of 3D five directional rectangular braided composites," Composites part B, vol. 42, pp. 1373 - 1385, 2011.

[10] P. Lapeyronnie, P. Le Grognec, C. Binetruy and F. Boussu, "Homogenization of the elastic behavior of a layer-to-layer angle interlock composites," Composite Structures, vol. 93, pp. 2795 - 2807, 2011.

[11] F. Stig and S. Hallstrom, "A modelling framework for composites containing 3D reinforcement," Composite Structures, vol. 94, no. 9, pp. 2895 - 2901, 2012.

[12] M. Ansar, W. Xinwei and Z. Chouwei, "Modeling strategies of 3D woven composites: A review," Composite structures, vol. 93, no. 8, pp. 1947 - 1963, 2011.

[13] P. Badel, S. Gauthier, E. Vidal-Sallé and P. Boisse, "Rate constitutive equations for computional analyses of textile composite reinforcement mechanical behavior during the forming," Composites part A, vol. 40, no. 8, pp. 997 - 1007, 2009.

[14] A. Charmetant, E. Vidal-Sallé and P. Boisse, "Hyperelastic modelling for mesoscopic analyses of composite reinforcements," Composites Scicence and Technology, vol. 71, no. 14, pp. 1623 - 1631, 2011.

[15] P. Badel, E. Vidal-Sallé, E. Maire and P. Boisse, "Simulation and tomography analysis of textile composite reinforcement deformation at the mesoscopic scale," Composite Science and Technology, vol. 68, no. 12, pp. 2433 - 2440, 2008.

[16] S. Buchanan, A. Grigorash, J. Quinn, T. McIlhagger and C. Young, "Modeling the geometry of the repeat unit cell of three dimensional weave architecture," Journal of Textile Institute, vol. 7, no. 101, pp. 679 - 685, 2010.

[17] S. Lomov, G. Perie, D. Isanov, I. Verpoest and D. Marsal, "Modeling three dimensional fabrics and three dimensional reinforced composites: challenges and solutions," Textile research Journal, vol. 81, no. 1, pp. 28 - 41, 2011.

[18] Y. Mahadik, K. Robson-Brown and S. Hallett, "Characterization of 3D woven composite internal architecture and effect of compaction," Composites part A, vol. 41, no. 7, pp. 872 - 880, 2010.

[19] A. K. Pickettt, J. Sirtautas and A. Erber, "Braiding simulation and prediction of mechanical properties," Applied Composite Materials, 2009.

[20] M. Duhovic and D. Bhattacharyya, "Simulating the deformation mechanisms of kintted fabric composites," Composites Part A: Applied Science and Manufacturing, 2006.

[21] RADIOSS Theory Version 100 Manual, 2009.

[22] S. Lomov, D. Ivanov, I. Verpoest, M. Zako, T. Kurashiki, H. Nakai and S. Hirosawa, "Meso-FE modelling of textile composites: road map, data flow and algorithms," Composites Science and Technology, vol. 67, pp. 1870 - 1891, 2007.

[23] I. Verpoest and S. Lomov, "Virtual textile composites software WiseTex: Integration with micro-mechanical, permeability and structural analysis," Composites Science and Technology, vol. 65, pp. 2563 - 2574, 2005.

[24] S. Lomov, A. Gusakov, G. Huysmans, A. Prodromou and I. Verpoest, "Textile geometry preprocessor for meso-mechanical models of woven composites," Composites Science and Technology, vol. 60, pp. 2083 - 2095, 2000.

[25] M. Sherburn, A. Long, A. Jones, J. Crookston and L. Brown, "Prediction of textile geometry using an energy minimization approach," Journal of Industrial textiles, vol. 41, no. 4, pp. 345 - 369, 2012.

[26] G. Hivet and P. Boisse, "Consistent 3D geometrical model of fabric elementary cell. application to a meshing preprocessor for 3D finite element analysis," Finite Element Analysis Design, vol. 42, pp. 25 -49, 2005.

SESSION

VISUALIZATION, GRAPHICAL USER INTERFACE, TOOLS AND TECHNIQUES

Chair(s)

TBA

Triangular Prism Element Optimization for Mesh Visualization of Printed Circuit Boards

A. Karen Daniels[1] and B. Shu Ye[2]

[1,2]Computer Science Department, University of Massachusetts Lowell, Lowell, MA, USA

Abstract—*Prism elements arise in some printed circuit board modeling contexts, such as visualization and electromagnetic field modeling. Here we consider prisms built by extruding from triangular bases which result from constrained 2d Delaunay triangulation. The goal is to partition each extruded prism into sub-prisms of high quality that fit within the given printed circuit board layers. A prism quality measure is introduced and, from it, optimal prism height is derived given a triangular base. Given a printed circuit board's layer heights and optimal prism heights, we provide a method for determining the height of each prism element. The overall prism mesh quality is evaluated, which examines the tradeoff of prism element quality versus the number of elements. The new method also compares favorably with respect to a prior prism mesh generation method that does not involve optimizing prism heights.*

Keywords: Meshing, Visualization

1. Introduction

In recent years, the interconnect modeling on Printed Circuit Board (PCB) and in packaging has become a bottleneck for successful high-speed circuit design [1] and visualization. The signal integrity issues, such as the signal propagation time, the digital pulse distortion, and the cross-talk, all effect the quality of the digital signal and can cause integrated circuit gate misswitching and introduce large bit rate error [2]. Therefore, simple physical constraints on the routing rules are no longer sufficient. For critical nets, accurate circuit simulation is needed, which requires accurate electromagnetic (EM) characterization on interconnects. The finite element based full-wave EM field solver can be applied to perform such tasks which, in turn, rely heavily on the quality of the finite element mesh generation [3]. Figures 1 and 2 (both images courtesy of Cadence Design Systems) provide meshing examples for two common PCB structures: coupled serpentine lines and coupled vias. The PCB has a layered structure. A serpentine line is a transmission line, embedded in a single layer, containing turns to control signal propagation time over a line segment. A via is a vertical signal connection between layers. In this paper we focus on prism mesh generation, as discussed in Section 1.1 and illustrated in Figures 1 and 2. The goal is to provide a high-quality prism mesh which can be used for mesh visualization as well as techniques such as finite element modeling. Part

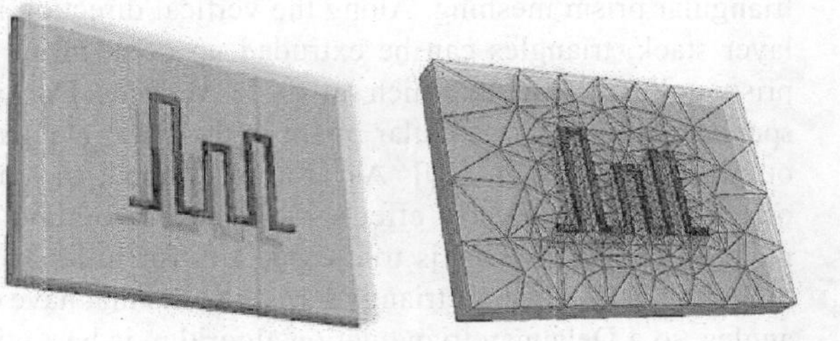

Fig. 1: PCB coupled serpentine line feature (left) with mesh (right).

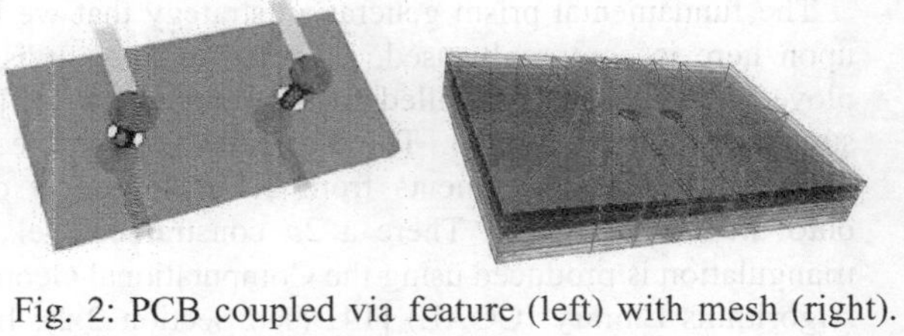

Fig. 2: PCB coupled via feature (left) with mesh (right).

of this process involves creating sublayers of layers, where appropriate. One important goal of mesh visualization is verification of the model structure.

1.1 Prism Mesh Generation

Mesh generation for finite elements has been widely studied (see [4] for a survey). The following mesh definition is given in [4]. T_h is a mesh of Ω if:

- $\Omega = \cup_{K \in T_h} K$.
- The interior of every element K in T_h is non-empty.
- The intersection of the interior of two elements is empty.

Techniques for mesh generation in general have been studied extensively in the geometric modeling and computational geometry communities [4], [5], [6], [7]. Geometric and topological underpinnings of mesh generation are explored in [8]. In some cases, mesh generation is tightly coupled with the EM simulation method (e.g. in [9] there is tight coupling of mesh generation with Finite Element Method (FEM) simulation).

Here we perform mesh generation separately from the EM simulation in order to allow our mesh results to be used as a starting point for mesh visualization or other techniques such as FEM. We primarily focus on mesh visualization, but we use quality measures that should be valuable across multiple contexts.

Due to the layered specialty of those interconnects on PCB and in packaging, a mesh consisting of triangular prisms is very efficient and sufficient to meet our meshing needs (each prism has triangular top and bottom and three rectangular sides.) On each layer, the vertical height of the interconnect is thin and the shape is irregular, which is very suitable for triangular prism meshing. Along the vertical direction in the layer stack, triangles can be extruded up or down to build prism volume elements which satisfy FEM needs. Due to this special property, a triangular prism is the basic element for our mesh generation [10]. As aforementioned, the quality of triangulation directly effects the accuracy of EM computation for FEM. This is true especially for full-wave EM modeling [11]. The best triangles are the ones that have equal angles, so a Delaunay triangulation algorithm is best utilized (see Section 2.1). Furthermore, PCB feature boundaries must be included in the triangulation, so a *constrained* Delaunay triangulation is used (see also Section 2.1).

The fundamental prism generation strategy that we build upon here is commonly used, as noted in [12]. It is employed in [9], and is detailed in our prior work [13] and summarized in Section 3. The first step is to project all PCB features' line segments from $3d$ orthogonally down onto the $2d$ x-y plane. There a $2d$ constrained Delaunay triangulation is produced using the Computational Geometry Algorithms Library (CGAL) [14] (see Section 2.2). In [9] the Triangle software by Shewchuck [15], [16] is used to generate a constrained Delaunay triangulation. While this is a strong approach, we find that CGAL is adept at handling segment intersection other than at their endpoints. In both our work and [9] edges of the triangulation are extruded up through the layers to construct prisms. In [9] each prism is subdivided into tetrahedra. In contrast, we subdivide the prisms horizontally to preserve the prism mesh structure. Within a given sublayer all of the prisms must have the same height. This is because if prisms have different heights within a sublayer, the generated prisms may not produce a conformal prism mesh. For us, the height of the prisms is a key decision and a crucial contributor to the quality of the overall mesh. The focus of this paper is producing a high-quality mesh by optimizing prism height and relating it to the selection of quality criteria fed as inputs to CGAL.

Other prism meshing research includes [12], [17], [18]. Motivated by problems in biology and medicine, Whitaker *et al.* [12] use iterative relaxation of point samples to create thin layers of triangular prisms. Their triangular quality measure is discussed in Section 4.1. In [17] Yamakawa and Shimada transform a tetrahedral mesh into a hybrid prism-tetrahedral mesh, motivated by FEM applications. They use prisms to reduce the number of elements and provide more accurate FEM analysis. Layers of prisms are created. Prism height can be governed by user input or can be derived "from the average edge length of the triangular faces." They provide a prism quality measure that we discuss in Section 4.1. For thin-walled solids, Yamakawa and Shimada [18] create prisms as an intermediate step in a process that begins with a tetrahedral mesh and ends with a hexahedral mesh. A layer of prisms is added to the boundary of the tetrahedral mesh. Some prisms are converted to hexahedral elements to form a mixed mesh. Finally, midpoint subdivision of the mixed mesh generates a hexahedral mesh. No pyramid elements are generated by this process; they can be a FEM concern.

1.2 Contribution and Overview

In [13] we based prism height inside each PCB layer solely on the thinnest height among the layers. Our triangle quality criteria for input to CGAL were related to the length of a triangle's longest edge and its aspect ratio. We used a triangle quality measure from [19] to evaluate the results. In [13] the focus was on triangle quality for successive refinements of an elliptical pad with a circle as a special case. Prism mesh quality was not evaluated. In this paper we present several contributions beyond the basic prism meshing algorithm. The first idea maximizes prism quality by formulating a prism quality measure based on the regular prism; this is based on the triangle quality measure from [19]. Next CGAL provides a $2d$ constrained Delaunay triangulation. Then we show how to, given a triangle as the prism's base, find the prism height that maximizes prism quality. The optimal height of the individual prism elements can then be used to determine a common prism height. A variety of strategies can be applied to derive common prism height. We give 5 choices and provide guidance on how to select a strategy. The next step produces sub-prisms within each PCB layer guided by the common prism height. Note that this approach is semi-automatic and involves optimizing prism quality. In contrast, the prism height selection method of Yamakawa and Shimada [17], while also semi-automatic, does not appear to select prism height to optimize prism quality. We compare their approach of the average triangle edge length measure with our strategy.

Finally, we perform the following post-processing step. We supply the common prism height to CGAL as a maximum edge length constraint. Thus, CGAL again creates a constrained Delaunay triangulation. We show that our approach compares favorably with respect to the results in [13]. We also examine the trade space of prism element quality versus number of prism elements. Some applications may need to apply further post-processing of the prism elements that we construct using quality criteria. For example, in FEM for PCB structures, the shape functions describing the field (e.g. EM) can further influence the number of prism sublayers required.

The remainder of the paper is structured as follows. First, Section 2 gives background on constrained triangle

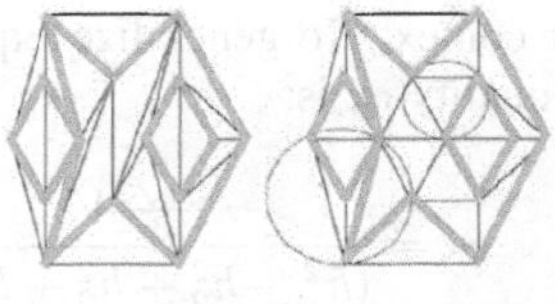

Fig. 3: A constrained triangulation (left) with a constrained Delaunay triangulation (right) (modified from [14]).

meshing, including the definition of a constrained Delaunay triangulation, and brief introduction to CGAL. Section 3 gives the original $3d$ triangular prism meshing algorithm, which uses constrained Delaunay triangulation, as in [13], and its choice of CGAL triangle quality criteria, as well as the triangle quality measure from [19].

Our new algorithm's primary goal is to provide good prism mesh quality. Section 4 presents our prism quality measure and shows how to maximize this measure by deriving optimal prism height given the base triangle. We compare this with the strategy used in [17]. Section 5 describes our revised prism meshing algorithm, including the post-processing step of using prism height to supply CGAL with revised quality criteria. Section 6 presents some results of our revised prism meshing algorithm on PCB examples and shows that it compares favorably with the standard approach. Section 7 concludes the paper and outlines future work.

2. Constrained Triangle Meshing

Here we give background for the prism meshing algorithms in this paper. We define Delaunay and constrained Delaunay triangulation in Section 2.1. Then we discuss CGAL's support for this functionality in Section 2.2.

2.1 Constrained Delaunay Triangulation

Delaunay triangulation ([3], [6], [8], [10]) has the empty circle property: each triangle's circumcircle's interior contains no vertices. The Delaunay triangulation also maximizes the minimum triangle angle size, which supports our $2d$ quality criteria.

Because we must include edges of structural features in the triangulation, we use a constrained Delaunay triangulation [8]. "It is convenient to think of constrained edges as blocking the view. Then, a triangulation is constrained Delaunay if and only if the circumscribing circle of any facet encloses no vertex visible from the interior of the facet" [14]. Among all constrained triangulations of a given set of vertices, the constrained Delaunay triangulation maximizes the minimum angle [8]. Figure 3 illustrates the constrained empty circle property of a constrained Delaunay triangulation, where thick segments are the constrained edges.

2.2 CGAL

CGAL's $2d$ constrained refined meshing [14] is utilized to respect input line segments and control the size of the triangles [15]. A CGAL constrained Delaunay triangulation satisfies the constrained empty circle property stated above in Section 2.1. The CGAL provides easy access to efficient and reliable geometric algorithms in a C++ library. For Delaunay triangulation and mesh generation, we find that CGAL can handle segment intersection other than at their endpoints better than other similar software, such as [16], which is used in [9]. CGAL does not yet support $3d$ constrained Delaunay triangulations (although it does support basic $3d$ triangulation), so we use their $2d$ constrained Delaunay functionality.

CGAL uses shape criterion lower bound B and size criterion of longest edge length to control triangle elements. The lower bound B is the ratio between the circumradius and the shortest edge length. The size criterion is an upper bound on the longest edge length of a triangle element. This criterion can allow users to define small triangles. In Section 3.2 we describe the choices available in the basic prism meshing algorithm.

3. Basic Prism Meshing Algorithm

Section 3.1 summarizes the algorithmic starting point for this paper. Section 3.2 discusses the CGAL triangle quality criteria used in this algorithm. Section 3.3 introduces the chosen triangle quality measure.

3.1 Algorithm

BASIC_PRISM_MESHING_ALGORITHM

$E_{xy} \leftarrow$ Initial set of structural feature edges, projected orthogonally onto the x-y plane
$l \leftarrow$ number of layers
$quality\_criteria \leftarrow$ $2d$ triangle quality criteria
$T_{xy} \leftarrow$ 2D_CONSTRAINED_TRIANGULATION ($E_{xy}, quality\_criteria$)
for $i = 1$ to l **do**
  Extrude and create prisms for layer i using $2d$ triangles in T_{xy}. Thinnest height among the layers is found and used to divide each existing layer into sub-layers.
end for

The mesh examples of Figures 1 and 2 use this approach. The idea, which we employed in [17], comes from Lee's thesis [9] for FEM analysis. Even prior to that, the idea of extruding triangles to form prisms has appeared in the literature as a common approach to prism meshing [12]; in some cases the offset direction comes from surface normals. The components and layers are projected to a $2d$ surface, on which a triangle mesh is generated based on the certain mesh control criteria such as edge length and angle of the mesh triangle elements. Then, the triangle mesh is extruded vertically back to the original layers of $3d$ structure to form prism elements. Prisms are built by connecting vertically adjacent triangles vertically. The results of this strategy are examined in Section 6 as a baseline for comparison with our new approach. Examples are introduced there for those experiments.

3.2 CGAL Triangle Criteria

In the basic algorithm we used the CGAL default angle bound of 20.7 degrees, which guarantees termination of the constrained Delaunay triangulation algorithm [14]. Good mesh quality in FEM simulation for a PCB context not only relies on the shape of mesh elements, but also closely depends on the wavelength λ. Wavelength has the relationship $\lambda = \delta / f$, where δ is the speed of light and f is the frequency. Consequently, we model the longest edge of a mesh element to be close to or less than one third of the wavelength, $(1/3)\lambda$. In today's high-speed design, if we take 50GHz as an example, the longest edge of mesh elements should be at most 2mm. We initially use this criterion, motivated by FEM considerations, as the longest CGAL edge length.

3.3 Triangle Quality

There are many possible ways to measure quality for triangular elements to assess the success of the above algorithm and the choice of CGAL criteria. For example, Whitaker *et al.* [12] use a radius ratio $Q = 3r/R$. Here "r and R are the radii of inscribing and circumscribing circles, respectively." From [4], in an optimal mesh of triangles the triangles are equilateral and "the elements in the mesh have a quality close to 1." One triangle quality formula offered there involves a ratio of longest edge length to inradius.

Here we present the method from [19] that we used in [13]. It forms a solid foundation for the $3d$ extension to the prism case in Section 4.1 and facilitates optimization. For the triangle case [19] the element quality q_t is:

$$q_t = \frac{4\sqrt{3}A}{h_1^2 + h_2^2 + h_3^2} \tag{1}$$

where A denotes the area, and h_1, h_2 and h_3 are the edge lengths. When it is an equilateral triangle $q_t = 1$. This agrees with the view expressed in [4].

4. Prism Mesh Quality

We begin our prism quality discussion by first generalizing Eq. 1 from Section 3.3 to the prism case in Section 4.1. Section 4.2 shows how to maximize prism height given a base triangle, and Section 4.3 examines sensitivity of prism quality to changes in prism height. Section 4.4 discusses overall prism mesh quality.

4.1 Prism Quality

Similar to [12] we start with a triangle quality measure that encourages equilateral triangles and the side faces of our prisms will be perpendicular to the triangular faces. We generalize generalize Eq. 1 to the prism case to accomplish this, and the result lends itself to optimization, which is useful in our context. To generalize Eq. 1 to the prism case the element quality q_p is:

$$q_p = \frac{\frac{32\sqrt{3}}{3}V}{(h_1^2 + h_2^2 + h_3^2 + h_4^2)^{\frac{3}{2}}}. \tag{2}$$

where V denotes the volume, the h's are the edge lengths, and the coefficient of V follows from the constraint that $q_p = 1$ for a regular prism. We assume that h_1, h_2, h_3 are the known edge lengths for the base triangle of the prism, and h_4 is the unknown height which we would like to optimize.

4.2 Prism Quality Maximization

Starting with Eq. 2, for notational convenience let $\beta = h_1^2 + h_2^2 + h_3^2 \geq 0$. This can be calculated for a given base triangle. Our goal is to solve for positive h_4 which maximizes quality q_p. The result using calculus is:

$$h_4 = \sqrt{\beta/2} \geq 0. \tag{3}$$

Although we designed q_p to equal 1 for a regular prism, 1 is not the maximum value of q_p. For an equilateral base triangle with sides all equal to 1, we obtain $q_p = 1.0264$ from Eq. 2 when using Eq. 3 for the height. Using Eq. 2 for q_p, we randomly generated 20,000 triangles to select h_1, h_2, h_3 and with h_4 from Eq. 3. Results appear in the top line of Table 1. Our experiments support the conjecture that $q_p = 1.0264$ is the maximum value of q_p.

Using the fact that h_4 maximizes q_p, one can use calculus to show that the equilateral case when $h_1 = h_2 = h_3 = 1$ does indeed optimize q_p. Since the roles of h_1, h_2, and h_3 in Eq. 2 are symmetric, one can show that the partial derivative of q_p with respect to h_1 equals 0 when $h_1 = h_2 = h_3 = 1$, so that this yields a critical point. These results suggest that the behavior of Eq. 2 makes it a useful prism quality measure.

Table 1: q_p for 20,000 randomly generated triangles using Eq. 3 for h_4 and using average triangle edge length.

method	$max\ q_p$	$min\ q_p$	$avg\ q_p$
Eq. 3	1.02638	1.91483 $e-4$	.528858
Avg. edge length	.999977	2.92361 $e-5$	.506697

Table 1 (bottom line) also shows 20,000 random trials for calculating prism height by averaging triangle edge lengths (an approach from [17]). Note that the average quality is smaller here than when using Eq. 3 for h_4. The maximum quality is also smaller and appears to have an upper limit of 1 rather than the upper bound of 1.0264 when using Eq. 3 for h_4. These differences can be justified algebraically.

4.3 Prism Quality Sensitivity

For the purpose of the revised prism meshing algorithm in Section 5, it is useful to examine the sensitivity of Eq. 2 to the value of h_4. A small random example is presented in Figure 4. In that example a triangle's edge lengths are

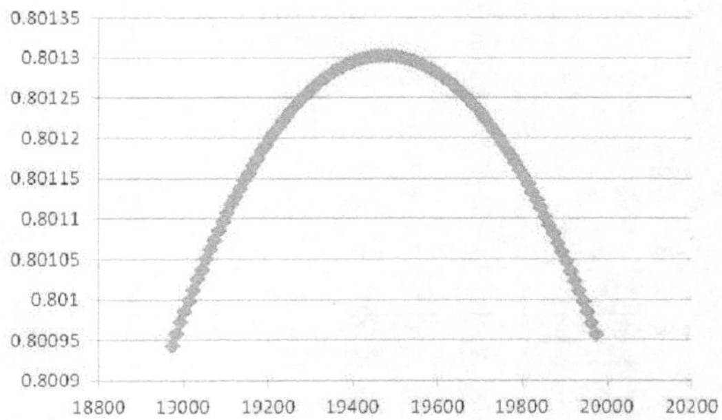

Fig. 4: Prism quality vs. h_4 for a randomly generated triangle.

randomly generated, h_4 is calculated using Eq. 3, and then prism quality is plotted using Eq. 2 for a range of h_4 values near the optimal value. Note the difference in scale for the two axes in the figure. This suggests that, for this sample triangle, prism quality is not very sensitive to changes in h_4. For a collection of triangles, it is possible to compare sensitivity by calculating the second derivative of q_p and then comparing the results across the triangles. This can be used to guide the overall prism quality policy choice in Section 5.

4.4 Overall Prism Mesh Quality

In assessing the results of Section 5's new algorithm in Section 6, we will evaluate the average prism quality across the mesh using Eq. 2. However, this is not the only criterion. From [4]: "An optimal mesh is that for which the chosen quality function is optimal while, at the same time, its number of vertices (elements) is minimal." Thus, we must take the number of prism elements into account in addition to the quality of the prism elements. There is a tradeoff between number of prism elements and prism element quality, which we explore in Section 6. The number of prism elements is addressed in some literature. Yamakawa and Shimada [17] give an example from computational fluid dynamics in which 42,304 elements provided good analysis results.

As noted in Section 1.2, some applications may need further post-processing of the prism elements that we construct. For example, in FEM for PCB structures, wavelength or choice of FEM shape functions may impose a lower bound on the number of prisms within a layer. This lower bound is often small and is satisfied in our work.

5. Revised Prism Meshing Algorithm

Here we introduce our new approach in REVISED_PRISM_MESHING_ALGORITHM. An important challenge is how to select sub-layer heights during the extrusion process so that overall high prism quality is achieved. Step 6 of the algorithm presented in Section 3 used the thinnest height among the layers to produce conformal prisms with a common height inside each sub-layer. Other choices of sub-layer height are possible, and here we use our prism quality maximization from Section 4.2 as the basis for 5 policy choices in CALCULATE_PRISM_HEIGHT. While this choice is user-defined, it can be guided by the sensitivity analysis suggested above in Section 4.3.

REVISED_PRISM_MESHING_ALGORITHM

$E_{xy} \leftarrow$ Initial set of structural feature edges, projected orthogonally onto the x-y plane
$l \leftarrow$ number of layers
$l_h \leftarrow$ layer heights
$c \leftarrow$ user's choice of height policy
$quality\_criteria \leftarrow$ 2d triangle quality criteria: $longest\_edge\_length$ and $angle\_bound$
$T_{xy} \leftarrow$ 2D_CONSTRAINED_TRIANGULATION ($E_{xy}, quality\_criteria$)
$h \leftarrow$ CALCULATE_PRISM_HEIGHT(T_{xy}, l, l_h, c)
if $c \neq 1$ and $h < longest\_edge\_length$ **then**
    $longest\_edge\_length \leftarrow h$
    $quality\_criteria \leftarrow$ 2d triangle quality criteria with adjusted triangle $longest\_edge\_length$
    $T_{xy} \leftarrow$ 2D_CONSTRAINED_TRIANGULATION ($E_{xy}, quality\_criteria$)
end if
for $i = 1$ to l **do**
    Extrude and create prisms for layer i using 2d triangles in T_{xy} and height h.
end for

CALCULATE_PRISM_HEIGHT(T_{xy}, l, l_h, c)

switch (c)
case 1:
$h \leftarrow$ height calculated as in Step 6 of BASIC_PRISM_MESHING_ALGORITHM
case 2:
$h \leftarrow$ average optimal prism height in T_{xy} using Eq. 3
case 3:
$h \leftarrow$ maximum optimal prism height in T_{xy} using Eq. 3
case 4:
$h \leftarrow$ minimum optimal prism height in T_{xy} using Eq. 3
case 5:
$h \leftarrow$ minimum layer height
end switch
return h

This new method gives users an opportunity to tune prism mesh quality over the given model structure based on optimal heights of prism meshing. The difference between cases 1 and 5 in CALCULATE_PRISM_HEIGHT is that case 1 does not have the feedback into CGAL triangulation criteria that case 5 has. Cases 2 through case 5 provide feedback for $longest\_edge\_length$ criteria to refine triangle

Table 2: Resources for Prism Meshing

Resources	List
Operating System	Windows 7: 64-bit
Machine	PC
Programming Language	C++ (STL)
Development Environment	Microsoft Visual Studio 2005
Existing Libraries	Qt 4.6.2 Desktop Edition
	CGAL 4.0
	Boost Library 1_51
	VTK 5.8.0

Fig. 5: PCB with single serpentine line (left) and single via (right), used examples in our experiments.

meshing again. Cases 2 through case 5 also give suggestion of more realistic heights for prism meshing. Later on, the prism quality tables show very positive results.

6. Quality Results

We begin by listing in Table 2 the resources that we use to implement and test our algorithm. This includes the visualization toolkit VTK. Section 6.1 describes our test cases and examines their layer heights. Section 6.2 discusses the optimal heights associated with the prisms formed by our new algorithm. Section 6.3 tabulates quality results for our test cases and illustrates visualization results.

6.1 Test Cases

To evaluate our new algorithm we use one single serpentine line PCB and one single via PCB (Figure 5, courtesy of Cadence Design Systems). Since layer height is the basis for cases 1-5 in CALCULATE_PRISM_HEIGHT, we briefly discuss layer height for these 2 examples. The serpentine line resides in a 5 layer structure. Top and bottom layers are the shield layers, while the middle layers are the dielectric layers. Of the 5 layers, the thickness of 3 of them is 1mm and the other 2 are each 4 mm thick. The via model is a 11 layer structure. The 11 layer structure has two shield layers in the middle of the layers; other layers are the dielectric layers. The via model itself has two traces, a drill, two pads and two anti-pads (void or hole features). We approximate a pad using a regular octagon. Two anti-pads are on the shield layers. Two traces are used to connect other devices, via models or transmission line models. The minimum of the layer heights for this via example is 2mm.

6.2 Optimal Prism Heights

The other key ingredient to the revised algorithm in Section 5 is the calculation of optimal prism element height

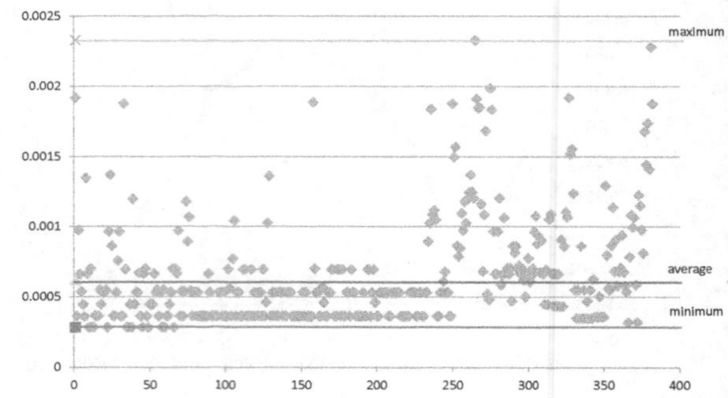

Fig. 6: Scatter plot of optimal prism heights using Eq. 3, in centimeters, for example in Figure 5, using 20.7 degree angle bound and 2mm longest edge length criteria in CGAL. There are 382 triangles (horizontal axis).

for cases 2-4. In our two examples the optimal prism heights are calculated using Eq. 3. For a 20.7 degree angle bound and 2mm longest edge length criteria in CGAL we discuss optimal prism height results. A scatterplot of optimal prism height for the triangles in the serpentine line case appears in Figure 6. In this case, there are 382 triangles. The minimum height is 0.282843 mm, the maximum height is 2.32849 mm and the average height is 0.659132 mm. 62.8% of optimal triangle heights in this case are smaller than the average. In the single via case, we obtain minimum optimal prism height of 0.019614 mm, maximum height of 1.18 mm, and the average is 0.196417 mm. Similar to the serpentine line case, the majority (68.8%) of optimal triangle heights in the single via example are smaller than the average. In the via case, the layer heights are all smaller than the average optimal prism height; this will influence the choice of case in CALCULATE_PRISM_HEIGHT.

6.3 Quality and Visualization Results

Mesh quality and visualization results for the 5 cases in CALCULATE_PRISM_HEIGHT for our serpentine line and via cases appear in Tables 3 and 4 and Figures 7 and 8 (both images courtesy of Cadence Design Systems). The last column is average prism quality across the mesh. In both of our examples the best case is always better than case 1. The percentage improvement is 94.4% and 87.5%, respectively. In the serpentine line example, the best triangle and prism quality is provided by case 4, which uses minimal optimal prism height across the triangles. Note that the number of triangles and prisms is of moderate size, which facilitates fast mesh visualization (144 seconds).

In the via example, the best triangle and prism quality is provided by case 5, which uses minimum layer height. Unfortunately, in this situation the number of triangles and prisms is quite large, which presents a challenge for mesh visualization. We plan to address this in future work.

Table 3: Single serpentine line results for example in Figures 5 and 7.

Case	Longest Edge (meters)	# Triangles	Triangle Quality	# Prisms	Prism Quality
1	0.002	382	0.845355	3056	0.359807
2	0.000659132	717	0.899001	2868	0.594523
3	0.00232849	382	0.845355	1524	0.521804
4	0.000282843	3350	0.907986	13400	0.699492
5	0.0001	27121	0.911653	108484	0.555146

Table 4: Single via results for example in Figures 5 and 8.

Case	Longest Edge (meters)	# Triangles	Triangle Quality	# Prisms	Prism Quality
1	0.002	324	0.8088	3888	0.3728
2	0.000196417	1097	0.8927	13164	0.3177
3	0.00118	324	0.8088	3888	0.3728
4	0.000019614	90376	0.9142	1084512	0.68273
5	0.00002032	84199	0.9143	1010388	0.699

7. Conclusion

The goal of new prism meshing approach is to improve the quality of meshing. Here, we obtain optimal heights of prism elements by maximizing prism quality. Our experimental results show significant quality improvement of the revised method. In the future we plan to expand our set of test cases beyond the single serpentine line and via feature cases to multiple serpentine lines and coupled vias. Also, as indicated in Section 6.3, in some cases the number of elements can be large enough to induce visualization difficulty with our use of the visualization toolkit VTK. To address this, in future work we plan to investigate using VTK in a parallel environment. The authors thank Michelle Daniels for helpful suggestions on prism quality sensitivity.

References

[1] R. Tummala, "SOP: What is it and why? A new microsystem-integration technology paradigm-moore's law for system integration of miniaturized covergent systems of the new decade," *IEEE Transactions on Advanced Packaging*, vol. 27, no. 2, pp. 241–249, 2004.

[2] J. Thompson and N. Weatherill, Eds., *Handbook of Grid Generation*. CRC Press, 1999.

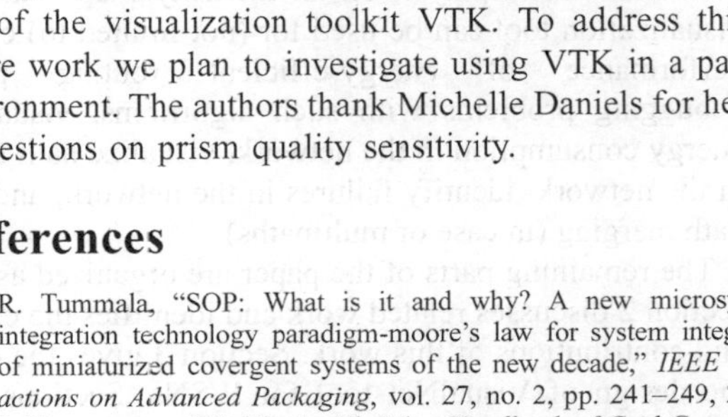

Fig. 7: PCB single serpentine line mesh result from Figure 5 with case 4 and zoomed in view.

Fig. 8: PCB single via partial mesh result from Figure 5 with case 5 and zoomed in view. 30000 out of 1010388 prisms are supplied to VTK.

[3] I. Tsukerman, "A General Accuracy Criterion for Finite Element Approximation," *IEEE Transactions on Magnetics*, vol. 34, no. 5, pp. 1–4, 1998.

[4] P. Frey and P.-L. George, Eds., *Mesh Generation: application to finite elements*. Paris: Oxford and HERMES Science Publishing, 2000.

[5] M. Botsch and et al., "Course 23: Geometric modeling based on polygonal meshes," in *Proceedings of ACM SIGGRAPH*, 2007.

[6] J. Goodman and J. O'Rourke, Eds., *Handbook of Discrete and Computational Geometry, second ed.* CRC Press, 2004.

[7] M. de Berg, O. Cheong, M. van Kreveld, and M. Overmars, *Computational Geometry: Algorithms and Applications*, 3rd ed. Springer, 2008.

[8] H. Edelsbrunner, *Geometry and Topology for Mesh Generation*. Cambridge University Press, 2001.

[9] S. Lee, "Efficient Finite Element Electromagnetic Analysis for High-Frequency/High Speed Circuits and Multiconductor Transmission Lines," Doctoral thesis, University of Illinois at Urbana-Champaign, Urbana Illinois, 2009.

[10] C.-T. Hwang and et al., "Partially Prism-Gridded FDTD Analysis for Layered Structures of Transversely Curved Boundary," *IEEE Transactions of Microwave Theory and Techniques*, vol. 48, no. 3, pp. 339–346, 2000.

[11] D. Rodger and et al., "Finite Element Modeling of Thin Skin Depth Problems using Magnetic Vector Potential," *IEEE Transactions on Magnetics*, vol. 33, no. 2, pp. 1299–1301, 1997.

[12] R. Whitaker, R. Kirby, and Z. Fu, "A Relaxation Method for Surface-Conforming Prisms," in *Proceedings of the 17th International Meshing Roundtable, Research Note*, 2008.

[13] S. Ye and K. Daniels, "Triangle-based Prism Mesh Generation for Electromagnetic Simulations," in *Research Note for the 17th International Meshing Roundtable*, Pittsburgh, Pennsylvania, 2008.

[14] M. Yvinec and et al., "CGAL User and Reference Manual, URL = http://www.cgal.org."

[15] J. Shewchuck, "Updating and constructing constrained delaunay and constrained regular triangulations by flips," in *19th Annual ACM Symposium on Computational Geometry*, San Diego, California, 2003, pp. 181–190.

[16] ——, "Triangle software. URL = http://www.cs.cmu.edu/~quake/triangle.html."

[17] S. Yamakawa and K. Shimada, "Converting a Tetrahedral Mesh to a Prism-Tetrahedral Hybrid Mesh for FEM Accuracy and Efficiency," in *Proceedings of the ACM Solid Modeling and Physical Modeling Symposium*, 2008, pp. 287–294.

[18] ——, "Automatic All-Hex Mesh Generation of Thin-Walled Solids via a Conformal Pyramid-less Hex, Prism, and Tet Mixed Mesh," in *Proceedings of the 20th International Meshing Roundtable*, 2011.

[19] E. Holzbecher and H. Si, "Accuracy Tests for COMSOL - and Delaunay Meshes," in *Proceedings of the COMSOL Conference 2008. URL = http://cds.comsol.com/access/dl/papers/5436/Holzbecher.pdf*, Hanover, 2007.

VisualNet: General Purpose Visualization Tool for Wireless Sensor Networks

S. Rizvi and K. Ferens
Department of Electrical and Computer Engineering
University of Manitoba
Winnipeg, Manitoba, Canada
Ken.Ferens@ad.umanitoba.ca

Abstract - In a large-scale Wireless Sensor Network, the main goal is to minimize node's energy consumption and maximize network lifetime. One way to achieve this is to develop energy-efficient routing algorithms. These algorithms are first implemented and tested using network simulators. Mostly, these simulators analyze the network in terms of protocol overhead, throughput, network latency, network lifetime, energy variance, and packet losses, generating log files for each of them. These files are later analyzed for results. However, an in-depth visual analysis is important during network operation to identify network behavior. This paper presents a visualization tool called "VisualNet" which generates intensity maps for network energy distributions. The software is developed in LabVIEW and was integrated with a Java-based network simulator to generate intensity maps and analyze large network data (energy distributions). The VisualNet tool can be used for plotting energy distributions, analyzing performance of a protocol, visualize load balancing, tracking path formation, and node failures in the network.

Keywords: wireless sensor network; energy consumption; network lifetime; energy efficient routing algorithm; intensity map; load balancing.

I. INTRODUCTION

A Wireless sensor Network (WSN) is a network of spatially dispersed sensor nodes that are normally deployed in an ad hoc manner (randomly scattered). A WSN is formed by hundreds or thousands of small, inexpensive, lightweight, autonomous nodes. Each node in a WSN comes with a drawback, which is its limited energy supply. For such a resource limited WSN, the main goal is to minimize energy consumption and maximize lifetime of the network. One approach to meet the requirement of extending lifetime is to design energy efficient routing algorithms that have the objective to balance the work load among the nodes in the network.

These routing algorithms are initially tested using different network simulators (e.g., ns-2[1]) available. These simulators mostly generate log files for the network operation, which are used to generate results for the network such as data rate achieved, packet losses occurred, protocol overhead, and delay. However, these simulators do not provide a tool for monitoring network's energy-efficiency. The energy-efficiency of the network can be monitored by monitoring residual energy value for each node in the network. The residual energy value for each node in the network can be logged periodically by the simulator during network operation. Since a WSN is a large-scale network, these energy values of the network constitute a large data, which needs to be properly sorted out and analyzed. One way of handling this large data is to feed it to a visualization tool. A visualization tool for monitoring energy-efficiency of the network can simply take this data set of network energy values and plot it over an intensity map to see the energy consumption across the network.

Such a visualization tool can be used by the researchers and academia to analyze large energy data from sensor networks and display it on an intensity map. This type of visualization tool can be used for (not limited to) evaluating performance of energy-efficient routing protocols, debugging problems with such algorithms, visually track energy consumption in the network, visualize path formation in the network, identify failures in the network, and find out path merging (in case of multipaths).

The remaining parts of the paper are organized as follows: section 2 discusses related work and identifies the extensions and contributions of this work. Section 3 gives the details of the design of VisualNet tool for WSNs. Sections 4 and 5 discuss the simulation experiments performed to test the visualization tool with data from some leading routing algorithms. Finally, conclusions and future work are given.

II. RELATED WORK

The main goal in developing VisualNet is to allow the users to visualize energy consumption in the network. The intensity maps would show energy variations within the sensor network area. By visualizing energy states of sensor nodes, a deeper understanding of the network can be achieved. Furthermore, the proposed software is a general purpose tool which can easily be integrated with a network simulator or a machine monitoring a real WSN. A lot of other visualization tools exist that allow the user to visualize different parameters of the sensor network. However, these softwares are both application as well as hardware specific.

SpyGlass [2] is extensible visualization software for WSNs. It uses a multi-layer mechanism to produce visualization. In SpyGlass, sensor nodes transmit data to a gateway node that is connected to a remote station using TCP/IP. The remote station runs the visualization software and characterizes network data. By processing sensor data, the graphical user interface of the visualization component presents readings on a canvas, textual information on a side bar, and line-based output at the bottom. SpyGlass shows important information about the network but does not explicitly display energy consumption graphically. The visualization tool proposed in this paper can easily run on a machine capturing sensor data, and generate intensity maps for the WSN in hand.

Mote-VIEW [3] is online monitoring software to visualize WSNs. The software gathers data from a gateway connected to a WSN. The software can only be used with Crossbow's products. The software allows the visualization of network topology and network statistics. The software logs data from a WSN into a database. This data can be analyzed and plotted using built in functions of the software. The software also uses intensity map for representing different parameters of the sensor node with colors. This is similar to the approach taken by the proposed software. However, ours is only focused on analyzing energy consumption of the network and deducing results from it. Also, Mote-VIEW is hardware specific software and only run with Crossbow's products and is not extensible.

A modular visualization tool for WSN is MonSense [4]. The software is extensible and is used to visualize data from a simulation as well as from a real test bed. The software is used for evaluating WSN algorithms. In its original package, the software does not indicate energy consumption on a separate map.

Another Sensor Network Analysis and Management Platform (SNAMP) is presented in [5]. The SNAMP is designed to provide researchers application specific visualization framework. The software runs with a real-time network and collects data for analysis. The software tells about network topology, sensor data, performance of the network, and hardware resources (as they are depleted). The software is complex and runs with a real-time network only.

In most of the visualization platforms, different parameters of the sensor network are analyzed visually. Mostly these platforms are hardware specific and are not extendable. Most of these visualization tools are very complex and are not general purpose. The proposed tool was therefore developed to assist in our research for WSNs. The proposed software however is a general purpose tool and can be extended with more visualization functions for different applications.

III. DESIGN OF VISUALNET

The main idea behind developing this tool is to read energy readings from a sensor network and plot them to have a graphical representation of node's energy. This can be done by representing energy values in terms of intensity, which are plotted on an intensity map. These energy values are residual energy values of nodes in the network, which are generated from simulations, or collected from a base station in an actual WSN. VisualNet therefore is a general purpose tool which can be used to analyze energy readings from any network. For most of the simulators, a small script needs to be written that would generate residual energy readings to a specific location in the computer, which are then read on the fly by the visualization tool.

The network visualization tool (VisualNet) is designed using NI LabVIEW 2012 development suite. The software is a simple yet novel virtual instrumentation implementation for Wireless Sensor Networks. The front panel of the software has an intensity graph, which plots the residual energy value corresponding to node's location. The intensity graph can be written with a 2-D array of P-values. Therefore, node's (x, y) coordinates are provided as array indices for a given P. The main front panel is shown in Fig. 1. The tool has two modes of operation, namely, online-mode and offline-mode. When the VisualNet is run, a 'vi' file is run which asks the user to select the mode of operation, shown in Fig. 2. These two modes are explained further as follows:

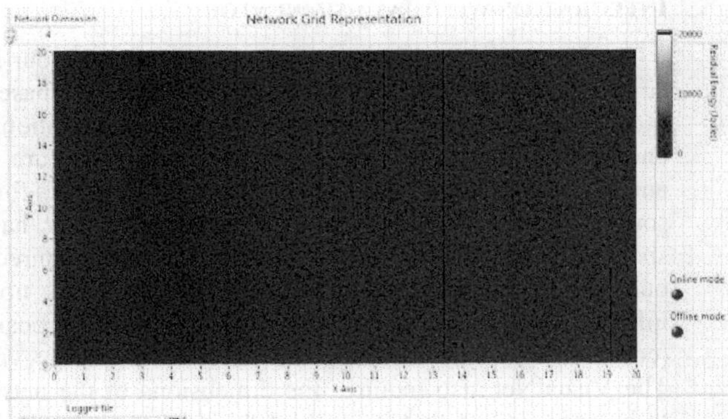

Fig. 1 Front panel of the VisualNet.

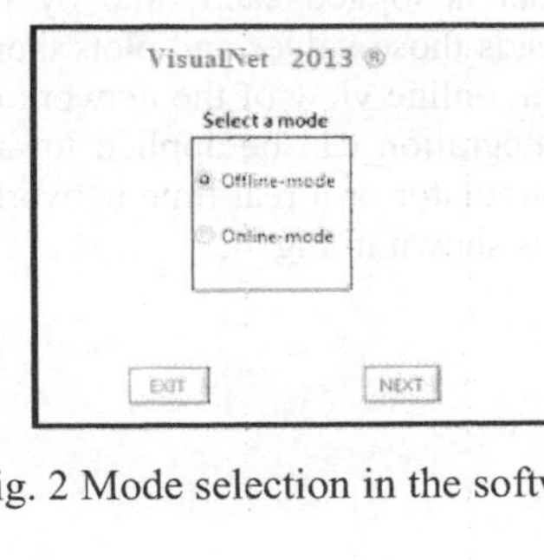

Fig. 2 Mode selection in the software.

ONLINE-MODE OF OPERATION

The online mode is used to integrate the tool with any network simulator (or a network) requiring a GUI for analyzing the network. The selection of the "Online-mode" opens the reference to the onlinemode.vi and invokes front panel of this file. The software finds the location of the file logged by the network simulator first and then defines its own directory for storing its files. The files generated by the software are the images of the intensity maps taken after a specified interval (5 s), and the information about the network (e.g., which node failed first, average network energy value). The software can also apply application specific function to analyze data. The software keeps checking if the file written by the network simulator is complete, and if the file has been logged, it reads those values and plots them on the intensity map. After plotting the acquired data, the software then grabs the image of the plot and stores it in its own directory for further use. The flow chart of the operation is shown in Fig. 3.

OFFLINE-MODE OF OPERATION

In the offline mode, the software simply reads the stored file from the specified location and plots the results on an intensity map. The plot is also saved as an image file. The offline mode can be used to analyze data from any type of network simulator or a real-time network.

INTEGRATION WITH JAVA SIMULATOR

The VisualNet tool can easily be integrated with our Java simulator based database or with any other database. In order to analyze data from a WSN, some simulations of energy-efficient routing protocols were run to capture data and to feed our visualization tool. The VisualNet asks for the source directory of the file to be read. The user has to specify the software where to look for the data required. In our case, we specify the logged text file containing node's information. This information is of node's position (coordinates x, y), node ID, and its residual energy value. The VisualNet also requires the dimensions of the network to be specified so that it can plot the data accordingly. The sampling time of the logged data is also required by the software so as to refresh the visualization maps accordingly. After the data is logged each time by the simulator, the VisualNet reads those values and plots them on the intensity map. Thus, an online view of the network can be visualized. The same integration can be applied to any other database from other simulator or a real time network. The integration architecture is shown in Fig. 4.

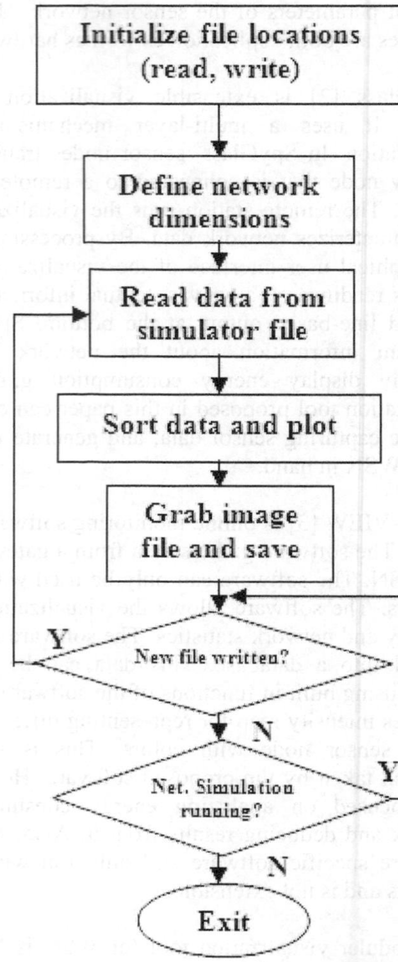

Fig. 3 Flow chart for online-mode operation

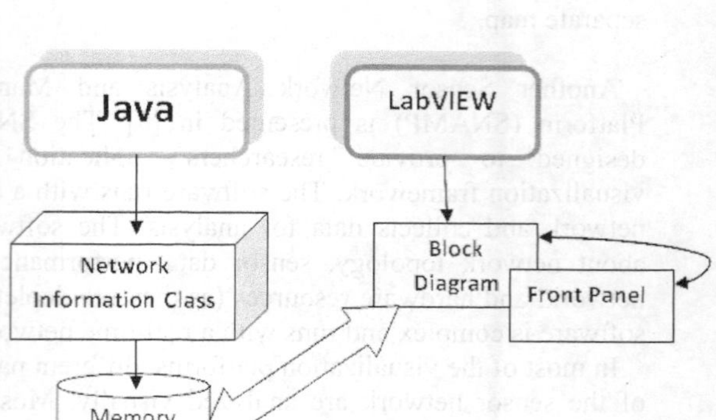

Fig. 4 The architecture of visualization integration.

IV. EXPERIMENTAL SETUP

In order to test the proposed visualization tool, we integrate it with a Java simulator. The simulator is used to test the performance of some energy-efficient routing algorithms and generate data, which can then be imported by the proposed tool. The simulation is designed for data centric routing protocols like Directed diffusion [6], Load balanced directed diffusion [7], and Multipath directed diffusion [8]. The simulator model which is used to model data-centric protocols is shown in Fig. 5.

The simulator uses object oriented programming power of Java to create objects, attributes, and events. The "Node" class is the class which is used to instantiate node objects. Instantiated sensor nodes are deployed over a square field area (*A*). Deployed *N* nodes in the network are scattered randomly over the field and are stationary. To ensure high network connectivity and avoid partitions in the network, the area of the network *A* is scaled to maintain a certain node density in the network. The network is simulated with one sink and one source node placed randomly in the network. The other important classes here are the "TransmitPacket" and "ReceivePacket" classes. These classes are used to pass the packet between nodes. Each node is assigned an initial energy of 5 J, and the transmission energy is computed using equation from [9],

$$E_{Tx}(k,d) = E_{elec} * k + \epsilon_{amp} * k * d^2 \qquad (1)$$

Whereas, for reception, the energy is given by

$$E_{Rx}(k,d) = E_{elec} * k \qquad (2)$$

A *25m* by *25m* grid was created and different numbers of nodes, ranging from *N* = *360, 400... 600* were placed in this area. Nodes were given a radio range of r = 4m. The event triggering times for interests, exploratory data, reinforcements and reinforced data were 5 s, 10 s, 15 s and 1 s respectively. The control packet size varies from 6 to 48 bytes for different protocol models. The data packet size packet size was fixed to 50 bytes.

The output of the simulation is captured in a log file which is generated by the Eclipse IDE platform for Java. Eclipse prints all the communication details of the network as a text file, which is helpful for traceability and verification of the simulation. Also, for all the experiments, the simulation itself generates multiple log files. These log files are appended every 20 s with the values of network such as energy variance, residual energy values of the nodes, average energy of the nodes, and energy samples used for intensity map plotting. These logged files can be used later for analyzing network lifetime and energy consumption. The simulation was run with one sink and source. The network lifetime for the simulations is defined as the time at which any one node in the network fails.

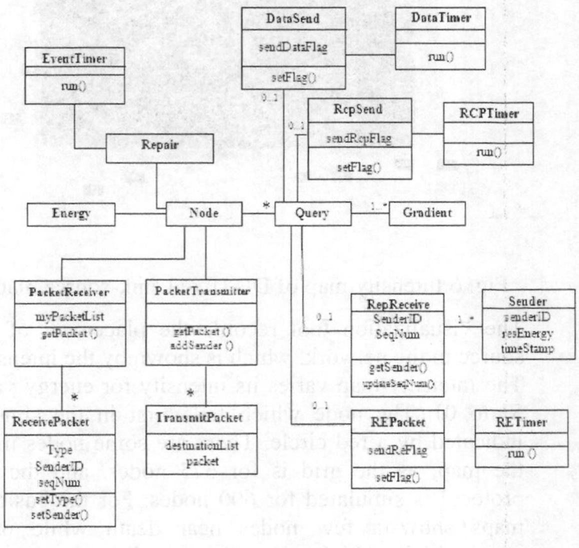

Fig. 5 Simulator model for data-centric WSN routing protocols.

V. EXPERIMENTAL RESULTS

In order to test the proposed software, we acquire energy readings from three energy-efficient routing protocols [7][8]. These protocols are energy-efficient methods developed for WSNs. The data from these simulations is then fed to the proposed software to visualize the network for different parameters.

DIRECTED DIFFUSION

The java based simulator ran simulations for the basic directed diffusion protocol. The simulation was run with one sink and source. During the simulation, residual energy values for each node is logged every 20 s. These readings are stored with node's location and its identity. For each protocol, two intensity maps are presented. These maps are maps generated at the time of network death. In one map, the sink and source nodes are placed randomly, while in the other map sink-source are placed on the extreme ends of the network. The results for these configurations are plotted in Fig. 6 and Fig. 7.

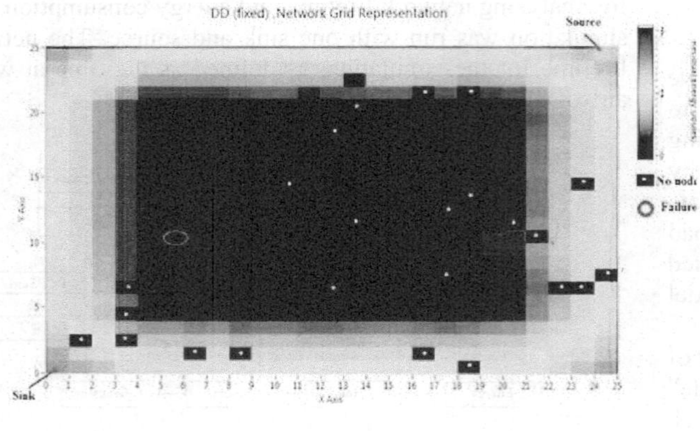

Fig. 6 Intensity map of DD (fixed sink-source placement).

The visualization tool records the placement of sink and source in the network, which is shown by the intensity maps. The intensity map varies its intensity for energy value from 5J to 0J. The node which fails first in the simulation is indicated by a red circle. There are some nodes missing on the map, as the grid is for 625 nodes, and the proposed protocol is simulated for 600 nodes. For the basic DD, the maps show a few nodes near death while others are contrastingly at higher intensity. Another thing to notice here is the outskirts of the network. It can be seen that the path formation takes place mostly in the centre of the network. The nodes at the outskirts of the network as well as in the centre are left with high energy and were not used properly. This indicates that the directed diffusion does not have load balancing.

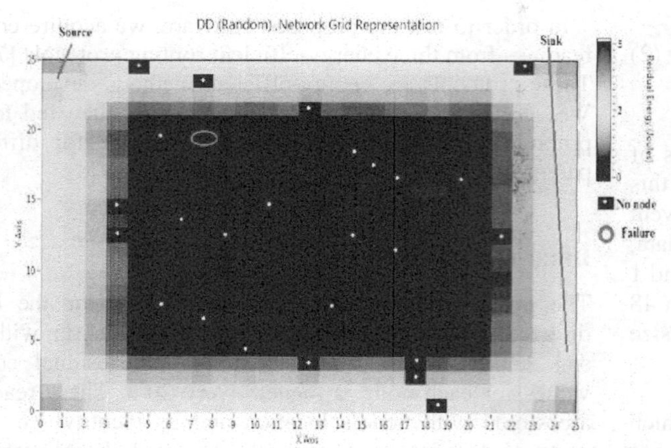

Fig. 7 Intensity map plot of DD (random sink-source).

Load Balanced Directed Diffusion

Another protocol simulated to acquire data for the proposed software was the load balanced directed diffusion [7]. Intensity maps generated from the results are shown by Fig. 8 and Fig. 9.

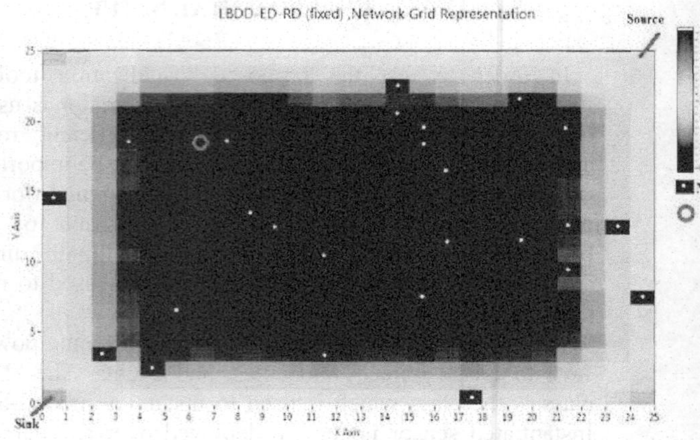

Fig. 8 Intensity map plot for load balanced DD, using fixed sink-source placement.

From Fig. 8 and Fig. 9, it is evident that for the load balanced DD network more nodes were used in the path formation and were near death (black boxed pixel) when network failed. This points out towards the fact that the load balancing allows each node to consume energy almost at the same rate and time, and at the time of network death more nodes were on the same level.

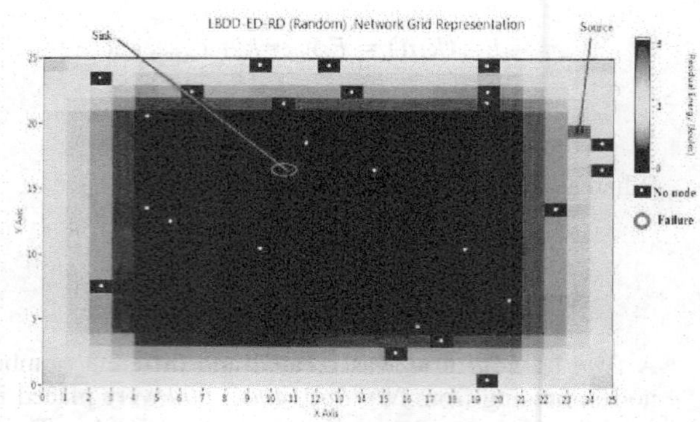

Fig. 9 Intensity map plot for load balanced DD, using random sink-source placement.

Multipath Directed Diffusion

The simulation was also run for the multipath directed diffusion which is an energy-efficient protocol for WSNs. The results from the simulation generated intensity maps shown in Fig. 10 and Fig. 11.

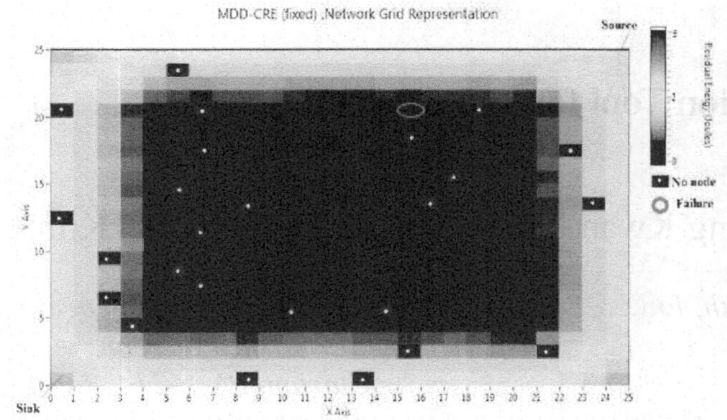

Fig. 10 Intensity map plot for multipath DD, using fixed sink-source placement.

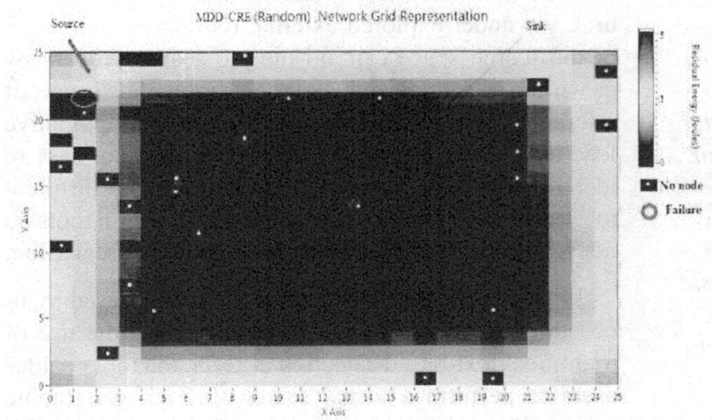

Fig. 11 Map for multipath DD, using fixed sink-source placement.

From results, it can be seen that the intensity contrast is deeper and more nodes have reached near death while being used. The load balancing cause considerable utilization of paths in the centre of the network. Another thing to notice is that the path formation is concentrated in the centre of the network. This is encouraging because no matter where the source and sink are placed in the network, the load balancing tries to construct different paths around them. The outskirts of the network has the least share in constructing paths. These portions are unused may be because the route construction packets when reaches the corners of the network may not find a node to forward the packet and the packet is dropped there.

VI. CONCLUSIONS AND FUTURE WORK

In this paper, a visualization tool for the Wireless Sensor Network is presented. The tool is tested by integrating it with a Java based network simulator. The visualization tool generates intensity maps by reading residual energy values of the network nodes. This intensity map can be used to evaluate performance of energy-efficient routing protocols, debugging problems with such algorithms, visually track energy consumption in the network, visualize path formation in the network, identify failures in the network, and find out path merging (in case of multipaths).

Future work involves using the proposed tool for monitoring an online sensor network. The software can also be expanded incorporating more visualization functions such as setting up alarms, indicator for node failures, and generating maps on the internet portals. The software can also apply application specific functions to analyze data.

VII. REFERENCES

[1] The Network Simulator, NS–2 [Online].: http://www.isi.edu/nsnam/ns/

[2] C. Buschmann, D. Pfisterer, and S. Fischer, "SpyGlass: A wireless sensor network visualizer," ACM SIGBED Review, Vol. 2, no. 1, 2005.

[3] Mote-VIEW Monitoring Software, Crossbow Technology Inc: [online] http://bullseye.xbow.com:81/Technology/UserInterface.aspx

[4] José Pinto, Alexandre Sousa, Paulo Lebres, Gil Manuel Gonçalves, and João Sousa, "MonSense- Application for deployment, monitoring, and control of wireless sensor networks," Poster in *ACM RealWSN'06*.

[5] Yu Yang, Peng Xia, Liang Huang, Quan Zhou, Yongjun Xu, and Xiaowei Li, "SNAMP: A Multi-sniffer and multi-view visualization platform for wireless sensor networks", In *Proc. of 1st IEEE Conf. on Industrial Electronics and Applications*, 2006, pp.1-4.

[6] C. Intanagonwiwat, R. Govindan, D. Estrin, J. Heidemann, and F. Silva, "Directed diffusion for wireless sensor networking," *IEEE/ACM Transactions on Networking*, vol. 11, no. 1, pp. 2-16, Feb. 2003.

[7] S. Wijedasa, S. Rizvi, and K. Ferens, "Load balancing algorithms for wireless sensor networks," in *Proc. Int. Conf. on Wireless Networks*, Las Vegas, Nevada, 2012, pp. 61-67.

[8] S. Rizvi, and K. Ferens, "Multipath route construction using cumulative residual energy for wireless sensor networks," In *Proc. of Seventh Int. Conf. on Systems and Networks Communications*, Lisbon, 2012, pp. 71-76.

[9] W. R. Heinzelman, A. Chandrakasan, and H. Balakrishnan, "Energy efficient communication protocol for wireless microsensor networks," in *33rd Annual Hawaii Int. Conf. on System Sciences*, 2000, pp. 3005-3014.

Effective Visualization Tool for Job Searching

Yilin Gu† Andries H. Smith†,1 Jong Kwan Lee† Xinyue Ye‡ Soo K. Kim*

†*Dept. of Comp. Science* ‡*School of Earth, Env. & Society*
Bowling Green State Univ.
Bowling Green, OH 43403
{guyil, smithah, leej, xye}@bgsu.edu

Dept. of Comp. Info. Science
Clarion Univ. of Penn.
Clarion, PA 16214
skim@clarion.edu

Abstract

In this paper, we introduce a web-based visualization tool that provides a new visuospatial and interactive platform for job searching. The tool supports not only the traditional text-based search queries, but also visual search queries based on interaction with geographic space. The job search tool allows users to explore spatial and multivariate information via a web interface that is based on widely-used information APIs. The effectiveness of the new visualization tool is evaluated by comparing it with other traditional job search tools.

Keywords– Information visualization, geovisualization, job search, web tool.

1 Introduction

When people search for a job, they are actually searching for a place to live. In other words, job searchers not only care about the job itself, but also consider a wide range of the other factors. One could be concerned with the number of similar jobs within that area (which could mean greater opportunities for professional development), or one could wonder about quality of life indices for that area, such as the crime rate or cost of living index. As a parent, one may care about if there are good schools within the area.

Yet searching for a place to work is a complicated and multidimensional information task. People need to synthesize a wide variety of relevant variables in order to make a good decision about where to live.

[1]Corresponding Author

— Manuscript submitted to The 2013 Int'l Conf. on Modeling, Simulation and Visualization Methods (MSV'13)

For a job search task, visualization represents a natural, yet under-explored external tool. A visualization of the search space can aid the job search process by providing a natural and intuitive geographic frame of reference. The visual medium also reduces cognitive load by making information and patterns more easy to identify for the searcher [9]. While there are different job search tools available, traditional job search tools do not support information-rich visuospatial job searching.

In this paper, we introduce a new web-based visuospatial job search tool. Stepping beyond the use of traditional text-based selection criteria, the tool enables users to perform a visual search through geographic space. The tool presents an interactive, visual interface that reveals many layers of quality of life indices, gives users the ability to compare regions, and lets users search by a freely defined geographic area. We also compare the functionalities of the new tool to traditional job search tools. The comparison shows that the new tool provides many significant and valuable features for the potential job searcher.

The paper is organized as follows. In Section 2, the related work in information visualization and job search tools are discussed. Section 3 introduces the new visualization tool. In Section 4, the new job search visualization tool is compared to other popularly used job search tools. Section 5 concludes this paper.

2 Related Work

In this section, we show some of the related information visualization methods and discuss other popularly-used tools for a typical job search.

Figure 1: A tag-based geovisualization from [19]. Each tag corresponds to a service directory query - red indicates queries that occurred more often than expected and blue indicates queries that occurred less often than expected. (Aerial imagery copyright 2007 NASA, Europa Technologies and TerraMetrics Inc.)

2.1 Information Visualization

Information Visualization aims to represent data in such a way that facilitates analysis and the generation of new insights using the visual sense as a filter [4]. Research in information visualization has produced both domain-specific and generic tools that present data with maximum transparency, while dealing with common implementation challenges such as performance, interaction, and extensibility.

One example of a information visualization tool was given by Bischof [2], who introduced *Spiegel*. Spiegel is a scientific information visualization runtime architecture that enables the creation of extensible and interactive visualization components. Spiegel serves as a kind of generic visualization operating system, linking together visualization components with a simple interface. Although Spiegel has been primarily applied to the modeling and visualization of astronomical processes, the tool is generic in that it allows for the creation of visualizations for any domain. However, while generic visualizations are often useful, there are also instances (e.g., [12, 18]) where domain-specific visualizations can better represent specific types of information.

Geovisualization, a subfield of information visualization, is an active research area drawing on advances in exploratory data analysis, with roots in the cartographic tradition [12]. Related work in geovisualization has produced tools that aid both researchers and laypeople in understanding, analyzing, synthesizing, and presenting complex geographical data [17, 11, 7].

There are many geovisualization toolkits grouped under the Geographical Information Systems (GIS) umbrella. Some common examples include ArcGIS [1], OpenJump [14], and LandSerf [8]. These toolkits tend to support generic visualizations of geographical data, but provide limited support for analysis of geo-annotated data outside their native formats, their integrations with external data sources notwithstanding. A study which leverages GIS technology for geomodeling and geovisualization has also been presented [3].

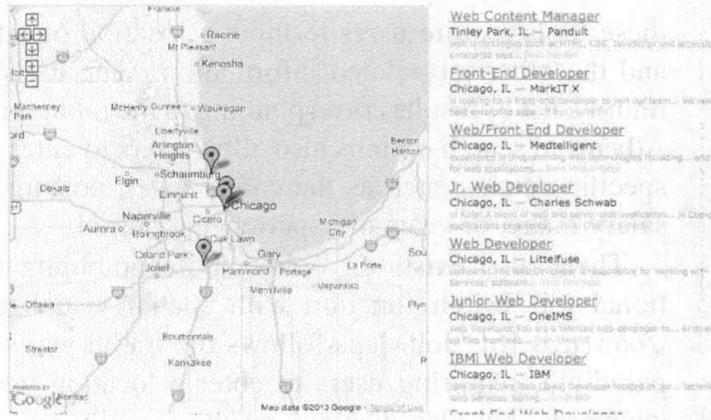

Figure 2: A list of job search results displayed on a map by JobMaps [6].

An integrated geovisualization tool in the health field is given by Robinson et al. [15], who present $ESTAT$– a geospatial toolkit for epidemiological research. ESTAT is capable of presenting scatter plots, bivariate maps, time series plots, and parallel coordinate plots for geo-referenced data. Each data analysis tool is fully interactive, allowing users to explore and manipulate data in real time.

$CrimeViz$ by Roth et al. [16] is a geospatial tool for analyzing and exploring crime data. In addition to visualizing spatial relationships in complex criminal incident data via the Google Maps API, the tool allows users to manipulate data dimensions through a data panel, and explore temporal relationships through a temporal panel.

Wood et al. [19] have developed a geovisualization mashup prototype based on de-facto standard technologies. It is capable of interactively mapping datasets with spatial, attribute, and temporal dimensions. The tool has been applied to the analysis of data from a mobile directory service. An example visualization from their paper is shown in Figure 1. The figure visualizes the subject of queries made to a mobile phone directory service by location.

2.2 Job Search Tools

There are various job search tools on web, including Indeed [5], Linkedin [10], and Monster [13]. Generally, these tools require users to input a location of interest and the other job-related information. The tools then return a list of results corresponding to the input criteria. Advanced search options also allow users to enter more specific details, such as the career level, posting date, salary range, or years of experience required.

There also exists an online tool combining traditional job search function with spatial visualization, *JobMaps* [6]. JobMaps follows the traditional search paradigm, requiring users to enter a location and job keywords, but also displays results visually on a map alongside the job listing (see Figure 2).

Although these tools perform a useful function, they are based on the premise that when searching for a job, one looks only for a company to work for. Yet intuition suggests a more likely premise: job searchers look for places to live, with a low cost of living, low crime rates, good schools, and hospitals, etc. The new job search visualization tool attempts to increase the breadth and depth of information available job searchers, and thereby overcome some of the weaknesses of traditional job search tools.

3 New Visualization Tool

Next, the new web-based job search visualization tool is presented. We first describe the technical description of the tool, followed by a behavioral description.

3.1 Technical Description

Figure 3 gives a technical overview of the new job search tool. The tool uses the standard client-server architecture to retrieve city and job information from the database via a PHP script running on the web server. The PHP server mediates client side requests for job, zip code, and quality-of-life indicator information from a MySQL database, while the client side makes direct requests to the Google Maps, Google Place, and Google Visualization APIs to manage the map display, manage user interaction with the map, display company positions, tables, and charts, and get local institution information.

To retrieve the job search data, we use two Python modules. The first module uses regular expressions to parse HTML from traditional job-search websites for key identifiers such as company name, experience, and job function. The second module downloads and parses zip code data from a zip information database. Both module store the resulting information in a server-side database. Further processing is done on the server by another Python module, which aggregates jobs in each city, saving city information in a separate table.

After the user selects a location, the client queries the database for job information corresponding to that location. Only the top twenty results are initially displayed to improve performance. When the user clicks on a job item in the displayed table, an event is triggered which passes the job place information to Google Place API, which returns the exact location of the company. The job description is also passed into Google Search API, which returns the search result of the job position and list on the left panel.

The tool also supports a one-hour-driving visualization from a specified company location. The visualization shows the approximated one-hour-driving range as a green-shaded area via a recursive call to the Google Maps API. The area is defined as the convex hull of seven 70-mile-away locations on the Google Map.

Another feature of the tool is the display of zip code and quality of life indicator information. For these displays, the client queries the databases on the server and displays markers on the map with varying intensities according to indicator rank. Searching for institutions (e.g., high schools, hospitals) is also supported by implementing a keyword search through the Google Place API.

The tool also allows users to compare multiple areas. The comparison component is primarily implemented using Javascript / jQuery and the Google Maps API. When a user clicks on the map, the client calls the Google Maps API to draw an adjustable circle which defines an area of interest. Then, the information queries are limited to the area through a client-side filter for the defined area. For the data comparison visualization, the tool utilizes the Google Visualization API.

3.2 Behavioral description

In the next section, the behavioral description of the tool is discussed.

When users first use the job search tool, two panels are displayed. One panel shows the controls for user queries and selections. Another panel shows the map of the search space with search results displayed on top of the map. One example is shown in Figure 4 (a) (with a zoomed-in map). On the map, red circles represent cities with job openings, and circle size indicates the total number of jobs within that city. Users can either select a city or select an area to search all the jobs within that city or area. In the control panel, users can also choose a job area, job type, and experience level to make their search more precise.

If users choose an area on the map, a table of job list-

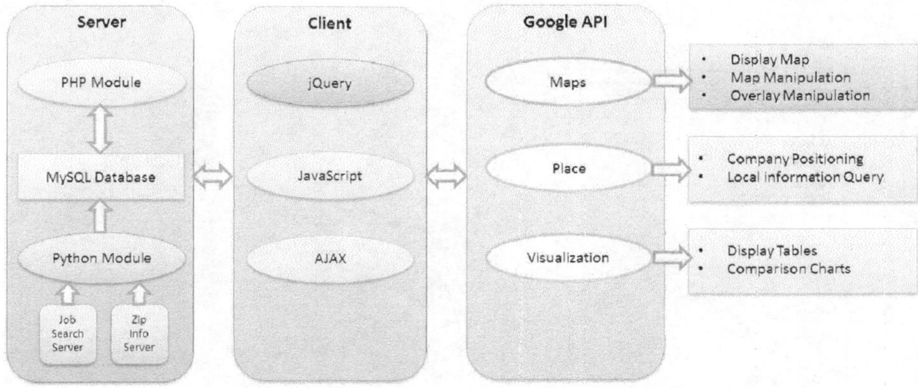

Figure 3: A technical overview of the visualization tool.

ings is displayed. At the bottom of the control panel, the user can click on interesting job positions to get more information, as shown in Figure 4 (b).

On the map, company location is indicated by a marker. When the user clicks on the marker, an option panel with three choices is displayed. The first choice allows the user to draw a circle with the company as its center, and adds the area to the comparison list, (which will be discussed later). The second choice allows the user investigate the one hour driving range from the company for quality of life indicators and other relevant information. Using the selected area as a reference, the user can inspect house prices, crime rates, the cost of living index, high schools or even restaurants. When the user investigates an area for related information, data aggregated by zip code are presented. Each zip code has a green marker located at its center, and the intensity of the marker indicates the rank of the zip code's index among all zip codes in the U.S. Users can also search for colleges, high schools, or other institutions within the selected area. The institutions' locations are marked on the map, while their names are listed in a table form. When the user clicks on an institution in the table, the corresponding marker on map bumps to highlight the institution's location. An example is shown in Figure 4 (c). In the figure, a company in Columbus, Ohio, is marked, and the one hour driving range is shown as a green shaded region, while nearby high schools are also marked with blue squares.

The comparison of multiple areas is also supported by the tool. To compare areas, users draw circles over the relevant areas, then select quality of life indicators (e.g., median income, cost of living index) to compare. The tool then displays three charts comparing the areas with respect to the information selected as well as the total job numbers. The first two charts are simple bar charts showing the comparison of job numbers and the selected information. The last chart is a bubble chart, which plots the comparison between the selected information on an X-Y scatter plot with the circle size indicating the number of jobs (see Figure 5 (a) and (b)).

4 Comparison of Job Search Tools

In this subsection, we compare our new visualization tool with other widely-used job search tools.

The fundamental difference between existing job search tools and the new tool is that the former provide a text interface and a table of listings, with relevant information such as company location and distance, but without a visual interface presenting the data in an intuitive spatial layout. The one exception is JobMaps [6], which presents job results visually on a Google API-enabled map. Yet JobMaps displays individual results, and not aggregate data, and does not allow user interaction–users cannot search by a freely defined geographical area. The new tool not only visualizes the geographic locations of job opportunities, but also offers an easily accessible, aggregate view of overall job distributions. While both traditional job search tools and the new tool offer users a listing of job opportunities, the new visualization tool presents results geographically and gives an immediate overall picture of where certain job type is aggregated.

The new visualization tool also offers users information often considered beyond the scope of traditional job search tools. As noted in Section 2, traditional job search tools have relatively narrow view of the job search– finding a job is, simply, finding a company to work for. On the other hand, the new job search vi-

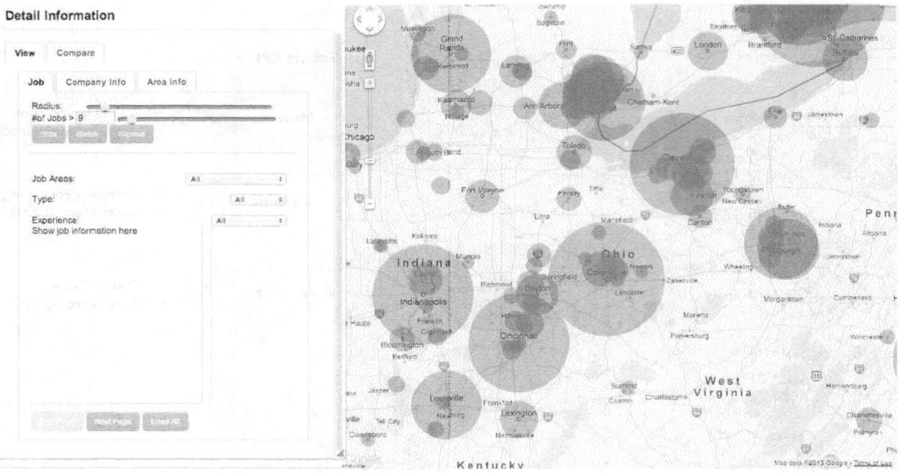

(a) Control panel (left) and map panel (right); sizes of red circles are proportional to the number of available jobs.

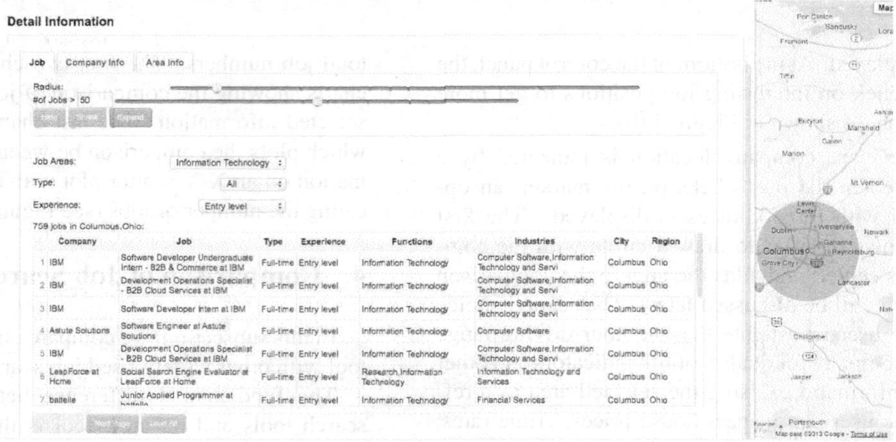

(b) Job listing in table form.

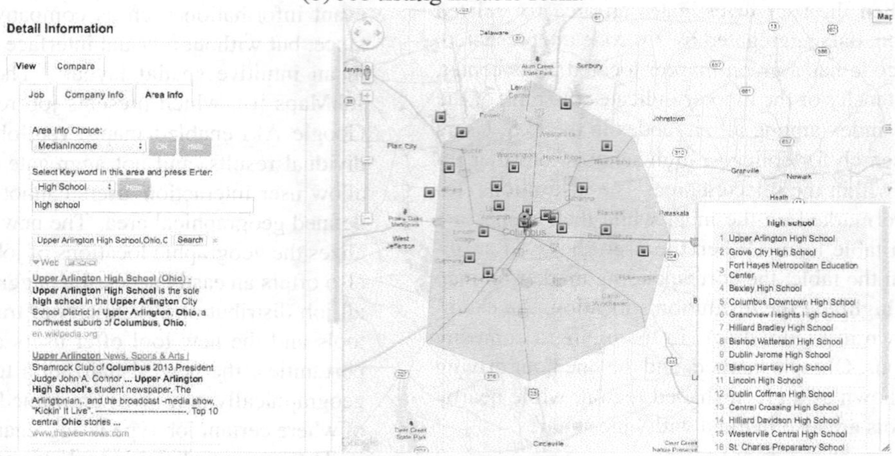

(c) One hour driving range and nearby high schools for a user-selected company.

Figure 4: Functionalities of the new tool.

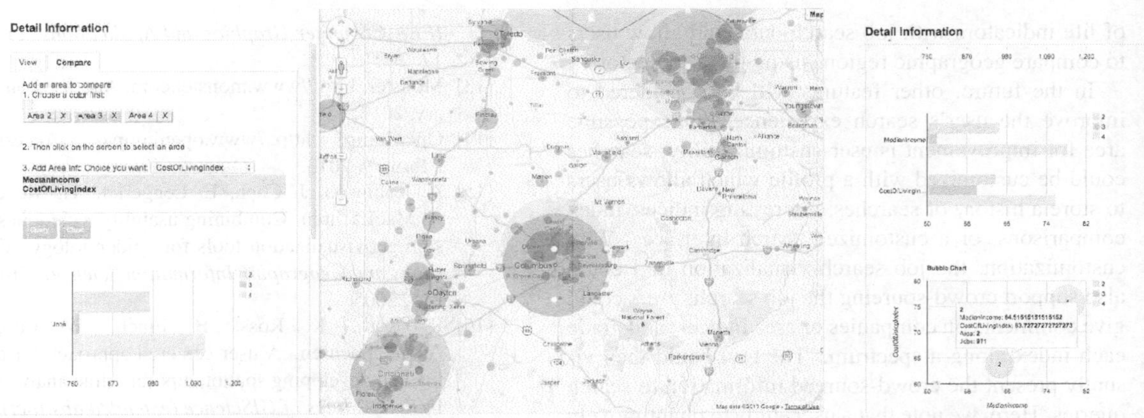

(a) Three-city comparison: map selection and a comparison chart (b) Other comparison charts

Figure 5: The area comparison functionality of the tool

sualization tool is motivated by the intuition that job searchers search for places, in addition to companies to work for. Thus, the new tool gives users immediate, visual access to a wealth of area information, so that the user can easily acquire a comprehensive summary knowledge of the potential work place.

In addition to providing area information, the new job search visualization tool also provides users with the ability to analyze information relevant to the job search through area comparisons. This interactive feature, missing from traditional job search tools, extends and deepens the tool's motivating idea that users search for a place to live; the tool provides users a means to inform themselves on the differences between places. The ability to compare greatly aids their decision making– users can highlight two, three, or more areas which they are considering, and compare them using the indices made available by the tool, thereby gaining an appreciation for the relative qualities of each selected area.

Table 1 summarizes the contrasts between the new visualization tool and LinkedIn, Monster, and JobMaps. Like traditional tools, the new visualization tool supports job searching and filtering, but it also supports

Functionalities	LinkedIn, Monster	Job-Maps	New Tool
Provides job search listings	√	√	√
Allows user to filters listings	√	√	√
Displays aggregate job information	×	×	√
Displays zip/area information	×	×	√
Allows user to view jobs by area	×	×	√
Allows for comparison between areas	×	×	√
Displays company locations	×	√	√
Provides social networking services	√	×	×

Table 1: Functionalities of different job search tools

visualization of company locations, job aggregations, zip/area information and area comparisons, as well as filtering jobs by a freely defined geographic area. However, the job search visualization tool does lack some features widely available among popular search tools (e.g., providing social networking services).

One feature that is currently missing from the job search visualization tool, but found in many traditional tools, is the ability to create a searchable profile and the ability to connect this profile to other job searcher or employer profiles. Implementing this feature was not considered a high priority, since its absence does not detract from the main contribution of the new visualization tool– features like visual searching, visualization of area information, and area comparisons. The employee profile features, best demonstrated by LinkedIn [10], could also be added in the future.

5 Conclusion and Discussion

In this paper, we have presented a new job search visualization tool that gives users access to a wide spectrum of useful information relevant to the job search. In addition to giving users the ability to search through geographic space using an interactive map, the tool can visually reveal multiple indices relevant to the job search. The tool also lets users compare regions across a range of indices.

Although many job search tools already exist and some have geographical components, these tools either have limited support for location-based searching, or statically present job place information. We are unaware of any other tools that let users interactively search using a visual interface, present multiple quality of life indicators with job search data, and allow users to compare geographic regions using these indicators.

In the future, other features will be considered to improve the user's search experience. One possible area for improvement is user-customizability; searches could be customized with a profile which allows users to store a history of searches, interesting indices, index comparisons, or a customized search interface. With customization, the job search visualization tool could also support crowd-sourcing the job search; users could give comments on companies or area indices, and grade each index along a spectrum. The tool could then visually present the crowd-sourced information to search queries. Here, we note that a user study to quantitatively evaluate the new tool is being conducted. The result of the user study will also be considered to improve the tool.

References

[1] ArcGIS. http://www.esri.com/software/arcgis. Accessed on February, 2013.

[2] H. Bischof. Visualization done right! In *Proceedings of 2008 International Conference on Modeling, Simulation, and Visualization Methods*, pages 109–115, 2008.

[3] P. Dergel and P. Fuks. Modeling and visualization of the traffic system with multi-agent system and GIS. In *Proceedings of 2008 International Conference on Modeling, Simulation, and Visualization Methods*, pages 292–297, 2008.

[4] J. Fekete, J. van Wijk, J. Stasko, and C. North. The value of information visualization. In *Information Visualization : Human-Centered Issues and Perspectives*, chapter 1. Springer Berlin Heidelberg, 2008.

[5] Indeed. http://www.indeed.com. Accessed on February, 2013.

[6] JobMaps. http://www.jobmaps.us. Accessed on February, 2013.

[7] E. Koua and M. Kraak. Geovisualization to support the exploration of large health and demographic survey data. *International Journal of Health Geographics*, 3(12):19, 2004.

[8] LandSerf. http://www.soi.city.ac.uk/ jwo/landserf/. Accessed on February, 2013.

[9] J. Larkin and H. Simon. Why a diagram is (sometimes) worth ten thousand words. *Cognitive Science*, 11:65–99, 1987.

[10] LinkedIn. http://www.linkedin.com. Accessed on February, 2013.

[11] A. MacEachren, F. Boscoe, D. Haug, and L. Pickle. Geographic visualization: designing manipulable maps for exploring temporally varying georeferenced statistics. In *Proceedings of the IEEE Symposium on Information Visualization*, pages 87–94, 1998.

[12] A. MacEachren, M. Gahegan, W. Pike, I. Brewer, G. Cai, E. Lengerich, and F. Hardisty. Geovisualization for knowledge construction and design support. *IEEE Computer Graphics and Applications*, 24(1):13–17, 2004.

[13] Monster. http://www.monster.com. Accessed on February, 2013.

[14] OpenJump. http://www.openjump.org. Accessed on February, 2013.

[15] A. Robinson, J. Chen, E. Lengerich, H. Meyer, and A. MacEachren. Combining usability techniques to design geovisualization tools for epidemiology. *Cartography and Geographic Information Science*, 32(4):243–255, 2005.

[16] R. Roth, K. Ross, B. Finch, W. Luo, and A. MacEachren. A user-centered approach for designing and developing spatiotemporal crime analysis tools. In *Proceedings of GIScience (extended abstract)*, 2010. accessible at http://www.geovista.psu.edu/CrimeViz/.

[17] T. Vance, N. Merati, S. Mesick, C. Moore, and D. Wright. Geomodeler: Tightly linking spatially-explicit models and data with a GIS for analysis and geovisualization. In *Proceedings of the 15th Annual ACM International Symposium on Advances in Geographic Information Systems*, pages 244–251, 2007.

[18] X. Wang, P. Chen, and W. Ding. Web-based interactive visualization of data cubes. In *Proceedings of the 2005 International Conference on Modeling, Simulation and Visualization Methods*, pages 136–143, 2005.

[19] J. Wood, J. Dykes, A. Slingsby, and K. Clarke. Interactive visual exploration of a large spatio-temporal dataset: Reflections on a geovisualization mashup. *IEEE Transactions on Visualization and Computer Graphics*, 13(6):1176–1183, 2007.

Development of the Web-Based Structure and Form Analysis System (SAFAS) for Architectural Education

M. Setareh[1], F. Bacim[2], N. Polys[2], and B. Jones[3]
[1]School of Architecture and Design, Virginia Tech, Blacksburg, Virginia, USA
[2]Department of Computer Science, Virginia Tech, Blacksburg, Virginia, USA
[3]School of Education, Virginia Tech, Blacksburg, Virginia, USA

Abstract - *This paper presents a collaborative effort among the Schools of Architecture and Design, Computer Science, and Education at Virginia Tech, Blacksburg, Virginia, to develop the web-based Structure And Form Analysis System (SAFAS) for the education of architects. The details of the software architecture, operations, and graphical user interface of SAFAS are discussed.*

Keywords: SAFAS, Web-Based Application, Architectural Structures, Architectural Education, Spatial Structures

1 Introduction

During the past decade there have been a number of attempts to use computers to enhance building design education. The target audiences for these software tools have been architecture, building construction, and engineering students (Messner and Horman [1]; Moloney and Amor [2]; Sulbaran and Crosby [3]; Kalisperis, et. al. [4]; Chou, et. al. [5]; Stojadinovic [6], and others).

Before the beginning of modern architecture, buildings were designed and built by master builders. They were in charge of creating the building from preliminary sketches to the final design and construction. However, due to the complexity of modern construction, the design process is now fragmented among several trades with each expert professional being responsible for his/her own part of the overall design and construction. Therefore, the modern building design process is an integrated collaborative effort, in which architects still have a major role; however, their main responsibility is limited to issues related to building aesthetics and function.

Even though structural engineers are generally responsible for the overall design of structural elements, architects must be familiar with the concepts related to building structures, and in particular, the inter-relationship between form and structure. For this reason the National Architecture Accreditation Board (NAAB) has mandated that all students in accredited architecture programs have instruction related to structural analysis and design.

There have been a few attempts and experimentations with the application of computer visualization and simulation as tools to teach structural behavior to architecture students with some success (Black and Duff [7]; Vassigh [8]; Setareh, et. al. [9,10]).

A collaborative effort supported by the National Science Foundation started in 2009 among the faculty members from the Schools of Architecture, Computer Science, and Education at Virginia Tech with the overall goal of integration of structures in architecture education. For the next three years, the team developed and tested the Structure and Form Analysis System (SAFAS). SAFAS is mainly the result of an attempt to close the gap between architecture and engineering education using an intuitive three dimensional (3D) graphical application. To ensure that SAFAS will be accessible to as many students as possible, a web-based approach was adopted. Upon the completion of the SAFAS development, it was used and tested by students of three architecture programs at the University of Illinois, Urbana-Champaign, Hampton University, and Virginia Tech.

This paper discusses the overall design of the SAFAS and focuses on the various aspects of software architecture and its graphical user interface. The application of the software in several architectural structures courses and different rounds of changes made to the SAFAS based on the analysis of the formative and summative evaluations can be found elsewhere (Setareh, et. al. [11]; Jones, et. al. [12]).

2 SAFAS and Spatial Structures

The main objective of this project is to help architecture students and architects to better comprehend the inter-relationship between building structure and form. The reader should note that in the context of this paper, "spatial structures" refer to structural systems made of interconnected linear elements. These systems are made of steel, aluminum, plastic or wood. They create architecturally appealing forms and are mostly used as long-span roof systems. It is assumed that the spatial structures are pin-connected and loads are applied at their connections (nodes or joints) only, thus, their members are under axial (tensile or compressive) forces only. This aspect of the spatial structures make them ideal candidates to be used for visualization of the inter-relationship between the form and structural behavior by the novice users.

3 Design of SAFAS

SAFAS consists of two main modules: Module One (Knowledgebase) and Module Two (Structure and Form Experimentation). SAFAS can be found at: http://legacy.caus.vt.edu/setareh/archresearch/

3.1 Module One (Knowledgebase)

This module includes several web pages with informative and educational materials as related to the various aspects of spatial structures.

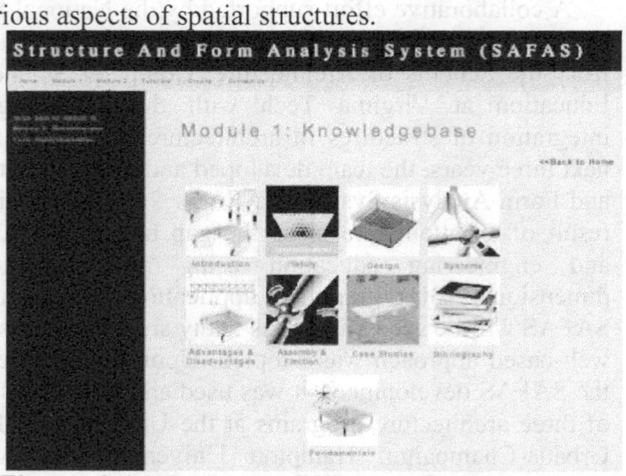

Figure 1. Links to the Different Sections of the SAFAS-Module One

As mentioned by Setareh, et. al. [11], this includes: Introduction, History, Design, System, Advantages and Disadvantages, Assembly and Erection, Case Studies, Bibliography, and Fundamentals. Figure 1 shows the webpage which includes the links to the above mentioned sections of the SAFAS Module One.

A Dublin-Core metadata was used as a means to publish these resources in an accessible and searchable format (Web Consortium, www.w3c.org; National Science Digital Library, www.nsdl.org).

3.2 Module Two (Structure and Form Experimentation)

This module consists of software that can be used to: (1) create computer models of spatial structures, (2) subject them to various loading conditions, and (3) simulate the structural behavior by displaying the internal member forces and joint deformations. All the spatial structures used here are made of double-layer grids. This module was developed using Web3D standards and open source libraries using Java (Web3D Consortium, www. Web3d.org; Xj3D Java Toolkit, www.xj3d.org) to create a versatile software to be used on a wide variety of client platforms. The project development platform used Net Beans and SVN.

The main objective was to design user friendly software since the target audience was undergraduate architecture students with limited knowledge of structures and computer science. Another important software design goal was to create a portable, durable, and interoperable software tool. The interactive 3D contents of this module is portable as the open-source Xj3d rendering library (Java and OpenGL) provides cross-platform client application to visualize spatial structural models and their behavior under the applied loads. The 3D model visualization uses Extensible 3D (X3D) application, which is an open, royalty-free standard developed through the Web3D Consortium and ratified through the International Standardization Organization (ISO). This has made SAFAS durable as the models created through this application will be reproducible for many years to come. The import/export of the models using the X3D and VRML emphasizes the software interoperability.

SAFAS Module Two consists of two modes:

(1) Pre-Analysis Mode - This mode is used to define the structure and the applied loads.

(2) Post-Analysis Mode - This mode is used to simulate the effects of loads on spatial structures to assist student learning.

The software launches in the "Pre-Analysis" mode. Here, the user can build models of rectangular flat double-layer grid spatial structures using several different configurations. The software allows the user to create his/her own structural model, define the section properties, apply loads, and show the internal forces and structural deformations based on the results of the analysis by the structural analysis software. The user can also compare the results of the analysis of two different spatial structures.

Two structural analysis programs were used as the analytical engines for this module of SAFAS: (1) The open-source, PC-SAP4 [13], and (2) The commercial software, SAP2000 [14]. The development of SAFAS started with using the PC-SAP4 as a proof of concept, and was later replaced by the SAP2000. Both computer software reside on a remote server, and a username and password are required to gain access to them. The structural analysis program PC-SAP4 was originally developed in the early 1970's at the University of California, Berkeley, California. The SAP2000 is the commercial version of PC-SAP4 developed by the Computers and Structures, Inc. (CSI), Berkeley, California.

The simulation service is managed by a queue and each user's results are saved on both the client and the server. The communications between the SAFAS and SAP2000 are conducted using the SAP2000 API functions within a Visual Basic application.

3.2.1 SAFAS Module Two User Interface and Software Operations

Pre-Analysis Mode

Upon launching the software, the user can create a new project by clicking on the "create new structure" icon or by selecting "New" from the "File" menu bar. This opens a dialog box, as shown in Figure 2, which includes eleven different configurations of spatial structures in four groups, according to the top and bottom layer grid patterns.

The user can select one of the configurations and specify the total length, width, depth, and height. He/she can also define the number of modules to be used in each direction. The superimposed (S.I.) dead load and snow load will be entered and the support locations and types can be selected (corner, pyramid, tree or edge).

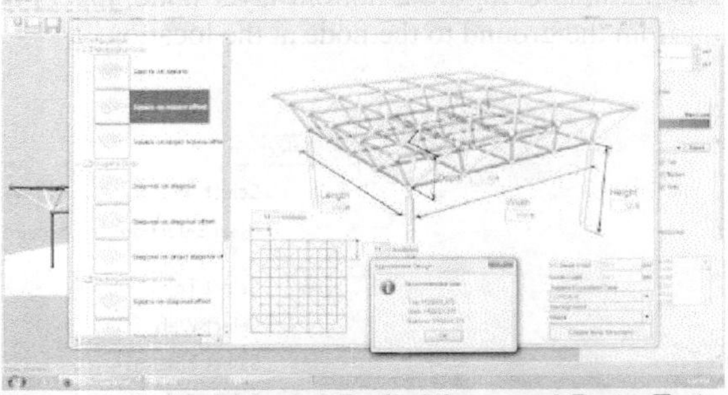

Figure 2. Initial Model Definition and Data Entry Control Panel

Also, several background options are provided for enhanced visualization of the model. These include: blank, grass, grass with trees, and user-specified. Based on the entered information, SAFAS conducts an approximate design and recommends member sizes for the top, web and bottom layers. At this point, the structural model is shown in the SAFAS main display (Figure 3). The load control panel (Figure 4), located on the right side of the display, allows the user to change the values of the applied loads. In addition, the nodal loads can be shown using the Glyph representation (arrows) or by coloring the nodes.

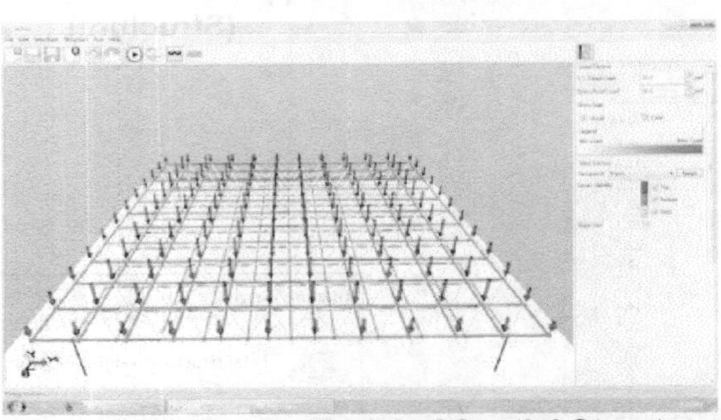

Figure 3. Complete Model of Spatial Structure

The heaviest-loaded node is colored in dark red and the lightest-loaded node in white. Various shades between these two limits are used for the remainder of the nodes.

The View Control panel (Figure 4) allows the user to define the viewpoint (front, rear, left, right or top) and the layer to be visible (top, bottom or web). These options can help the user turn on and off selected layers of the structure for enhanced visualization. The user can also place a continuous membrane on the top layer which helps visualization of the roof profile.

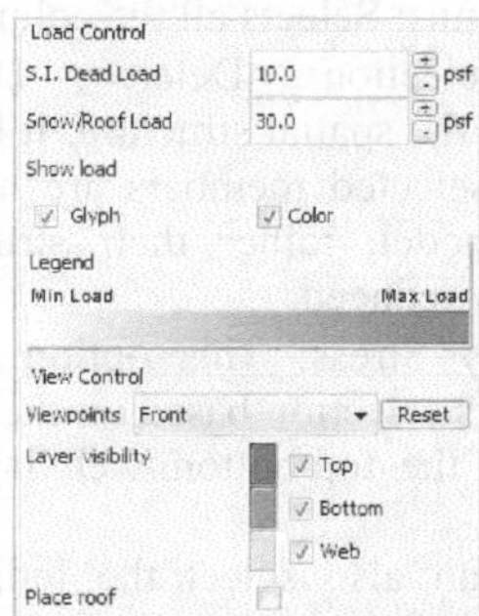

Figure 4. Load and View Control Panels

The user can manipulate the created structure using the options in the toolbars and control panels. The software has a conventional user interface in which the main menu, located at the top left corner of the window, includes: File, Edit, Selection, Structure, Run, and Help menu bars. At the bottom of the window, a status bar indicates the current state of the operations of the software. There is also a toolbar under the main menu bar which includes active buttons for the most commonly used tasks included in the main menu bar.

The following is a brief description of the various functions of the main menu bar (note that most actions within each drop-down menu include shortcut equivalents, as indicated below):

File: When this drop-down menu is selected, the following options will appear (Figure 5a):

- New <Ctrl/N>: This command creates a new file.
- Open/Manage <Ctrl/O>: This command opens an existing file, previously created by the software.
- Save <Ctrl/S>: This saves an existing file.
- Close <Ctrl/W>: This closes an existing file.
- Export: This saves the created file in a user-specified directory to be submitted to the SAP for analysis. This feature facilitates portability of the generated files to other instances of the software or a separate computer.
- Export X3D: This allows the software output to be viewed by any other X3D viewer application. It can also be imported into a Computer-Aided-Design (CAD) application.

Edit: This drop-down menu includes (Figure 5b):

- Undo <Ctrl/Z>: Undoes the last five tasks.
- Redo <Ctrl/Shift/Z>: Redoes the last five tasks.

Selection: This drop-down menu allows different selection options (Figure 5c):

- Select All <Ctrl/A>: Selects the entire model including all the nodes and members.
- Clear Selection <Escape>: Clears the selected parts of the structure.

- Select Top, Select Web, Select Bottom: Selects the top, web, and bottom layers of the structure, respectively.
- Select Columns: Selects all the columns in the structure.
- Remove Selection <Delete>: Deletes the selected members of the spatial structure. It has to be noted that in reality the selected members are not removed from the structural model, rather their structural properties are substantially reduced.
- Selection by Stress: This option opens a dialog box, which allows selection based on the user-defined range of stresses for the top/bottom/web layer members (Figure 5d).

The user can also select the individual members and nodes by clicking on them or drawing a box around them to select a group of members. The color of the elements turns into red upon selection. Structure: This drop-down menu allows changes to the structure geometry, support conditions and applied loads, assigning member sizes, and computing the total structural weight. The various options include (see Figure 5e):

- Add single Column(s) to Selection <Ctrl/J>: After selecting node(s) from the bottom layer, using this option adds a column from the ground to the selected node(s).
- Place Columns Manually <Ctrl/K>: After selecting this option, clicking on a bottom layer node, places a column from the ground to the node at the location.

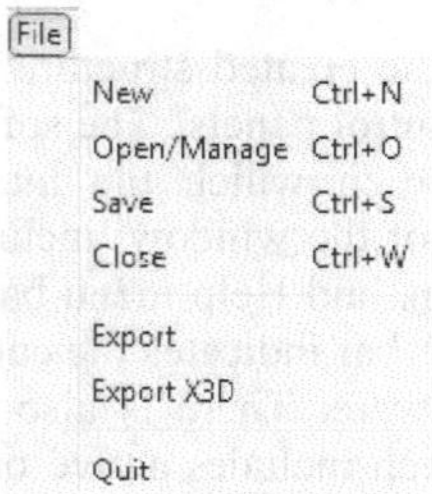

(a) File

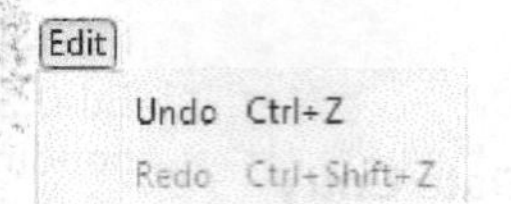

(b) Edit

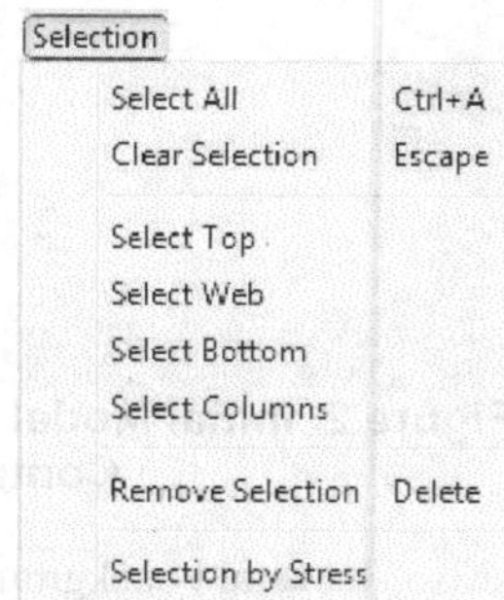

(c) Selection

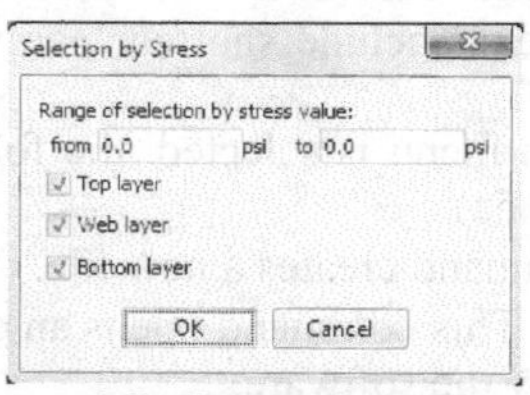

(d) Selection by Stress (Selection)

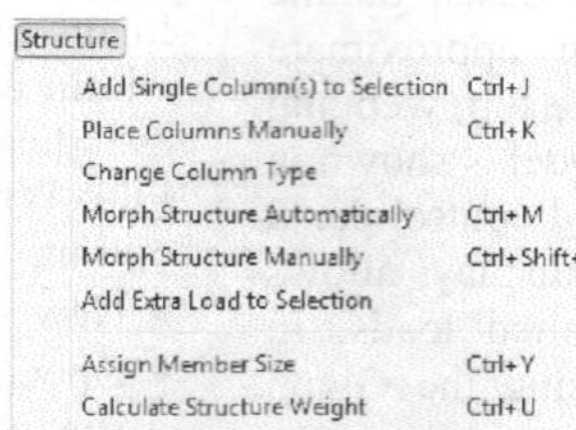

(e) Structure

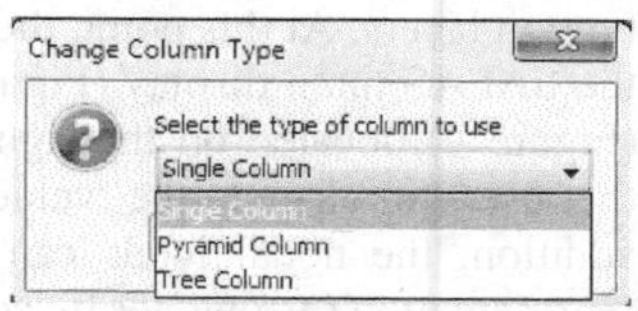

(f) Column Type (Structure)

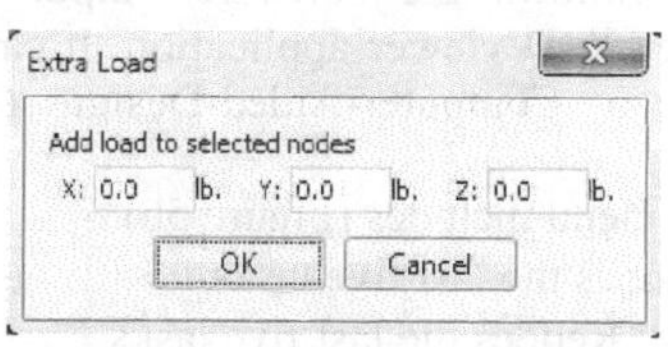

(g) Add Extra Load to Selection (Structure)

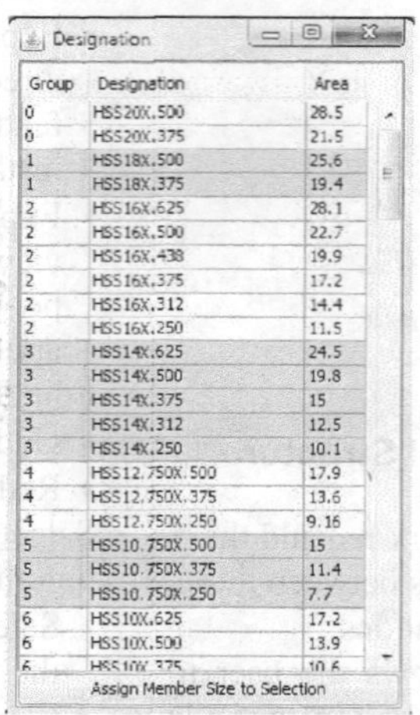

(h) Assign Member Size (Structure)

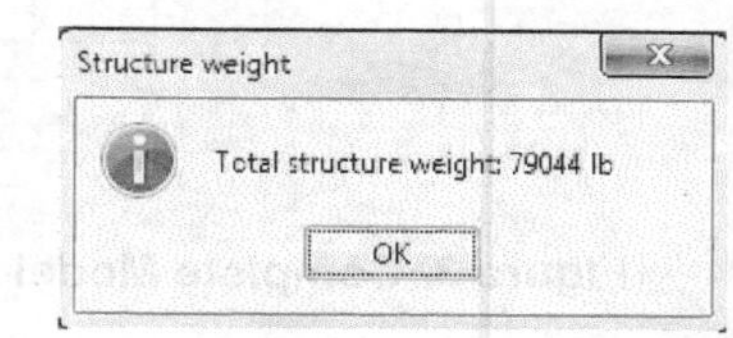

(i) Calculate Structure Weight (Structure)

Figure 5. Pre-Analysis Mode Menus and Options

- Change Column Type (see Figure 5f): This works in conjunction with the above two options for placing columns, and has to be selected first before adding columns. There are three possible choices: Single Column (a straight column from the ground to the node), Pyramid Column (a straight column connected to a module), or a Tree Column. Figure 6 shows the pyramid and tree column options
- Morph Structure Automatically <Ctrl/M> (Figure 5e): Activating this option, opens the "Morph Control Panel" (Figure 7a.), on the right side of the window. The software allows two morph geometries: Dome (representing a sphere-like deformation) and Vault (representing a cylindrical deformation). Each morph option includes three pre-defined functions for morphing the structure (see Figure 7a): Smooth (a bell-curve roof profile), Linear (a linear, double-pitch roof profile), Barrel Vault (a parabolic roof profile), and Uniform (a flat roof profile).

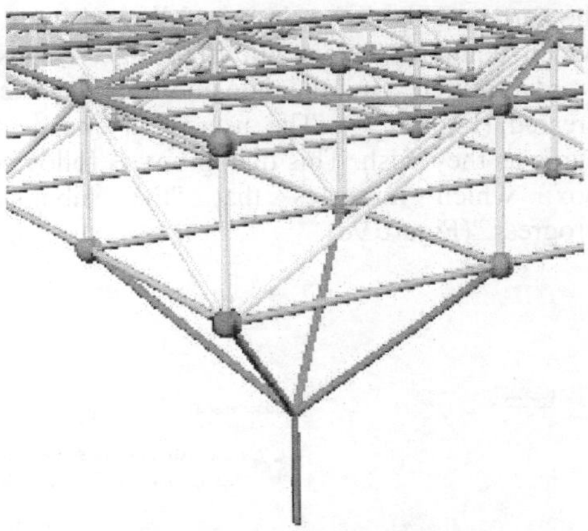

(a) A Pyramid Column

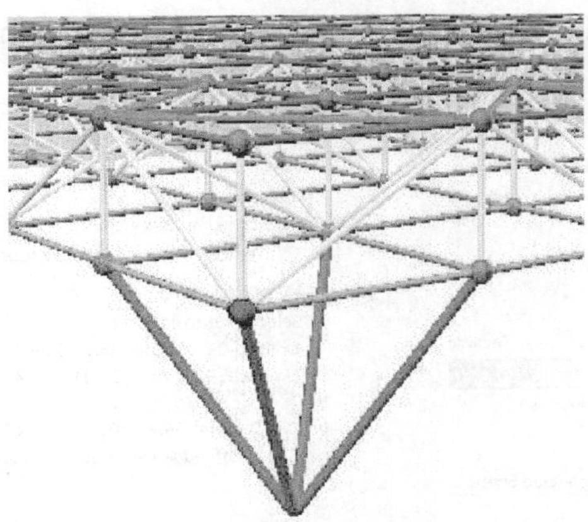

(b) A Tree Column

Figure 6. Pyramid and Tree Columns

The morph control panel allows the changes to the shape of the selected parts of the structure to be applied along a particular axis by using the "Axis Lock" option. The user can define the morph radius from the selected node (extent that the morph function is applied). The "Max" button selects the entire roof structure. The morphing function can be applied to an individual layer or both layers by selecting the choice from the "Apply to" option. The default orientation of morph is along the x-axis; however, it is possible to modify this by changing the value in the "Orientation (deg)" box. This changes the orientation of morph with respect to the x-axis.

The automatic morph allows the user to change the shape of the structure by moving the selected nodes by a fixed value along the x, y, and z axes. Upon selecting the "Automatic Morph (selected)" in the "Morph Control Panel", a dialog box opens (Figure 7b.), which allows the user to enter the desired amount of morphing along the three axes.

- Morph Structure Manually <Ctrl/Shift/M> (Figure 5e): This allows the user to place the cursor on a node from which an area is selected (this is identified by changing the color of the nodes), set by radius. The user can then move the cursor and deform the structure using the various curve options of the automatic morphing that was explained above.

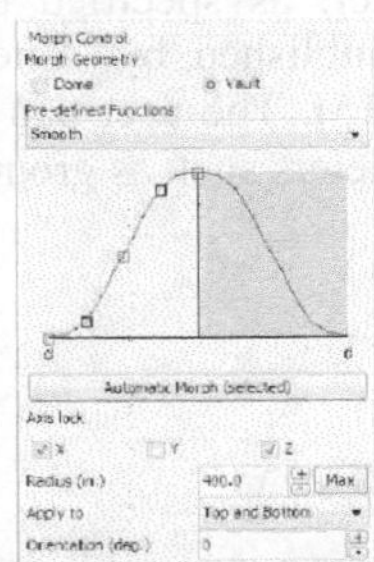

(a) Morph Control Panel

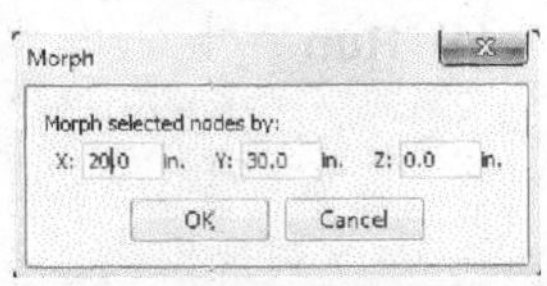

(b) Automatic Morph Dialog box

Figure 7. Morph Control Panel and Automatic Morph Dialog box

The amount of displacements along the three axes and the coordinates of the selected node during the morphing process are shown in a text box located at the upper right corner of the window. The status bar at the bottom of the screen shows the current mode of the software. Figure 8 shows a morphed spatial structure.

- Extra Load to Selection (Figure 5e): This option allows the user to apply additional loads (in addition to the gravity loads) along the x, y, and z axes. The user first selects the individual or a group of nodes, and then uses this option, which opens a dialog box (Figure 5g) to enter additional loads on the structure.

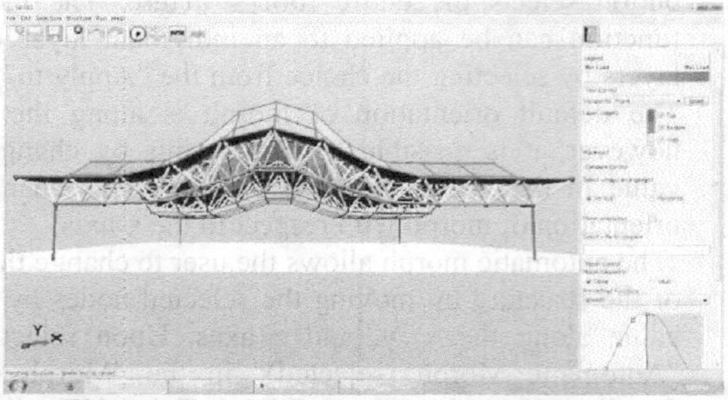

Figure 8. A Morphed Spatial Structure

- Assign Member Size <Ctrl/Y> (Figure 5e): Upon selection of members and using this option, a "Designation" dialog box opens (see Figure 5h). This dialog box includes a list of the available standard steel Hollow Structural Shapes (HSS) that can be used for the spatial structure members. This list includes the designation and cross-sectional area of each shape. All the shapes are placed in groups that have the same nominal outside diameter, as specified by the Manual of Steel Construction published by American Institute of Steel Construction [15]. The user can sort this table based on different parameters such as group number, designation or the cross sectional area by clicking each header. To complete the member size assignment, the user must select "Assign Member Size to Selection" in the Designations dialog box.
- Calculate Structure Weight <Ctrl/U> (Figure 5e.): This option computes the total weight of the structure based on the member sizes used (Figure 5i).

Post-Analysis Mode

Run: This option includes the submission of the model to SAP for the structural analysis, and comparison of the results of two spatial structures:

- Analyze <Ctrl/R> (Figure 9a): This options is used when the modeling is complete and the user intends to submit the structure to the SAP, structural analysis program, for computation of nodal displacements and member forces. Upon choosing this option, a dialog box opens in which the user enters his/her assigned username and password (Figure 9b). This feature ensures the security of access to the server. This dialog box is followed by a second box which contains the default file name, consisting of the word "untitled", and the date and time that the model was created (Figure 9c). The users can change this default name as they wish. This dialog box is followed by a third box, which indicates that "the submission is in progress."(Figure 9d).

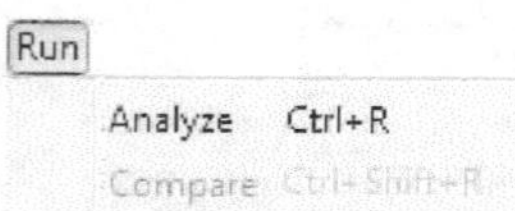

(a) Run

(b) User Information Check for file Submission

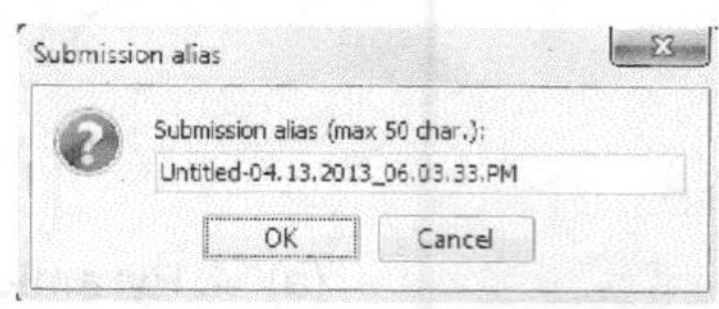

(c) Setting Filename

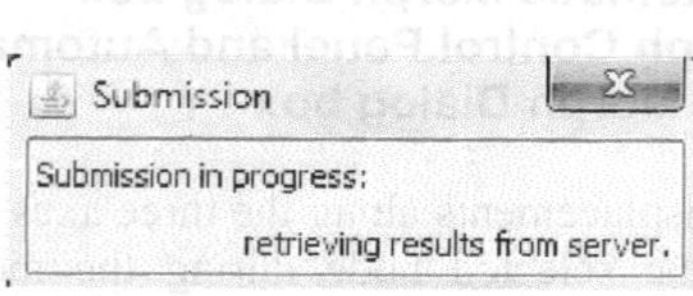

(d) SAP Analysis in Progress

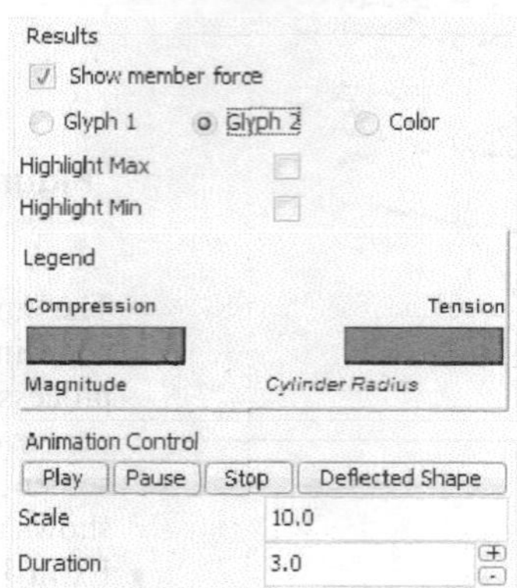

(e) Results and Animation Control Panels

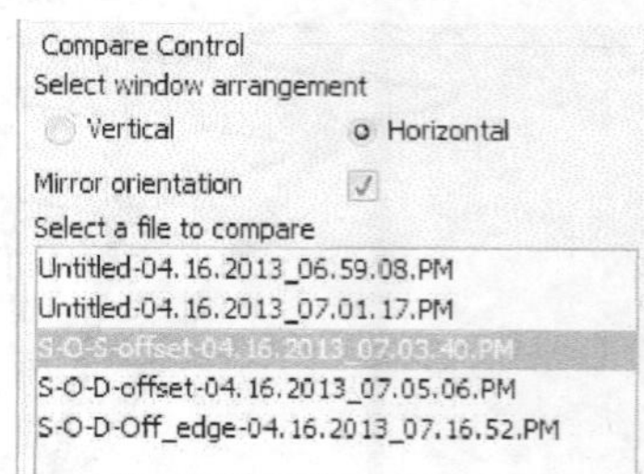

(f) Compare Control Panel

Figure 9. Post-Analysis Mode Menus and Options

At this time, the SAP input file is created and submitted to the server that the PC-SAP4 or SAP2000 computer software resides on. Upon the completion of the analysis, this dialog box is automatically closed. This also changes the status of the software to the "post-analysis" mode, and adds the post-analysis controls to the panel on the right side of the screen. This includes the "Results" and "Animation" controls. The "Results" allow the user to select how the member forces are to be shown. These include two glyph options: Glyph 1 (using cones to demonstrate if the member is in tension or compression and their size to indicate the relative size of the internal force) (Figure 10a), Glyph 2 (shows the member forces by coloring them, "red" to represent compression members and "blue" for tensile members (Figure 10b). The diameter of cylinders represents the relative internal force magnitude). The third option is "color", which colors the compression members in red and tensile members in blue. The color shading changes based on the member force magnitude (Figure 10c). The "Highlight Max", and "Highlight Min" in the Results Control Panel can be used to identify the members having the largest and smallest forces (Figure 9e.)

Upon placing the cursor on a member, the internal forces and stresses are given in a textbox located at the top right corner of the screen. Also, when the cursor is placed on a node, the deflection and position of node are shown (see Figure 10.)

To help visualize the deformation of the structure, the animation control shows moving images of the structure when subjected to loads. The video can be started, stopped, and paused at any time by the user. The static deflected shape can also be displayed. The amplitude of the deformation can be increased for very stiff systems or reduced for unusually flexible structures. The animation duration can also be changed by the user for better visualization (see Figure 9e).

- Compare <Ctrl/Shift/R> (Figure 9a): Once the analysis is complete, the user can compare the results of the behavior of two structures using the Compare control panel (Figure 9f). Upon activating the compare option (Figure 9a), a split window appears. The user can then select a second structural model from the compare control panel "Select a file to compare" (see Figure 9f). The split window can be oriented horizontally or vertically. The images in the two windows can be linked so that the two structures will be observed from the same viewpoint. This is accomplished by selecting the "mirror orientation" in the compare control panel (Figure 9f). Figure 11 show the comparison of two structural models in a horizontally split window.

4 Summary and Conclusion

This paper presented the details of the software architecture, operations, and the graphical user interface of the "Structure And Form Analysis System (SAFAS)." SAFAS was developed through a collaborative efforts by a team of researchers at Virginia Tech to help architecture students better understand the inter-relationships between structure and form. This web-based software was used in several architectural structures courses at Virginia Tech and two other universities. The analysis of students' performance showed that SAFAS is an effective educational tool for learning about structural performance.

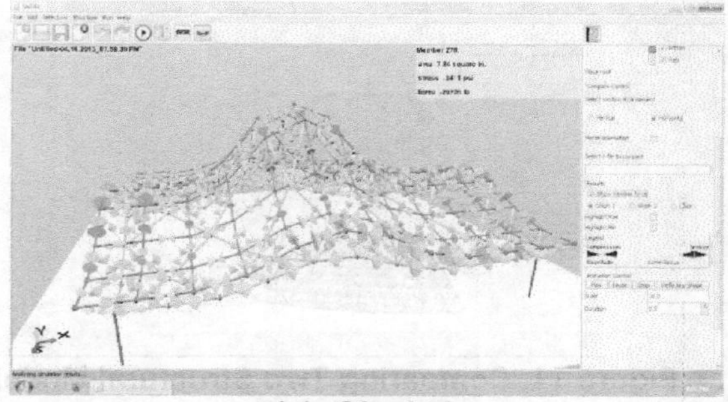

(a) Glyph 1

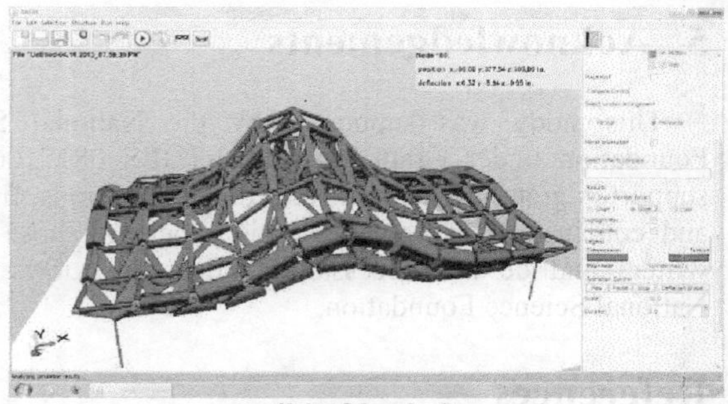

(b) Glyph 2

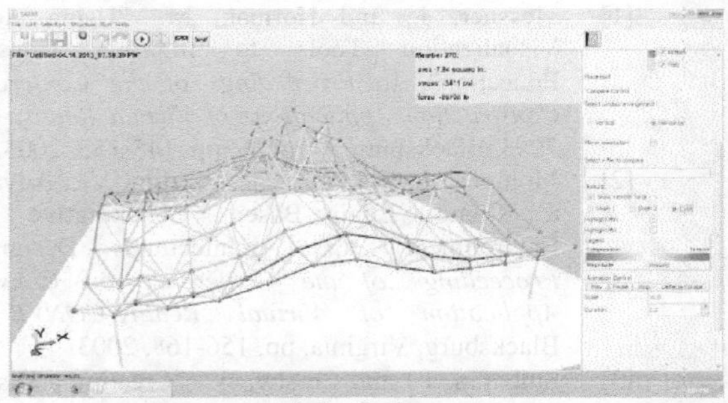

(c) Color

Figure 10. Various Modes of SAFAS Results Representations

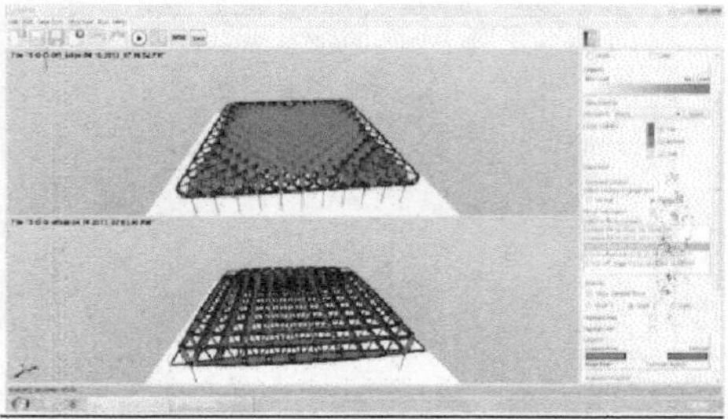

Figure 11. Comparing Two Structural Models in SAFAS

5 Acknowledgements

This study was supported by the National Science Foundation under Grant No. CCLI/TUES 0817106. This support is gratefully acknowledged. Any opinions, findings, and conclusions expressed in this paper are those of the writers and do not necessarily reflect the views of the National Science Foundation.

References

[1] Messner, J., and Horman, M., "Using Advanced Visualization Tools to Improve Construction Education", In *Proceedings of the Conference on Construction Applications of Virtual Reality-CONVR 2003,* Blacksburg, Virginia, pp. 145-155, 2003.

[2] Moloney, J., and Amor, R., "StringCVE: Advances in a Game Engine-Based Collaborative Virtual Environment for Architectural Design", In *Proceedings of the Conference on Construction Application of Virtual Reality-CONVR 2003,* Blacksburg, Virginia, pp. 156-168, 2003.

[3] Sulbaran, T., and Crosby, W., "Creating a Distributed Virtual Reality Environment to Enhance Engineering Students' Abilities in Crane Selection", In *Proceedings of the Conference on Construction Application of Virtual Reality-CONVR 2003,* Blacksburg, Virginia, pp. 169-178, 2003.

[4] Kalisperis, L., Otto, G., Muramoto, K., Gundrum, J., Masters, R., and Orland, B., "An Affordable Immersive Environment in Beginning Design Studio Education", In *Proceedings of the 2002 Annual Conference of the Association for Computer Aided Design in Architecture,* Ponoma, California, pp. 49-56, 2002.

[5] Chou, C., Hsu, H., and Yao, Y., "Construction of a Virtual Reality Learning Environment for Teaching Structural Analysis", *Computer Applications in Engineering Education,* Vol. 5, pp. 223-230, 1997.

[6] Stojadinovic, B., "Conceptual Design of a Haptic Interface for Structural Analysis Software", In *Proceedings of the ASCE 2000 Structures Congress,* Philadelphia, Pennsylvania, 2000.

[7] Black, R. G., and Duff, S., "A Model for Teaching Structures: Finite Element Analysis in Architectural Education", *Journal of Architectural Education*, Vol. 48, No. 1, September, 1994.

[8] Vassigh, S., "Interactive Structures: Visualizing Structural Behavior", CD-ROM, *John Wiley and Sons, Inc.*, Hoboken, New Jersey, 2005.

[9] Setareh, M., Bowman, D., and Kalita, A., Gracey, M., and Lucas, J. "Application of the Virtual Environments in Building Sciences Education and Practice", *Journal of Architectural Engineering*, American Society of Civil Engineers, Vol. 11, No. 4, pp. 165-172, 2005.

[10] Setareh, M., Bowman, D., and Kalita, A., "Development of a Virtual Reality Structural Analysis System", *Journal of Architectural Engineering*, American Society of Civil Engineers, Vol. 11, No. 4, pp. 156-164, 2005.

[11] Setareh, M., Bacim, F., Jones, B., Polys, N., Geng, T., and Orsa, B., "Integrating Web-Based Visualization with Structural System Understanding to Improve the Technical Education of Architects", *Journal of Online Engineering Education*, Vol. 3, No. 1, 2012.

[12] Jones, B., Setareh, M., Polys, N., and Bacim, F., "Application of an Online Interactive Simulation Tool to Teach Engineering Concepts Using 3D Spatial Structures", *International Journal of Technology and Design Education,* Springer Publishing Company, under review, 2013.

[13] Maison, B., "PC-SAP4. A Computer Program for Linear Structural Analysis", *Earthquake Engineering Research Center,* University of California, Berkeley, California, 1994.

[14] Computers and Structures, "SAP2000 – Linear and Nonlinear Static and Dynamic Analysis and Design of Three-Dimensional Structures", *Computers and Structures, Inc.*, Berkeley, California, 2011.

[15] American Institute of Steel Construction, "Manual of Steel Construction", *AISC*, Chicago, Illinois, 2010.

Visualization of Mobility-Density Relation in a Modified Percolation Agent-Based Model

Bruce Paizen, M.Eng., Jay Kraut, Ph.D., Marcia R. Friesen, Ph.D., and Robert (Bob) D. McLeod,
Department of Electrical and Computer Engineering, University of Manitoba

Abstract-- **A modified percolation theory model was developed to incorporate agent mobility on the grid. In this agent-based model (ABM), the impact of agent density was found to significantly influence agent mobility. The visual representation software tool developed provides an intuitive understanding of the ABM simulation dynamics and mechanisms. The software tool visually illustrates that there is a relationship between mobility and density that would have to be taken into account for research into connectedness or connectivity (i.e., epizootic modeling) involving percolation models. Visualization is a common method that is often employed in many percolation models and studies as it helps in narrowing down regions of interest that can be followed up on in a more systematic manner.**

Index Terms-- **Visualization; percolation theory; epizootic; agent-based model (ABM)**

I. INTRODUCTION

Percolation theory is not a new modeling method as a variety of models have already been created [1]. However, percolation models typically do not include mobility, and so that is the novelty introduced and explored here. The purpose of this research is to qualitatively examine the extent to which increasing agent population density limited mobility and to illustrate this through visualization software.

A percolation model involves a simple grid of interconnected nodes. Each node has adjacent nodes that they can affect and in turn are indirectly able to affect their adjacent nodes. Phenomena such as connectedness or connectivity related properties can be studied as second order phase transitions. In this way a phenomena can expand on the grid or eventually sputter out and stop. These transitions are associated with critical parameters such as the percolation threshold. The percolation threshold for an infinite grid would be the threshold for the occurrence of long range behaviour or long range patterns to emerge. The most common phenomena studied with percolation models are the formation of the largest cluster of connected components.

A common use of a percolation model is the modeling of forest fires. In this model the percolation threshold would translate to the tree density above which the entire forest will be consumed by fire [2]. In mathematical terms, the percolation threshold is the critical value of occupation probability so that boundless connectivity occurs.

The two main types of percolation are bond percolation and site percolation. As shown in Fig. 1, site percolation considers lattice vertices as the relevant entities and bond percolation considers the edges as the relevant entities. This paper will use site percolation with each site representing an agent in an agent-based model (ABM).

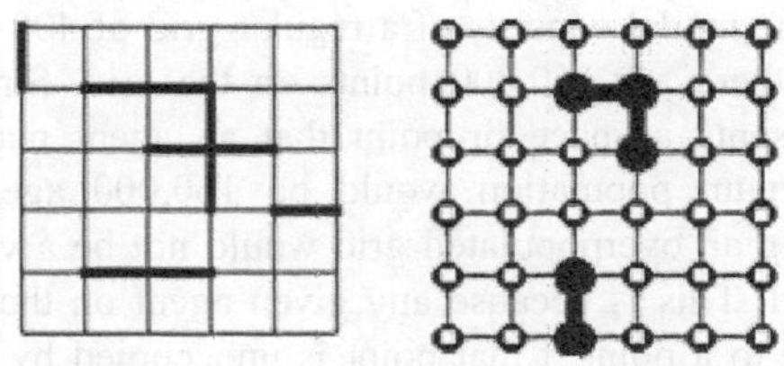

Fig. 1. Bond percolation (L); site percolation (R) [1].

Oleinikova used percolation theory to apply second order phase transitions to the process of cooling a liquid to the point where it froze; aggregating previously isolated microcrystalline structures into a larger frozen solid [3]. Recently, percolation theory is becoming more applied to epizootic research including work on plague bacteria passed by gerbils and the impact on the percolation threshold from gerbil tunnel connectivity [4].

II. ABM DESIGN AND VISUALIZATION

ABM is an area of increasing interest for modeling and simulation of human and animal phenomena, including disease spread. However, it is necessary to select the correct algorithm or model depending on the application. Some algorithms sacrifice precision for performance with techniques as simple as updating only a certain number of agents per simulation time step [5]. This increases performance but decreases precision, thus diminishing output data quality. Choosing an

Corresponding author: Robert (Bob) R. McLeod, Department of Electrical and Computer Engineering, University of Manitoba, Winnipeg, Canada, R3T 5V6; e-mail: mcleod@ee.umanitoba.ca.

Affiliation footnotes:

Bruce Paizen is currently employed at Associated Engineering Group Ltd.

Jay Kraut is presently a Postdoctoral Research Associate at the Laboratory for Surgical Modeling, Simulation and Robotics, Health Sciences Centre, Winnipeg, Manitoba, Canada algorithm to use in an ABM simulation therefore depends on the aim of the simulation. For instance, particle simulations bear performance problems and a lack of system size scaling due to particle interaction with every other particle inducing an O(N2) complexity. Even for a minimal interaction such as a nearest neighbour interaction, it is still necessary to perform Euclidean distance calculations for every combination of two particles [5]. Our modified percolation model presents a novel method that may be suited to problems in particle simulation and ABM design.

Visualization methods may increase intuitive understanding of complex phenomena. For example, most timeline drawing or planning software uses temporal logic in order to visualize cases and Seker [6] introduces a visualization tool to illustrate his novel framework for relational event representation. Vespa [7] shows that Apollonian Packings and Networks are useful structures that may be used to solve many problems and having a tool to visually explore these structures is imperative for furthering research in this area. Likewise, our [8] visual software allows exploration of epizootics in a novel way and similarly [9] has a graphical user interface to allow interaction with a visualization tool.

III. MODIFYING PERCOLATION MODEL TO INCORPORATE MOBILITY

The model consists of a regular grid of 400-by-400 nodes, thus there are 160,000 points on the grid. Since each point represents a space or point that an agent may occupy, the maximum population would be 160,000 agents. However, having an overpopulated grid would not be a very interesting model. This is because any given agent on the grid can only move to a point if that point is unoccupied by another agent. Thus, the population used in this simulation is limited to allow for the observation of critical phenomena during the simulation.

Mobility is the associated with probability that an agent will move to a different location on the next simulation step or iteration step. For each iteration or loop through the program, a random number will be generated for each agent. The speed multiplier, as named on the program graphical user interface in previous work [8], is the mobility. Mobility can be set from "one" through "five". A setting of "one" means that there is a twenty percent chance that the agent will attempt to move one grid unit in an arbitrary direction (20% x, 20% y) on the next program iteration, and "five" means that there is a one-hundred percent chance that an agent will attempt to move a grid unit in an arbitrary direction (100% x, 100% y) on the next program iteration. Zero mobility was not considered in detail here as it corresponds to the well-studied case associated with traditional percolation models.

The agent will not move to a given point if another agent already occupies that point. Thus, agent population density factors in adversely affecting the mobility. In terms of neighbourhoods, the mobility of the agent is restricted to a stochastic Moore neighbourhood, while its ability to spread a more conventional Moore neighbourhood [1].

TABLE I

PROBABILITY AN AGENT RELOCATES ON THE NEXT ITERATION.

Mobility	Movement in x or y	Agent movement
1	20 %	36 %
2	40 %	64 %
3	60 %	84 %
4	80 %	96 %
5	100 %	100 %

Table 1 illustrates the probability that an agent will move on the next iteration [8]. For the mobility setting of "one" (mobility = 1), there is a probability (p) of 0.2 that the agent will move along the x-axis. It will move either negative one (p=0.1) or positive one (p=0.1) along the x-axis. There is also an equivalent calculation for the y-axis. Thus, there is also a probability (p) of 0.2 that the agent will move along the y-axis; either negative one (p=0.1) or positive one (p=0.1) along the y-axis. This means that there is a 0.04 probability that the agent will simultaneously move along the x-axis and y-axis and this corresponds to a diagonal movement. As can be seen in Fig. 2, the 0.04 probability of moving diagonally is split equally by the four corners. Furthermore, there is a 64% chance the agent will remain in the same place.

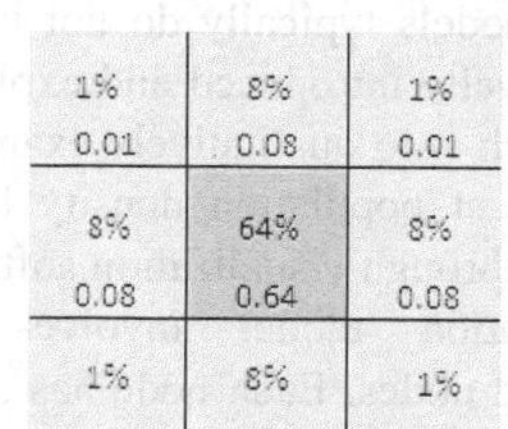

Fig. 2. Mobility set to "one".

This agent mobility analysis can be applied to the other mobility settings. Figure 3 shows the probabilities for the mobility setting of "three". Mobility incorporated into the traditional percolation model suits many ABM applications.

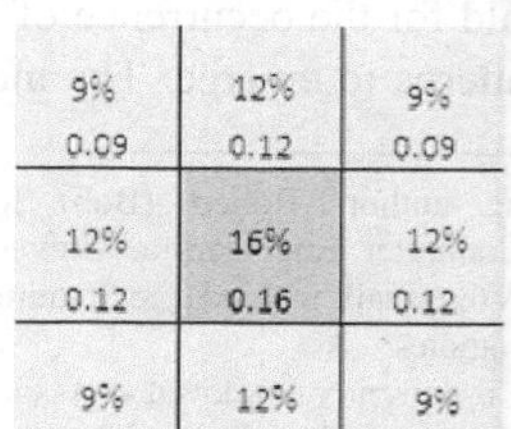

Fig. 3. Mobility set to "three".

IV. EXPERIMENTS WITH A SINGLE AGENT

The simulation with a single agent (population set to one agent) verifies that with a higher mobility the agent is able to visit more unique points on the grid in a given number of iteration steps. As a corner case, this provides some basic validation of software tool mobility feature and the result is graphed in Fig. 4.

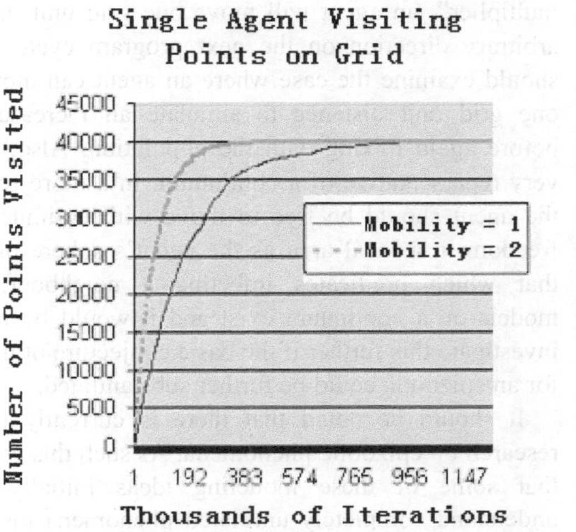

Fig. 4. With higher mobility the agent traverses more points.

Simulations were also performed to examine the path of a single agent and the area that it covered on a 200-by-200 grid. Figure 5 follows the path of an agent roaming in a free range that would represent a single agent in a given predefined space. Percolation models typically do not include mobility, which is the novelty investigated here.

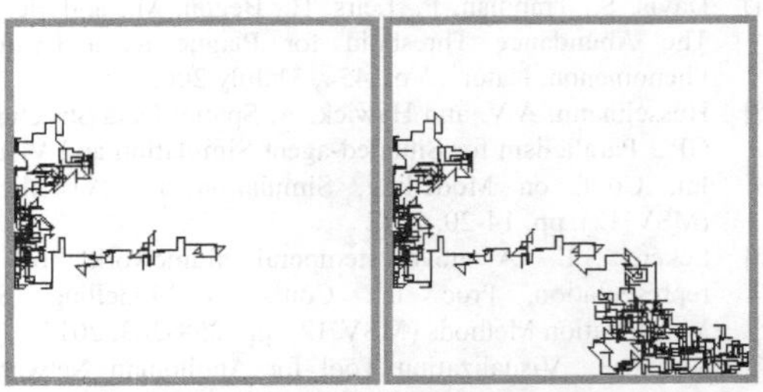

Fig. 5. Agent traversed 1389 points after 7214 iterations (left) and 3123 points after 15115 iterations (right).

V. VARIATION OF AGENT DENSITY

Simulations were done for varying agent population densities. The purpose was to qualitatively examine the extent to which increasing agent population density limited mobility. With increasing density, agent mobility is decreased since the area roamed after 3000 simulation iterations decreases. This validates our conjecture that population density adversely influences agent mobility and is plotted in Fig. 6.

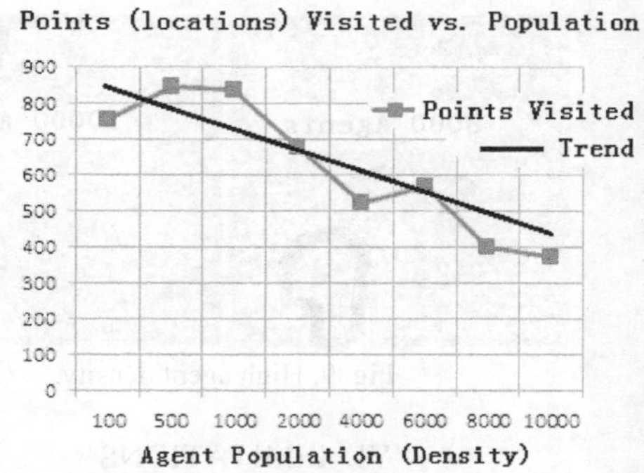

Fig. 6. Increasing agent density decreases agent mobility.

At all degrees of agent density (low, intermediate, and high), the trend is upheld that increasing density will decrease agent mobility. Figures 7 through 9 are snapshots from the simulation tool that depicts this finding. In Fig. 7, 846 locations on the grid were visited at a 500 agent population, and 835 locations on the grid were visited at a 1000 agent population. In a 200-by-200 grid, an agent population of 1000 or less is considered sparse.

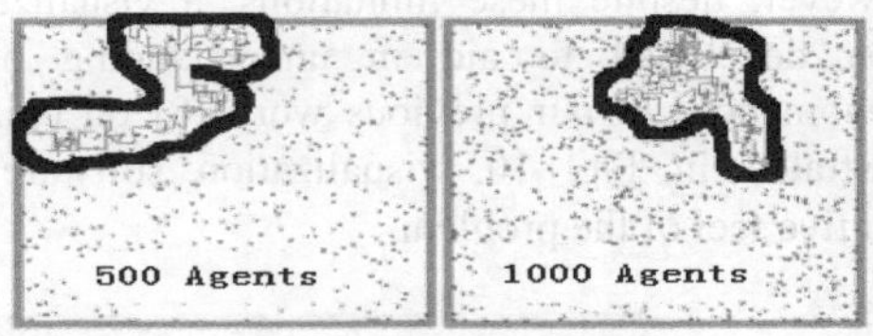

Fig. 7. Low agent density.

In Fig. 8 for intermediate densities, 675 locations on the grid were visited with an agent population density of 2000. With a density of 6000 agents on the grid, only 567 locations were visited. This may suggest that sensitivity analysis is needed for ABM output data when variables are interdependent.

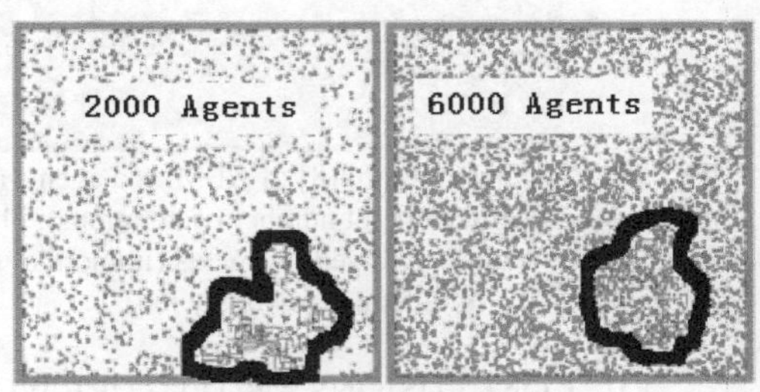

Fig. 8. Intermediate agent density.

In Fig. 9 at high agent population densities, 398 locations are visited by the agent at 8000 agent density and only 374 locations are visited at 10000 agent density. These results are all for 3000 iteration steps.

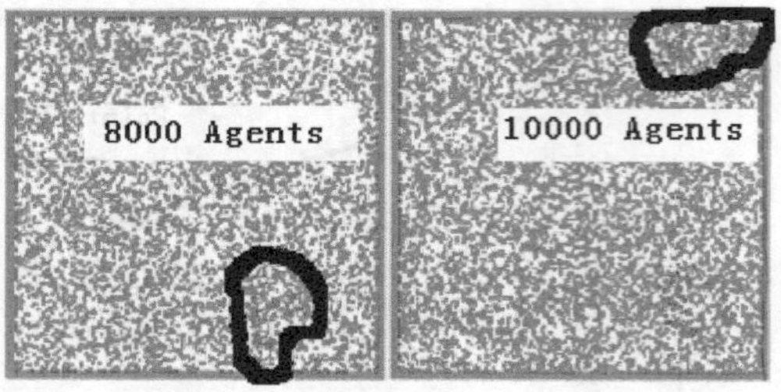

Fig. 9. High agent density.

VI. LIMITATIONS

There are some limitations associated with simplified scenario, if considering a deployment to a scaled-up ABM for epizootic research. In [8] it was suggested that the period of an agent being in a contagious state should be governed by a distribution as opposed to a specific duration. This also applies to the mobility and the neighbourhoods investigated in this study. It would also be interesting to track the movement of an agent within a facility using video or technologies related to Real-Time Location Systems perhaps using Wi-Fi tracking or ultra wide band tracking [9] to refine the mobility model. However, despite these limitations, a visualization tool has been developed to aid in understanding of a complex phenomenon. In our previous work [8] on epizootic spread, illustrated in Fig. 10, visualization software provides an intuitive feel of the problem.

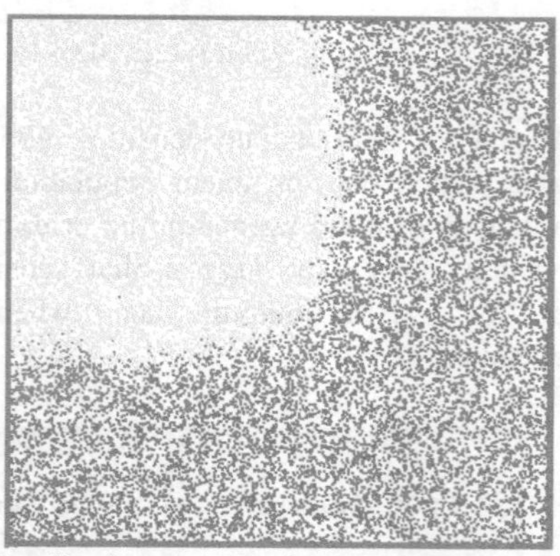

Fig. 10. Visualization tool [8] of ABM: red agents (mobile) are infected (contagious for set number of iterations); blue agents (mobile) not yet infected; yellow agents (immobile) died after infection (previously red).

VII. CONCLUSIONS AND FUTURE WORK

Our work shows a visual representation of agent mobility being impacted by increasing agent density in a modified percolation model. This ABM is a novel approach to disease spread research, both epidemic and epizootic, and may be well-suited for other research areas. For future work, several grid areas could be incorporated and linked through real-life links that exist in intensive unit production. This would require additional programming to model the various intensive unit production connectivity schemes that affect the spread of the disease on a larger scale, and to add other elements of fidelity and realism to an ABM built on percolation theory.

Mobility is the probability that an agent will move on the underlying grid and for each loop through the program, a random number will be generated to govern the probability. Based on this random number, and the setting of the "speed multiplier", an agent will move one grid unit in a somewhat arbitrary direction on the next program cycle. Future work should examine the case where an agent can move more than one grid unit distance to simulate an increase in mobility before again mixing with the population. Also, a grid is not very representative of a continuum. In a more realistic model the agent should be free to move with unlimited degrees of freedom in a local area as the agent's sphere of influence is that which predicates infecting a neighbour. Percolation models on a continuum exist and it would be worthwhile to investigate this further if the basic conjecture of using an ABM for an epizootic could be further substantiated.

It should be noted that there is currently limited ABM research on epizootic phenomena. As such this work illustrates that some of these modeling ideas initially intended to understand completely unrelated phenomena may have place in epizootic research.

VIII. REFERENCES

[1] Stauffer, D. and Aharony, A. Introduction to Percolation Theory, 2nd ed. London: Taylor & Francis, 1992.

[2] Niessen, W.V. and Blumen, A. Dynamics of forest fires as a directed percolation model, J. Phys. A: Math Gen. 19 L289-L293, 1986.

[3] Oleinikova, A., and Brovchenko, I. Percolating networks and liquid-liquid transitions in supercooled water. Journal of Physics: Condensed Matter 18, S2247-2259, 2006.

[4] Davis, S., Trapman, P., Leirs, H., Begon, M., and Heesterbeek, J.A.P. The Abundance Threshold for Plague as a Critical Percolation Phenomenon, Nature, Vol. 454, 31 July 2008.

[5] Husselmann, A.V. and Hawick, A. Spatial Data Structures, Sorting and GPU Parallelism for Situated-agent Simulation and Visualisation, Proc. Int. Conf. on Modelling, Simulation and Visualization Methods (MSV'12), pp. 14-20, 2012.

[6] Seker, S.E. A novel temporal framework for relative event representation, Proc. Int. Conf. on Modelling, Simulation and Visualization Methods (MSV'12), pp. 258-263, 2012.

[7] Vespa, L. Visualization Tool for Apollonian Network and Packing Analysis, Proc. Int. Conf. on Modelling, Simulation and Visualization Methods (MSV'12), pp. 54-58, 2012.

[8] Paizen, B., Kraut, J., Friesen, M., and McLeod, R.D. Epizootic Agent-Based Modeling: The Mobility Threshold for Disease Spread as a Critical Percolation Phenomenon, Biological Engineering Transactions. 5(3): 109:121, 2012.

[9] Laskowski, M., Demianyk, B.C.P., Witt, J., Mukhi, S.N., Friesen, M.R., and McLeod, R.D., Agent-Based Modeling of the Spread of Influenza-Like Illness in an Emergency Department: A Simulation Study, IEEE Transactions on Information Technology in Biomedicine - TITB, 15(6), pp. 877-889, 2011.

[10] Youn, J., Ali, H., Sharif, H., Deogun, J., Uher, J., and Hinrichs, S.H. WLAN-based Real-time Asset Tracking System in Healthcare Environments. Third IEEE Conference on Wireless and Mobile Computing, Networking and Comm. (WiMob 2007), 2007.

MARWind: Mobile Augmented Reality Wind Farm Visualization

Gerald Dekker[1], Qiuhao Zhang[1,2], John Moreland[1], Chenn Zhou[1,3]
[1]Center for Innovation through Visualization and Simulation
[2]Electrical Engineering
[3]Mechancial Engineering
Purdue University Calumet
Hammond, IN, USA

Abstract - *Wind is increasingly being used as an alternative source of energy across the globe. The placement of wind turbines is often done so as to optimize the amount of energy harvested from the wind. When planning a wind farm, this process is referred to as siting. The siting of wind turbines is both highly visible to the public and can also have direct effects on the efficiency of a wind farm.*

A mobile augmented reality application for wind farm siting is being developed as part of a larger project titled "Mixed Reality Simulators for Wind Energy Education". The application has many potential benefits both for students, the public, and wind energy professionals. Using global positioning system and compass for registration, users can use mobile devices to view what a proposed wind farm will look like at a given location. Additional functionality will combine wind flow visualization.

Keywords: Augmented Reality, Wind Farm, Wind Turbine, Siting, Mobile Augmented Reality, Visualization

1 Introduction

Mixed Reality Simulators for Wind Energy Education is a project funded by the Fund for the Improvement of Postsecondary Education (FIPSE) comprehensive program of the US Department of Education. It is a multi-year project that covers five wind turbine simulators and will also include related curricular materials. These will accompany each simulator to assist and enhance the education and training of qualified wind energy professionals. The simulators are using a variety of technologies and available on multiple platforms. Mixed Reality Simulators for Wind Energy Education is divided into five phases: 1) Developmental; 2) Implementation; 3) Evaluation & Refinement; 4) Dissemination; and 5) Community Building Sustainability.

In the wind industry, there are two serious nation-wide problems: Limited training for students to transfer learned concepts to practical applications, and Lack of educated professionals in wind energy. This proposed project seeks to implement an innovative solution using Mixed Reality Simulators for Wind Energy Education that will address the issue of knowledge transfer, while simultaneously increasing the number and quality of critically needed wind energy professionals. Such a solution would not be limited only to the wind energy industry, but could be expanded or modified to address knowledge transfer across multiple domains.

The goals of this project are to:

- To provide an innovative solution for optimizing learning effectiveness and improving postsecondary education by developing mixed reality simulators that can be easily used and integrated into existing curriculum.
- To apply the mixed reality simulators to train postsecondary students and professionals in nationwide wind energy education.
- To provide experiential learning opportunities for students in the field of modeling, simulation, and visualization.

Augmented Reality (AR) is a type of technology that allows the user to see the real world, with virtual objects superimposed upon or composited into the real world [1,2]. The typical hardware components for AR technology are sensors, a processor, a display and input devices. These components are usually standard equipment in smartphones, which makes them a prospective AR platform. With the development of smartphones, mobile augmented reality (MAR) becomes an important category in AR systems. There have been many AR systems with different methods for visualizing the augmented scene. Most AR Applications use two technologies to register a camera for tracking: markers and images. Markers are quick and convenient for registration, however this approach works only if there are prepared markers in the view. Image recognition can eliminate these restrictions, but at the cost of computational resources. Typical mobile devices continue to get faster, but still have limited CPU and memory capabilities. For these and other reasons, utilization of built-in sensors in mobile devices is beneficial.

In recent years, there has been much research on the application of AR to education [3–6]. This technology shows promise in usage for wind energy education. The mobile augmented reality wind farm application is one of seven simulators currently being developed through the Mixed Reality Simulators for Wind Energy Education project. The purpose of these simulators is to provide training and enhanced interaction when dealing with operations and maintenance of wind energy systems. Separate simulators are being developed to focus on different aspects of wind energy including wind farm siting, wind turbine design, control &

monitoring, aerodynamic wake effects, and safety training. Additionally, a template will be available for educators and wind professionals to create further simulators that may be better suited for specific training. This paper discusses the work being done to create a simulator for wind farm siting that will be used on mobile devices.

The application will allow the user to create virtual turbines and display them within a real environment to view the distribution of turbines when planning wind farm. Users can do the following:

- Choose different turbine models, which are created in Autodesk's 3ds Max modeling software and loaded into the application.
- Decide the GPS coordinates for each turbine and view the distribution both on the Google map view and rendering window.
- Inspect detailed information of turbines, such as GPS coordinates, the distance of the user from the turbine, turbine model type and so on.

2 Related Work

Smartphones with cameras and positional sensors (e.g. GPS, compass and accelerometer) are becoming ubiquitous; this is why mobile devices are emerging as the most convenient platform on which to do augmented reality. Most AR applications which track mobile device position and orientation send data to a remote server which processes the data and sends the result back to the mobile device .This job offloading is due to the computation limitation of the mobile device. Some devices are capable of using only the local CPU for data processing , but a fast look-up resource, such as a database, is then required for camera registration [7] .

Location based systems consider the user's current location when presenting the information. Those systems fall into two categories: indoors and outdoors. There are many approaches for indoor applications: these are not relevant to the work being done and so will not be discussed. Outdoors environments present many challenges. . The complexity of a typical outdoor scene often dictates that a database for camera registration is beyond the capacity of the mobile devices. Assigning all computation to a remote server is also a problem as there is no guarantee of Internet access . The best solution is to use local resources such as the sensors on the mobile device. Some applications use a device's GPS, accelerometer, and hardware compass to register the camera rather than image processing to reduce the computational stress. Nevertheless, use of these sensors alone cannot provide sufficient registration accuracy. Civilian GPS has relatively poor accuracy, with a projected error of several meters. A typical built-in accelerometer has a significant degree of accumulated drift. Additionally, a hardware compass provides orientation information on only one axis. If a high accuracy application is needed, image processing is required when calculating camera pose[8], [9].

Wind farm planning with virtual reality is a new representation and discussion tool for sustainable landscape [10], [11]. AR technology is also widely used in education field, like engineering, mathematics, biology and so on. Mobile devices are never used in the wind energy for education although there are millions of applications on smartphones platforms. Since AR is a very useful technology for wind farm planning, and the smartphones platforms become more ubiquitous, combining them is a nice attempt.

3 Methodology

The mobile augmented reality wind farm application creates virtual wind turbines based on GPS and associates them with the existing environment. These are then displayed

Figure 1. MARWind being used at the site of a real wind farm showing both real and AR wind turbines.

The current location of the user is updated and reflects the changes of the distance and angle between the user and virtual turbines in the scene . This will show users what the wind farm will look like, and how turbines will be distributed in the farm. Through this application, users can visit a future wind farm before it actually exists.

3.1 System architecture

This application relies on the Apple iOS platform. Due to hardware limitations, the application only can be launched on iPhone 4, iPhone 4S, and iPad 2(3G version). The primary hardware limitation is availability of a built-in GPS module. Although all iOS devices can use Wi-Fi data to determine the current location, a GPS module can provide more stable and precise geographical information: this precision is essential to the proper functioning of the application. . Moreover, to view the virtual wind farm, a user may be confronted with a remote location where there is no Wi-Fi coverage. Another restriction is the gyroscope : to acquire precision movements of the device, this application utilizes the three-axis gyroscope which previous iOS devices do not support.

The Unity game engine, an integrated development environment for creating 3D animations and interactive models, is utilized in this application. Unity applications can be deployed to many platforms, including the Apple iOS mobile runtime. Moreover, Unity offers many pre-fabricated plugins which can greatly reduce the time and effort spent on software development . Prime31, a plugin which supports Unity access to mobile device features such as the gyroscope, GPS, and the hardware compass ,was used in the development of this application.

3.2 Design

The entire project was designed in the Unity iPhone development environment. The real-time visual data is captured from the camera of the device and rendered as a plane texture. In front of the plane, various virtual turbines are created and assigned a corresponding location. A virtual camera is utilized to simulate a real device camera for rendering virtual objects.

A simple Graphical User Interface (GUI) was designed for users to input the location of turbines. 3D rendering components are implemented with C# script, and GUI components are mainly developed using iOS native code .

Native location services and the gyroscope integrated into the device are used to estimate the camera's motion so that the virtual turbines' geographic position and pose may be registered without using image processing. This method reduces computation requirements and so enhances the overall perceived fluidity of the displayed composite image. The two positioning methods used are available through the Prime31 plugin. Specifically, the *DeviceMotion* and *CoreLocation* modules facilitate access to these items from within the Unity environment.

3.2.1 Location services

Through the use of location services an accurate geographic position of the mobile device can be ascertained. The objects of the virtual and the real world must be perfectly aligned at all times or the illusion of coexistence will fail. The location services Apple provides rely on both GPS and a public WiFi access point registration database. The GPS position data is preferred, but if no GPS signal is available (such as indoors) location data based on routers or base station identifiers can be used. This mechanism insures the application can run in any situation, even though the location data accuracy is degraded. .

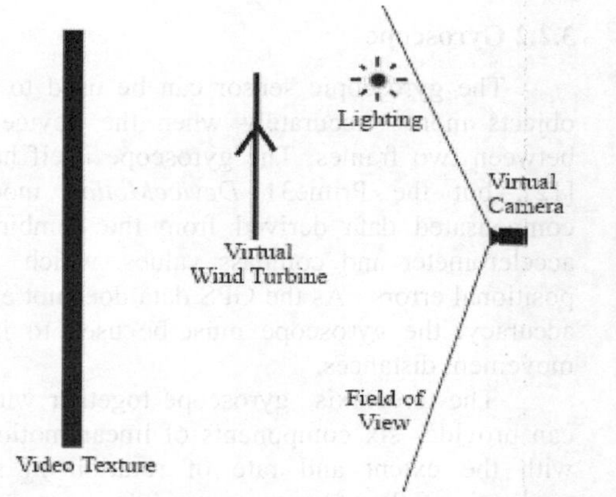

Figure 2. Layout of main objects in Unity, with real world imagery being displayed as a video texture background.

Users have the ability to specify multiple types of turbines when placing wind farms. During placement, users are able to specify longitude, latitude, and altitude to populate a wind farm, or they can manually place turbines through a touch map interface.

To determine the exact location of an object, two factors are needed. A polar coordinate system is used in this application; therefore, two parameters are the distance from a fixed point and an angle from a fix direction. With two coordinates, the user's location and the turbine's location, we calculate the distance and the true north angle.

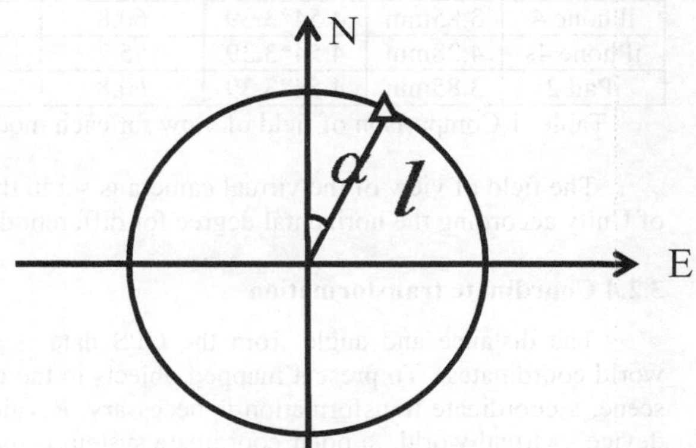

Figure 3. Polar coordinate system of real world.

When the user is moving, the GPS data is updating continually, and the device will re-calculate the distance and angle to present correct virtual turbines in the scene. Using this method, we initially register virtual objects to the real-time environment. The calculated positions are prone to drift, however, due to floating point round-off errors. It was determined that the data from GPS should have at least six decimal places to ensure the accuracy of the positions on a one meter scale.

3.2.2 Gyroscope

The gyroscopic sensor can be used to register virtual objects more accurately when the device moves rapidly between two frames. The gyroscope itself has inherent drift [12], but the Prime31 *DeviceMotion* module provides compensated data derived from the combined gyroscope, accelerometer and compass values, which reduces overall positional errors. As the GPS data does not exhibit one meter accuracy, the gyroscope must be used to interpolate small movement distances.

The three-axis gyroscope together with accelerometer can provide six components of linear motion data, , along with the extent and rate of rotation in space. In this application, the gyroscope mainly processes the rotation angle.. . Linear interpolation of small movements using local sensors reduces the number of calls to the GPS unit, which improves overall application performance.

3.2.3 Field of view

For the augmented reality application, a virtual camera, a simulation of the real device's camera, is created to combine the virtual and real world . To ensure the virtual camera appears similar to a real one, we calculate an appropriate field of view for each device.

Model	Focal length (mm)	CCD size (mm^2)	Horizontal degree	Vertical degree
iPhone 4	3.85mm	4.54*3.39	60.8	47.5
iPhone 4s	4.28mm	4.54*3.39	55.7	43.2
iPad 2	3.85mm	4.54*3.39	60.8	47.5

Table 1 Comparison of field of view for each model.

The field of view of the virtual camera is set in the scene of Unity according the horizontal degree for different devices.

3.2.4 Coordinate transformation

The distance and angle from the GPS data is in real world coordinates. To present mapped objects in the device's scene, a coordinate transformation is necessary. Recall, in the device's virtual world, a polar coordinate system is used. The angle of the virtual object in the scene depends on the initial device face. Through the gyroscopic data of the device's rotation angle, we calculate the angle in the mobile scene. The virtual object's distance must appear coincident with the real world distance; to accomplish this, , a fixed linear offset was used, and the turbine's size was scaled to simulate the perspective of the distance. This method was originally designed to avoid occlusion of virtual objects by the real world texture plane This solution works when turbines are far from the user , but when the user is extremely close to the turbine, such as 5 meters, the texture plane will occlude the top of the turbine. To deal with this problem, two cameras are set to render different objects. One is only responsible for virtual turbines; the other is for the real world capture: the two parts will never affect each other. Since this method has solved the interference of turbines and environment rendering, the original design is no longer necessary, we use the real distance and let the camera present the perspective, which may give a more realistic experience.

3.2.5 GUI design

A simple GUI was implemented for users to input GPS data and choose different models. Due to the limitations of Unity, pure iOS native code was used to achieve this functionality. Unity iPhone functions are actually wrappers around underlying native iOS code. Unity provides methods for sending messages between Unity and the native iOS runtime. . . These methods were utilized to communicate with the native user interface.

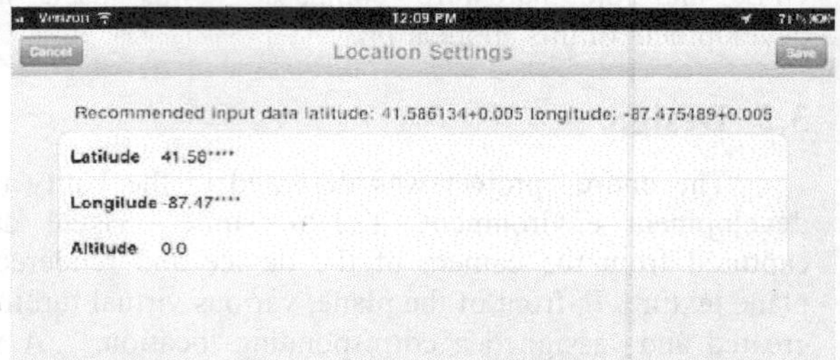

Figure 4. GUI to input wind turbine locations by longitude, latitude, and altitude.

In the second revision of the application , a Google map based GUI was implemented. For this GUI design, a map is used to show the locations of all turbines and the user. Users can not only view turbines in the rendering window , but also have an overall impression of the turbines' distribution on the landscape. Also, users can inspect detailed information related to each turbine, and edit each turbine's model and location. Additionally, the user can create various wind farms with different turbine distributions.

4 Results

4.1 Augmented reality

In our test, we loaded two different virtual turbine models. These models were created in 3ds Max, and imported into Unity. Figure 4 shows the rendering result of differing orientations of turbines Two camera rendering insures that both the camera capture texture and the turbine models are not distorted.

4.2 Localization

GPS data is collected only when user's movement is larger than one meter. This prevents visible jitter: GPS values taken at this small of a scale are well below the advertised civilian accuracy of the positioning system, and typically full of random noise.

4.3 GUI

A simple GUI in the rendering window is used to control the augmented reality settings. The "Start Motion" and "Stop Motion" buttons are designed to run and stop the gyroscope. "Reset Motion" is used to acquire the ground surface reference plane for the gyroscope. The "Start capture" and "Stop capture" buttons control the camera .

Figure 5. Rendered turbines with different orientation in the real environment.

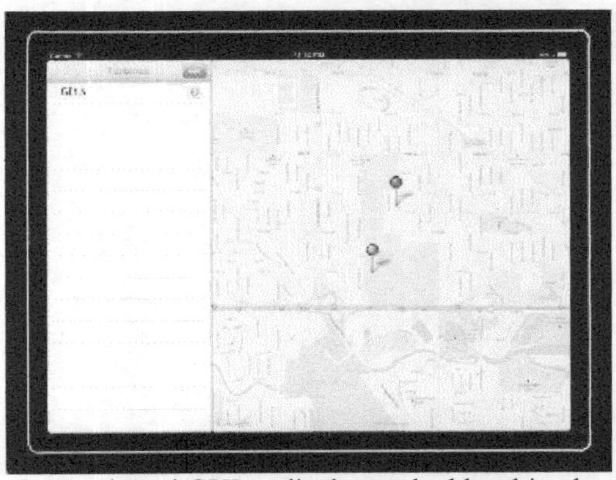

Figure 6. Map based GUI to display and add turbine locations.

The application's map view user interface utilizes a split view mechanism to present a comprehensive summary of the current state of virtual objects and registration points. In Figure 6, the left part of the split view interface shows turbine characteristics such as model type and location. The right part of the view shows the distribution of turbines in this wind farm.

5 Conclusion

This project has developed an augmented reality wind farm siting application for mobile devices. The resulting application can be used to visualize potential wind farm locations by overlaying 3D wind turbines at locations specified through either longitude and latitude coordinates, or through manual placement with a map interface. Although the computational limitations of current mobile devices are pronounced, these negative factors can be reduced by leveraging the speed of built-in hardware accelerated sensors. Future functionality will combine pre-computed wind-flow visualizations with turbine configurations to provide useful information for wind energy professionals such as the boundary of individual turbine wake effects.

6 Acknowledgements

The contents of this paper were developed under grant P116B100322 from the U.S. Department of Education. However, those contents do not necessarily represent the policy of the U.S. Department of Education, and you should not assume endorsement by the Federal Government.

7 References

[1] R. T. Azuma, "A Survey of Augmented Reality," *Media*, vol. 4, no. August, pp. 355-385, 1997.

[2] R. Azuma, Y. Baillot, R. Behringer, S. Feiner, S. Julier, and B. MacIntyre, *Recent advances in augmented reality*, vol. 21, no. 6. IEEE Computer Society, 2001, pp. 34-47.

[3] M. Dunleavy, C. Dede, and R. Mitchell, "Affordances and Limitations of Immersive Participatory Augmented Reality Simulations for Teaching and Learning," *Journal of Science Education and Technology*, vol. 18, no. 1, pp. 7-22, Sep. 2008.

[4] H. Kaufmann and D. Schmalstieg, "Mathematics and geometry education with collaborative augmented reality," *Computers & Graphics*, vol. 27, no. 3, pp. 339-345, 2003.

[5] F. Liarokapis et al., "Web3D and Augmented Reality to support Engineering Education," *Engineering and Technology*, vol. 3, no. 1, pp. 11-14, 2004.

[6] D. Schmalstieg and I. Systeme, "Geometry Education with Augmented Reality," *Technology*, no. 9225889. 2004.

[7] M. Turk, "Location-based augmented reality on mobile phones," *Cell*, pp. 9-16, 2010.

[8] G. Takacs, V. Chandrasekhar, and N. Gelfand, "Outdoors augmented reality on mobile phone using loxel-based visual feature organization," *Proceeding of the 1st*, pp. 427-434, 2008.

[9] G. Reitmayr, "Location based Applications for Mobile Augmented Reality," *Reproduction*, 2001.

[10] J. Jallouli, G. Moreau, and R. Querrec, "Wind turbines' landscape: using virtual reality for the assessment of multisensory perception in motion," *Proceedings of the 2008 ACM symposium on Virtual reality software and technology*, vol. 16, no. 2, pp. 257-258, 2010.

[11] N. Yabuki, D. Ph, and J. T. B. West, "VIRTUAL REALITY SIMULATION OF WIND POWER PLANTS USING SOUND AND 3D ANIMATED GRAPHICS," in *10th International Conference on Construction Applications of Virtual Reality*, 2010.

[12] T. H. Höllerer and S. K. Feiner, "Mobile Augmented Reality," *Telegeoinformatics LocationBased Computing and Services*, vol. 20, no. 8, pp. 1-39, 2004.

How Data can become Data a Movie Star?

H.-P. Bischof
Department of Computer Science,
Center for Computational Relativity and Gravitation,
Rochester Institute of Technology, Rochester, NY, US

Abstract— *Visualization of scientific data is the art of converting numerical values into an image, which can be comprehended by a human visual system. The conversion process can lead to a movie or an individual image. The creation parameters, like light, viewing position, etc. typically do not change. A movie can be assembled out of images where the creation parameters for each individual image does not change, or each image may have different creation parameter set. This article discusses the second approach, which is a significantly more dynamic and creative approach. We will analyze what existing visualization systems are capable of, and we will present a unique way how to create accurate, but very dynamic movies.*

Keywords: Visualization Framework, Animation

1. Introduction

This conversion of numerical data into visuals makes it sometimes possible to understand complex relations, but it is no replacement for an analytical analysis. A histogram, for example, is the appropriate to tool to convey statistical information to statistically untrained people[10]. A visualization of the functions $f(x) = e^{-1}$ and $g(x) = 1x$ is helpful in order to see that $f(x)$ and $g(x)$ for x close to 0 are nearly identical. The proof for the birthday paradox[11] becomes a bit easier if this fact is know.

The visualization of scientific data should not be confused with the generation of a visual for a movie. The outer space scene generated for the movie WALL-E[5] is wonderful, but not based on data generated by an experiment or a simulation. A visualization of scientific data needs to be true to the science, but can also be exiting from an experience point of view. In order to do so, it must be possible to control viewpoint, color, light, size of objects and other attributes used to control the creation of the visualization.

For a moment picture the following visualization problem. A tiny black hole is merging with a very large black hole, and for the scientist it is important to show the correct size of the objects. In order to see the path of the small black, the viewpoint has to be so far away that the small black hole becomes invisible, because its appearance is smaller than one pixel from the desired viewpoint. One solution of this problem would be something like this: The viewpoint moves from a viewing point far away to the original sized tiny black hole. The at first invisible black hole will became visible during the movement of the viewpoint. After the final viewpoint is reached, the size of the tiny black hole is increased to a size, which makes it visible form the original viewpoint. The viewpoint then moves to the desired viewpoint. The merger of the black holes continues and shortly before the merger takes place we use a similar technique as described before to show the actual merger. The viewpoint moves close to where the merger takes place, then the size of the tiny black hole shrinks to its real size and the merger continues from there on. It is obvious that the movement of the viewpoint have to be smooth in order to create a pleasant viewing experience. For example, the movement cannot come to a abrupt stop at the end of a movement.

The rest of the paper explores three selected visualization systems in terms of their functionality and their capability to create more animated visualizations. The systems chosen are visit[1], ParaView[2] and Spiegel[7].

2. Architecture

All three visualization systems are using similar data flow architecture. The raw data is read, and filtered if the raw data cannot directly be used for the visualization. This data is then converted into geometric objects. These objects will then be visualized according to the chosen algorithms and then stored, shown, or assembled to a video.

ParaView is normally controlled via GUI, but the engine can be programmed using the scripting languages pvbatch[3] or pvpyhton[4]. The batch programs allow creating, connecting, and controlling the data flow and the components used in the process. The flavor of scripting language is similar to other scripting languages. The use of it requires a significant understand of the available ParaView components and their communications and control. The scripting languages are the path to the creation animated movies. This aspect will be explored in chapter Architecture.

The Spiegel visualization framework is a Unix pipeline inspired architecture. Similar to ParaView a GUI is used to create the data flow. A scripting langue used to create and connect the components, and the resulting program is then stored in a file. The scripting language is extremely simple and does not have control structure, or variables differently to the scripting languages used for VisIt or ParaView. The creation of more dynamic movies is controlled by a Spiegel component which if programmable. This aspect will be explored in chapter Animation Language.

VisIts dataflow is based on operators, which are performed on the data, like slicing, etc., before the modified data actually gets visualized. Like the other two systems, a GUI controls visit. VisIt is using a scripting language or a GUI component in order to create animated video. The GUI component allows very simplistic animations; the language needs to get used in order to create sophisticated animated movies.

3. Visualization Components

A Spiegel visualization component[7] has typed input, output and argument channels; k input channels, l output channels and m argument input channels. The output of a component can be connected to the argument of a component, which allows reaching into the data stream and modifying the visualization based on the data. Lets assume we would like to follow a black hole with a cameras viewfinder. In order to do so one component of the visualization program would reach in the data stream and send out the position of the black hole we are looking for. This position would be sent as an argument input to the camera, and the viewpoint would follow the black hole. The camera itself would be at a fixed position in space, but the cameras viewfinder, or look-at-position would follow a particular black hole. This functionality alone would not do, because the black hole may ay be in a less than desirable lighting situation. One solution would be to point a light source to the same position as the look-at-position of the camera. Figure 1 illustrates this concept. The dashed lines connect output channels with a argument channel, and the solid lines connect output with input channels. The Stars component send out all stars to the Visualizer and the component, which extracts the position of the black hole, we are interested in, in this case number 3.

This "hello world" program illustrates one design principle behind the Spiegel system. The Spiegel program language is simple; it allows only creating and connecting components. Every functionality else need is implemented in Java, which allows to use object oriented program paradigms and the power of existing Java frameworks. This concept allows to add functionality very easily, because the Spiegel specific communication part can be learned in less than 5 minutes. My students have proven this many times.

VisIt and ParaView are using well known scripting languages, mainly python. The connection of data output and argument does not really exist. The burden of the functionality of the visualization program is divided into scripting and the components. This means, the same functionality can be achieved in many different ways. Adding new components into the ParaView or VisIt environment is doable, but very difficult. My students have proven this many times. In other words, an animation is most likely done in a scripting

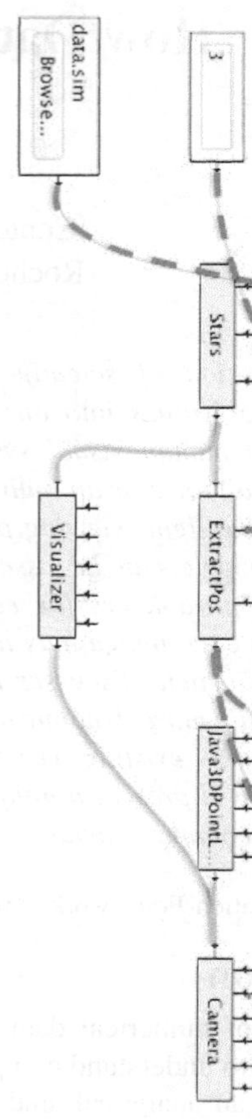

Fig. 1: How to change the viewpoint based on the location of a black hole

environment, and it is not easy to re-use established ideas, from one visualization to an other.

4. Visualization Algorithms

The basis for visualizations is obviously the available algorithms. VisIt and ParaView trump Spiegel in this regard significantly. Benger at all[6] describe in detail the usual implemented visualization algorithms. VisIt and ParaView implement a super set of these algorithms. Both systems have been developed to be a production tool. Spiegel, on the other hand, was and is developed as research system and its main purpose is to understand design criteria's for visualization systems. Spiegel has been successfully used to create visuals as shown on History Channel.

5. Animation 1.0

The animation of a scientific data visualizations can enhance the understanding of the data[8]. The result of an animation is a movie; therefore we must keep in mind how many frames per second the animation creates. In other words, the number or frames used for the simulation is know before the animation is created.

The most simplistic animation of a supernova simulation of a stellar explosion is keeping every thing constant, viewing position, lighting condition etc. The input parameter for this animation would be t, meaning we create a frame for t starting at the beginning, and then the next value of t would be calculated by t = t + Δ t. This might not the most desirable animation because at the beginning at the end of the simulation nothing of interested may happen. In other words, it is known when and where the visualization shows an interesting situation. Therefore it would be better if Δ t would not be a constant, but rather be calculated as Δ t = F(simulation time) in order to fast forward the time of show the simulation in slow motion. If this is done, then we introduce the concept of a simulation time and visualization time. The simulation time is the time of the simulation, which created the data; the visualization time is the wall time passing while the animated movie is running. Scalars like time are very obvious and easy to understand and to use. The visualization time moves forward in constant units; the simulation time is calculated based on a function. At this point the how to calculate the simulation time is not important. We will be discussed in the next chapter.

Is a scalar, like time, the only kind of data which drives an animation. For example, lets assume you would like to visualize how a projectile rips a balloon apart. It might be preferable to use the x/y/z position of the projectile to drive the simulation and not the time. This is most likely not the path to go, because if the time is know, then it is know there the projectile is, because the projectile has to follow the laws of physics. The author has never found a need to use to anything else than a scalar value to control the animation. Nevertheless the following chapter will not use this restriction.

6. Animation 2.0

Animation always require at least on input parameter, i, to drive the animation, which at the end controls the change of the attributes used to create single frames. We assume at this point, that the input parameter is a scalar value. A function is needed for every attribute controlled by i.

For this example we would to adjust the viewpoint of a camera. The viewpoint should follow a path in 3d. We assume i moves forward by a constant Δ i. We will later show that this is a fair assumption. The path p, is defined by a function $f(i)$. We need to know the values of $f(i)$ for a few fixed values of i. These values are called the anchor points. For example:

```
I = 0: p = (0, 0, 255)              // a
I = 1: p = (0, 255, 0)              // b
I = 3: p = (255, 0, 0)              // c
I = 4: p = (255, 255, 255)          // d
```

The question is how do we calculate the value for p(i), at i = 2? Some kind of interpolation has to happen between the anchor points. If the values represent the RGB values for a color, then a linear interpolation between the points is the one to choose. TCP-splines[9] would be the right choice, if the values represents the path of a flying seagull, because the flight seagull does not include sharp kinks.

The Δ for i is: 1, 2, 1. Lets follow the flight of the seagull for a moment. We note that the speed of the seagull between point a and b is twice as fast as the flight from point c and b. This technique would be used to create a speed up or slow-motion view of the simulation.

It is obvious that the described algorithm can be implement in any reasonable language, which includes the scripting language used in ParaView or VisIT. The question is would be worthwhile to implement a tiny specialized language animation language.

7. Animation Language

The input for an animation language is one input value. The outputs can be many attributes as a function of the input. The values of the attribute are controlled by the input value, the anchor points, and the interpolations used for a given attribute. We have to keep in mind, that the final result will be a movie; therefore we have to define how many frames per second the animation should generate: The animation language must allow for the following:

1) Define the outputs attribute by names, we call this objects output streams
2) Define the anchor points for each output stream
3) Define the interpolation algorithm for each output streams

An example is shown in Fig xxx and the use case is show in Fig .. The keywords of the language are: fps, stream, name, type, interpolator, and the parenthesis. TCB is an index in a table defining the one used for the position stream.

```
fps 25.0

stream position {
        name "position"
        type vector interpolator TCB
}
time 0 { position(0, 0, 255) }
time 1 { position(0, 255, 0) }
time 3 { position(255, 0, 0)
time 4 { position(255, 0, 0) }
```

The component Flythrough gets the input parameter from the Clock component and sends out the position parameter calculated based on the animation program shown in Figure 2. The clock ticks forward in time, and this will trigger a change of the output attribute position.

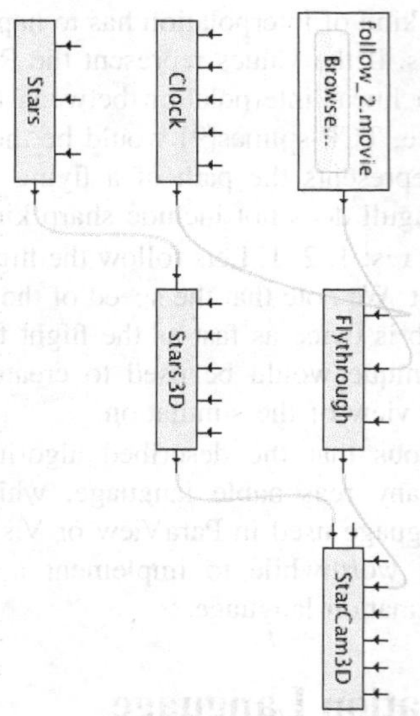

Fig. 2: How to change the viewpoint based on the location of a black hole

8. Extension

The component parsing the animation programs needs to get modified, if the grammar of the animation language needs to change. This might be a serious undertaking, highly depending on the new grammar. Adding new interpolators, or new type is trivial; it just requires the creation of a interpolator class and an extension of an array to connect the identifier with the interpolator.

9. Future Work

Incorporating of the Spiegel animation philosophy in ParaView or VisIt should be done as a proof concept. The animation language does not make it easy to modify the program after it is written because the language does not have variables and arithmetic build in. The language would benefit from adding these two ideas. Rather complicated animated movies have been produced with this technology, but none of them had audio attached to it. It would be interesting to understand if this language could support the creation of audio for the animation.

10. Conclusion

The use of this or any other animation language could be added to ParaView or VisIt. Animation in these two environments is difficult to create. Therefore it would be beneficial for the users to add visualization language as described

References

[1] The visit home page @ONLINE. March 2012.

[2] Paraview - open source scientific visualization tool@ONLINE. March 2013.

[3] Paraview/users guide/batch processing @ONLINE. March 2013.

[4] Praview/python scripting paraview @ONLINE. March 2013.

[5] Wall-e@ONLINE. March 2013.

[6] Werner Benger, Markus Haider, Josef Stoeckl, Biagio Cosenza, Marcel Ritter, Dominik Steinhauser, and Harald Hoeller. *Visualization Methods for Numerical Astrophysics*. InTech - Open Access Publisher, 2012.

[7] Hans-Peter Bischof, Edward Dale, and Tim Peterson. Spiegel - a visualization framework for large and small scale systems. In *In MSV âĂŹ06: Proceedings of the 2006 International Conference of Modeling Simulation and Visualization Methods*, 2006.

[8] Danyel Fisher. Animation for visualization: Opportunities and drawbacks @ONLINE. March 2013.

[9] Doris H. U. Kochanek and Richard H. Bartels. Interpolating splines with local tension, continuity, and bias control. In *SIGGRAPH '84: Proceedings of the 11th annual conference on Computer graphics and interactive techniques*, pages 33–41, New York, NY, USA, 1984. ACM Press.

[10] Douglas C. Montgomery. *Introduction to statistical quality control*. Wiley, New York, NY [u.a.], 3. ed edition, 1997.

[11] Kazuhiro Suzuki, Dongvu Tonien, Kaoru Kurosawa, and Koji Toyota. Birthday paradox for multi-collisions. *IEICE Trans. Fundam. Electron. Commun. Comput. Sci.*, E91-A(1):39–45, January 2008.

Integration of Augmented Reality with Computational Fluid Dynamics for Power Plant Training

John Moreland[1], Jichao Wang[1,2], Yanghe Liu[3], Fan Li[1,2], Litao Shen[1,2], Bin Wu[1], Chenn Zhou[1,2]
[1]Center for Innovation through Visualization and Simulation
[2]Electrical and Computer Engineering
[3]Mechancial Engineering
Purdue University Calumet
Hammond, IN, USA

Abstract— *This research describes the motivations and technical approach for combining Augmented Reality with Computational Fluid Dynamics to develop materials for training on a large boiler of a coal-fired power plant. A number of different software were used for this approach including Gambit and Fluent for numerical simulation, 3dsMax for 3D modeling and visualization, and D'fusion for Augmented Reality. The result leverages the benefits of existing simulation methods and emerging interactive technologies to allow presenters to show characteristics of any numerical simulation in a vivid and convenient way.*

The technical description of the simulation and visualization contains a series of complex steps and components, including the integration of the data, the construction of the geometry, and the analysis of the properties of flow within the boiler. The methods used to present this data with augmented reality can be expanded to many different areas.

Keywords: Augmented Reality, Training, Power Plant, Boiler, CFD, Visualization

1 Introduction

Trainees at a coal-fired power station typically receive comprehensive training in boiler operation procedures through traditional two-dimensional (2D), non-scaled representations of components in a classroom environment. It is difficult to fully understand the complex workings of boiler operation in such environments. In general, there is a known issue in transferring learned concepts from a classroom setting to practical application in real world settings [1,2]. Improvements for the boiler training are being sought the development of computer simulations and different forms of interaction to enhance instruction. Initial efforts have already been made at Purdue University Calumet's Center for Innovation through Visualization and Simulation to combine computational fluid dynamics (CFD) and immersive 3D Visualization to enhance understanding of complex industrial processes [3]. These have been applied to develop a virtual boiler unit using Virtual Reality (VR) and CFD so that a 3D model could be used in the training process. However, the developed virtual package still has some limitations due to the necessity of specialized 3D display. This can limit the accessibility for trainees to gain the full benefits of the VR model.

With the purpose of optimizing and maximizing the advantages of CFD and 3D visualization, a further effort is underway to develop methods to use standard equipment such as laptops and mobile devices to extend the training capabilities of the virtual boiler outside of a dedicated VR environment. The goals of this research are:

- To create a turbulent reacting CFD model for a specific boiler at a coal-fired power plant.
- To integrate CFD flow data and VR visualization models to provide a 3D representation of the boiler unit.
- To construct an AR environment to display and interact with simulation data combined with live elements.
- To provide a more efficient training media and software for the boiler operation crew.

Augmented Reality (AR) is being utilized to provide easy access to all the details of a virtual model in a 3D environment. This will provide a unique and intuitive method for trainees to interact with boiler components as well as simulated combustion and flow data. Initial efforts are utilizing printed 2D schematics of the boiler and components as the physical interface upon which 3D representations of the boiler and related data are displayed. Work is underway to integrate this method of interaction with 3D printed models of the boiler and components to increase the intuitive nature of the method even further. Trainees will then be provided with a variety of physical objects with which to explore the various operating conditions of the boiler.

2 Background

There are a number of technologies available to provide users with an interactive and immersive experience. While this study focuses on augmented reality, it is important to understand the relationship of augmented reality to related technologies such as virtual reality, augmented virtuality, and mobile devices. Through understanding the differences between these technologies, it becomes easier to utilize the strengths of each for specific purposes, thus increasing the benefit to the users. Milgram proposed a Mixed Reality Continuum (figure 1) which categorizes technologies on a scale ranging from a completely real environment through a completely virtual environment [4]. It is important to note that in virtual reality, the user is immersed in computer generated imagery and is cut off from the real world. While this is beneficial in many circumstances, it also creates some issues such as potential disconnects between the virtual objects and their real world counterparts.

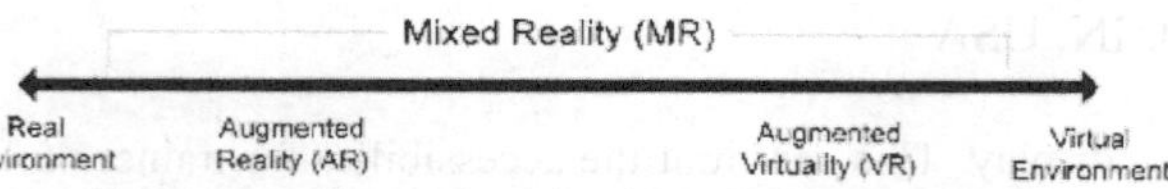

Figure 1. Milgram's Mixed Reality Continuum.

With AR, a user is able to maintain a connection with real world, while still enjoying the benefits of 3D models and useful infromation from the virtual world. AR is type of technology that combines 3D virtual objects with real world imagery in real time [5]. A typical implemenation of AR uses a camera connected to a computer to recognize patterns from the real world and then display useful information on top of the live video display. With the advances in mobile technology in recent years, Mobile AR applications are surfacing for phones and tablets to provide augmented interfaces for maps, social networking, gaming, and educational training [6-9]. One study of particular note explored the usage of augmented reality for maintenance within a power plant. This effort focused on developing a protoype system to assist with actual maintenance operations by displaying relevant text and schematic information on-site [10]. While this wasn't specifically an educational application, it provided useful insights into the implementation of a mobile augmented realiy system within the power plant environment.

This paper focuses on more detailed operations and the phenomena occurring within the power plant boiler and turbine. The combination of augmented reality for educational training is explored by combining the technology with computer simulated combustion and fluid flows and Photorealistic representations of the boiler at a coal-fired power plant.

3 Methodology

3.1 Simulation

Gambit® is used to preprocess the model. The geometry obtained from Gambit® will be imported into Fluent® for the fluid computation [11,12]. In order to get correct results in Fluent®, inlets, outlets and other conditions must be set up appropriately while building the geometry of the boiler.

The simulation was divided into two activities:

Build the geometry: The model of the boiler was built based on the data provided by CIVS. Each cyclone has four inlets, three of them are for air input, and the other is for coal. Figure 1a shows a 2D cross-section of the boiler model in ANSYS, while figure 1b shows post-processed results within Paraview.

The Geometry obtained from Gambit® was meshed and imported into Fluent® to simulate the all characteristics inside the boiler, such as temperature distribution, velocity temperature and tracks of discrete particles. Since further calculation and analysis would be based on the meshed geometry, the meshed graph needs to be as accurate as possible.

The graphic of the component will be calculated for the detailed flow characteristics and detailed reaction. In this case, the velocity and flow turbulence characteristics are calculated.

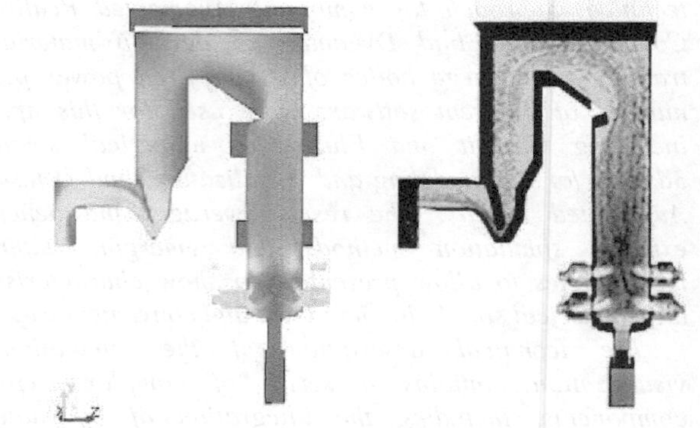

Figure 2. A 2D cross-section of the boiler CFD results in ANSYS (left), and 3D results visualized in Paraview (right).

Procedures included the following steps:

1. Read the data: First, the data of the meshed geometry of the boiler should be loaded into Fluent®. This will ensure that the mesh is correct and is able to be processed

2. Check the dimensions: Before beginning calculations, checking needs to be done to make sure all the scale and dimensions are correct. In order to get the precise calculation, the dimensions in Fluent® should correspond to the geometry drawn in Gambit® before setting data [13].

3. Set data: In Fluent®, the properties and boundary conditions (including pressure, temperature, velocities of the inlets and the outlet) of the system should be set first to enable the model to flow.

The air inlets of the boiler should be a velocity-inlet, the coal inlet needs Discrete Particle Model (DPM in Fluent®) and the outlet should be set as a pressure-outlet. The material used in the calculation is air and coal.

4. Check data: After setting the data, all the data should be checked to ensure the correct characteristic of the flow.

Otherwise, the flow will not display the actual situation of the actions taken in the power plant, and the data may not be correct.

5. Calculate: In this case, the velocity of the flow is calculated. The number of iterations is 10,000 in order to get the converged results. Usually, if the continuity shown in the figure can be stable and be below 1e-3, the results would be accurate enough

6. Display the calculation: The results show the detailed velocity changes inside the boiler.

3.2 Visualization

The simulation results were brought into Paraview for post-processing and to generate 3D models representing certain aspects of the data such as temperature and velocity using vectors, streamlines, and color gradients to represent varying data values [14].

The resulting models were exported from Paraview and brought into 3dsMax to integrate with additional models for trainees to better understand simulation results in the context of the real boiler in the field [15]. 3D models of the surrounding structure and equipment was created and registered with the boiler simulation results based on drawings and specification provided by the power plant. Additional elements such as animated processes and flame particle effects were also included to increase the realism of the model.

In addition to the facility model and processes, aerial imagery of the real facility was imported and registered to align with the structures. This provided additional elements of realism for the trainees to relate the simulation results to the real environment.

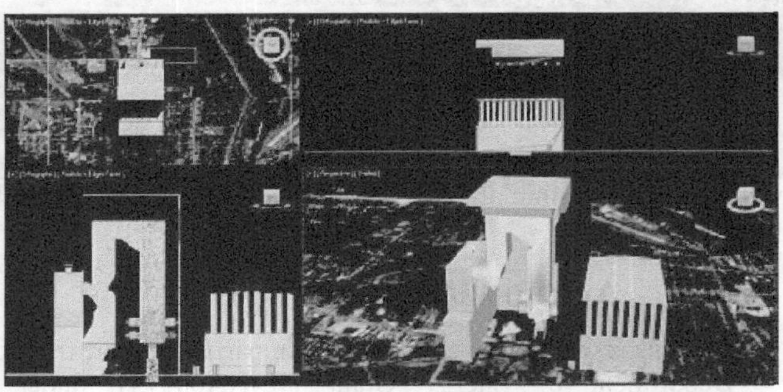

Figure 3. 3D CFD results from Paraview are combined with a photorealistic model of the surrounding structure in 3dsMax.

Once simulation and photorealistic models were combined, the models were exported and used as input for AR software. Several AR software were evaluated for this research. The high-level AR tool D'fusion® was selected for its flexibility and ease of development.

By using D'fusion®, a real-time AR environment can be set up and rendered [16]. The tracking system needs a tracker such as a paper with special marks, a camera to capture the tracker's information and source code files that tell the system to build certain models based on the tracker's location [17].

First, a meshed model of the virtual scene is imported into D'fusion. Then several camera drivers and tracking code will be linked into the system. Finally, after multiple tests, the software is able to display the operation and the case on the screen

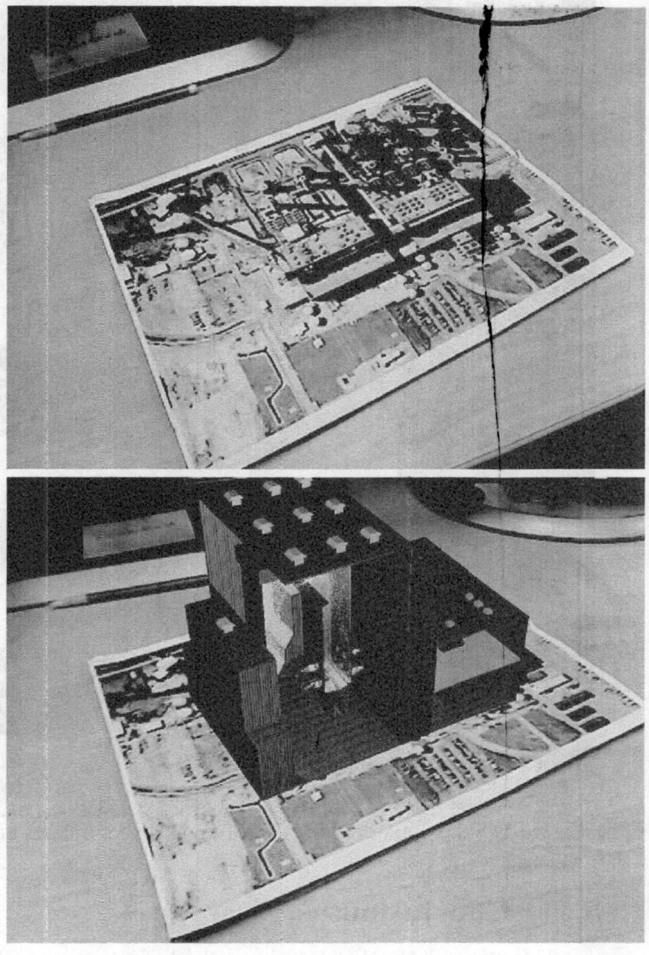

Figure 4.Aerial photograph of the power plant serves as the target image for the AR software (Top). The Boiler CFD results and and surrounding structure are registered and displayed over top of the image (Bottom).

4 Results

The CFD simulation method, 3DS Max modeling, and D'fusion toolkit themselves have been used for many years. But this project is the first time to make it an integrated system for engineering projects. The transition between software is the main problem. Because of the rapid development of techniques, file formats are different for 3D model. Thus, details are being lost during converting files such as textures and the directions of some patterning. New algorithm is highly expected in order to uniform the format.

Another problem to be optimized is the function of the outcome system. By using packaged software to develop the AR environment has its limitation. Further powerful function like regional / full view switch of a model or all dimensional tracking was not achieved.

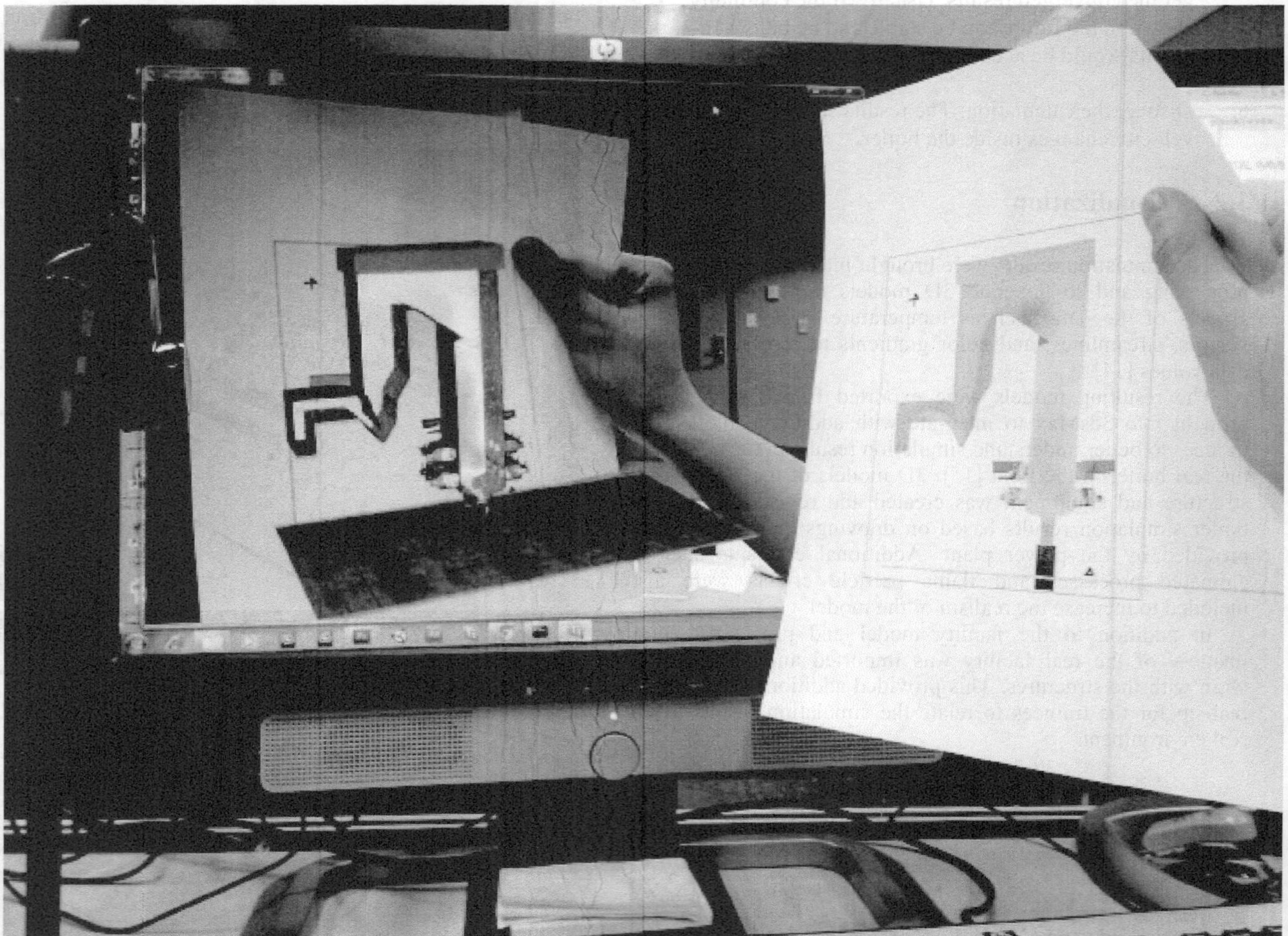

Figure 5. Schematic drawings are used as target images and registered to align simulation results with relevant drawing details.

5 Conclusions

This research has developed a method of integrating CFD simulation results with photorealistic 3D models for the purpose of power plant training using augmented reality. The method includes numeric simulation, post processing, modeling of associated 3D structures, and registration with relevant technical drawings.

Future work will build additional options to interface with CFD data through AR, explore additional methods to integrate AR into training and assess their effectiveness.

6 Acknowledgment

This research was conducted with partial support from U.S. Department of Energy Grant DE-NA000741 under the administration of the National Nuclear Security Administration.

7 References

[1] Norman, G., & Schmidt, H. (1992) The psychological basis of problem-based learning: a review of the evidence. *Academic Medicine*, 67(9), 557-565.

[2] Resnick, L. (1987) The 1987 Presidential Address: learning in school and out. *Educational Researcher*, 16(9), 13-20.

[3] Fu, D., Wu, B., Moreland, J., Chen, G., and Zhou, C. Q., 2009, "CFD Simulations and VR Visualization for Process Design and Optimization", Proceedings of the Inaugural US-EU-China Thermophysics Conference, Beijing, China, UECTC-RE '09, UECTC-RE T5-S6-0298, (7 pages).

[4] Milgram, P., & Kishino, F. (1994) A taxonomy of mixed reality virtual displays. IEICE Transactions on Information and Systems, 12, E77-D9.

[5] Azuma, R. T. (1997). A survey of augmented reality. *Presence-Teleoperators and Virtual Environments*, *6*(4), 355-385.

[6] Morrison, A., Oulasvirta, A., Peltonen, P., Lemmela, S., Jacucci, G., Reitmayr, G., ... & Juustila, A. (2009, April). Like bees around the hive: a comparative study of a mobile augmented reality map. In *Proceedings of the SIGCHI Conference on Human Factors in Computing Systems* (pp. 1889-1898). ACM.

[7] Schmalstieg, D., Langlotz, T., & Billinghurst, M. (2011). Augmented Reality 2.0. In *Virtual Realities* (pp. 13-37). Springer Vienna.

[8] Ebling, M. R., & Cáceres, R. (2010). Gaming and augmented reality come to location-based services. *Pervasive Computing, IEEE*, *9*(1), 5-6.

[9] Smith, P., & Brown, V. (2011, March). Mobile Augmented Reality as an Emerging Technology in Education. In *Society for Information Technology & Teacher Education International Conference* (Vol. 2011, No. 1, pp. 3362-3365).

[10] Klinker, Gudrun, Oliver Creighton, Allen H. Dutoit, Rafael Kobylinski, Christoph Vilsmeier, and B. Brugge. "Augmented maintenance of powerplants: A prototyping case study of a mobile AR system." In *Augmented Reality, 2001. Proceedings. IEEE and ACM International Symposium on*, pp. 124-133. IEEE, 2001.

[11] Guide, G. M. (1998). Fluent Incorporated. *Lebanon, NH*, *3766*.

[12] Fluent. (2011). 13.0. ANSYS. *Inc., Canonsburg, PA, USA*. http://www.ansys.com

[13] I. Tari. "CFD Analyses of a Notebook Computer Thermal Management System and a Proposed Passive Cooling Alternative." *Components and Packaging Technologies*. IEEE Transactions.

[14] Ahrens, J., Geveci, B., & Law, C. (2005). Paraview: An end-user tool for large data visualization. *The Visualization Handbook*, *717*, 731.

[15] 3dsMax. (2013). Autodesk Inc. http://www.autodesk.com

[16] D'Fusion. (2013). Total Immersion. http://www.t-immersion.com/

[17] W. Matcha. Development and preliminary investigation of Augmented Reality Experiment Simulation (AReX) interface. National Postgraduate Conference (NPC). 2011.

SESSION

MODELING

Chair(s)

TBA

Effective Early Stage Model-Based Testing for an IT UI Application

Xin Bai
Alexander Ivaniukovich

The Microsoft Corporation
Redmond, WA 98052
xinbai@microsoft.com
aivan@microsoft.com

Abstract

Model-based testing is a technique which has been practiced by many software test teams. A prototype has been developed as a proof of concept (POC) for a User Interface (UI) application by many of the development teams. A combination of the two gives the project teams a capability to virtually work on an IT UI application at the early stage of design purely based on the function specification and come up with a solution with high confidence from both sides of development and quality assurance.

Keywords: Model-Based Testing, software testing, Spec Explorer, Visual Studio, UI, Sketchflow.

I. Introduction

In the world of software testing, the UI automation is always a challenge. Not only because it is hard to maintain the automated codes to accommodate a frequent UI change on its nature; but also, it is difficult to obtain the development codes, which contain the required components for UI automation at the early stage of the project cycle. As a result, we often observed that the UI automation work cannot be completed until the end of the project cycle and thus it provided a little value to the current project release (it may add more value to the next release as part of regression).

Although many project teams have tried to solve the issues by a team effort, model-based testing is an effective and proven strategy to tackle on the problem.

By practicing model-based testing, in the design phase of the software development, developers focus on creating a UI prototype to mimic the real UI and navigation, in the meanwhile, testers just focus on authoring a machine readable model based on requirements by using a tool to generate a complete and maintainable test case suite [1].

The strategy and solution presented in this article facilitates the project teams with a method to test a UI application with automation at the early stage of a product development cycle. The paper presents a case study of model-based testing, using Microsoft Visual Studio add-on Spec Explorer [2] as a tool to create a machine readable model based on requirements. The combination of the two efforts provides the project teams with the capability to create an UI application prototype at the early stage even without any production codes, to discover inconsistent and missing requirements in building a model, and to ensure the quality by finding the issues in the design phase.

II. Today's Automation

In today's software testing against an UI application, automation is not possible to accomplish at the early stage of design phase of the project cycle. It has always been a challenging task for testers to work on UI test automation while developers are working on a prototype in the software design phase. Even during the build phase, if the needed UI properties, for example, automation id, name, and class name for UI controls, are missing, it will block testers from continuing any UI automation work.

Traditionally, testers create test cases and automation test scripts per user behaviors based on the existing requirements. As a result, a static set of test cases with scripting are created during the build and stabilization phases. If UI design is changed, which is a normal practice during the development of an UI application, the test scripts need to be updated frequently and manually. It results in much maintenance work and is the number one complaint during UI automation. The same issue occurs when a new release comes into the picture.

Furthermore, testers manually design test cases and write test scripts based on requirements. In fact, each tester may create a different set of test cases based on one's experience. As a result, some use cases may be missed during this manual test case design and creation process.

In Figure 1, it displays the traditional software testing activities at different phases of Requirement, Design, Build, and Stabilization. It shows that testers normally start writing test automation scripts at the Build phase and they have to continue updating the scripts through the Stabilization phase, which is the later stage in the project cycle.

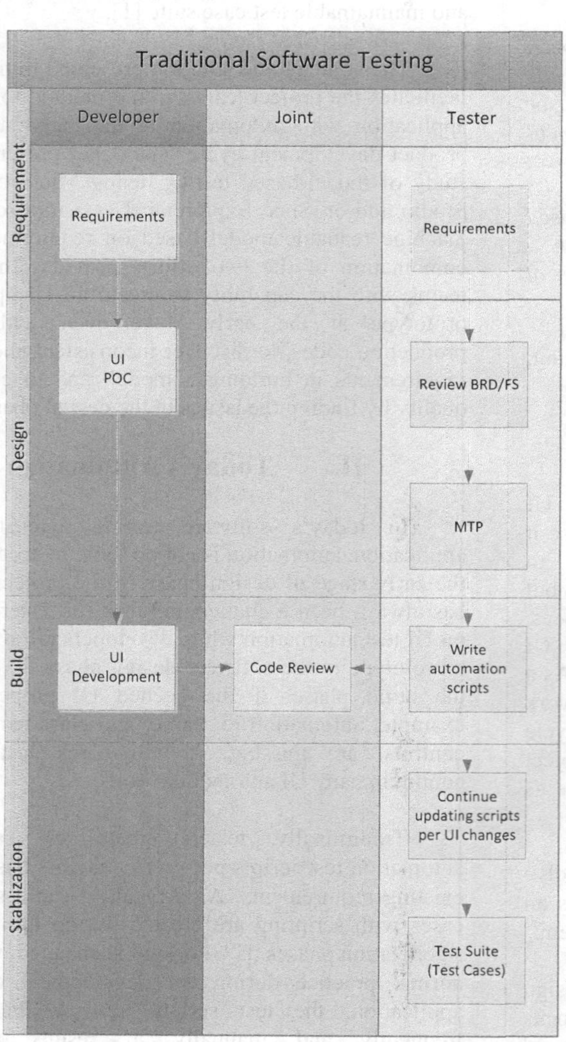

Figure 1 Traditional Software Testing

Basically, there are three major problems by using this traditional software testing process:

- Limited test automation against System Under Test (SUT) at the early stage of the software development cycle.
- High maintenance cost of UI test automation.
- No complete and automatically generated suite of test cases, which cover user behaviors hundred percent.

The vision and recommendation presented in the paper is to use a Model-Based testing technique as an alternative test method to fill the gaps above. Model-based testing is a test technique that system behavior is checked against a model. And the model can be built against the requirements as early as at the design phase.

Since the model is a simpler description of the system under test, it can help us to understand and predict the system's behaviors at the early stage.

It does not need to be an all or nothing approach while testers try to leverage model-based testing. At least, it can help them to fill the existing gaps in the traditional software testing. Particularly, it is feasible to be applied to a complex, state rich, and UI based application due to its internal nature.

III. Model-Based Testing

Model-based testing is a new level of testing, although it has been around for many years. It simulates the user behaviors based on a well-built model by testers. The model is an abstraction of the system under test from a particular perspective.

In Figure 2, it displays a high level conceptual architecture of model-based testing and its related activity components. It shows that testers can start building a system model at the design phase when developers are working on a POC solution, for example, an UI prototype using MS Sketchflow [3].

Testers may have already found some inconsistent, unclear, even missing requirements while building the model. The testers would feedback the findings to the project teams, which should have tremendously improved the requirement inspection effectiveness since it is at the early stage of bug detection process. Of course, it requires the testers to put some up-front effort in the project cycle.

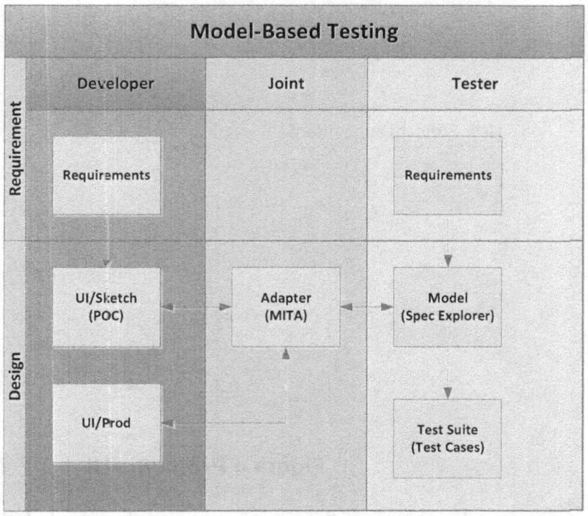

Figure 2 Model-Based Testing

IV. Benefits

A. Benefits

There are a couple of immediate benefits for the project teams by using model-based testing:

- Early stage testing to reduce costs
- Early automaton to detect bug
- Automatic generation of test cases
- 100% coverage of user behaviors
- Easy test script maintenance

In model-based testing, the suite of test cases is automatically generated out of the model by a tool. For example, MS Spec Explorer, it has been integrated with Visual Studio as an extension. There are some advantages by using this tool:

- The test cases are automatically generated.
- The suite of generated test cases covers the most complete paths, and thus it has a better coverage.
- It is easier to maintain the test cases. Each time when a new feature is added, we just need to update the model and re-generate test cases.

B. Challenges

There are some obstacles, especially when it is the first time testers use the model-based testing methodology. Basically, an adapter needs to be developed as a bridge between the UI Prototype and the MS Spec Explorer model.

- Testers are not comfortable to use it at beginning since they are not familiar with the technique.
- The initial effort to build a model is high.
- Need dedicated resources to work on it. A limited tester resource may have assigned to work on requirement inspection as well as the test plan.
- Specific technical skills and tools are required. Testers need to learn those technical skills.
- Testers are capable of making a design suggestion based on the practice of building a model.

In the next section, a case study will be presented on how to create a model, to generate test cases, to bind the model with a system adapter to generate some real test cases against the prototype, and finally to achieve the goal of performing an early stage automation and testing for an UI application.

Although there are some other tools in the market to help with the model-based testing. Here, we use Microsoft Spec Explorer 2010 to demonstrate a case study since it is integrated with Visual Studio well and a VS solution is presented in this case study.

V. A Case Study

A Silverlight UI application is used as an example to elaborate the major steps during a model-based testing.

As a case study, all solution details assume that Microsoft Visual Studio 2010 or greater and .Net are in use. Also, it assumes that Microsoft Spec Explorer 2010 Visual Studio Power Tool and MS Sketchflow are in use.

A. Prototype

In the design phase, developers usually develop a prototype for the purpose of POC based on the existing requirements. By using MS Sketchflow, developers can quickly create a UI prototype which closely mimics the behaviors of a real UI application. It is not required to develop a middle tier or/and backend code.

In Figure 3, it shows a prototype solution named 'Solution MitaApplication' in Visual Studio. For simplicity, it includes a project named

'MitaApplcation', which has only one static class – 'MitaClass' with one static method – 'MainMethod ()'.

MITA (Microsoft Internal Test Automation) is a UI automation framework. In the case study, MITA is leveraged for creating a sample application adapter code. Actually, in the real world, testers can use any other UI automation framework, for example, they can use the Coded UI feature in Visual Studio [4]

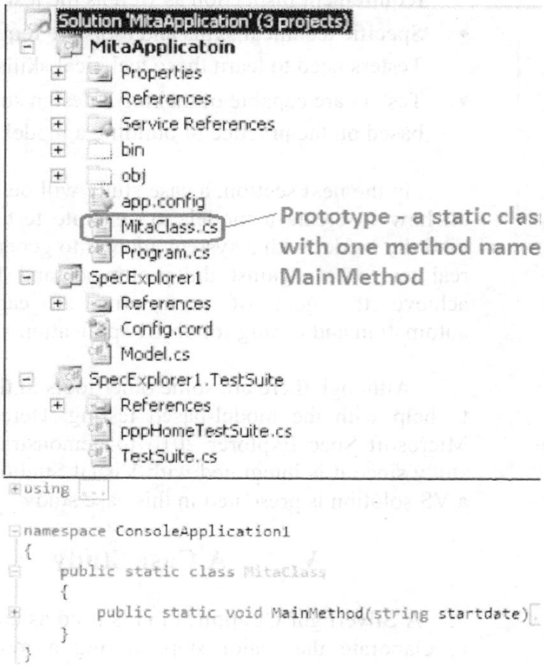

Figure 3 Sample of Prototype Solution

The method MainMethod () represents a test scenario for a UI dashboard prototype in Figure 4, which basically performs the following actions:

1. Launch a Silverlight UI application.
2. Create a new project.
3. Enter the project name and other required items for the project.
4. Enter Start Date for the project.
5. Save the launch project onto the dashboard.

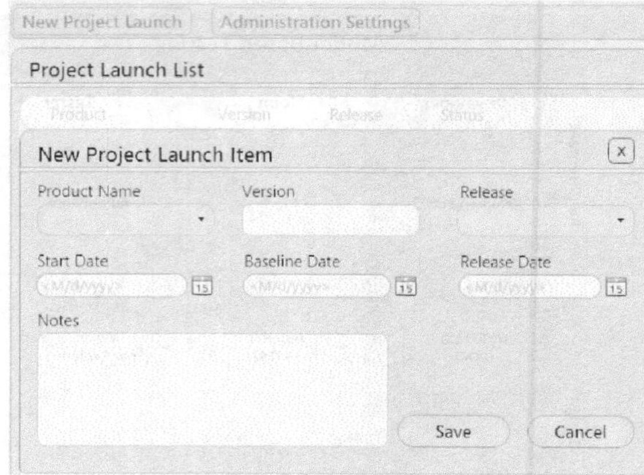

Figure 4 Prototype UI

In practice, there are some tools which help the developers to develop the POC of an UI application, for example, Microsoft Expression Blend [5], which is a design tool to help with creating an UI sketch at the early stage of the project. The tool is easy to use and it has rich feature to create an UI sketch without any middle tier and database associated with it. It enables a developer to deliver on the ideas faster.

B. Model

At the same period of time when developers work on a POC of the application, testers can work on a model per existing requirements, which simulates the system and incorporates all user behaviors. The task is beyond the traditional activities a tester normally works on at the design phase, which is only to inspect the requirements and write a master test plan.

Microsoft Spec Explorer 2010 Visual Studio Power Tool is a tool that extends Visual Studio for modeling software behavior, analyzing that behavior by graphical visualization, model checking, and generating standalone test code from models [2]. Although some initial effort need to be put in building a model, the tool itself is relatively easy to use and the test cases can be automatically generated. Besides, the suite of test cases is more complete than those manually created, and it is designed to cover user behaviors 100%. As a result, it enables testers to detect the bugs at the early stage, in the meanwhile, to maintain the test cases with a better flexibility.

Since Spec Explorer has been integrated with Visual Studio, after its installation, a 'Spec Explorer' menu is created within Visual Studio client as in Figure 5.

Figure 5 Spec Explorer Menu in VS Client

Now, testers can also add a new project of 'Spec Explorer Model' type as shown in Figure 6, which holds a C# model file as well as a configuration coordination file.

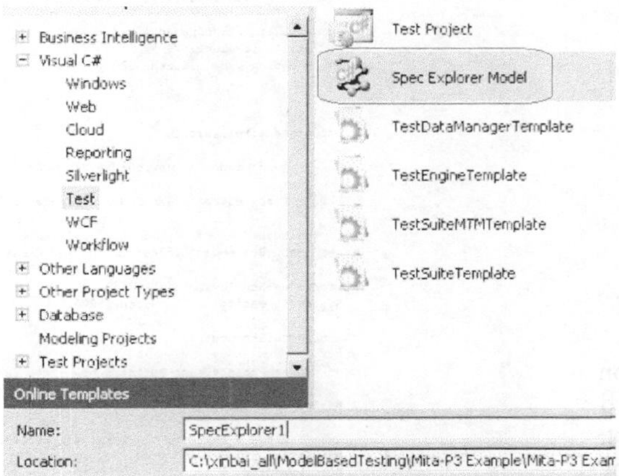

Figure 6 Spec Explorer Model project

While the project is created, there is an option to create a separate test suite project, which holds all of the auto-generated test cases out of the model by Spec Explorer.

In Figure 7, it shows the two projects described above in Visual Studio: SpecExplorer1 and SpecExplorer1.TestSuite.

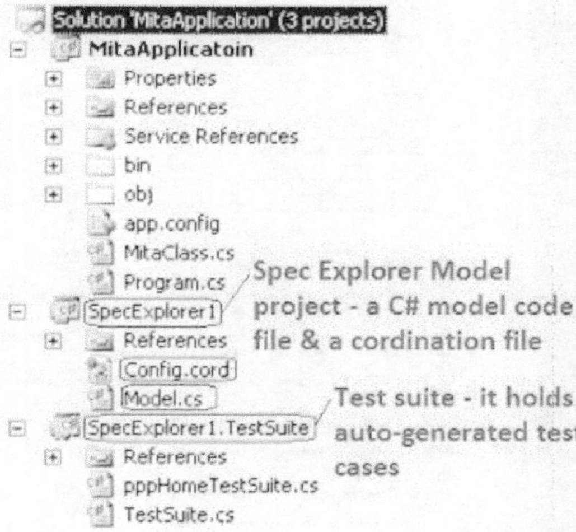

Figure 7 Spec Explorer Model project and Test Suite project

In the project SpecExplorer1, two files are created by defaults: one is 'Model.cs', which holds the C# model codes representing different rules; the other is 'Config.cord', which holds all actions, bounds, switches, and the state machine definitions.

In Figure 8, it displays the content of the model program 'Model.cs' for the case study. The rule in the model program is represented by the test method, here, it is 'MainMethod ()'.

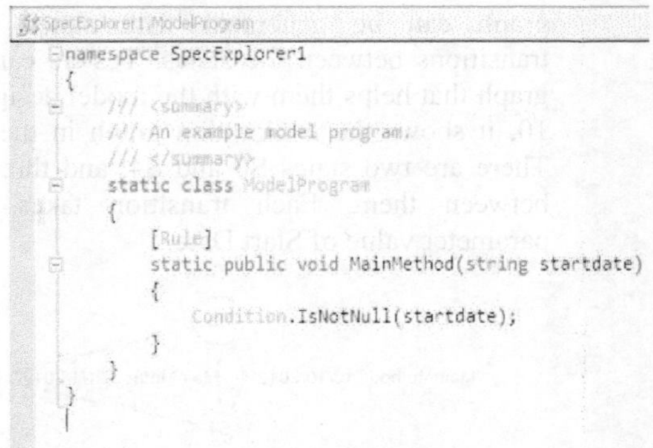

Figure 8 Sample of Model Program

In Figure 9, it displays the content of coordination file 'Config.cord'. It contains actions of the model which is to bind to either a model program or adapter functions. It also defines all of the switches, configurations, main state machine, sliced machines for specific scenarios.

```
// This is a Spec Explorer coordination script (Cord version 1.0)
// Here you define configurations and machines describing the
// exploration task you want to perform.

/// Contains actions of the model, bounds, and switches.
config Main
{
    action all ConsoleApplication1.MitaClass;
    switch StepBound = 10;
    switch PathDepthBound = 10;
    switch GeneratedTestPath = "..\\SpecExplorer1.TestSuite";
    switch GeneratedTestNamespace = "SpecExplorer1.TestSuite";
    switch TestEnabled = true;
    switch TestClassAttribute = "Microsoft.VisualStudio.TestTools.UITesting.CodedUITest";
}

/// This configuration provides a domain for parameter in the previous one.
config ParameterCombination: Main
{
    action abstract static void ConsoleApplication1.MitaClass.MainMethod(string startdate)
        where startdate in {"12/12/2010", "1/1/2011", "3/3/2011"};
}

machine pppHomeModelProgram() : Main where ForExploration = true
{
    construct model program from ParameterCombination where Scope = "SpecExplorer1.ModelProg
}

machine createLaunchProject() : Main where ForExploration = true
{
    (MainMethod) || pppHomeModelProgram
}

machine slicedModelProgram() : Main where ForExploration = true
{
    createLaunchProject || pppHomeModelProgram
}

machine pppHomeTestSuite() : Main where ForExploration = true, TestEnabled = true
{
    construct test cases where strategy = "ShortTests" for slicedModelProgram()
}
```

Figure 9 Sample Coordination File

C. Test Suite

As soon as a model is built based on requirements, Spec Explorer can generate automated test codes and save them in the Test Suite project, which is created in previous Section B. Here, it is the project of 'SpecExplorer1.TestSuite'.

While a model is being built, an exploration graph can be generated with states as well as transitions between the states. Testers can review the graph that helps them with the model design. In Figure 10, it shows the exploration graph in the case study. There are two states S0 and S4, and three transitions between them. Each transition takes a different parameter value of Start Date.

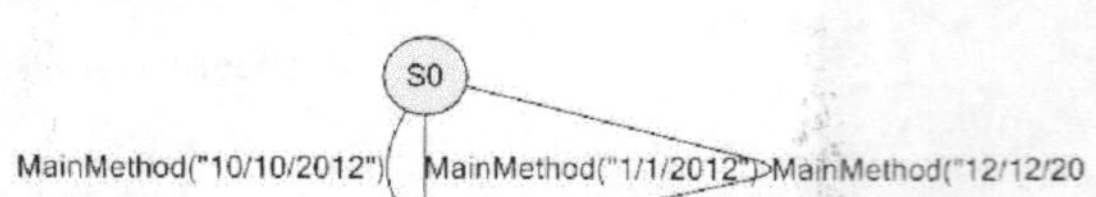

Figure 10 Sample of Exploration Graph

D. Adapter

In previous Section C, a set of test cases are generated by Spec Explorer after a model is developed. Within such a test case, action invocations don't call the system under test directly because they belong to modeling. In order to call a real SUT, an adapter must be developed upon the prototype so that Spec Explorer generates a new set of test cases by binding to the adapter. In Figure 2, it shows how UI/Sketch, Adapter, and Spec Explorer play together.

The adapter codes are part of prototype project 'MitaApplication', which is mentioned in the Section A. For a UI application, the adapter codes hold any functions and user behaviors based on the requirements. Figure 11 shows a sample code of the adapter.

```
namespace ConsoleApplication1
{
    public static class MitaClass
    {
        public static void MainMethod(string startdate)
        {
            WindowOpenedWaiter wmpOpenedWaiter = new WindowOpenedWaiter(UICondition.
            Process.Start("iexplore.exe");
            System.Threading.Thread.Sleep(5000);

            try
            {
                wmpOpenedWaiter.Wait();

                UIObject wmpWindow = wmpOpenedWaiter.Source;

                UIObject addressbar = wmpWindow.Descendants.Find(UICondition.CreateF

                //wmpWindow.Descendants.Find(UICondition.CreateFromName("Address and
                wmpWindow.Descendants.Find(UICondition.CreateFromName("Address and s

                wmpWindow.SendKeys("{ENTER}");
                System.Threading.Thread.Sleep(15000);

                wmpWindow.SetFocus();

                Button newProjectLaunchButton = new Button(wmpWindow.Descendants.Fir

                newProjectLaunchButton.Click();

                ComboBox box = new ComboBox(wmpWindow.Descendants.Find(UICondition.C
                box.SetFocus();
                box.Expand();

                ListBoxItem productitem = new ListBoxItem(box.Descendants.First());
                System.Threading.Thread.Sleep(2000);
                productitem.Select();

                System.Threading.Thread.Sleep(1000);
                box.Collapse();

                UIObject versiontxt = wmpWindow.Descendants.Find(UICondition.CreateF
                versiontxt.SendKeys("1.1");
```

Figure 11 Sample Code of Adapter

Here, in the study case, the adapter codes are in a C# file named 'MitaClass.cs', which has been discussed in the Section A. But for a complex application, it is better to separate the UI element codes. The definition of those UI element objects can be generated by using a tool, for example, the Coded UI feature in Visual Studio.

The Adapter codes for sketch UI can be leveraged to access the production UI controls for automation purpose if the AutomationId and other control properties of the sketch UI are designed to be the same as those of production UI. In Figure 2, it shows how UI/Prod, Adapter, and Spec Explorer play together.

VI. Summary

In software development life cycle (SDLC), early test automation and bug detection are always challenging, but badly desired by the teams since it is going to save many costs and ensure product quality. But, in the early stage, testers may not have access to the development codes, even the prototype codes. Therefore, testers are blocked from starting their test automation. This requires testers to think creatively and work out a different way to do testing. The model-based testing is a strategic methodology to tackle on the challenge.

Traditionally, on one hand, testers create test cases and automation scripts manually based on ones' experience. During the process, some of the important use cases may be missed. On the other hand, the test scripts are piled up as testers try to cover more and more use cases, which make it harder to maintain them, especially for a UI application.

The proposed 'early stage model-based testing for an UI application' can fill these gaps as an alternative way of testing. Testers can start doing some preliminary testing based on the model that they have built and thus find some design bugs at the early stage. Also, by leveraging some tools, such as, Spec Explorer, a complete suite of test cases can be generated automatically and maintained easily.

Finally, testers will achieve a better job satisfaction by doing a model-based testing since they are going to be more involved in creative architecture and design process. Also, they will learn new technology and tools and do more coding by working on the model and adapter with developers.

VII. Acknowledgements

We would like to thank Mrs. Poorvi Shrivastav and Mr. Raghavender Anegouni, the software development engineers in test, and Mrs. Swati Kaul, the team's test manager, in Microsoft MSIT, took time to review the paper or listen to the presentation demo, and provided some valuable feedback.

VIII. References

[1] Nico Kicillof, "What is Model-Based Testing?" http://blogs.msdn.com/b/specexplorer/archive/2009/10/27/what-is-model-based-testing.aspx

[2] MSDN, "Spec Explorer 2010 Visual Studio Power Tool." http://visualstudiogallery.msdn.microsoft.com/271d0904-f178-4ce9-956b-d9bfa4902745

[3] Expression Team, "SketchFlow: An Overview", http://expression.microsoft.com/en-us/ee215229.aspx

[4] Junfeng Dai, "Use Spec Explorer to do UI automation test", http://blogs.msdn.com/b/junfengdai/archive/2010/08/02/use-spec-explorer-to-do-ui-automation-test.aspx

[5] Wikipedia, "Microsoft Expression Blend", http://en.wikipedia.org/wiki/Microsoft_Expression_Blend

Survey of Techniques to Increase Accuracy of Touch Screen Devices

Xiaoyuan Suo
Xiaoyuansuo51@webster.edu
Assistant Professor, Department of Math and Computer Science, Webster University, Saint Louis, MO, USA

Abstract- *The objective of this project is to conduct exploratory research into the effort of increasing accurac on touch screen devices. Graphical password schemes have been proposed as a possible alternative to text-based schemes. Human can remember pictures better than text, thus may contribute to a more positive user experience. Graphical password techniques include recall-based click password (e.g. imposing background image so user can click on various locations on the image), and recognize-based selection password (e.g. selecting images or icons from an image pool).*

Keyword: Touch Screen Design, Human Computer Interactions, Touch Screen Device Accuracy

1 Introduction

Touch-Screen interface designs have attracted rising attention in recent years; devices such as ATM (automated teller machines), ticket machine, PDA (personal digital assistant), have been widely used in various occasions. Lately, Touch-Screen devices are technologically becoming more accurate, usable and popular in any size; such as smart phones, or Apple's iPad, iPhone, and iPod touch [1] etc. Media report estimates that Touch-Screen devices will account for more than 80 percent of mobile sales in North America by 2013[2, 3]. The worldwide market for Touch-Screen mobile devices will surpass 362.7 million units in 2010, a 96.8 percent increase from 2009 sales of 184.3 million units, according to Gartner, Inc. By 2013, Touch-Screen mobile devices will account for 58 percent of all mobile device sales worldwide and more than 80 percent in developed markets such as North America and Western Europe. [2] By 2013, Touch-Screen mobile devices will account for 58 percent of all mobile device sales worldwide and more than 80 percent in developed markets such as North America and Western Europe. [3]

One difficulty for interface design on mobile computers is lack of screen space caused by their small size. Small screens can easily become cluttered with information and widgets, which presents a difficult challenge for interface designers. [4] Small displays and multiple inputs require users to select menus and enter data with pinpoint accuracy. These challenges are especially exacerbated when a user is in motion. Human factors researchers propose improving Touch-Screen targets through a variety of design innovations. Areas of inquiry include changing graphical target size and location, employing mathematical models to expand the target area, minimizing errors with target-specific prompts, and basing outputs on gestures and user histories. [5]

This research involves building surveying existing works on improving accuracy for touch screen devices. In addition, we try to gain a more complete understanding on the following:

a. <u>*Approaches of overcoming limitations of a touch screen computer for graphical password designs.*</u>
Touch screens have special limitations such as: user's finger, hand and arm can obscure part of the screen; and the human finger as a pointing device has very low "resolution". It is also difficult to point at targets that are smaller than the users' finger width.

b. <u>*The relationship between the background color, image choice and the accuracy of touch screen devices.*</u>
When properly selected, we expect background image to positively increase the accuracy of touch screen devices. we define the complexity of an image is as a combinational quantitative measure of the number of objects presented, the number of major colors, and the familiarity of the image to users and other factors. Careful selected background images can enhance effective graphical password design

c. <u>*The relationship between different types of gestures and accuracy*</u>
Users can benefit from using different types of gestures for different purposes on touch screen devices. Although a large screen on a PC would provide more pixels, it allows less interactive methods. We anticipate different types of gestures would provide different user experiences, thus provide different types of accuracy.

2 The Survey

Recent work by Diller [5] studied various techniques to improve input areas of touch screen mobile devices; in this work, multiple approaches and studies were discussed. Our work differs from this work by having a more comprehensive discussion and classification of techniques to increase accuracy of touch screen devices. The intention of this work is to provide fellow researchers and practitioners in the field with a more complete guide to achieve more usable touch screen device designs.

In addition to analyzing properties of tabletop displays and summarizing existing text entry methods for tabletop use; Work by Go et al. [6] also proposed a new keyboard design. In addition to the new design, the work primarily discussed touch screen keyboard use for finger typing; the analysis is from five aspects: screen size, touch screen keyboard types, number of keys, typing devices, and technique. Our work will focus more on the precision of Touch-Screen input.

2.1 Touch Screen Precision

The Touch-Screen device size and the Touch-Screen's effective area affect the Touch-Screen keyboard design. The device sizes can be small, medium, or large. Small Touch-Screen devices[7], such as mobile and smart phones, Personal Digital Assistants (PDAs), and handheld computers, have a smaller Touch-Screen area and smaller onscreen objects. Even though manipulations on smaller devices primarily relied on stylus, finger use has become more popular in the research community since Apple's iPhone and iPod touch were released. Medium-size Touch-Screen devices include standard PCs and tablet PCs. Finally, large Touch-Screen devices contain table-top displays, wall-sized displays and projectors [8]. Recently, researchers started to examine text entry specifically for tabletop displays [9].

There are two types of keyboard: soft keyboard and gesture-based keyboard (menu based) [6]. Soft keyboards can have various keyboard layouts; and a gesture-based keyboard allows the user inputting a gesture, drawing a line without lifting up the finger or stylus.

The QWERTY layout is the standard for soft keyboards, but an alphabetical layout is used as a selection keyboard in some cases. These two layouts are suitable for walk-up-and-use scenarios. [9] Two typical cases for the number of keys include alphabetical (full-size) keyboards such as the 101 keyboard for standard PCs and the numerical 10-key pad for mobile phones. [6]

The work by Parhi et al. [7] is presented to determine optimal target sizes for one-handed thumb use of mobile handheld devices equipped with a touch screen using a two phase study. The study primarily focused on small sized screen. Phase 1 of this study is intended to determine size recommendation for widgets used for single-target tasks, such as activating buttons, radio buttons and checkboxes; while phase 2 is trying to evaluate required key sizes for widgets used for text or numeric entry. The study concluded that no key size smaller than 9.6mm would be recommended for serial tapping tasks, such as data or numeric entry. A 9.2 mm target size for discrete tasks would be sufficiently large for one-handed thumb use on touch screen devices.

Investigations by Sears, A., et al. [10] showed the effect keyboard size has on typing speed and error rates for touch screen keyboards using the lift-off strategy. A cursor appeared when users touched the screen and a key was selected when they lifted their finger from the screen. Four keyboard sizes were investigated ranging from 24.6 cm to 6.8 cm wide. Results indicated novice users can type approximately 10 words per minute on smallest keyboard and 20 words per minute on the largest. Experienced users improved to 21 words per minute on smallest keyboard and 32 words per minute.

Work by Colle and Hiszem estimates the smallest key size that would not degrade performance or user satisfaction. The results showed participants entry times were longer and errors were higher for smaller key sizes, but no significant differences were found between key sizes of 20-25mm. participants also preferred 20 mm keys to smaller keys, and they were indifferent between 20 and 25 mm keys. The work concludes a key size of 20 mm was found to be sufficiently large for land-on key entry. [11]

Three experiments conducted by Lee and Zhai focused on the operation of soft buttons (either using a stylus or fingers). The study showed button size affects performance, particularly when buttons are smaller than 10 mm. Styli can more accurately handle smaller buttons and they depend less on synthetic feedback than fingers do, but they can be lost easily and require an acquisition step that bare fingers do not. The two types of touch sensors explored, capacitive and resistive, afford very different behavior but only subtle performance difference. The first can be operated by fingers with very sensitive response, but is more error prone. [12]

Work by Brewster [4] describes a small pilot study and two formal experiments that investigate the usability of sonically-enhanced buttons of different sizes. An experimental interface was created that ran on a 3Com Palm III mobile computer and used a simple calculator-style interface to enter data. The buttons of the calculator were changed in size between 4x4, 8x8 and 16x16 pixels and used a range of different types of sound from basic to complex. Results showed that sounds significantly improved usability for both standard and small button sizes – more data could be entered with sonically-enhanced buttons and subjective workload reduced. More sophisticated sounds that presented more information about the state of the buttons were shown to be more effective than the standard Palm III sounds. The results showed that if sound was added to buttons then they could be reduced in size from 16x16 to 8x8 pixels without much loss in quantitative performance. This reduction in size, however, caused a significant increase in subjective workload. Results also showed that when a mobile device was used in more realistic situation (whilst walking outside) usability was significantly reduced (with increased workload and less data entered) than when used in a usability laboratory. These studies show that sound can be beneficial for usability and that care must be taken to do testing in realistic environments to get a good measure of mobile device usability.

3 Efforts to Improve Touch-Screen Input Precision

3.1 Tactile Feedback

Many researchers have shown the benefits of tactile feedback for touch screen widgets in all metrics: performance, usability and user experience [13-20]. Koskinen et. al, [20] showed people perceive some tactile feedbacks more pleasant than others when virtual buttons are pressed with fingers on a touch screen.

3.2 Add Sound to Improve Precision

The results from Brewster [4] showed that if sound was added to buttons then they could be reduced in size from 16x16 to 8x8 pixels without much loss in quantitative performance. This reduction in size, however, caused a significant increase in subjective workload.
Early portable computers used either a joystick or trackball as the pointing device. This changed in 1994 when Apple Computer, Inc. [1] introduced the PowerBook 500 series of notebook computers, the first commercial computer with a built-in touchpad as a pointing device[21]. Since then, numerous notebook computer manufacturers also adopted this technology. Today, the trackball is all but extinct in notebook computers. Joystick usage is also down, with IBM and Toshiba remaining as the key players. The touchpad is now the predominant pointing technology for notebook computers. [22]

Being direct between control and display, touch screens also have special limitations. First, the user's finger, hand and arm can obscure part of the screen. Second, the human finger as a pointing device has very low "resolution". It is difficult to point at targets that are smaller than the finger width. These limitations have been realized and tackled before, mostly notably by Sears, Shneiderman and colleagues [10, 23]. Their basic technique, called *Take-Off*, provides a cursor above the user's finger tip with a fixed offset when touching the screen. The user drags the cursor to a desired target and lifts the finger (takes off) to select the target objects. They achieved considerable success with this technique for targets between finger size and 4 pixels. For very small targets (1 and 2 pixel targets), however, users tended to make a large amount of errors with *Take-Off*. To handle small targets, Potter and colleagues [24] used techniques relying on the system's knowledge of target locations, which essentially avoided the need of precise pointing. However, there are many situations where the system cannot know what objects are users' targets. Instead of using a bare finger, in some cases the user may use a stylus (pen) to interact with touch screens. A stylus is a much "sharper" pointer than a finger tip, but its resolution may still not be as good as a mouse cursor. Ren and Moriya investigated different strategies for handling small targets and reported that 1.8 mm (5 pixels) was a crucial limit beyond which special needs arise. [25]

This work [25] also proposed several techniques to improve bare hand pointing on touch screens. The goal is to design techniques allowing users to precisely point at single pixels without resolving to zoom. User studies proved "precision-handle" have promising attributes considering speed, accuracy and comfort. "Precision-handle" is done by using a handle with a smaller scaled tip for increased precision. The handle can stretch or shrink as the user manipulates it. [25] The user studies indicate that the bandwidth of the unsupported index finger is approximately 3.0 bits/s while the wrist and forearm have bandwidths of about 4.1 bits/s. [26]

Subjects attempted to recognize simple line drawings of common objects using either touch or vision. [27]
The author proposed three strategies in this paper:
1. land-on: uses initial touch of the touch screen for selection
2. First contact: user makes selections by dragging their fingers to the desired item.
3. take off: when user make contact with the touch screen, a cursor (<+>) will appear to assist the user, after dragging the cursor, when user is satisfied with its placement, they confirm the selection by removing their finger from the touch screen.

User studies showed the take off strategy had a significantly higher rating of satisfaction; it also showed less errors. [24] The work proposed a pointing technique, which is called *Shift* that is designed to address these issues. When the user touches the screen, Shift creates a callout showing a copy of the occluded screen area and places it in a non-occluded location. [28]

The study by Sears et. al [23]explored touch screen keyboards using high precision touch screen strategies. The work demonstrates touch screen keyboards provided slower speed compare to traditional keyboard. Touch-Screen keyboards may be useful when limited text entry is needed or keyboard is awkward. [23]

Many other works[29] also reconfirmed the fat finger problem through user study. The work also presented two devices that exploit the new model in order to improve touch accuracy. RidgePad prototype extracts posture and user ID from the user's fingerprint during each touch interaction. In a user study, it achieved 1.8 times higher accuracy than a simulated capacitive baseline condition. [29]

The work by Karlson et. al [30] involves the study of a new software based interaction technique called "Thumb Space", which provides general one-handed thumb operation of Touch-Screen based mobile devices. The process includes a few major steps:

1. Defining the ThumbSpace, in this phase, user drag the thumb to define a rectangular shape that user will be comfortable with tapping.
2. Guess, aim and lift. The guess phase requires user to make an initial guess about the sub region with his thumb corresponds to the intended target, and touch the sub-region. in the aim phase, user rolls or drags his thumb to make object cursor animate to the closest displace space object. Finally, user confirms the selection by lifting his thumb.

The user studies showed the ThumbSpace design improves accuracy for selecting targets that are out of thumb reach, and makes users as effective at selecting small targets as large targets. [30]

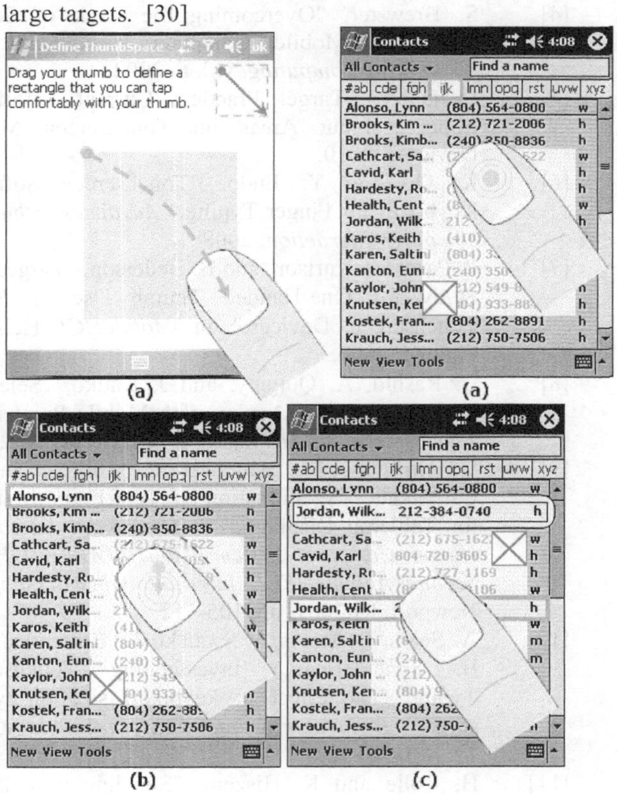

Figure1 : Defining the ThumbSpace. Selecting objects with ThumbSpace. Assuming the user wants to select the first name in the list, he first (a) *guesses* the location of the ThumbSpace proxy for 'Alonso'; (b) the initial ThumbSpace point of contact maps to 'ijk' so the user *aims* for the intended target by dragging his thumb downward. The user confirms the selection by lifting his thumb, or cancels the selection by dragging his thumb to the X before lifting; (c) ThumbSpace occlusion correction. [30]

This user study later conducted about "Thumb Space" [31] was performed on different target size, position and different hand use under walking or standing positions. With a few limitations such as study environment, control of walking pace etc, the conclusions are as follow:

1. Preferred vs. non-preferred hand: about a third of the users sometimes use their non-preferred hand to dial their mobile phones; this finding is different from the use of a mouse, pen or stylus.
2. Standing vs. walking: with limited space of walking (with no real world physical obstacles), the studies suggested walking by itself does not affect performance.
3. Target position and size: the largest target size of 11.5mm in this study generated a 95% accuracy rate. While positions on the left and right edge were not preferred, these provided accuracy rates about 10 percent than those int he middle. Such result confirms that when participants perceived a task to be more difficult and uncomfortable they took longer to thumb tab and were able to be more accurate. [31]

Schildbach and Rukzio [32] used three moderately different target sizes—6.74 mm, 8.18 mm and 9.50 mm in width—per Apple's iPhone Human Interface Guidelines. To extend the real-world environment and determine the impact target size had on cognitive functioning, they asked participants to interact with the device while walking along a pre-determined course. 4 Results showed that increasing target size by up to 40 percent—i.e., from 6.74 x 6.74 mm to 9.5 x 9.5 mm—had a significant impact on decreasing error rates and mitigating the cognitive load demands of walking. Users slowed their normal walking pace when they encountered small targets, and essentially switched focuses from navigating through their environment toward interacting with their Touch-Screen devices. The researchers noted that such a change of attention outside of a controlled experiment might put users at a higher than normal risk for accidents. Therefore, they proposed creating a "walking mode" that presented larger input targets when the user was in motion. Their suggestion attempts to address the balancing act that designers face when trying to optimize a mobile device's Touch-Screen interface: large targets are not always optimal when display space is at a premium, even when they convey significant advantages to users. This complication called for some researchers to investigate mathematical alternatives to interpreting target selection.

Strategy	Details
Land-on 1	Target selected when stylus hits it
Land-on 2	Similar to Land-on 1. but this time the stylus must start outside the target and then move into it
Take-off 1	Target is highlighted when stylus is touching it. selection is made when pen is taken off the target
Take-off 2	Similar to Take-off 1. but the target is selected when the stylus is removed from any point on the screen (either inside or outside the target area)
Space 1	Pen approaches from above. target highlights when stylus is within 1 cm above the target. Selection occurs as soon as the stylus lands on the target
Space 2	Similar to Space 1. except that the selection is made when the pen lands anywhere on the screen (either inside or outside the target area)

Table 1: Selection strategies from Ren *et al.* [33].

In Ren *et al.'s* experiments [34], participants had to select individual targets that appeared in different locations on screen as fast as possible. Their results showed that the Land-on 2 strategy gave the best balance between speed of selection and error rate. This strategy has some problems in real situations as, if there were many targets close together, one might inadvertently select the wrong one by moving over it on the way to the target required. Not all of these strategies are currently implemented on mobile devices (for example, the space strategies relied on an electromagnetic tablet which could sense the stylus when it was above the surface – no current mobile computers work in this way). Many mobile devices implement just the Land-on 1 or Take-off 1 strategies (in the work described below the Take-off 1 strategy was used as the 3Com Palm III only provides this technique).

Some researchers have claimed that the current touch screen technology would not allow high resolution selection, saying that selection of a single character with a touch screen would be slow if it is even possible (Sherr, 1988; Greenstein & Arnaut, 1988). Others have blamed the size of the human finger for the lack of precision, claiming that the size of the user's finger limits the size of selectable regions (Beringer, 1985; Sherr, 1988; Greenstein & Arnaut, 1988). Previous studies have made no attempt at evaluating a touch screen for high resolution tasks, restricting targets to relatively large sizes ranging from a square that is 0.25 inches per side, to targets that were approximately 1.0 x 1.6 inches. In addition, many of these studies have indicated that touch screens result in significantly higher error rates than many other selection devices, including the mouse [24].

4 Conclusion

Touch screen devices represents exciting new frontiers in research and technologies. Touch screen devices are ubiquitous: they encompass portable audio and video players, digital cameras, tablet PCs and PDAs, as well as cell phones and smart phones. A Sept. 2006 *Cellular News* story [35] estimated that there are more than 2.5 billion mobile phones worldwide. In the upcoming decade, we do believe by improving touch screen devices accuracy, user experiences on touch screen devices will be dramatically improved.

5 Reference

[1] Apple, "http://www.apple.com."

[2] Gartner, "Gartner Says Touchscreen Mobile Device Sales Will Grow 97 Percent in 2010," in *http://www.gartner.com/it/page.jsp?id=1313415*, 2010.

[3] K. Fleming, "Report: Touch Screen Mobile Device Sales Booming," in *CRN*, 2010.

[4] S. Brewster, "Overcoming the Lack of Screen Space on Mobile Computers," *Personal and Ubiquitous Computing,* vol. 6, 2002.

[5] F. Diller, "Target Practice: Current Efforts to Improve Input Areas on Touchscreen Mobile Devices," 2010.

[6] K. Go and Y. Endo, "Touchscreen Software Keyboard for Finger Typing," *Advances in human-computer interaction,* 2008.

[7] P. Parhi, A. Karlson, and B. Bederson, "Target Size Study for One-Handed Thumb Use on Small Touchscreen Devices," in *MobileHCI* Helsinki, Finland, 2006.

[8] U. Rashid, A. Quigley, and J. Kauko, "Selecting Targets on Large Display with Mobile Pointer and Touchscreen," in *ITS* Saarbrucken, Germany, 2010.

[9] U. Hinrichs, M. Hancock, C. Collins, and S. Carpendale, "Examination of Text-Entry Methods for Tabletop Displays " in *Horizontal Interactive Human-Computer Systems, 2007. TABLETOP '07. Second Annual IEEE International Workshop on* Newport, RI 2007, pp. 105-112.

[10] A. Sears, D. Revis, J. Swatski, R. Crittenden, and B. Shneiderman, "Investigating Touchscreen Typing: The effect of keyboard size on typing speed " *Behaviour & information technology,* vol. 12, p. 17, 1992.

[11] H. Colle and K. Hiszem, "Standing at a kiosk: Effects of key size and spacing on touch screen numeric keypad performance and user preference," *Ergonomics,* vol. 47, p. 17, 2004.

[12] S. Lee and S. Zhai, "The Performance of Touch Screen Soft Buttons," in *CHI* Boston, MA, 2009.

[13] I. Poupyrev and S. Maruyama, "Tactile interfaces for small touch screens," in *16th annual ACM symposium on User interface software and technology* New York, NY, 2003.

[14] J. C. Lee, P. H. Dietz, W. S. Yerazunis, and S. E. Hudson, "Haptic pen: a tactile feedback stylus for touch screens," in *17th annual ACM symposium on User interface software and technology* 2004.

[15] M. Fukumoto and T. Sugimura, "Active click: tactile feedback for touch panels," in *CHI '01 extended abstracts on Human factors in computing* 2001.

[16] A. Nashel and S. Razzaque, "Tactile virtual buttons for mobile devices," in *CHI '03 extended abstracts on Human factors in computing systems* 2003.

[17] S. Brewster, F. Chohan, and L. Brown, "Tactile feedback for mobile interactions," in *SIGCHI conference on Human factors in computing systems* 2007.

[18] E. Hoggan, S. A. Brewster, and J. Johnston, "Investigating the effectiveness of tactile feedback for mobile touchscreens," in *annual SIGCHI conference on Human factors in computing systems* 2008.

[19] I. Poupyrev, S. Maruyama, and J. Rekimoto, "Ambient touch: designing tactile interfaces for handheld devices," in *15th annual ACM symposium on User interface software and technology* 2002.

[20] E. Koskinen, T. Kaaresoja, and P. Laitinen, "Feel-good touch: finding the most pleasant tactile feedback for a mobile touch screen button," in *10th international conference on Multimodal interfaces* 2008.

[21] M. R. McNeil, A. Kim, J. E. Sung, S. R. Pratt, N. Szuminsky, and P. J. Doyle, " A comparison of left versus right hand, and mouse versus touchscreen access methods on the Computerized Revised Token Test in normal adults and persons with aphasia ".

[22] M. Akamatsu and I. S. MacKenzie, "Changes in applied force to a touchpad during pointing tasks," *International Journal of Industrial Ergonomics,* vol. 2, p. 11, 2002.

[23] A. Sears, "Improving Touchscreen Keyboards: Design issues and a comparison with other devices," *Interacting with computers,* vol. 3, p. 253, 1991.

[24] R. L. Potter, L. J. Weldon, and B. Shneiderman, "Improving the Accuracy of Touch Screens: an Experimental Evaluation of Three Strategies," in *CHI* 1988, 1988.

[25] P.-A. Albinsson and S. Zhai, "High Precision Touch Screen Interaction," in *CHI* Ft. Lauderdale, Florida, USA, 2003.

[26] R. Balakrishnanl and I. S. MacKenzie, "Performance Differences in the Fingers, Wrist, and Forearm in Computer Input Control," in *CHI* Atlanta GA, 1997.

[27] J. M. Loomis, R. L. Klatzky, and S. **J.** Lederman, "Similarity of tactual and visual picture recognition with limited field of view," *Perception,* vol. 20, p. 10, 1991.

[28] **D. Vogel** and **P. Baudisch**, "Shift: A Technique for Operating Pen-Based Interfaces Using Touch," in *CHI* San Jose, California, USA, 2007.

[29] C. Holz and P. Baudisch, "The Generalized Perceived Input Point Model and How to Double Touch Accuracy by Extracting Fingerprints," in *CHI* Atlanta, GA, 2010.

[30] A. Karlson and B. Bederson, "ThumbSpace: Generalized One-Handed Input for Touchscreen-Based Mobile Devices," in *INTERACT'07 Proceedings of the 11th IFIP TC 13 international conference on Human-computer interaction* 2007.

[31] K. Perry and J. P. Hauracade, "Evaluating One Handed Thumb Tapping on Mobile Touchscreen Devices," in *Graphics Interface Conference* Ontario, Canada, 2008.

[32] B. Schildbach and E. Rukzio, "Investigating Selection and Reading Performance on a Mobile Phone while Walking," in *MobileHCI* Lisbon, Portugal, 2010.

[33] X. Ren and S. Moriya, "The Best among six Strategies for Selecting a Minute Target and the Determination of the Minute Maximum Size of the Targets on a Pen-Based Computer," in *INTERACT '97 Proceedings of the IFIP TC13 Interantional Conference on Human-Computer Interaction* Chapman & Hall, Ltd., 1997.

[34] X. Ren and S. Moriya, "Improving selection performance on pen-based systems: a study of pen-based interaction for selection tasks," *ACM Transactions on Computer-Human Interaction (TOCHI) - Special issue on human-computer interaction with mobile systems,* vol. 7, 2000.

[35] http://www.cellular-news.com/story/19223.php, "2.5 Billion Mobile Phones In Use," in *Cellular News*, 2006.

[36] L. Kulik, "Mobile Computing Systems Programming: A Graduate Distributed Computing Course," *IEEE Distributed Systems Online,* vol. 8, p. 5, 2007.

Translating MOKA based Knowledge models into a Generative CAD model in CATIA V5 using Knowledgeware

Lohith ML[1], Laxmi Prasanna[1] and Devaraja Holla Vaderahobli[1]
[1]Engineering Unit, Infosys Limited, Bellevue, Washington, USA

Abstract - *Knowledge based engineering (KBE) is an engineering product development methodology wherein the knowledge of the engineering product and its design process is captured and embedded into a software system (known as KBE applications or systems) and use this system in the design and development of similar new products. Methodology and tools oriented to Knowledge based Engineering Applications (MOKA) provides a consistent methodology for structuring and representing engineering knowledge for the purpose of developing KBE applications. This involves in first building the Informal Knowledge model and then translating this into Formal Knowledge model comprising of the Product Model and the Design Process Model. This Formal Knowledge model can be used for developing the KBE applications in any of the CAD platforms and software technologies. This paper discusses the translation of the MOKA knowledge model into a Generative and Reactive CAD model of the product in a CAD system, specifically in CATIA V5.*

Keywords: KBE, MOKA, CATIA V5 Knowledge-ware.

1 Introduction

In recent years, knowledge based engineering (KBE) has gained significant focus amongst many aerospace and automotive industries in order to have competitive advantage. Significant increase in productivity has been realized through KBE approach by many of these organizations. In this approach advanced software techniques are used to capture and reuse product and process knowledge in an integrated way. KBE is an engineering product development technology wherein the knowledge of the engineering product and its design process is captured and embedded into a software system (known as KBE applications or systems) and use this system in the design and development of similar new products. Stokes et. al [8] have conducted a detailed study of Knowledge Based Systems. These KBE applications usually are tightly integrated with any of the CAD systems (mostly the commercially available CAD systems such as CATIA V5) for the purpose of representing the product specific design data generated by the KBE systems. CAD system vendors have enabled their CAD systems to be customizable for specific needs of the designer. They exposed several programming interfaces (commonly known as Application Programming Interfaces or APIs) and created specific workbenches/tools for customization. Customizations helped the designers to build KBE applications that are tightly integrated with CAD system. But, in recent years, many commercial CAD systems have offered good features and tools that enable efficient modelling of engineering knowledge within CAD system itself, thus significantly reducing the effort required for customization. Knowledge-ware workbenches of CATIA V5 is one such platform that provides good tools and features for building efficient and good KBE applications [2].

Most of the engineering products and their design processes are knowledge intensive. The idea behind KBE is to capture this generic knowledge of the product family within KBE applications and re-use these KBE applications efficiently in the development of new products of similar product family [6], [8]. To enable this to happen, it is essential that these KBE applications have to be continuously enhanced to keep it updated with respect to the continuously evolving and enhancing engineering product design and development methodologies. In addition, software and CAD systems/technologies are also evolving with frequent updates and versions that significantly impacts integrated KBE applications. A structured development methodology for translating the engineering knowledge into software applications (KBE applications) significantly helps to take care of the continuously evolving engineering knowledge and CAD/Software technologies. This ensures re-usability of KBE applications to realize significant productivity improvement over a long period of time. There are several research work reported in the literature related to capturing and representing engineering knowledge corresponding to geometric feature. Bidarra R. et. al [1] have detailed out Semantic Feature Modeling and its advantages over conventional modeling. As part of the semantics, they store heterogeneous data such as, material properties, manufacturing details, as well as topology information. Liu Y. et. al [5] dealt with the implementation of the semantic feature model. They describe semantic feature in a language representation which is defined across different domains in a concurrent engineering environment. Stokes et. al. [8] describe a structured methodology (MOKA) for representing the knowledge from the perspective of building the software applications and is very relevant from KBE perspective. It also supports the representation of various types of knowledge that are involved in the design of any product – structure, function, behavior, representation, manufacturing as well as design process. MOKA (Methodologies and tools Oriented to Knowledge based engineering Applications) involves in first building the Informal Knowledge model and then translating this into formal knowledge model which comprises of the Product Model and the Design Process Model. Creation of these Knowledge models is dealt in detail by Stokes et. al. [8]. The Formal knowledge model can be used for developing the KBE applications in any of the CAD platforms and software technologies.

This paper discusses the approach of translating MOKA based knowledge model into generative CAD model for building KBE application within Knowledge-ware workbenches of CATIA V5. The translation methodology ensures that there is traceability of knowledge between the Knowledge Model and the Generative CAD model, so that any changes in the knowledge (such as rules, constraints) can be easily carried out.

Next section gives an overview of MOKA knowledge models and describes various elements of these models that will be used for building the Generative CAD model. Subsequent section describes the mapping approach for translating various elements of knowledge model using Knowledge-ware tools/features. Finally, this approach has been illustrated with an example and then concluded.

2 Knowledge representation in MOKA knowledge models

KBE technology involves in both the development as well as use of KBE software applications for the design and development of engineering products. Typical life cycle of a KBE application development has been shown in Figure 1, which has been dealt in detail by Stokes et. al [8]. At a higher level, this is similar to any general software development life cycle. However, the methodology for capturing and formalizing the engineering knowledge and how this is translated into KBE software application is unique considering the nature of engineering product development. MOKA provides a structured methodology for structuring and representing the engineering knowledge in the form of Informal and Formal knowledge models which is to be developed during the capture and formalize phases of the KBE life cycle. These knowledge models are independent of any CAD or software technologies. These knowledge models are used as input for developing the KBE software models in specific CAD or software technologies in which the KBE application is intended to be integrated or developed [7], [8]. The various steps involved and the different knowledge models to be developed are shown in Figure 1.

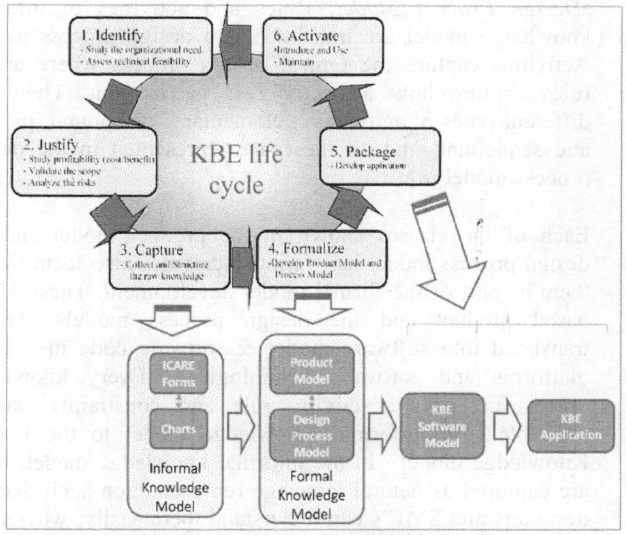

Fig. 1: Overview of KBE Life Cycle

KBE software models and KBE applications are CAD and software technology specific and are built from the Formal knowledge model. There could be more than one KBE software model and application that corresponds to one formal knowledge model.

The first step involved in knowledge modeling is to build the Informal knowledge model, which in turn involves in structuring the knowledge into five categories – Entities, Constraints, Rules, Activities and Illustrations. The first four of these categories are used in building the informal knowledge model and illustrations are like supporting examples to enhance the understanding about the knowledge objects that belong to first four knowledge categories. Apart from identifying various entities, constraints, rules and activities, the relationships amongst these knowledge objects is also identified and represented in the form of charts. Multiple types of charts can be used to represent various knowledge objects and their relationships [8].

Formal knowledge model has two components – product model and the design process model. These models are built using MOKA Modeling Language (MML) which is an extension of Unified Modeling Language (UML) that is typically used in any software design / modeling. Various stereotypes of classes and diagrams are defined as part of MML and these are used in building the formal knowledge model. Informal model is taken as the input for building the formal knowledge model.

•*Product Model*: Entities and constraints of informal knowledge model are translated into Product model. Entities are classified into multiple types – structural, functional, behavioral, representation and technology and then used in various views of the product model. Structural entities form the core of the product model where the structural break-down of the product i.e. various assemblies, parts and features are represented [8].

•*Design Process Model*: Rules and activities of informal knowledge model are translated into design process model. Activities capture the typical design process where as the rules capture how an activity is carried out. There are different types of activities – elementary, compound, parallel and sequential; and all these are represented in the design process model [8].

Each of the classes shown in the product model and the design process model has various attributes also identified in them as part of the formal model development. These MML based product and the design process models can be translated into software model & software code in specific platforms and software technologies. Every knowledge object (i.e. entity, activity, rule and constraint) can be traceable from Informal Knowledge model to the Formal Knowledge model. In the informal knowledge model, these are captured as natural language representation such that the designers and SME's can understand them easily; whereas in the formal knowledge model, these are UML based representations such that the software designers can understand them well; yet maintaining the traceability between Informal and formal knowledge models. The focus of current paper is translating this Formal knowledge model into a Generative CAD model within CATIA V5 Knowledge-ware workbenches by ensuring the traceability of knowledge between Formal Knowledge model and the Generative CAD model.

3 Features of Catia V5 knowledgeware to enable knowledge intensive product design

As mentioned earlier, most of the commercial CAD systems such as CATIA V5 are enabled to be customizable by the designers. Since most of the KBE software applications are built using the customization tools, they are tightly integrated with the CAD system. CATIA V5 provides rich set of Application Programming Interfaces (API's) to customize and build KBE applications on it. In addition, CATIA V5 provides several specialized features in the form of various Knowledge-ware workbenches to enable modeling the knowledge intensive products in an efficient way. Accordingly, there are two ways in which Knowledge models can be used for designing the products in CATIA V5.

3.1 Development of KBE Application using API's

This involves developing the KBE software model by extending the Formal knowledge model and then building the software application using various required API's from CATIA V5 in specific languages such as Visual Basic [10] or C++. The KBE applications thus developed will take the required specific design input such as specifications and then generate the specific design output or CAD model in CATIA V5. As mentioned by Van der Laan et. al [9], ICAD is also used to create KBE application for parametric models.

3.2 Development of Generative models using Knowledgeware

This involves building the generative CAD model of the product (including Assemblies and parts) with all the design knowledge modeled within CATIA V5 using Knowledge-ware features and tools. This Generative CAD model is then instantiated for designing the product with specific design inputs or specifications. The input design parameters and constraints of the generative CAD model are replaced with the actual input specification values to get the corresponding design output or CAD model. All the rules are evaluated automatically within the generative model.

This paper discusses the 2nd approach where the Formal knowledge model is translated into a Generative product model using CATIA V5 Knowledge-ware.

CATIA V5 Knowledge-ware workbenches provide several specialized tools with many features to enable modeling the knowledge intensive products in an efficient way. It defines an Engineering Knowledge Language (EKL) that provides syntax for encoding the engineering knowledge within these workbenches. There are two levels of EKL - Core EKL and the Advanced EKL based on the available key words and symbols in dictionary. Advanced EKL has additional key words and symbols available in the dictionary when compared to Core EKL. Advanced EKL enables the use of advanced features of Knowledge-ware for engineering knowledge representation [2]. Following are some of the important workbenches that are used in building of the Generative model.

1. Knowledge Advisor (KWA)
2. Knowledge Expert (KWE)
3. Product Knowledge Template (PKT)
4. Business Process Knowledge Template (BKT)

Each of these tools has several features that can be directly used for translating various elements of knowledge model into a generative CAD model. The features that are relevant for the current work have been outlined below [2].

3.2.1 Knowledge Advisor (KWA)

Knowledge Advisor workbench allows users to incorporate knowledge within design models and leverage it to assist in engineering decisions, automate repetitive design tasks. Users can incorporate knowledge in design through relations such as formulas, advisor rules, advisor checks, reactions and leverage it as and when required. Advisor Rule is a set of instructions, prescribed based on design conditions.

Advisor Check is used to analyze the value of specific design condition. Advisor Check is basically a set of instructions that are validated whenever there is a change in related parameters. It will not cause any events. A Reaction is similar to Advisor Rule except that it's triggering can be controlled by a defined event. Changes in the event will cause the Reaction to trigger. Reaction is designed to create an associative and reactive model.

3.2.2 Knowledge Expert (KWE)

Similar to KWA, Knowledge Expert workbench allows users to incorporate knowledge within design models. KWE defines a way to specify design rules, checks which must be implemented across the organization so as to ensure best methods and established standards are followed. We can create Expert Rules based on design conditions. Rule Set gathers Expert Rules and Expert Checks. A Rule Base is created at root level in KWE workbench. Rule Base contains several Rule Sets related to Product

3.2.3 Product Knowledge Template (PKT)

Product Knowledge Template as the name suggests enables us to create Templates. These Templates can encapsulate the design methodology at feature, part and assembly level. User defined features (UDF) are created at feature level; Document Templates are created at Part and Assembly levels. UDF's are similar to Power copies with additional capability of encapsulation. We can edit the templates easily through parameters as we do in part design.

3.2.4 Business Process Knowledge Template (BKT)

BKT is oriented towards design process. We can define design process sequence and execute the design process. Technological objects are created in BKT and it contains behaviors. Knowledge elements like rule, check etc can be incorporated through behaviors.

4 Translating MOKA knowledge model into Generative CAD model in Catia V5 knowledgeware

There have been several attempts made earlier, as reported by Emberey et. al, [3] and Skarka et. al. [7], to create KBE applications in CATIA V5 by referring to MOKA based knowledge models. Most of these approaches use Informal Knowledge Model for building the KBE application. Skarka et. al. [7] describes the way the Informal knowledge model has been used for building the generative model in CATIA V5 Knowledge-ware. The focus of this paper is to logically extend the Formal Knowledge model to build the generative CAD model by maintaining the traceability beyond Formal Knowledge Model. Various elements of Knowledge-ware tools such as Rules, Checks and Reactions has been mapped to various elements of Formal Knowledge model. Details of this mapping and other mechanisms for translating Formal Knowledge Models into CATIA V5 Generative Model have been explained in the following sections.

4.1 Translation Method

The overall relationship between various elements of Knowledge model can be illustrated as follows- ***Activity*** creates or modifies an ***Entity***. ***Activity*** is governed by a ***Rule***. ***Entities*** and ***Rules*** are constrained by ***Constraints***. ***Entity*** can be an input for an ***Activity***. This broad level relationship amongst ***Activity-Rule-Constraint-Entity*** (ARCE) has been maintained while arriving at the translation method.
Design Process Model explains the relationship between ***Activity & Rule*** as well as ***Activity &Entity***. Product Model explains the relationship between ***Entity & Constraint***. The two models are connected through relations existing between ***Entity & Activity***. Similar construction is possible in CATIA V5 through Knowledge-ware features. Knowledgeware Behaviors, Rules, Product template/Part template/UDF/Power-copy, and Checks can be used to represent ***Activity***, ***Rule***, ***Entity***, and ***Constraint*** of Formal Knowledge model. These CAD features are connected through formula relation in CATIA V5. Formula relations in CATIA V5 are used to implement the Knowledge relations of Formal Knowledge model. Figure 2 depicts the high level mapping between various elements of the two models.

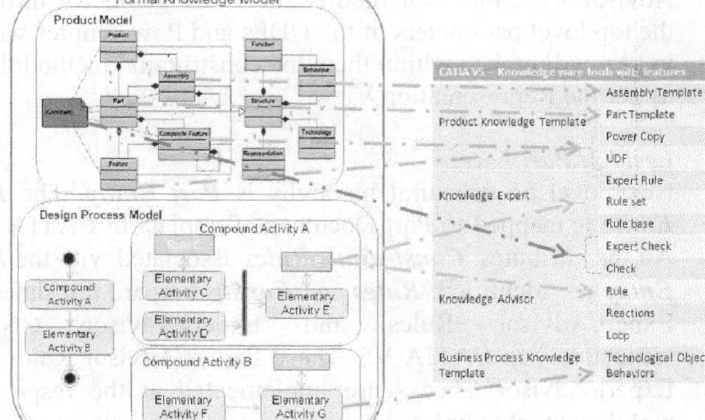

Fig. 2: Mapping of various elements of knowledge models to Knowledge-ware features and tools for implementation.

As mentioned in Section 2, Formal knowledge models have two components, Design Process model and Product model. When starting from Product Model, ***Entities*** are taken as the starting point for modeling. ***Entities*** of ***Product*** and ***Assembly*** types are translated to Product Document Templates in CATIA V5. ***Entities*** of ***Part*** type are translated to Part Document Templates in CATIA V5. ***Entities*** of ***Composite Feature*** & ***Feature*** types are translated to either UDF or Powercopy. Structure View of the product model shows the structural decomposition of the Product. Product Model translation is done at three levels based on the Structural decomposition of the Product.

1. ***Composite Features*** and ***Features*** Level
2. ***Part*** Level
3. ***Assembly*** Level

*Level 1: **Composite Features** and **Features** Level*

For every ***Features*** and ***Composite Feature***, all of the relevant ***Rules*** and ***Constraints*** are first identified. All the identified ***Rules*** are translated to Expert / Advisor Rules. Similarly, all the identified ***Constraints*** are translated to Expert/Advisor Checks. The attributes of ***Constraints*** and ***Rules*** are translated to parameters in Advisor Check/Expert Check and Expert/ Advisor Rules respectively. These Expert /Advisor Rules and Expert/Advisor Checks are implemented at the part document template level where the corresponding ***feature*** or ***composite feature*** resides. Corresponding to this ***feature*** or ***composite feature***, either a UDF or a power copy is created such that the CAD geometry construction methodology of the UDF/Powercopy is in line with the Representation view of the ***feature*** or ***composite feature***. The Expert/Advisor Rules themselves will modify the related parameters that in turn drive the CAD geometry. The sequence of ***activities*** are indirectly realized though the dependencies of the parameters as far as possible. For ***Activities*** that could not be realized through the parameter dependencies, it is realized by creating Advisor Reactions, whose triggering can be controlled. Advisor reactions can also drive CAD geometries. The Expert/Advisor Rules or Advisor Reactions can modify the CAD geometry through the top level parameters of the UDFs and Powercopies which in turn will embed within them the construction methodology as per the Representation View.

*Level 2: **Part** Level*

Next level of structural hierarchy is ***Part Entity***. The ***Part Entity*** is mapped to Part Document Template in CATIA V5. All the attributes, ***Constraints***, ***Rules*** associated with the ***Part Entity*** are identified. ***Rules*** and ***Constraints*** are translated to Expert/Advisor Rules and Expert/Advisor Checks respectively in CATIA V5. These Expert/Advisor Rules and Expert/Advisor Checks are implemented at the respective part document template level. The interaction between Expert /Advisor Rules, Expert/Advisor Checks, Advisor reaction and UDFs/Powercopies is similar to that mentioned in "***Composite Features*** and ***Features*** Level" section. The CAD geometry construction methodology of this part document template is in line with the Representation view of the ***Part Entity.***

*Level 3: **Assembly** Level*

Next higher level of structural decomposition is ***Assembly Entity***. The ***Assembly Entity*** is mapped to Product Document Template in CATIA V5. All the Attributes, ***Constraints***, ***Rules*** associated with the ***Assembly Entity*** are identified. ***Rules*** and ***Constraints*** are translated to Expert/Advisor Rules and Expert/Advisor Checks respectively in CATIA V5. These Expert/Advisor Rules and Expert/Advisor Checks are implemented at the respective product document template level. The attributes of ***Constraints*** are translated to parameters in Advisor Check/Expert Check. The Expert/ Advisor Rules themselves will modify the related parameters that in turn drive the assembly level instances and their relationships. The sequence of ***activities*** are indirectly realized though the dependencies of the parameters as far as possible. For ***Activities*** that could not be realized through the parameter dependencies, are realized by creating Advisor Reactions at product template level, whose triggering can be controlled. Advisor reactions can also drive the assembly level instances and their relationships. The assembly construction methodology (instances and their relationships) will be such that it is in line with the Representation view of the ***Assembly Entity.***

While starting from Product Model, ***Entity-Rules-Constraints*** are created first which to some extent captures the ***Activity*** flow through parameter dependencies. Then for the ***Activities*** that are not captured through parameter dependencies, Advisor Reactions are used to complete ARCE relationship.

This approach is a template based approach, where the entire assembly structure is created upfront with all the embedded rules and constraints where as the previous approach is a creation from scratch approach where the CAD geometries are created when the technological object is instantiated.

As mentioned in the previous section traceability has been the key consideration in arriving at the mapping methodology between Formal knowledge model and CATIA V5 Knowledge ware features. Various knowledge objects such as ***Activity***, ***Entity***, ***Constraint***, ***Rules*** that are present in the Informal knowledge Model, could be traceable to the Formal Knowledge Model. Similar traceability is maintained while translating Formal Knowledge Models into CATIA V5 Generative Model. At a high level, Product knowledge model gets translated through PKT and Design process Model gets translated through BKT. There is a one to one correspondence between ***Rule*** of knowledge model to the Rule within Knowledge ware. All the ***Constraints*** are mapped to the Checks of Knowledge ware. All the parameters of ***Entity***, ***Rule*** or ***Constraint*** are translated as Parameters of CATIA V5 with proper categorization. Change in parameter of any CAD geometry is reflected through dependent parameters because parameters are linked through formulae. The parameter linkages follow ARCE relationship thus ensuring traceability.

5 Conclusion

Though Knowledge based engineering approach stresses more on the re-use of knowledge and the KBE applications, there have been lots many challenges in realizing this especially because of frequent enhancements/changes in the software technology as well as product development technologies. Structured KBE application development methodology with traceability of knowledge across the KBE life cycle will play crucial role in ensuring that the knowledge is made re-usable over a long period of time. MOKA based Knowledge modeling methodology provides a very good foundation in terms of Informal and Formal knowledge models having very good traceability amongst them. This paper focuses on logically extending this to create the generic CAD model within CATIA V5 by translating Formal Knowledge model; by ensuring that the knowledge is traceable till the generic CAD model. Though the CAD model can be generated in many ways and many other CAD systems, the focus of this paper was specific to CATIA V5 – Knowledge-ware. However, the similar approach can be thought of for other CAD systems as well.

6 References

[1] Bidarra R., Bronsvoort W.F.: Semantic feature modeling, Computer-Aided Design 32 (2000) 201–225 doi:10.1016/S0010-4485(99)00090-1

[2] Dassault Systemes, http://www.3ds.com/ , CATIA CAD Software, Version 5 Release 21

[3] Emberey C.L., Milton N.R.: Application of Knowledge Engineering Methodologies to Support Engineering Design Application development in Aerospace, American Institute of Aeronautics and Astronautics, 2007

[4] IBM, http://www.ibm.com/, Rational Rhapsody Software, Version 7 Release 1

[5] Liu Yong-Jin, Lai Kam-Lung, Dai Gang, and Yuen Matthew Ming-Fai: A Semantic Feature Model in Concurrent Engineering, IEEE TRANSACTIONS ON AUTOMATION SCIENCE AND ENGINEERING, VOL. 7, NO. 3, JULY 2010

[6] Pinfold M., Chapman Craig, Preston Steve: Knowledge acquisition and documentation for the development of a KBE system for automated FE analysis, Int. J. Knowledge Management Studies, Vol. 2, No. 2, 2008, 163-174 doi:10.1504/IJKMS.2008.018319

[7] Skarka Wojciech: Application of MOKA methodology in generative model creation using CATIA, Engineering Applications of Artificial Intelligence, 20, 2007, 677–690 doi:10.1016/j.engappai.2006.11.019

[8] Stokes, M.: Managing Engineering Knowledge, MOKA: Methodology and Tools Oriented to Knowledge Based Engineering Applications, Professional Engineering Publishing Ltd, London, United Kingdom, 2001

[9] Van der Laan A.H., Van Tooren M.J.L.: Parametric Modeling of Movables for Structural Analysis, American Institute of Aeronautics and Astronautics, 2004

[10] Vermeulen B., Van Tooren M.J.L.: Implementation of an Automated Detailed Design Tool (ADDET) in the Design Process for FML/Glare Fuselage Panels, American Institute of Aeronautics and Astronautics, 2007

FPGA Synthesis of Glucose-Insulin Feedback System

Sourav Dutta[1] , Nazeih M. Botros[2]

Abstract—**Goal of this paper is to develop a hardware realization of Insulin-Glucose feedback system based on FPGA. Behavioral modeling of the mechanism is developed with the aid of Hardware Description Language(HDL). Digital Differential Analyzer (DDA) algorithm is used in order to solve the mathematical model of insulin glucose dynamics. The simulation is synthesized using Xilinx Design Suite (9.1i) and downloaded into a Combinational Complex Programmable Logic Device (CPLD) / Field Programmable Gate Array (FPGA) Xilinx XSA-50 microchip.**

***Keywords*—Insulin-Glucose feedback system, FPGA synthesis, Digital Differential Analyzer, Pulsatile Insulin.**

I. INTRODUCTION

As with the design of any compound engineering system, realistic computer simulation can provide vital information about the safety and confines of algorithms, can guide and focus the emphasis of clinical studies, and can out-rule unrealistic scenarios in a cost-effective manner prior to human use. In the area of diabetes, accurate computer-simulation prediction of clinical trials has been done by the Archimedes diabetes model [1, 2]; a company—Entelos Inc. specializes in predictive bio simulation and in particular has developed a diabetes simulator. The ability of recent diabetes simulators are narrowed to prediction of average population that would be observed during clinical trials because these simulators are based on population models. For this reason a different kind of computer based simulator is needed in order to realize the function of artificial pancreas which should be capable of simulating the glucose–insulin dynamics of an individual. Various glucose–insulin models [6], [7-9] have been developed to serve this purpose.

In the glucose–insulin endocrine metabolic regulatory system, the two pancreatic endocrine hormones, insulin and glucagon, are the primary regulatory factors. Numerous in vivo and in vitro experiments have revealed that insulin secretion consists of two oscillations occurring with different time scales: rapid oscillations having a period of 5–15 min [10] and ultradian oscillations occurring in the period of every 50–150 min [11-13]. Considerable amount of work has been done in the field of biological simulation. Botros et al modeled biological mechanism such as human growth hormone secretion and simulated it using FPGA [3- 5].

In this paper we synthesize the glucose-insulin model developed by Tolic et al. The FPGA chip is tested by comparing its output with that of the afore mentioned paper [tolic]. In the paper Tolic et al developed a set of differential equations which can successfully describe the glucose – insulin feedback system. Solving these differential equations in a digital environment is a challenge because digital computing has also its limitations. Thus, recently some researchers are exploring ways to return to the use of the analog computing method again [14], especially in cases where ultrafast speed of the solving process is needed (real-time simulation).

II. MATHEMATICAL MODEL OF GLUCOSE – INSULIN MECHANISM

Numerous in-vivo and in-vitro experiments have shown that insulin concentration oscillates in two different time scales: rapid oscillation with a period of 5-15 minutes and ultradian oscillation with a range of 80-150 minutes ([11], [10], [13] and [15]).Ultradian oscillations of insulin concentration are believed to be mainly due to glucose interaction in the plasma and instability in the insulin-glucose feedback system([11], [12], [13] and [16]).

To determine whether the ultradian oscillations could result from the interaction between insulin and glucose, a parsimonious nonlinear mathematical model consisting the six ordinary differential equations including the major mechanisms involved in glucose regulation was developed by J. Sturis, K. S. Polonsky, E.Mosekilde and E. Van Cauter ([11]) in 1991 and recently simplified by I. M. Tolic, E. Mosekilde and J. Sturis ([12]) in 2000. The purpose of these two models was to provide a possible mechanism for the origin of the ultradian insulin secretion oscillations.

To determine whether the ultradian oscillations could result from the interaction between insulin and glucose, a parsimonious nonlinear mathematical model consisting the six ordinary differential equations including the major mechanisms involved in glucose regulation was developed by J. Sturis, K. S. Polonsky, E.Mosekilde and E. Van Cauter ([11]) in 1991 and recently simplified by I. M. Tolic, E. Mosekilde and J. Sturis ([12]) in 2000.

[2]Professor Nazeih M Botros is with Department of Electrical and computer Engineering , Southern Illinois University, Carbondale.IL-62901-6603. He is a senior member of IEEE and the coordinator of Biomedical Engineering at SIUC.
Email : botrosn@siu.edu

[1]Sourav Dutta is a PhD student at Department of Electrical and computer Engineering , Southern Illinois University, Carbondale.IL-62901-6603
Email : sourav@siu.edu

The simplified model takes the form:

$$\frac{dI_p}{dt} = aI_p + bI_i + cG + d \quad (1)$$

$$\frac{dI_i}{dt} = eI_p + fI_i \quad (2)$$

$$\frac{dG}{dt} = gI_iG + hG + kx_3 + p \quad (3)$$

$$\frac{dx_1}{dt} = r(I_p - x_1) \quad (4)$$

$$\frac{dx_2}{dt} = r(x_1 - x_2) \quad (5)$$

$$\frac{dx_3}{dt} = r(x_2 - x_3) \quad (6)$$

The model has three main variables: the amount of glucose in the plasma and intercellular space, *G*, the amount of insulin in the plasma, I_p ,and the amount of insulin in the intercellular space, I_i. In addition, there are three variables x_1, x_2 and x_3 that represent the delay between insulin in plasma and its effect on the hepatic glucose production.
Values of the parameters *a,b,c,d,e,f,g,h,k,p,r* are taken from the paper [9].

III. FPGA IMPLEMENTATION AND ARCHITECTURE

In order to synthesize the glucose – insulin system using FPGA, Digital Differential Analyzer (DDA) algorithm is used to write the Hardware Description Language (HDL).
A digital differential analyzer (DDA), also sometimes called "digital integrating computer", is a digital implementation of the differential analyzer. The integrators in DDA are implemented as accumulators, whereby the numeric results are converted back to a pulse rate by the overflow of the accumulator. The main advantage of the digital integrator, when compared to an analog integrator, is the scalable precision. Also, in a digital integrator based on DDA, we don't have drift errors and noise [17] due to the imperfection of electronic components. By accumulation over time of values in a register we can calculate the integral of signals. The basic digital integrator is expressed by (7).

$$V_{n+1} = V_n + K.S \quad (7)$$

In (7), Vn+1 denotes the next state of the accumulator used for calculating the integral. The coefficient of *K* is a constant factor that is less than 1; it is used for time scaling. In this equation *S* denotes the input signal for integration. We can map this technique on FPGA very easily by writing a behavioral code. After each rising clock pulse, the equation updates the integral value. In this integrator, Rounding or truncation errors are only due to the limitation of registers.
Fig 1 shows the architecture of the DDA based differential equation solver which is downloadable to the FPGA chip.
The multiply is replaced by a shift-right as `dt` is chosen to be a power of two.

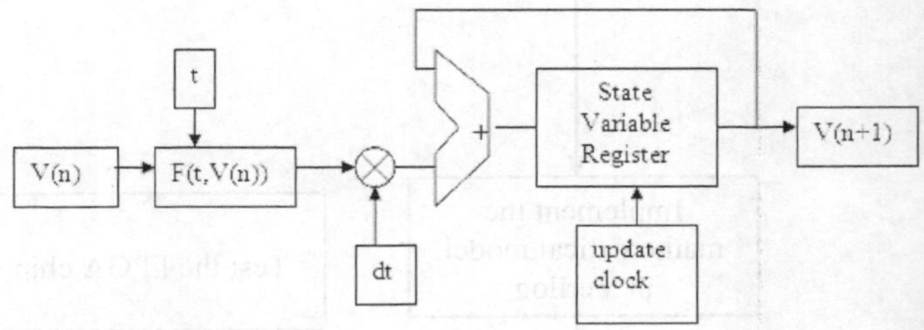

Fig 1: Hardware architecture of Digital Differential Analyzer

We can rewrite equations (1) – (6) by applying DDA as follows:

$$I_{p(n+1)} = I_{p(n)} + \left(aI_{p(n)} + bI_{i(n)} + cG(n) + d\right) \times dt \quad (8)$$

$$I_{i(n+1)} = I_{i(n)} + \left(eI_{p(n)} + fI_{i(n)}\right) \times dt \quad (9)$$

$$G(n+1) = G(n) + \left(gI_{i(n)}G(n) + hG(n) + kx_3(n) + p\right) \times dt \quad (10)$$

$$x_1(n+1) = x_1(n) + r\left(I_{p(n)} - x_1(n)\right) \times dt \quad (11)$$

$$x_2(n+1) = x_2(n) + r(x_1(n) - x_2(n)) \times dt \quad (12)$$

$$x_{3(n+1)} = x_{3(n)} + r\left(x_{2(n)} - x_{3(n)}\right) \times dt \quad (13)$$

IV. EXPERIMENTAL RESULTS

The FPGA technology provides a programmable interface to enable us to synthesize complex behavior models. FPGA chips Configurable Logic Blocks (CLBs) can be personalized to represent different models. The three distinguishing features of FPGAs chip: ***architecture, function-unit granularity and intra/inter-chip wiring organization*** can be fine-tuned to represent complex models in a fairly short period of time. Combined with HDL tools, we have a powerful tool to represent and synthesize the mathematical model.
In this experiment we used Xilinx ISE design suit 9.1i and the XSA-50 board which is equipped with *SPARTAN-2* type FPGA. The inbuilt clock signal is used to perform the experiment in a real time environment.
The steps of the experiment are shown in the Fig. 2 and Table 1 shows the numerical values of glucose and insulin after FPGA synthesis.

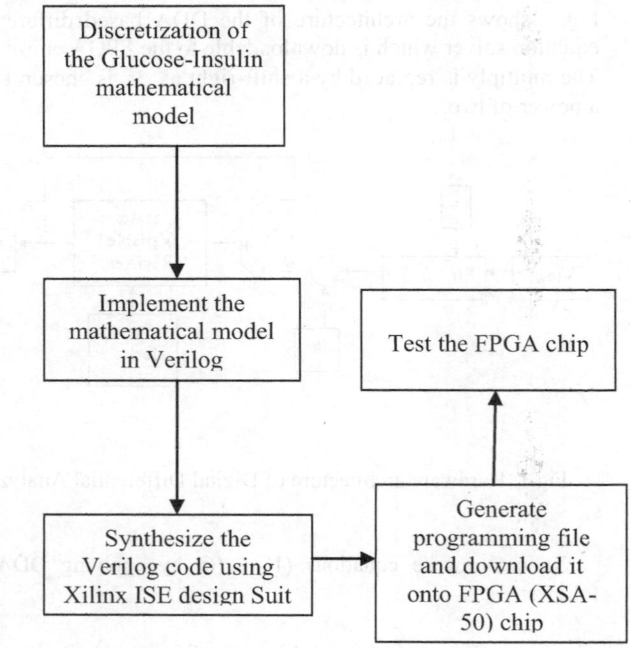

Fig 2. Implementation of the mathematical model onto the FPGA chip.

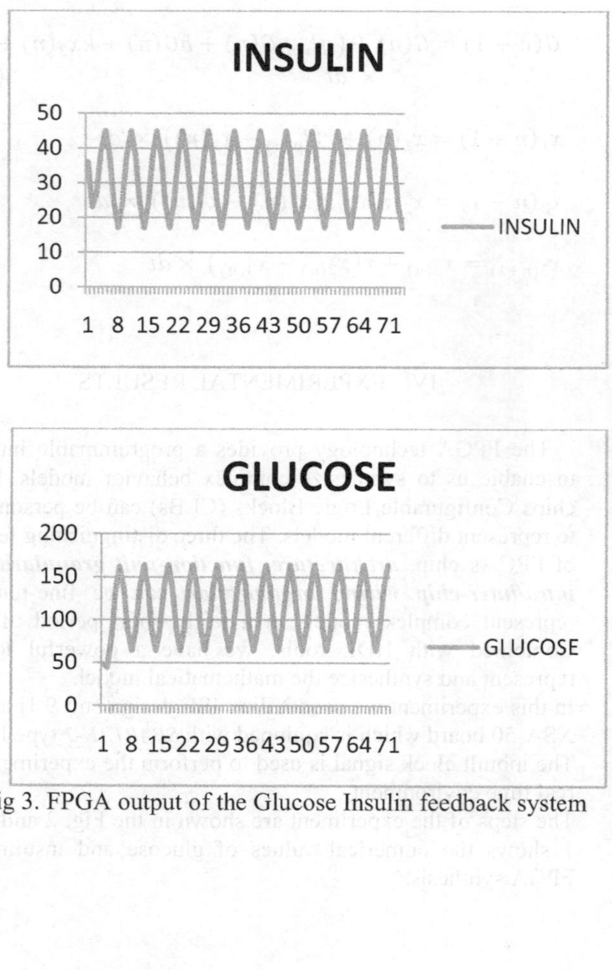

Fig 3. FPGA output of the Glucose Insulin feedback system

TABLE 1. Numerical values of glucose and insulin

TIME	INSULIN (Mg/dl)	GLUCOSE (Mg/dl)
1	36	48
2	23	44
3	27	79
4	39	134
5	45	162
6	38	138
7	24	89
8	17	64
9	24	89
10	38	139
11	45	164
12	38	139
13	24	89
14	17	64
15	24	89
16	38	139
17	45	164
18	38	139
19	24	89
20	17	64
21	24	89
22	38	139
23	45	164
24	38	139
25	24	89
26	17	64
27	24	89
28	38	139
29	45	164
30	38	139
31	24	89
32	17	64
33	24	89
34	38	139
35	45	164
36	38	139
37	24	89

Fig 3.illustrates the numerical values of Glucose and Insulin. We used Microsoft excel in order to visualize the glucose insulin oscillations as described in the paper [9].

TABLE 2. Resources used by FPGA

Device Utilization Summary (estimated values)			
Logic Utilization	**Used**	**Available**	**Utilization**
Number of Slices	48	768	6%
Number of Slice Flip Flops	32	1536	2%
Number of 4 input LUTs	83	1536	5%
Number of bonded IOBs	9	92	9%
Number of GCLKs	1	4	25%

The number of resources used after synthesis for solving the Gluocse Insulin dynamical equations, Flip-Flop slices and 4-Input LUT Slices are shown in the Table 2.

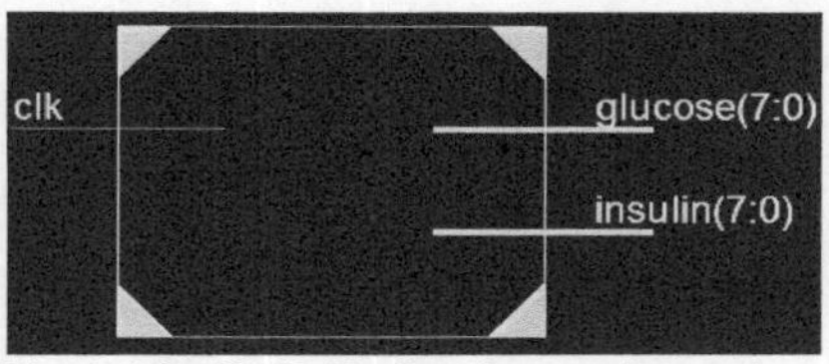

Fig 4. The RTL Technology schematic

Fig 4. Illustrates the chip developed by the Xilinx ISE design suite. The input is the clock signal and output is the glucose and insulin signals. Each of them is 8 bits wide.

The following figure shows the input clock signal and the output Glucose and Insulin signal after simulation using the Isim simulator provided by Xilinx ISE .

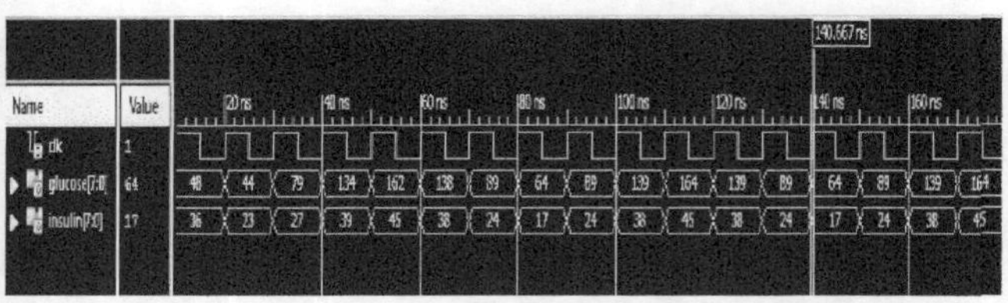

Fig 5.Isim simulation output of the Glucose Insulin feedback Model.

V. FUTURE WORK

In this paper we synthesized a constant glucose insulin feedback system. It is possible to see the response of insulin after meal injection or random glucose input. From hardware design perspective, generating the HDL code for solving dynamic equations by a flow diagram can be done in future. For modeling a complex system the future program will be node-based. After coupling nodes by either code or a GUI, the program will be able to generate a gate level HDL code for direct programming on FPGA. By this technique we can speedup the design and implementation process of analog computing solvers on FPGA, which will be capable of solving complex differential equations and simulating complex systems in real time on FPGA.

VI. CONCLUSION

We have used a previously successful mathematical model that describes the Glucose - Insulin feedback system patterns in humans to generate a blueprint for a microchip and generated a bit file to the prototyping board and produced some simulated hormone level figures from the chip. The result shows that the FPGA chip can successfully mimic the ultradian oscillation as described in the paper [12]. In future this research can lead us to develop a pocket friendly easy to maintain insulin pump which can secret insulin based on the meal injection in a purely digital environment.

REFERENCES

[1] Eddy DM, Schlessinger L. Archimedes: a trial-validate model of diabetes. Diabetes Care. 2003;26:3093–3101

[2] Eddy DM, Schlessinger L. Validation of the archimedes diabetes model. Diabetes Care. 2003;26(11):3102–3110.

[3] Botros, N., Akaaboune, A., and Alghazo, J., "Modeling, Synthesis And Realization of HGH Mechanism Using VHDL And FPGAs," International Journal on Simulation and Modeling, Vol. 25, No. 4, pp.285-290, 2005.

[4] Botros, N., "Modeling and Realizing Biological Mechanisms On FPGAs Chip," Proceedings of the World Congress on Medical Physics and Biomedical Engineering, Chicago, IL, July24-27, 2000.

[5] Botros, N., Akaaboune*, M., Alghazo*, J., and Alhreish*, M., "Hardware Realization of Biological Mechanisms Using VHDL and FPGAs," Proceedings of the Third International Conference on Modeling and Simulation of Microsystems, San Diego, CA, March 27-30, pp. 233-236, 2000

[6] Sorensen JT. A physiologic model of glucose metabolism in man and its use to design and assess improved insulin therapies for diabetes. Ph.D.

[7] Dalla Man C, Rizza RA, Cobelli C. Meal simulation model of the glucose–insulin system. IEEE Trans Biomed Eng. 2007;54(10):1740–1749.

[8] Dalla Man C, Raimondo DM, Rizza RA, Cobelli C. GIM, simulation software of meal glucose–insulin model. J Diabetes Sci Technol. 2007;1(3):323–330.

[9] Hovorka R, Canonico V, Chassin LJ, Haueter U, Massi-Benedetti M, OrsiniFederici M, Pieber TR, Schaller HC, Schaupp L, Vering T, Wilinska ME. Nonlinear model predictive control of glucose concentration in subjects with type 1 diabetes. Physiol Meas. 2004;25(4):905–920.

[10] N. Pørksen, M. Hollingdal, C. Juhl, P. Butler, J. D. Veldhuis and O. Schmitz, Pulsatile insulin secretion: detection, regulation, and role in diabetes, Diabetes, 51 (2002), S245–S254.

[11] J. Sturis, K. S. Polonsky, E. Mosekilde, E. Van Cauter, Computer-model for mechanisms underlying ultradian oscillations of insulin and glucose, Am. J. of Physiol., 260 (1991), E801–E809.

[12] Tolic, I.M., Mosekilde, E., Sturis, J., 2000. Modeling the insulin Glucose feedback system: the significance of pulsatile insulinsecretion J Theor Biology. 207, 361- 375 .

[13] C. Simon and G. Brandenberger, Ultradian oscillations of insulin secretion in humans, Diabetes, 51 (2002), S258–S261

[14] Bruce J. MacLennan, "Review of Analog Computing". Technical Report,Department of Electrical Engineering & Computer Science Universityof Tennessee, Knoxville (2007).

[15] E. T. Shapiro, H. Tillil, K. S. Polonsky, V. S. Fang, A. H. Rubenstein, and E. Van Cauter, Oscillations in insulin secretion during constant glucose infusion in mormal man: relationship to changes in the plasma glucose, J. Clin. Endocrinol.Metab., 67 (1988), 669–674.

[16] A. Mari, Mathematical modeling in glucose metabolism and insulin secretion, Curr. Opin. Clin. Nutr. Metab. Care, 5(2002), 495-501.

[17] K. Sivaranjani, J. Venkatesh and P. A. anakiraman, "Realization of a Digital Differential Analyzer using CPLDs," in International Journal ofModeling and Simulation 27(3), 280 (2007).

SESSION

VISUALIZATION, HCI, FUZZY LOGIC, MANET, AND APPLICATIONS

Chair(s)

Prof. Hamid Arabnia
University of Georgia

Fast detection and visualization with Parallel Coordinates of Automated Living Context-Awareness Environments

Pei Ling Lai[1] Jin Fu Chen[2] Shih Chung Chen [2] Jin Liang Yang[1]
[1]Dept. of Electronics Engineer
[2]Dept. of Electrical Engineer
Southern Taiwan University of Science and Technology, Tainan, Taiwan, R.O.C.
Correspond email: pllai@mail.stust.edu.tw

Alfred Inselberg
School of Mathematical Science, Tel Aviv University, Tel Aviv Israel, aiisreal@math.tau.ac.il

Abstract—This paper presents *The parallel Coordinates Automated Living Context-Awareness Visualization (PCALCAV)*. The system applies to the maintenance of health care for disabled/elderly people by monitoring their health status and their caretakers activities daily routines in their own environment. This includes, the number and time of door openings, the length of sleep, absences from the house and much more are clearly identified directly or from combining several sensor outputs. We monitored the daily behavior of four caretakers of the patients having is serious illness needing to stay in bed at all times. Several sensors were installed and integrated with an embedded system and which uses wired or wireless communication technology such as ZegBee and RFID. Data gathered are then stored in a storage device or transferred via Local Area Network (LAN) to a remote storage location where separate analysis and planning can be performed. Furthermore, the degree of dependence and usage of the subject on different household devices can be determined. This information is then be compiled and sent to the different units responsible such as household managers or family members in order to make informed decisions regarding the needs of the people under care. PCALCAV displays in house activities in parallel coordinates [2]. From the observation of each RFID for users tagged as #123, #121, #120, #117, we develop hypotheses and the monitor mechanism based on an efficient hashing algorithm. Using the graphical signatures, PCALCAV can quickly find patterns which seem abnormal enabling members of the family via text message or voice contact to intuitively recognize and respond to the matter in hand. Compared with existing visualization works, PCALCAV can handle hyper dimensions, i.e. can visualize many more than 3 parameters if necessary. This significantly reduces false positives obtained based on incomplete information. As a consequence, abnormal behavior is more precisely detectable by machine and more easily recognizable by human. Another strength of PCALCAV is handling of two device ZigBee and RFID sensors time flows. Pre-flow visualization greatly reduces the processing time and further provides compatibility with two sensors which export flow information. We demonstrate the effectiveness of PCALCAV using real-life data activated monitoring traces so of the so-called "Smart housekeeping system with a network of living-context awareness assistive service".

Key words—Parallel Coordinates, Automated Living Context-Awareness Visualization, Health monitoring at home, Remote Monitoring.

I. INTRODUCTION

Recognizing human activities using sensors is currently a major challenge in research[6]. Typically, the information extracted directly from sensors is either not clear enough or is too noisy to accurately infer activities occurring in the scene. Human activities are complex and evolve dynamically over time. To overcome these drawbacks a promising approach is the visualization of complex situations in a simple and intuitive way as in [1].

Visualization is not about seeing zillions but rather perceiving relations among them. With Parallel Coordinates (abbr. ||-coords) the search for multivariate relations is transformed into a 2-dimensional pattern recognition problem [2]. For a multivariate dataset, in general, our goal is to concentrate the relational information into clear patterns eliminating the polygonal lines altogether. The methodology's foundations are quickly reviewed and then our vision for the future is illustrated with a challenging example ([3], [4]), interesting in its own right, and having important applications from regression to machine learning [5] .

The novelty of the paper is two-fold: a) We present the first work in applying the ||-coords methodology for activity recognition, and b) we analysis and compare the different days (or users) to better understand the dataset.

.

The organization of the paper is as follows. In the next section related work is reviewed. Section 2 presents the basic concept of ||-coords detailing how visualization methodology is employed to detect the relationship between dataset's parameters.. Section 3 goes into the details of efficient simulations. We then describe our experiments and results in applying the model to home care based human activity recognition in an indoor environment. The conclusions is given last section..

II. Smart Housekeeping System with a Network of Living Context –Awareness Assistive Service

A. The Smart Housekeeping System

The monitoring system was designed 'to work long term, without any human operation throughout its operational period. The system included a personal computer, different sensors integrated with an embedded system and uses wired or wireless communication technology such as ZigBee and RFID, amplifiers, a network and an ISDN modem. In the current system, Microsofi Windows XP was used as the operating system. The system consisted of two components: data acquisition and data transfer.

1) Data Acquisition

In order to devise a visual mechanism for the smart housekeeping system, their characteristics need to be considered in terms of visualization. RFID and ZigBee are chosen. The selected sensors were both easy to install and use, and they did not disturb the daily behavior of the subjects. The following sensors were selected.

1. Pyroelectronic Infrared Photoresister sensors were used to detect doors opening and closing.
2. Hall Currency sensors were used for detecting electricity socket.
3. Reed Switch is used for detecting door opening/closing.
4. Infrared sensor were used to mark and detect the locations in the house.
5. Interrupt sensors were used to detect the passage of a human.
6. RFID's tags are carried by 4 person (#123 father, #121 sister, #120 mother, #117 uncle, the patience stays in his room all the time so that he does not carry the RFID tag)

Figure 1: The schema of house and two devices installed

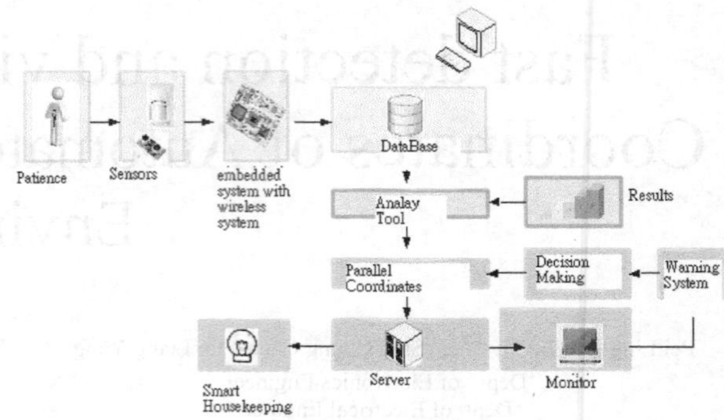

Figure 2: The schema of the Smart Housekeeping System with a Network of Living Context-Awareness Assistive service system design of PCALCAV

The output data gathered are then stored in a storage device.

2) Data Transfer

To achieve remote monitoring, the data were automatically transferred daily to another site ***via*** the Internet via Local Area Network (LAN) to a remote storage location to perform separate analysis and planning.

3) Parallel Coordinates

One important aspect of information visualization is scalability. Parallel coordinates provide great scalability to multiple dimensions. They are not complex, yet allow hyper dimensional patterns to be analyzed, They lead to a quick intuitive understanding of the information. This technique has no theoretical limit in the number of parameters that can be visualized. Therefore, we can scale up the application by incrementally introducing new visualization parameters as necessary. Moreover, it does not introduce bias for any specific dimension, while showing prominent trends, correlations and divergences from the raw data. These advantages enable us to gain critical insight into the dataset for the different RFID's tag users being tested and establishing reliable hypotheses. Even if an abnormal behavior occurs a specific image pattern can be obtained and the behavior can be detected then (and later) in a timely manner.

III. Simulation

A. Dataset

The Automated Living Context-Awareness dataset was collected. Data was collected automatically during the experiment, and the data transfer process was deemed successful. During the long-term monitoring (in total, over about three months), the system sometimes experienced troubles. However, we were able to fix these, and so demonstrate the robustness of the system. The computer sometimes stalled, and this was considered the biggest problem of the system. The shut down of the computer may have been due to instability of the Microsoft Windows XP operating system with long-term operation. The next version will use LINUX or Microsoft Windows XP as the operating system.

Fig. 3 shows The schema of the Smart Housekeeping System with a Network of Living Context-Awareness Assistive service, how the dataset can be obtained during a day from the house of subjects.

RFID's tags are carried by 4 person (#123 father, #121 sister, #120 mother, #117 uncle, the patience stays in his room all the time so that he does not carry the RFID tag) who take care of Patience (author) by 24 hours in shift. Sensors were installed in main entrance, back door, sister room, author room, bathroom at the upstairs , toilet at the upstairs and stair. The quality of RFIF performance are measured by distance, LQI (Link Quality Index) and Power. The system is monitoring the whole RFID's tags users daily behavior. Using the system, the 4 subjects were monitored from September 22nd, 2012 to January 2013. The subjects signed consent forms. Fig. 1 shows the floor plan of the house with the installed sensor locations. Each data set obtained was checked daily by a research student. When a problem was found the research student would make a telephone call to the subject to discuss the situation.

B. Data Preprocessing

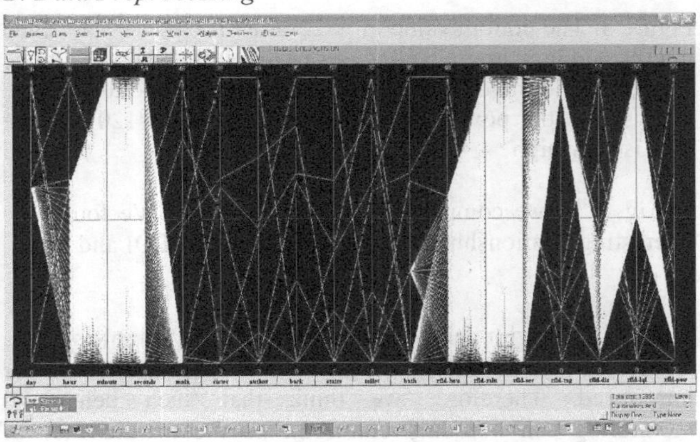

Figure 3: 9/22/2013 dataset-Original with 13995 data entries, note outliers

Fig 3 shows the parallel coordinates (abbr.||-coords) [2] method to perform the dataset. A dataset *P* with *N* variables is transformed into a set of points in *N* dimensional space. Information of daily behaviors, such as the number of door openings, the length of sleep, absences from the house, use of a bathroom or toilet, walking on the stairs were clearly identified using either a single sensor output, or by combining several sensor outputs.

C. Patitioning the Problem

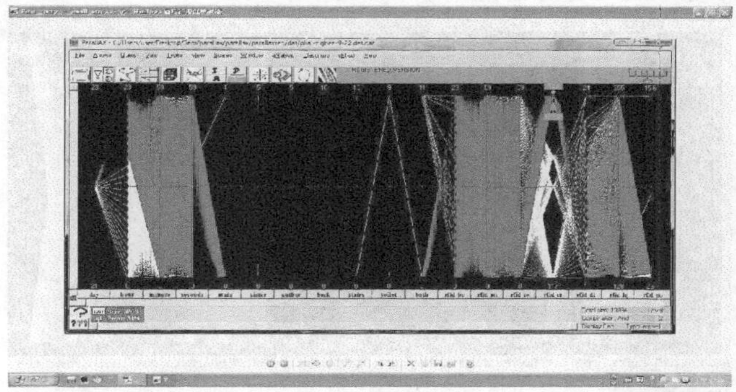

Figure 4: After cropping outliers there are 13984 data entries

We want to look into the dataset according the RFID users now. After cropping the outliers, there are 13984 data entries as Fig 4. It is easy to estimate that some regular daily behaviors can be observed from the sensor outputs as Fig 5. We found RFID users #123, #121, #120 and #117 turned up the house at different CONSECUTIVE times for 24 hours.

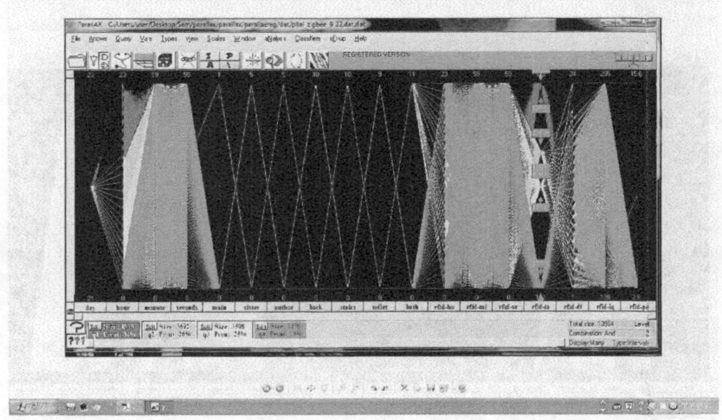

Figure 5 Each RFID users from #123 #121 #120 and #117 shows in house for the duty one after the other round 24 hours.

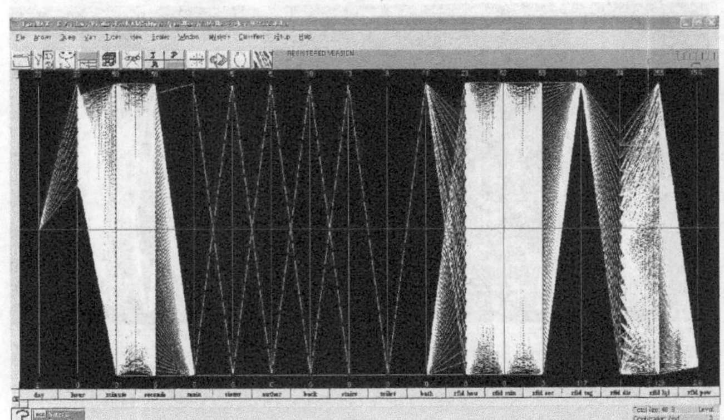

Figure 6(a): #123 activity in the house environment.

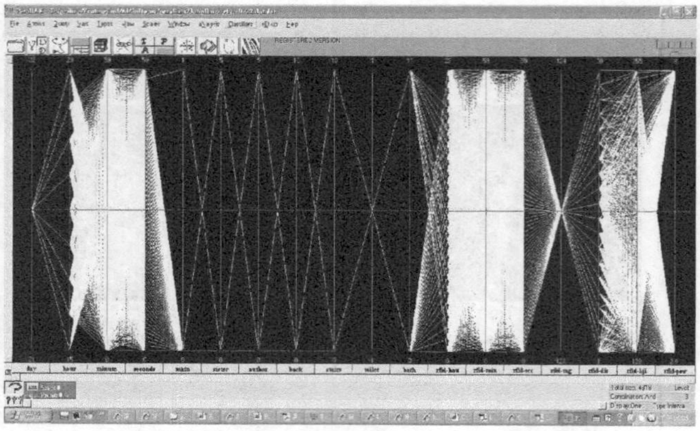

Figure6(b): Byisolating and rescaling the activity of user #123 one can easily to see that he stayed in house between 15 to 23 hours, entered from main door, went to the sister and author's room, went to upstairs to the bathroom and used back door as well. He was a very active person.

Similarly we also can see from the data that #121, #120 and #117 stayed in house 6 hours, 6 hours and 4 hours respectively.

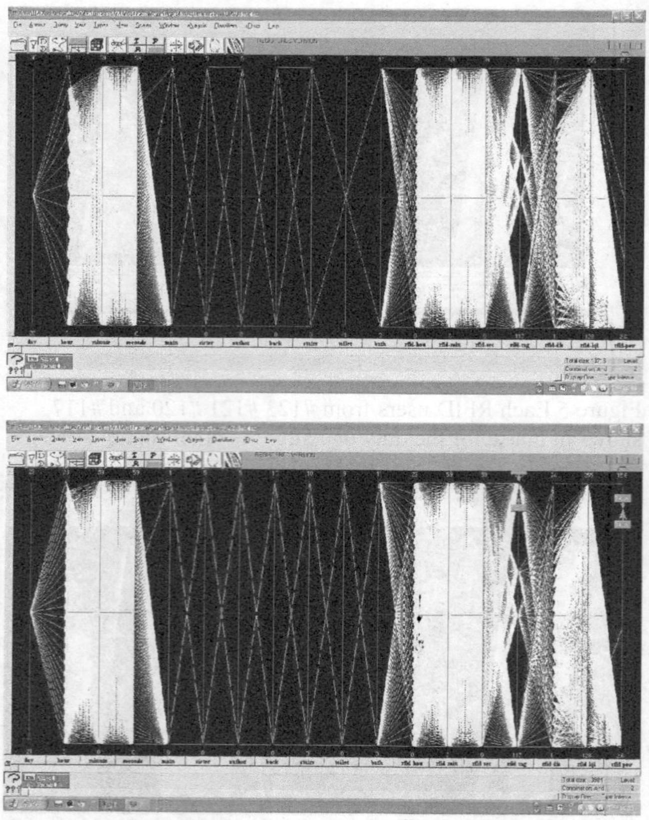

Figure 7 comparing two day 9/22 and 9/29, the last colum of RFID power

.

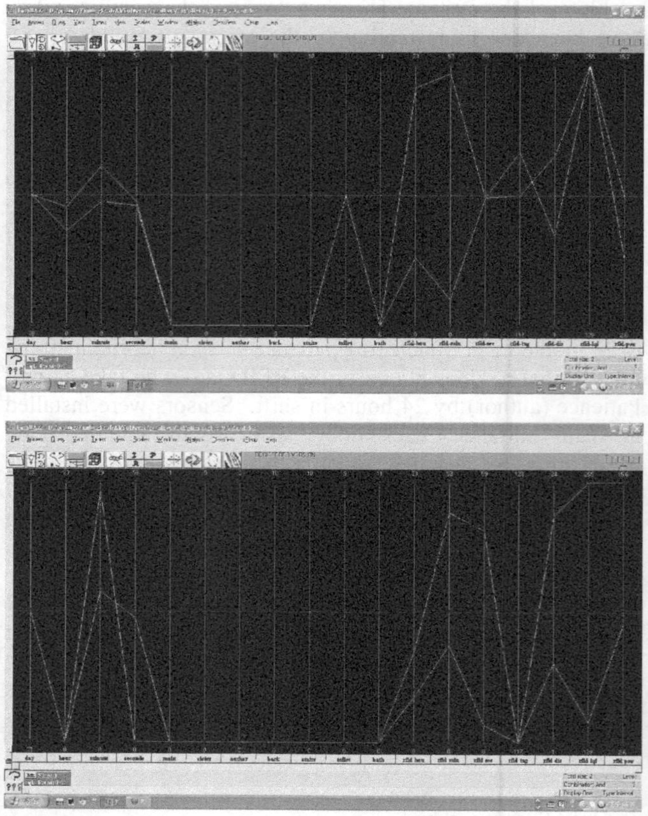

Figure 8: The bottom value in 9/22 of RFID power happened middle and high are related with #117 and LQI shows that one is good while the other one is low. Moreover the top picture 9/29 shows the power separately by #121 and #120 and the LQI is very high

In Fig. 7, 8, we compared the different days. We found the interesting relationship between RFID powder, LQI and users.

The daily behavior can be monitored with only simple sensors and a commercial industrial network. No special devices were introduced. Therefore, we think that such behavioral monitoring can not only contribute to the maintenance of health but other activities such as posting moving guards in building facilities for example.

IV. Conclusion

Research on the "Smart housekeeping system with a network of living-context awareness assistive service" by using several simple sensors was selected with a data acquisition system designed for monitoring daily behavior in the home. In addition, to achieve remote monitoring, data were transferred to another host via the Internet using wired or wireless LAN. The monitoring was evaluated practically with an experiment involving one domestic house that was inhabited by a seriously ill person with four caretakers.. Data originating from their daily behaviors were obtained automatically from a remote location. Some daily behavior patterns could be recognized from the data showing that such monitoring can greatly aid in the maintenance of a home care system.

REFERENCES

[1] P. L. Lai Jin Liang Yang and A. Inselberg, Geometric Divide and Conquer Classification for High-Dimensional Data, in Proc. Of DATA 2012: 79-82, 2012J. Clerk Maxwell, A Treatise on Electricity and Magnetism, 3rd ed., vol. 2. Oxford: Clarendon, 1892, pp.68–73.

[2] Inselberg, A. (2009). Parallel Coordinates : ***VISUAL*** Multidimensional Geometry and its Applications. Springer-Verlag, New York.

[3] Chatterjee, A. (1995). Visualizing Multidimensional Polytopes and Topologies for Tolerances. Ph.D. Thesis, Dept. Comp. Sci., Univ.

[4] Matskewich, T., Inselberg, A. and M. Bercovier. (2000). Approximated Planes in Parallel Coordinates. Proc. of Geometric Model. Conf., St.

[5] Lai, P.L., Fyfe, C. (2001). A Family of Canonical Correlation Anaylysis Networks. Neural Processing Letters, Volume 14 Issue 2, October 2001 Pages 93-105

[6] Ogawa, M.; Suzuki, R.; Otake, S.; Izutsu, T.; Iwaya, T.; Togawa, T., 2002, “Long term remote behavioral monitoring of elderly by using sensors installed in ordinary houses”, Microtechnologies in Medicine & Biology 2nd Annual International IEEE-EMB Special Topic Conference, 2-4 May 2002 , Page(s): 322 –325

Monitoring of Mixing Process by Visualization of Stirred Bio-diesel Production Reactor Using Electrical Capacitance Tomography

Syed F.A. Bukhari[a] **and Adesoji A. Adesina**[b]
[a]Department of Computer Engineering, Sir Syed University of Engineering & Technology, University Road, Karachi-75300, PAKISTAN
[b]Reactor Engineering & Technology Group, School of Chemical Engineering, The University of New South Wales, Sydney, NSW 2052, AUSTRALIA

Abstract - *Biodiesel are long chain fatty acid alkyl esters produced from the alcoholysis of triglycerides (or esterification of free fatty acids) in stirred vats. Non-edible (or waste cooking) oil and bioethanol are used as reactants in the second generation biodiesel technologies. As a result, complex multiphase (oil-aqueous-solid) mixing is inevitable (where the solid phase is the suspended catalyst particles). In order to improve production performance, this study deals with the non-invasive measurement of the phase hold-up and mixing attributes via electrical capacitance tomography (ECT).*

Keywords Biodiesel, electrical capacitance tomography, multiphase mixing, phase hold-up

1 Introduction

In a recent study, it has been shown that the world's oil resources are expected to meet the global demand until next few decades only [1]. According to World Energy Outlook (WEO) 2007, oil and gas supplies will reach 61 million barrels per day by 2030. On the other hand, in 2006 the forecast about available reserves of oil and gas are 1300 billion barrels and 6100 trillion cubic feet respectively. This alarming fossil fuel depletion rate has triggered the world to start research and development for alternate renewable energy sources. Bio-energy (e.g. biodiesel) is considered to be one of the potential renewable energy sources. The concept of biodiesel is not new as Rudolf Diesel invented a diesel engine running on vegetable oil in the year 1900 [2]. Biodiesel is considered superior to conventional diesel based on degree of pollution, sulphur content, aromatic content and flash point [3].

Nowadays, the most popular and commonly used methodology for second generation biodiesel production is transesterification. Conventionally homogeneous base catalyst under mild heating condition (50–60 °C) was used for biodiesel production. The transesterification processes are affected by main factors such as, reaction temperature, alcohol/oil molar ratio, type and concentration of catalyst as well as purity of reactants [4]. The cost of production of biodiesel can be reduced by using waste cooking oil as raw material since it is cheaper than virgin vegetable oils [5]. An increase in food consumption with the rise of world's population has created significant disposal problems for waste edible oils. For example, in USA waste cooking oil per year is about 4.5-11.3 million litres and in Japan it is $4x10^5$-$6x10^5$ tons [6]. Because waste cooking oil and bio ethanol (with alumina as catalyst) are used as reactants for the production of biodiesel therefore complex multiphase (oil-aqueous-solid) mixing phenomena is involved. It is essential to monitor the process of biodiesel production for the improvement of industrial performance. This study deals with the non-invasive measurement of the phase hold-up and mixing attributes via electrical capacitance tomography (ECT).

2 ECT System

ECT has been used effectively for monitoring of mixing processes in the past [7] [8]. In a conventional ECT system, the sensor takes the form of an array of electrodes placed around an insulating pipe and surrounded by a grounded screen. The data acquisition unit measures the capacitance of all possible electrode pairs, thus producing total measurements of n(n-1)/2, where n is the number of electrodes. In this work, the ECT system is used for non-invasive monitoring of phase hold-up and mixing attributes. Experimental work was carried out in a mechanically-agitated 2L reactor containing oil-ethanol-alumina mixture in various ratios. This reactor was fitted with an external 12-electrode copper belt sensor tightly wrapped around its acrylic glass wall (Fig. 1). All measurements were taken and analysed on the dual-mode M3000 module ECT system. A glass stirrer was used with speed up to 1300 rpm. The solid alumina (catalyst) was loaded in an amount of 0-100 grams/litre.

3 Eclectic data analysis approach

There are two main approaches for data analysis in process tomography: (1) raw measurement data analysis and

(2) visualisation of 2D or 3D images. Many algorithms have been developed for visualisation of ECT images but still quantitative errors exist associated with the image reconstruction techniques [7]. It has been shown that useful information about phase distribution can be obtained using raw data [9].

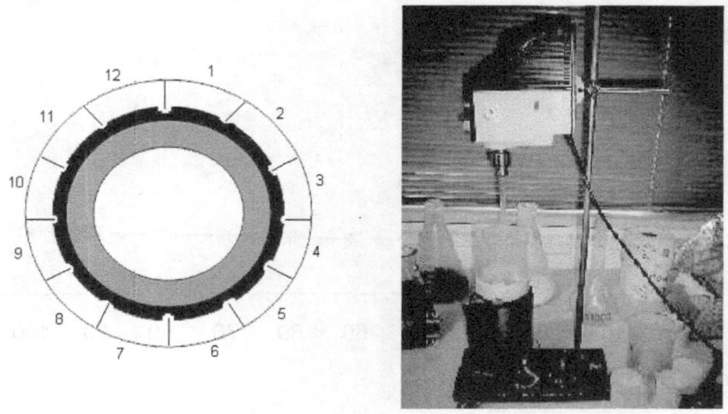

(a) Cross-sectional view (b) ECT sensor with stirrer

Fig. 1: ECT sensor test set-up

The Maxwell model can be applied to ECT measurements for calculation of dispersed phase hold up [10] [11] [12] which can be expressed in terms of measured capacitance (C_m) and high and low capacitance readings at calibration (C_h, C_l) by the following equation.

$$\text{Maxwell model: } \varepsilon_d = \frac{2C_l + C_h - 2C_m - C_m k}{C_m - k + 2(C_l - C_h)} \quad (1)$$

In above equation, k is the high to low permittivity ratio (C_h / C_l) and ε_d is the dispersed phase hold up. Banisi *et al.* [13] have shown that Maxwell's two phase model (Equation 1) can be modified for the three phase system (Equation 2). In this work this modified version has been used with the following assumptions.

1) Oil-ethanol (liquid-liquid) mixture has been treated as a continuous phase.
2) Solid particles of alumina are assumed to have a porous nature.

$$\varepsilon_g = \varepsilon_{s'} = \frac{1 - k_m / k_s}{1 + 0.5 k_m / k_s}$$

(2)

Where

k_m Measured permittivity of mixture

k_s Permittivity of alumina (solid)

$\varepsilon_{s'}$ Gas holdup

The estimation of $\varepsilon_{s'}$ requires two permittivity measurements, that of the liquid-liquid phase alone and that of the liquid-gas mixture (or dispersion).

The pressure difference between two vertically spaced points is given by

$$\frac{P_B - P_A}{L} = g(\rho_g \varepsilon_g + \rho_l \varepsilon_l + \rho_s \varepsilon_s) \quad (3)$$

Where

ρ_i Density of i (gas, liquid, solid) in g/cm^3

ε_i Holdup of i

g Acceleration due to gravity in cm/s^2

L Vertical distance between two points in cm

Since $\rho_g < \rho_s, \rho_l$, it is assumed that $\rho_g = 0$ and substituting ε_l for ε_s and ε_g using global volume balance equation, i.e. $\varepsilon_s + \varepsilon_g + \varepsilon_l = 1$. Equation (2) can be re-arranged to give ε_s

$$\varepsilon_s = \frac{\Delta P / L - g\rho_l(1 - \varepsilon_g)}{g(\rho_s - \rho_l)} \quad (4)$$

where $\Delta P = P_B - P_A$, since in this work pressure is assumed constant so $\Delta P = 0$.

4 Experimental data analysis and discussion

In this research, experiments were conducted in both 2-phase (oil-ethanol, alumina-oil and alumina-ethanol) and 3-phase (oil-ethanol-alumina) systems. An eclectic approach to the treatment of the raw dispersed phase data permitted the decoupling of oil phase hold-up and solid hold-up. The permittivity for ethanol, alumina and oil are 24.3, 9 and 3 respectively. The normalised measured values of permittivity for the mixture are shown in Fig. 2.

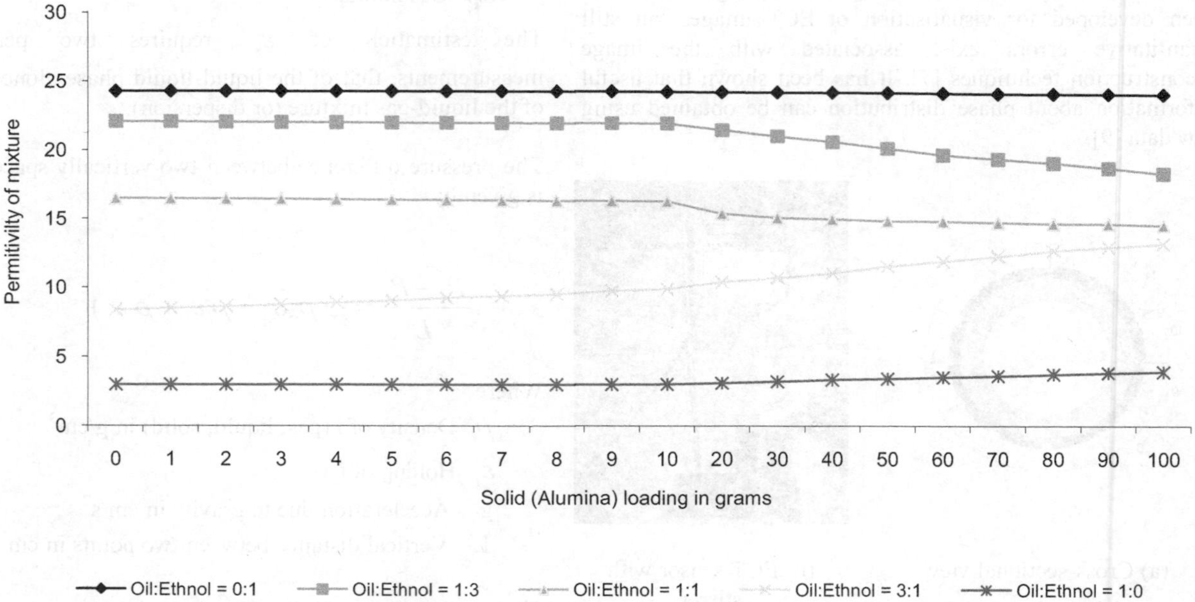

Fig. 2: Measured permittivity values for oil and ethanol mixture for different alumina loading

In the first case, oil:ethanol ratio was 0:1 and the observed change of permittivity was from 24.30 to 23.95 respectively on addition of alumina from 0 gram to 100 gram (in 20 steps). The reason for this decrease in permittivity was due to the addition of low permittivity material, i.e. alumina to high permittivity material, i.e. ethanol. The experiment was then performed for oil:ethanol ratio of 1:3. Here the permittivity was changed from 22.11 to 18.23 on addition of alumina similar to the previous case. The decrease in permittivity of the mixture was again dominated by alumina particles. The third experiment was performed on oil:ethanol ratio of 1:1. In this set of readings, the change of permittivity was from 16.50 to 14.48. The next experimental data were obtained for oil:ethanol ratios of 3:1 and 1:0 respectively. The change of permittivity values were from 8.39 to 13.13 and from 3.00 to 3.53 for oil:ethanol ratios of 3:1 and 1:0 respectively. The values of mixture permittivity were increased because mixture was dominated by oil having lower permittivity than alumina. Fig. 3-5 show effect on dispersed phase hold-up for different oil:ethanol ratios. These values are calculated using Maxwell model for three phases.

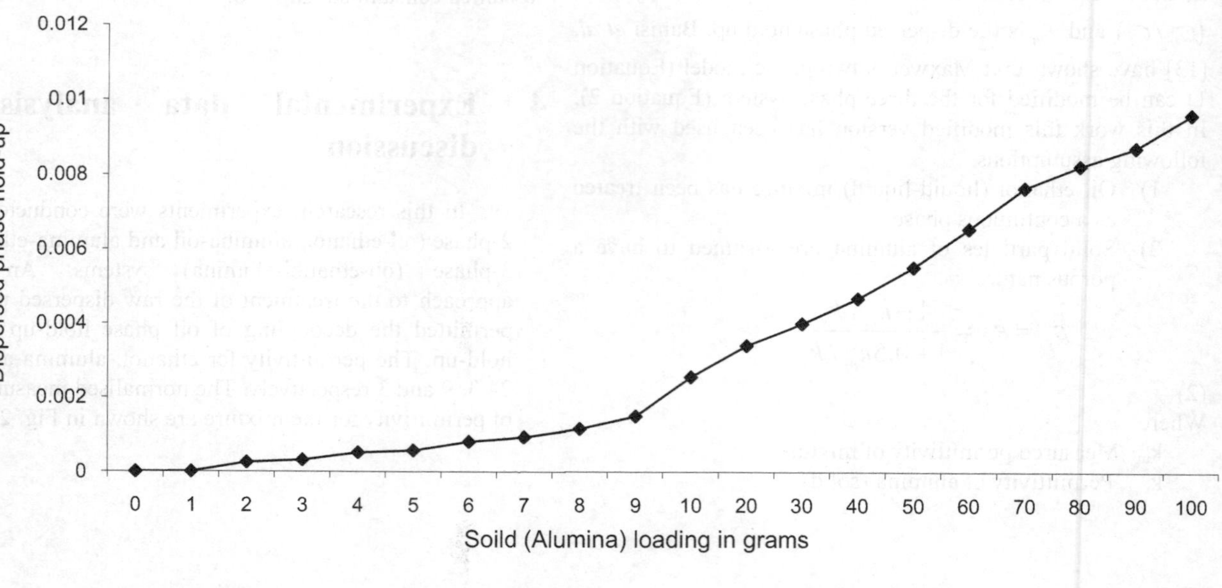

Fig. 3: Dispersed phase hold-up for oil:ethanol = 0:1 mixture for different alumina loading

Another set of experimental data were obtained with alumina loading at 20 grams/litre in different oil:ethanol ratios. The results are given in Fig.6, which show that the dispersed phase hold-up increased monotonically with solid loading, w, for all oil-ethanol ratios. In particular, the dispersed phase hold-up increased with increasing oil composition in the liquid phase suggesting that oil was dispersed as droplets in the continuous ethanol phase. This dependency was captured by the power-law relation:

$$\phi_{d/e} - \phi_{o/e} = aw^n \quad (5)$$

where, $\phi_{d/e}$ and $\phi_{o/e}$ are the dispersed phase hold-up and oil phase hold-up respectively (with ethanol as the continuous phase). Interestingly, both a and n are functions of the oil phase volume fraction, x_{oil}.

The effect of different stirring speeds on phase hold up with solid loading at 50 grams/litre was also observed. The results are shown in Fig. 7, which also reveals that the phase hold-up is strongly correlated with the impeller Reynolds number, Re_I. Indeed, as the oil volume fraction increased, the curves rose sharply suggesting that mixing would be better with very low oil:ethanol ratio. Incidentally, the transesterification reaction rate is favoured by ethanol:oil volume ratio greater than 6.

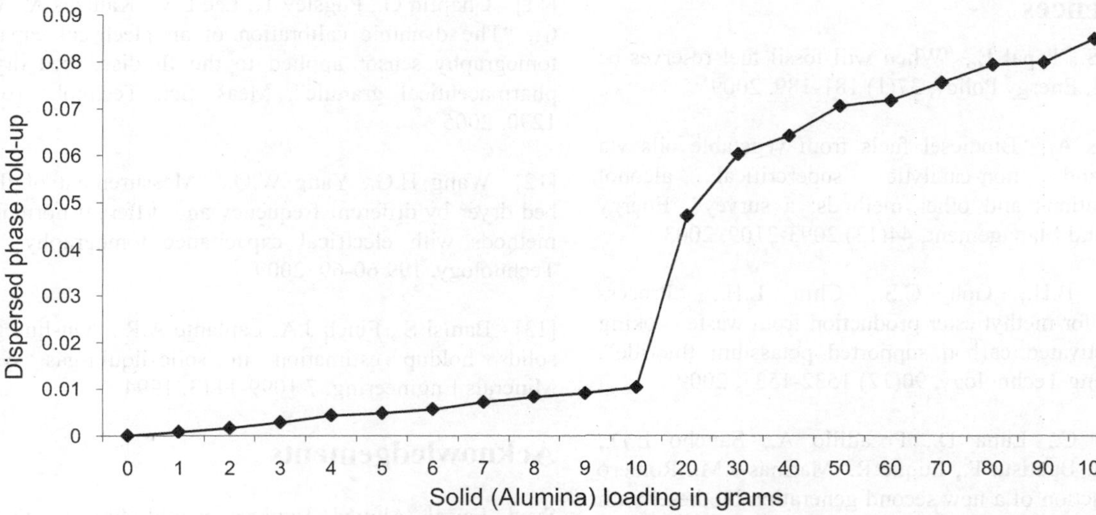

Fig. 4: Dispersed phase hold-up for oil:ethanol = 1:1 mixture for different alumina loading

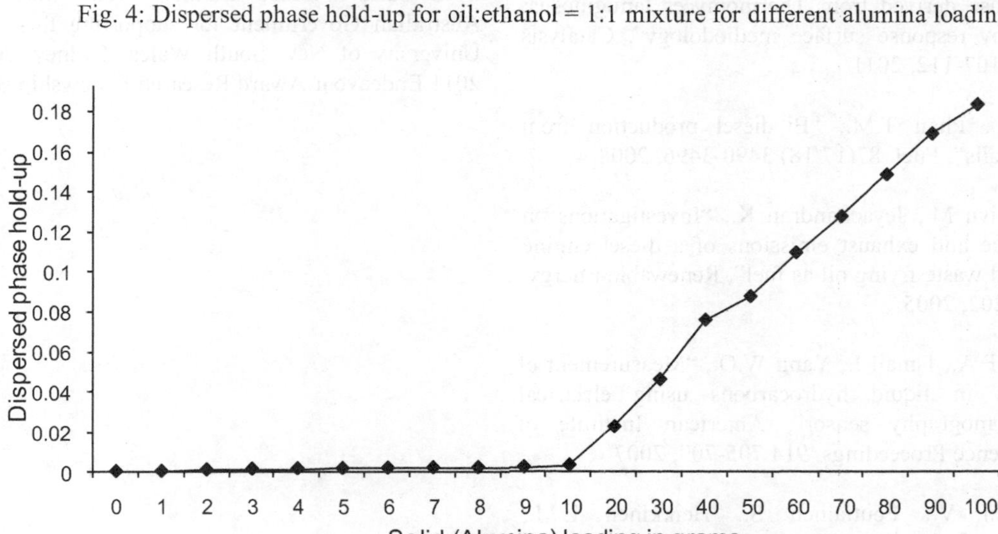

Fig. 5: Dispersed phase hold-up for oil:ethanol = 1:0 mixture for different alumina loading

5. Conclusions

In this work, an ECT-based system has been used to monitor the mixing and phase hold-up characteristics of a stirred bio-diesel production reactor. Experiments were conducted for different oil and ethanol ratios with different loading of alumina. Calculations were performed using Maxwell model for three phases. It was observed that the dispersed phase hold-up increases monotonically with solid loading for all oil-ethanol ratios. For the cases having high oil composition, it was noted that oil was dispersed as droplets in continuous ethanol phase. The experiments showed that ECT was also effective for sensing very low amount of alumina, i.e. in the range of 1 gram/litre.

6 References

[1] Shafiee S., Topal E., "When will fossil fuel reserves be diminished?", Energy Policy, 37(1) 181-189, 2009

[2] Demirbas A., "Biodiesel fuels from vegetable oils via catalytic and non-catalytic supercritical alcohol transesterifications and other methods: a survey", Energy Conversion and Management, 44(13) 2093-2109, 2003

[3] Hameed B.H., Goh C.S., Chin L.H., "Process optimization for methyl ester production from waste cooking oil using activated carbon supported potassium fluoride", Fuel Processing Technology, 90(12) 1532-1537, 2009

]4] Verdugo C., Luna D., Posadillo A., Sancho E.D., Rodriguez S., Bautista F., Luque R., Marinas J.M., Romero A.A., "Production of a new second generation biodiesel with a low cost lipase derived from Thermomyces lanuginosus: Optimization by response surface methodology", Catalysis Today, 167(1) 107-112, 2011

[5] Phan A.N., Phan T.M., "Biodiesel production from waste cooking oils", Fuel, 87(17/18) 3490-3496, 2008

[6] Pugazhvadivu M., Jeyachandran K., "Investigations on the performance and exhaust emissions of a diesel engine using preheated waste frying oil as fuel", Renewable Energy, 30(14) 2189-2202, 2005

[7] Bukhari S.F.A., Ismail I., Yang W.Q., "Measurement of water fraction in liquid hydrocarbons using electrical capacitance tomography sensor", American Institute of Physics Conference Proceedings, 914 705-709, 2007

[8] Rimpilainen V., Poutiainen S., Heikkinen L.M., Savolainen T., Vauhkonen M., Ketolainen J., "Electrical capacitance tomography as a monitoring tool for high-shear mixing and granulation", Chemical Engineering Science, 66(18) 4090-4100, 2011

[9] Grudzien K., Romanowski A., Aykroyd R.G., Williams R.A., "A novel approach to pneumatic conveying monitoring and control strategy development", Proc. 4th World Congress on Industrial Process Tomography, Aizu, Japan, 886-891, 2005

[10] Abdullah B., Dave C., Nguyen T.H., Cooper C.G., Adesina A.A., "Electrical resistance tomography-assisted analysis of dispersed phase hold-up in a gas-inducing mechanically stirred vessel", Chemical Engineering Science, 66 5648-5662, 2011

[11] Chaplin G., Pugsley T., Lee L.V., Kantzas A., Winters C., "The dynamic calibration of an electrical capacitance tomography sensor applied to the fluidised bed drying of pharmaceutical granule", Meas. Sci. Technol., 16 1281-1290, 2005

[12] Wang H.G., Yang W.Q., "Measurement of fluidised bed dryer by different frequency and different normalisation methods with electrical capacitance tomography", Power Technology, 199 60-69, 2009

[13] Banisi S., Finch J.A. Laplante A.R., "On-line gas and solids holdup estimation in soild-liquid-gas systems", Minerals Engineering, 7 1099-1113, 1994

Acknowledgements

Syed Faisal Ahmed Bukhari would like to thank the Australian Government for supporting this research at the University of New South Wales, Sydney, Australia under 2011 Endeavour Award Research Fellowship scheme.

The Transformation of Web Pages towards a Consistent Layout to Gauge the Change in User Performance

Gautham Krishna Mamidi and Ratvinder Singh Grewal
Department of Mathematics and Computer Science, Laurentian University, Sudbury, ON Canada

Abstract - *Websites are increasingly becoming the first source of information. There are many different categories of websites: News, Shopping, Information, and Entertainment. These different categories of websites in turn have different designs and layouts. The design and layout of these websites is not always consistent, which can lead to poor user performance, confusion, and complete rejection of the website by users. This research investigates the design of websites and the differences in design across the different categories of websites. In an attempt to improve user performance the introduction of consistency across websites was investigated. A program was written to convert particular websites so that they followed a consistent layout. This conversion was done in real time. In a consistent layout web page links are placed in a consistent manner, i.e. in a similar place on each and every Web page. The consistent-layout web page does not have any images or advertisements.*

Keywords: Human-computer interaction, web pages, consistency, no scrolling, layout

1 Introduction

Websites have become a rich source of information. About 697 million websites were found in a survey conducted by Netcraft in June 2012 [8]. In a vast increase from 2003, Netcraft received responses from 35 million websites. This shows that people are accessing websites more nowadays. Websites can be divided broadly into four genres: News, Shopping, Information, and Entertainment. News websites have news as their main source of information. There are different categories of news, including international, national, regional, sports, financial, and breaking news. These websites have the text, textual links, advertisements, photos, and videos. In contrast, Shopping websites have products as the main source of information. They have the product information, multimedia content, transaction pages, textual links, and images. Information websites for their part have information other than news, such as articles, tips, stories, and data. Finally, Entertainment websites have the information related to entertainment. They have large multimedia files, advertisements, images, and transaction pages. The News websites were chosen in my research as a starting point and the research can be extended to other categories of web pages.

As stated earlier, a web page is a combination of text, links, and graphical elements. The arrangement or formatting of these elements affects usability and accessibility of the web interface. Usability problems imply that a system cannot be used easily. It was observed in the literature review on web pages that users experienced usability problems because of variations in web page designs against usability recommendations [5]. Usability recommendations represent best practises that can reduce the problems faced by users when using an interface. In this work the authors presented a study of web page design patterns, changes in designs, and comparison of design patterns from 2000 to 2003 with previous research recommendations on web pages. In this study 56 web design features were used to assess website quality, usability, and accessibility quantitatively; the web pages were from 2000, 2002, and 2003. Some of the design features include fonts, colours, use of frames, and layouts.

The authors used an automated tool to collect website design patterns to judge the websites. The websites were divided by difference in design to denote good-, average-, and poor-rated websites. The web sites were rated good, average, and poor by panel of experts from Webby awards on a 10-point scale. This was to rate sites on overall experience and five specific criteria: content, structure and navigation, visual design, functionality, and interactivity. Webby awards are the source for rating websites based on above criteria. The design features were different in each of the rated categories suggesting that there was a major shift in website design features. The findings were compared with the design guidelines on web pages from previous studies. The results suggest that there is an increase in changes to the web page designs.

Users browse for information on web pages in various ways. Users do skimming and scanning for finding information on web pages. Skimming is a process of identifying main points of information on the web page quickly. Scanning is the process of identifying specific details of the information on the web page. Users' skimming and scanning time depends on how fast information can be found on a web page, and that depends on web page design, as stated earlier.

1.1 Problem Statement

User efficiency in finding information on the web page is hindered because of web page designs [5], [21]. Web pages have different designs, layouts, aesthetics, content, and links. This can cause usability problems for users when searching for information on a web page.

1.2 Proposed solution

The research above showed that the web page designs were not following usability guidelines in many of the design features. This caused usability problems for users when searching and scanning for information. In the case of some of the web pages, inconsistency in usage of colours, fonts, and layouts can be a potential usability problem. These usability problems can be reduced by modifying web page designs. A question was how a web page design can be used when searching for information.

In this study the original web page is referred to as the *original web page*. The research suggested that an excessive change in page layouts, images, and advertisements degrades the performance of users while searching for information. In this research project a system transformed the original web page to a web page with simple and consistent design with colours, fonts, and link placement. A web page with this simple and consistent design is called a consistent web page. The consistent web page does not have images and advertisements. The difference in users' performance when doing search tasks using original web pages and consistent web pages was determined.

2 Review of the Literature

2.1 Web Pages

Different factors affect the web page design. The properties of web interfaces include aesthetics, links, colours, advertisements, fonts, and layouts. The properties of web pages are studied in detail to understand about designs and user problems.

Aesthetics

Aesthetics deals with the human perception of beauty and how things are felt and judged. In one survey conducted by a Stanford research [10] it was found that the majority of respondents indicated that the design and look of the website mattered most, followed by the credibility judgement. However, the level of aesthetic treatment determines the credibility rating. The different aesthetic treatments of a website can generate different credibility ratings by the users. In a study [14], the higher aesthetically treated websites were termed as more credible than the lower aesthetically treated. The aesthetics of the web page and perceptions of usability are highly correlated [2]. The results from the experiment suggest that aesthetics and usability are positively correlated while the amount of information and usability correlated negatively. User satisfaction was also correlated with usability and aesthetics. The aesthetic treatment can be broadly divided into two categories and those can determine perceived usability.

The aesthetics of a web page has two categories; one is expressive aesthetics and the other is classical aesthetics. The expressive category represents the creativity of original design of the web page, whereas the classical category represents how clean, clear, and structured the web page is. The study [3], found that the classical category puts more emphasis on perceived usability of the web page whereas the emphasis on usability in the expressive category was less. The classical category also determines the level of trustworthiness of the web page. The design of the web page should be simple to be trustworthy [13]. The simple design refers to a web page without a lot of graphics, colours, and advertisements. The perception of the user on a web page depends on the aesthetics of the web page but the other question is how much time is needed to perceive it. The perception of users depends on the time the web page is exposed. The results indicate that the visual appeal was highly related to the design characteristics and 50 ms was enough to judge the web pages [11].

Links

Links can have different sizes and forms. The link size refers to the number of words in a link, and the form means whether it is text or graphics based. In one study [15] the effects of link size, link number, and clutter were studied to compare the performance of different age groups. The search performance was increased when there was less clutter, larger links, fewer competing links, and when the targeted links are in the left region of the web page. Another study [17], found that if links were text based rather than graphics based, this increased user performance. It was also found that the web pages that adopted an L-shaped navigation pattern also improved user performance.

Fonts

The web page contains text and the density of text varies on different web pages. A font has four features: font face, font size, bold, and italicization. There is an effect on users when different font types and sizes are used on the computer screen. Research on font types showed that on the computer screen the sans serif fonts are more legible than serif fonts [18]. The font type and font size have an effect on users when gender and age differences are considered. The sans serif font was preferred over serif font across all age groups for reading on the computer [19]. The size of font also affects readability; using font sizes from 9 pt to 14 pt was recommended.

Colours

Colours used on a web page are an important factor since the human eye is very sensitive to colour. In the research compilation by T. Billard [12], it was found that blue is a soft colour to use on the web page without much distraction to the user. Users are more sensitive to yellow, while green and red colours can cause fatigue. The colour combinations of higher contrast were studied using web pages [23]. The four colour combinations used in this study (font/background) were black/white, white/black, light blue/dark blue, and cyan/black. The users felt that the black on white is the most readable.

Advertisements

Research [21] shows that advertisements increase perceived workload and can hinder visual search. A study tested the effectiveness of advertisements on a goal-oriented task. Users perceived higher work load when flashing advertisements were present while searching for information. The other study [20] suggested minimal use of graphical advertisements if not avoidable. The placement of links and content can be achieved using different layout on web pages.

Layouts

Research on web page interface styles employed for testing users' perception of information quality has been done. In this study [4], two websites were used with similar content but different web page layouts. The interaction styles were menu based and metaphor based; the menu based interaction style was preferred to the other. Another study [1], found that the web page's level of complexity is related to the number of images, visible links, and number of words a web page has and the sections it is grouped into. The web page is assumed to be simpler if its layout is clear, clean, and well organized.

Other factors

The effects of visual complexity and order of the web pages on emotional responses have been studied. In this study [16], it was concluded that visual complexity and order design has carry-over effects on users' subsequent approach.

The above studies show the web page properties, designs and its effects on users. The credibility and usability of a web page can be improved or degraded by using aesthetics. The research on links shows that type of links, number of links, and clutter had an impact on users' performance. There was also difference in legibility of text on computer screens when different fonts were used. The colours used on the web pages determine users' ability to concentrate or distract. Advertisements used on web pages had impacted users' perceived work load. The different layouts of web pages were preferred by users which were clear, clean and well organized. The visual complexity and order of web pages had carry over effects on users. Type of users also affected preferences of elements on web pages. The effects on users can be minimized by choosing best practises or avoiding the problems mentioned in the above research review.

2.2 Human-Computer Interaction

Human-Computer Interaction (HCI) involves the study of interaction between humans and computers. It is concerned with the performance of those using computers and their by-products such as tablets, laptops, palm tops, and embedded systems. The other aspect is interaction, which can be direct or indirect. In the direct interaction, users receive feedback directly when using the system; in the indirect interaction users try to achieve something but might not get the feedback directly. Some of the important studies that have been done have focused on consistency and ease of design.

2.3 Consistency and Ease of Design

In *The Book of Everyday Things* by Donald Norman the author explains how poor designs in real life affect users' day-to-day life [9]. From physical devices to virtual devices the book describes how users face problems in everyday life, from unlocking doors to computer interfaces.

One of Nielsen's heuristics is making things visible [22] which also affects the usability of the object. The feedback given to the user after each action performed will also enhance the user's experience. The user should be able to understand the state of the device and alternatives for action by seeing it; this is a visibility factor. A good conceptual model for the user results in consistency in operations and results. Good mappings will also result in ease of use of the system. Human psychology, perceptions, and misconceptions, as well, will come into effect when using a system.

The user model developed by users who see the equipment will be a considerable factor. The design model is the model developed by the designer for the system where the user model is the mental model developed by users through the interaction with the system. The system image results from the physical structure of the system itself. In a well done conceptual model the system image makes the design model consistent and clear with the mental (user) model. However, a poor conceptual model can make the design model and mental model mismatch. Mismatched models can have an impact on users' ability to use an interface. The same principle can be applied to web page designs. As shown in research [5] the web page designs had problems that users had to overcome. The solution to this can be a consistent layout and consistent operations brought about by the design of a web page. If the layout of the web page is not different from other web pages then the user has the ability to adapt the system model to their mental model. When users begin to use the interface, they form a mental model, i.e. how they expect the interface to work. This mental model does not break down when users perform consistent operations.

By understanding both the website perspective and HCI, we can conclude that ease of design and consistency of operations will have an impact on the user's performance. Using the above web page studies and implementing consistency in web page designs usability problems and performance of users can be changed. The consistency in web page properties with emphasis on layout consistency was used in the solution.

3 System and Evaluation

As mentioned earlier, the original web pages will be transformed to consistent web pages. This can be done in two ways: one was automating the process, and the other was creating the web pages for experiment purposes. Automating the process of conversion from original to consistent saved time but took longer time in implementation whereas manual creation of consistent web pages was an easy process. However, it could have taken a longer time if implemented for more than one experiment. In this study the automatic conversion process was implemented. The research into system design was done by first studying web browsers.

The web pages are viewed from web browsers and there are many web browsers available and some of the popular ones are Internet Explorer, Mozilla, Maxthon, Chrome, Opera, and Safari. Mozilla Firefox is popular in the open source community because it can be programmed easily. There are many tools available in Firefox browsers to change how the web page looks and these are called add-ons. Add-ons were not suitable for complete web page transformations, so some of the other programs were looked into. The Application Programming Interfaces (APIs) is a protocol intended to be used as an interface by software components to communicate with each other. The Boilerpipe API and the HTML parser API were chosen to develop the conversion system. In our approach we selected multiple news web pages with different layouts. The selected web page was transformed to a specific layout based on best HCI practices. Usability studies done by Jakob Nielsen [6] indicated that users will perform searches in accordance with an "F" shaped or inverted "L" pattern. The study used eye tracking and heat maps to generate patterns when users scan the web page. In this study [6], users looked at thousands of web pages, however the dominant reading pattern looks similar like an F. Users first read in a horizontal movement, next they , moved down a bit to read across in second horizontal movement, and finally users scan the left side in as vertical movement. The same finding was used to build the system and this consisted of menu items on the left side and content links on the right side. The content from the web page will be on the top of the content links. The menu and content links lie side by side. The system was slow in doing the conversion.

Since my research focus was to show change in user performance if consistent layouts were used, the experiment version of the system was tweaked to work faster with only necessary menu and content links. It was also found no importance in quantitatively analyzing the consistent web page. It uses an offline version of the web page so as to provide the same work environment for all the users who participated in the experiment.

The pictorial representation of the system that converts different web pages into a same layout is in Figure 3.1, below.

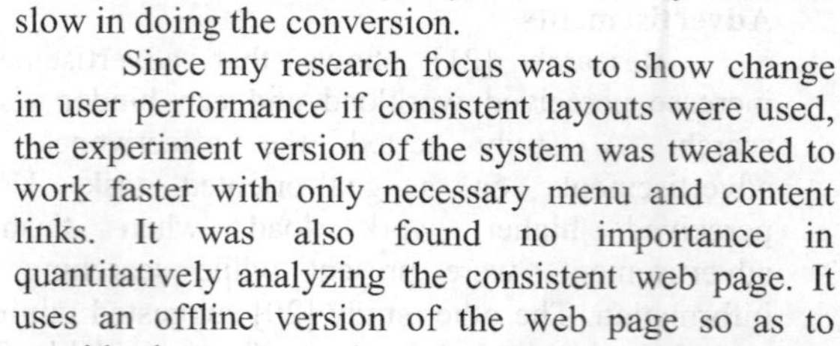

Figure 3.1 Pictorial version of converting different web page layouts to generic layout

The converted web page runs on a Tomcat server. Once the user logs in and enters the web page address, the conversion process initiates. The web page transforms to the consistent version removing all advertisements and images. If it is a content link then there was an option to view the preview of the content for that link.

The user evaluation technique was used to determine the change in users' performance when consistent and inconsistent layouts were used while performing tasks. There are two kinds of user evaluation one is lab studies and the other is field studies. The lab studies were conducted because more accurate data collection can be made without distracting users while performing the experiment.

4 Experiment

4.1 Objective

The objective of this experiment was to test users' performance differences when link search tasks were performed on the consistent and original layouts of a web page. As stated earlier, the original web page was an offline page that has links, content, images, and advertisements. In a consistent web page images and advertisements were removed and the same layout was used. Time duration to complete a task was used to measure performance.

4.2 Hypothesis

The Null Hypothesis: There is no difference in performance by users when searching for links on a consistent and original layout of a web page.

4.3 Setup and Analysis

A computer and mouse was used in a lab to conduct the experiment, users were given instructions on a Windows form application and they were asked to sign a consent form before the start of the experiment. The screen capture software records mouse movements and clicks. It was recorded as a video file which can be analyzed later. The video file was used to know the times when the user starts a task and finishes a task. The time duration was calculated by subtracting the finish time and start time of a task. The time duration for all tasks were calculated when the user completed successfully. If the user was not able to complete a task then it was termed as an error. The time taken for task completion and errors were entered into a spreadsheet for each user. The spreadsheet data was used for further statistical analysis. A total of 35 users' data was considered for analysis purposes. The computer monitor was in portrait mode and there was no scrolling on web pages.

A convention used for tasks: Task O represents a task performed on an original web page, and Task C represents a task performed on a consistent web page. The errors were discarded from data analysis as users committed few of them. The time taken by the user for performing the tasks was used for analysis purposes. The task was a content link search.

4.4 Results

Content link search

The statistics method was chosen by using quartile – quartile plot. The data distribution was not normal so non-parametric tests were chosen. The quartile – quartile plot for task O2.1 is shown in Figure 4.1.

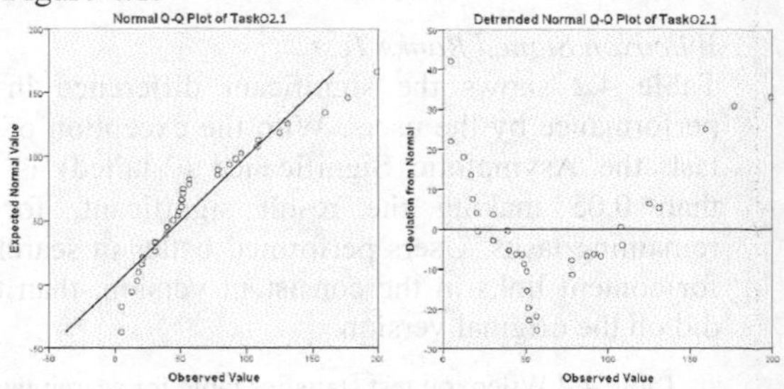

Figure 4.1 Q-Q plot for Task O2.1

In the non-parametric tests the Wilcoxon test was used to analyze the data. The dependent variables are tasks in consistent mode and original mode. The independent variable is time. Tasks performed by participants are mentioned below. Tasks and description can be found in Table 4.1. The task description was the same for tasks on both original web page and consistent web page.

Table 4.1 Tasks and Description: content link search

Tasks		Task description
Original web page	Consistent web page	
Task O2.1	Task C2.1	Search for content link “Hockey scores for today” on ESPN web page
Task O2.2	Task C2.2	
Task O2.3	Task C2.3	
Task O2.4	Task C2.4	
Task O2.5	Task C2.5	
Task O2.6	Task C2.6	
Task O2.7	Task C2.7	
Task O2.8	Task C2.8	

The link placement on the original web page and consistent web page is shown in Figure 4.2.

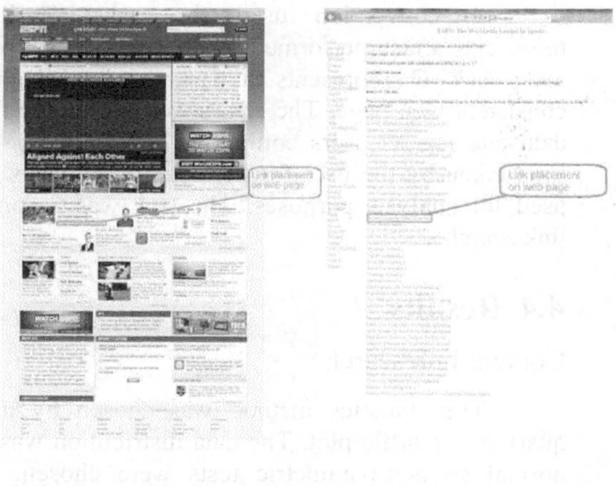

Figure 4.2 Original web page and consistent web page with search link shown in box

Wilcoxon Signed Ranks Test

Table 4.2 shows the significant difference in the performance by the users. With the exception of one task the Asymptotic Significance (2-tailed) is less than 0.05 making the result significant, for all remaining tasks. Users performed better in searching for content links in the consistent version, than they did on the original version.

Table 4.2 Wilcoxon test statistics table for search task

Tasks	Task C2.1 – Task O2.1	Task C2.2 – Task O2.2	Task C2.3 – Task O2.3	Task C2.4 – Task O2.4
Z	-3.800^{b}	-3.505^{b}	-4.078^{b}	-3.702^{b}
Asymp. Sig. (2-tailed)	.000	.000	.000	.000
Tasks	Task C2.5 – Task O2.5	Task C2.6 – Task O2.6	Task C2.7 – Task O2.7	Task C2.8 – Task O2.8
Z	-2.875^{b}	-1.769^{b}	-4.914^{b}	-3.284^{b}
Asymp. Sig. (2-tailed)	.004	.077	.000	.001

Over 70% of users felt text legibility was good in the consistent version compared to the original version.

4.5 Discussion

Users' performance in content link search tasks was measured and compared using two versions of web pages. The original web page contains images, advertisements, and the same layout, but the link placement on the web page varies. The consistent web page contains links and content with same layout. The task was searching for the content link in both the versions. Users performed better in searching for content links in the consistent version than with the original version. This result was as anticipated: the inconsistent content link placement made the search take longer as users had to learn the search pattern each time.

The content link can be anywhere on the web page in the original version whereas content link in the consistent version was placed consistently in a similar place. This had a learning effect on users and they performed better. The results were significant for all the tasks except one. Although users performed better in Task C2.6 compared to Task O2.6, the result was insignificant. With further analysis on Task O2.6 and Task C2.6, it was found that link placement of Task O2.5 is in the same quadrant as task O2.6. It can be inferred that users searched at the similar spot first as in the previous search task.

Based on the results, the null hypothesis is rejected in favour of alternative hypothesis: There is consistent improvement in performance of the user's ability to find the information faster in the consistent version of web pages compared to the original version of web pages. The results suggest there might be correlation between web page layouts and users' search patterns.

5 Conclusion

An experiment was conducted to test the hypothesis that users perform better when using the consistent version of web pages compared to the original version of web pages. To better understand results, tasks were developed for users to perform. The user evaluation technique was selected as an evaluation method. The experiment results disproved the hypothesis that users' performance on the consistent version of web pages and the original version of web pages is the same. The performance of users was measured by using time for completion of tasks. Time completion data results showed that a change in the user performance was observed between consistent and original web page.

The experiment without scrolling on web pages showed that there is an improvement in searching for links on consistent web pages.

6 References

[1] Eleni Michailidou, Simon Harper and Sean Bechhofer. Visual Complexity and Aesthetic Perception of Web pages. SIGDOC' 08, September 22–24, 2008.

[2] N. Tractinsky, A.S. Katz, D. Ikar. What is beautiful is usable. Interacting with Computers 13, 2000. 127-145.

[3] T. Lavie and N. Tractinsky. Assessing Dimensions of Perceived Visual Aesthetics of Websites. International Journal of Human-Computer Studies, Academic Press, Inc. Duluth, MN, USA, 2004. 60(3):269 – 298.

[4] Antonella De Angeli, et al. Interaction, Usability and Aesthetics: What Influences Users Preferences, 2006.

[5] Melody Y. Ivory, and Rodrick Megraw. Evolution of Website Design Patterns. ACM Transactions on Information Systems, Vol. 23, No. 4, October 2005. 463–497.

[6] Nielsen, J. F-Shaped Pattern for Reading Web Content. April 17, 2006; 2009 (01/28). http://www.useit.com/alertbox/reading_pattern.html

[7] Or Kaynar, and Yair Amichai-Hamburger. The effects of Need for Cognition on Internet use revisited. March, 2007. doi:10.1016/j.chb.2007.01.033

[8] http://news.netcraft.com/archives/category/web-server-survey/. Netcraft Ltd, 2012.

[9] Donald Norman. Design of everyday things. New York: Basic Books, 2001.

[10] Fogg, B. et al. Web credibility research: a method for online experiments and early study results. In Proceedings of CHI'01 extended abstracts on human factors in computing systems, 2001. pp. 61–68.

[11] Lindgaard, Fernandes, Dudek, and Brown. Attention web designers: You have 50 milliseconds to make a good first impression!. Behaviour and Information Technology, Vol. 25, No. 2, March-April 2006. pp. 115-126.

[12] Trish Ballard et al. Human Factors for Web Page Design,1997.

[13] Kristiina Karnoven. Beauty of simplicity. ACM, 2000.

[14] David Robins, and Jason Holmes. Aesthetics and credibility in website design. Elsevier Ltd. 2007.

[15] Michael Graham et al. Age differences in search of web pages: The effects of link size, link number and clutter. Human Factors, Vol. 46, No. 3, Fall 2004. 385-398.

[16] Liqiong Deng, and Marshall Scott Poole. Affect in web interfaces: a study of the impacts of web page visual complexity and order. MIS Quarterly Vol. 34 No. 4, December 2010. 711-730.

[17] Van Duyne, D. K., Landay, J. A., and Hong, J. I. The Design of Sites: Patterns, Principles, and Processes for Crafting a Customer-Centered Web Experience. Addison-Wesley, Boston, 2002.

[18] Schriver, K. A. Dynamics in Document Design. Wiley Computer Publishing, John Wiley & Sons, Inc., New York, NY, 1997.

[19] Bernard, M., Liao, C. H., and Mills, M. The effects of font type and size on the legibility and reading time of online text by older adults. In Proceedings of the Conference on Human Factors in Computing Systems. Vol. 2. Seattle, WA, 2001. 175–176.

[20] Flanders, V. and Willis, M. Web Pages That Suck: Learn Good Design by Looking at Bad Design. Sybex, San Francisco, CA, 1998.

[21] Burke M. et al. High-Cost Banner Blindness: Ads Increase Perceived Workload, Hinder Visual Search, and Are Forgotten. ACM Transactions on Computer-Human Interaction, Vol. 12, No. 4, December 2005. 423–445.

[22] Nielsen J. 10 Usability Heuristics, October 2012. http://www.nngroup.com/articles/ten-usability-heuristics/.

[23] Richard H Hall and Patrick Hanna. The impact of web page text-background colour combinations on readability, retention, aesthetics and behavioural intention. Behaviour & Information Technology. Vol. 23, Iss. 3, 2004.

[24] Wilcoxon, Frank. Individual comparisons by ranking methods. Biometrics Bulletin 1. Dec 1945. (6): 80–83.

Heart Disease Risk Detection with Competitive Learning and Adaptive Fuzzy Inference System, A Novel Approach

Hossein Shirazi[1], **S. M. R. Farshchi**[2]

[1]Department of Computer & Information Technology, MUT University, Tehran, Iran, Shirazi@MUT.ac.ir

[2]Social Network Laboratory, C4I Department, Tehran, Iran, Farshchi@ict.gov.ir

Abstract - *In this paper, we propose an adaptive method using a neural network to solve the heart disease risk detection. For the goal of heart disease risk detection, the statistical analysis is used to reduce the dimension of feature space and normalize each input feature; the novel fuzzy neural network with competitive learning are applied to realize the nonlinear mapping relationship between hemodynamic parameters and conclusions, which does not require predefining rules and subjective defuzzification. The preliminary testing results prove that the proposed method has a great accuracy for heart disease risk detection and it's promising for e-home healthcare usage. Experimental results on the RAZAVIs hospital databases have shown that the recognition rate achieved by the novel method (87.8%) outperforms the conventional approaches (82.9%and 82.3%).*

Keywords: competitive learning, fuzzy neural network, heart disease detection.

1 Introduction

The heart diseases (HDs) are the number one cause of death globally, more people die annually due to HDs than any other diseases [1]. Therefore, the demand of HDs risk detection is increasing in recent years. Among all kinds of HDs, coronary heart disease, hypertension and hyperlipaemia are three typical and frequently encountered HDs [2]. They result from the disorder of heart, vessel and blood separately, thus, selected as representative HDs for risk detection [3].

A wide variety of measurement has been used for CVD prediction, such as electrocardiography (ECG), magnetic resonance angiography etc. However, their application in home healthcare is limited due to inconvenient operation, invasive measurement and expensive cost [4]. Hence, the sphygmogram (SPG) is promising for home healthcare usage. After long-term exploration, the hemodynamic parameters (HDPs) derived from sphygmogram analysis are proved to reflect the cardiovascular status.

Various methodologies have been proposed to implement medical decision-making. Among them fuzzy neural networks (FNNs), which merge fuzzy logic (FL) and neural networks (NNs), draw great attention recently [5]. The NNs are in consideration due to its self-adaptation, robustness and performs the nonlinear mapping between the input features and the desired outputs. However, physicians do not favor it because it lacks a structural knowledge base for review and reference. In addition to NNs, FL is another popular solution for the task since it represents imprecise concepts through linguistic variables, such as "very", "middle", etc. There are various schemes to integrate FL and NNs for classification or diagnosis. A neuro-fuzzy model [6] is a fuzzy neural network model, that competing matching degrees of premise combinations as inference model provide the retrospection of the diagnosis evidence with comparable accuracy than conventional FNNs [7].

A conventional form of fuzzy systems for HD detection has low capabilities for learning and adaptation. Fuzzy mathematics provides an inference mechanism for approximate reasoning under cognitive uncertainty, while neural networks offer exciting advantages such as learning and adaptation, generalization, approximation. These networks are also capable of dealing with computational complexity, nonlinearity, and uncertainty [8]. A possible solution to overcome the above limitations of common HDs detection algorithms is the application of artificial intelligence approaches such as neural network and Fuzzy logic.

However, to the best of the authors' knowledge, the concept of FL has not been used for BP estimation [12]. In this paper, a novel expert system based on competitive learning and adaptive fuzzy inference system (CLAF) was adapted for data preprocessing, which categorizes input HDPs extracted from SPG into three groups named as sensitive, supporting and inertia group respectively, eliminates the random error effect and greatly reduces the dimension of input variable space. Then the features of sensitive group are used for HDs risk detection and then the fuzzy membership are constructed, which realize the nonlinear mapping relationship and map such reduced input symptoms to certain HDs efficiently. Moreover, the novel method is able to provide explanation in details about the deduced conclusion and its inference. The approach is tested and validated by the historical medical diagnosis records obtained from hospital.

The rest of this paper is organized as follows. The independent data analysis is given in Sections II. The structure of CLAF is given in Sections III. Section IV describes the experiment which is using the novel model and discusses the results. Conclusions are presented in Section V.

2 Preprocessing Of CVD's Data

The medical data consist of different sample's medical records, including each patient's original SPG data and physiological information. Denote the medical record space as $HDP \in R^N$ where N indicates the dimension of input variable space. In this research, there are 45 concerned practical input variables, including 6 physiological information and 32 extracted HDPs. Obviously, it is unwise and time-consuming to carry out the HDs risk detection via all these parameters, hence, the distribution verification and dimension reduction are required.

2.1 Classification of Hemodynamic Parameters

In order to minimize the dimension of feature space, it is necessary to conclude that which parameters are comparatively more significant. By means of variance analysis, the HDPs are divided into three groups, i.e. sensitive group, supporting group, and inertia group. Symbol F denotes the ratio of variance between different groups (HDG) and variance within same group (HSG).

$$F = \frac{HDG}{HSG} = \frac{Var\left(\frac{1}{n}\sum_{i=1}^{n} x_i\right)}{\frac{1}{m}\sum_{j=1}^{m} Var(x_j)} \quad (1)$$

Where m, n are the numbers of groups and records separately; the operator "Var" means the variance calculation [12]. Here, the F value is proportional to interrelationship between the parameter and HD. As a result, 38 HDPs are categorized according to different confidence coefficient [13]. Among them, 20 HDPs are classified as inertia parameters; 15 HDPs are classified as supporting parameters; and the remaining 10 HDPs are the sensitive parameters.

2.2 Fuzzy Variables for HDs Detection

To avoid sticking at meaningless accurate absolute values of HDPs, the FL is introduced. During fuzzification step, 4 prototypical functions are adopted for HD risk detection. The linguistic variables of fuzzification are defined as: "very low" (VL), "medium low" (ML), "normal" (N), "medium high" (MH), and "very high" (VH). Here, the Gaussian function is applied to represent the distribution of ML, N, MH and CHD.

Fig. 1 shows the membership functions of pulse rate (PR) according to this fuzzification.

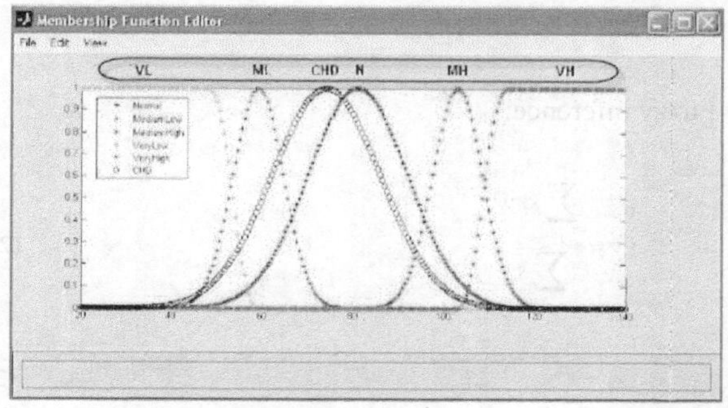

Figure 1. Membership function for fuzzification

The parameters of membership function are defined via great amount statistical analysis. For example, characteristics of Gaussian function depend on two key parameters, i.e. expected value (ξ) and standard deviation (τ). As shown in Table I, these two parameters are assigned through ξ=0 and τ =0, where are the mean and standard derivation of normal group respectively. The remaining definitions are listed in Table I.

TABLE I. PARAMETERS DEFINITIONS

Fuzzy Variable	Define Value	Parameter
Very Low	$\xi_0 + 3\tau_0$	Lower Value
	$\xi_0 - 2\tau_0$	Higher Value
Medium Low	$\xi_0 - 2\tau_0$	Lower Value
	$0.5\xi_0$	Higher Value
Normal	ξ_0	Lower Value
	τ_0	Higher Value
Medium High	$\xi_0 + 2\tau_0$	Lower Value
	$0.5\xi_0$	Higher Value
Coronary Heart Disease	ξ_C	Lower Value
	τ_C	Higher Value
Very High	$\xi_0 + 2\tau_0$	Lower Value
	$\xi_0 + 3\tau_0$	Higher Value

3 Structure of CLAF

Since the input and output data for fuzzy modeling are all crisp, the fuzzy system, which consists of fuzzy rule representation and fuzzy inference, can be simplified as follows:

Fuzzy rules:

$$if\ x\ is\ v_i, \Delta_i,\ \ then\ \ y = y_i \qquad i = 1,2,\ldots,\xi$$

Fuzzy inference:

$$y = \frac{\sum_i s_i y_i}{\sum_i s_i} \quad (2)$$

$$s_i = \begin{cases} 1 - \frac{\| x - v_i \|}{\Delta_i} & if \| x - v_i \| \leq \Delta_i \\ 0 & if \| x - v_i \| > \Delta_i \end{cases} \quad (3)$$

Where x is the crisp input vector, v and Δ are the center and the radius of each local input region, respectively, is the output center of each rule, is the number of fuzzy rules, and is the fuzzy membership function is used to measure the approximation degree of input in a fuzzy set. In general, only the approximation degree between input and the rule's premise is considered for fuzzy inference. It means that the strength with which a fuzzy rule is fired is assumed to be equal to the approximation degree of input in the rule's premise.

In contrast with that of traditional FNNs, the results of proposed methodology can be interpreted via the products of corresponding matching degrees, instead of a Boolean number (0 or 1) in output terminals merely. Providing an explanation in detail about the inference procedure that traditional FNNs do not provide is a novel feature of CLAF, since all knowledge is stored in the weights within the networks. The architecture of the novel CLAF is provided in Fig. 2. The number of CLAF input in first layer is equal to the dimension of feature HDPs. In its second layer, all features are fuzzified as fuzzy variables which are well defined in Table I and explained in section II. The third layer is used for evaluating matching degrees of all possible premises.

The first step of CLAF is the initialization of weights which is the process of filling the weight tables (PC1-PCn) which are empty initially. Each table corresponds to a predefined feature of HDPs, and it consists of entries. Each entry consists of a fuzzy variable and its weight. In this step, each weight is filled with the frequency of the corresponding membership in the category corresponding to the table. Therefore, all tables owned by the learning nodes are constructed in this step.

In order to obtain the optimum weight tables T, the competitive learning method is applied for training and adjusting the link weights. The error evaluation function E is defined as:

$$E = \frac{1}{2} \sum_{k=1}^{p} (y_O - y_N)^2 \quad (4)$$

Where O and N express the real output and current output respectively.

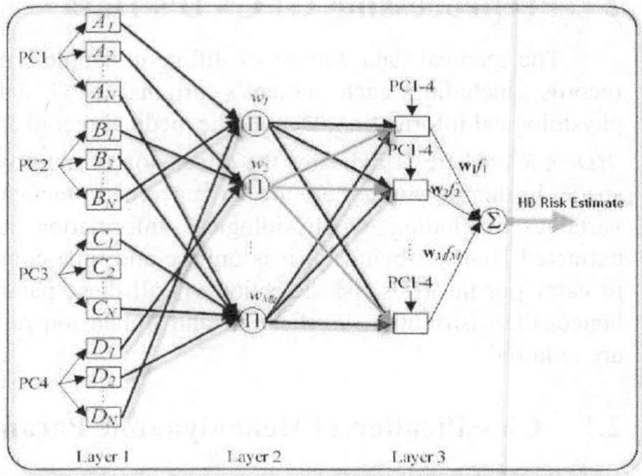

Figure 2. Architecture of the novel CLAF

4 Experimental Result

This section concerns experimental results of evaluating traditional and proposed approaches to HD risk detection on three test beds. In the experiments, two approaches, SVM, NB are evaluated as the approaches to HD risk detection. The parameters of the three approaches involved in this experiment are set by tuning them with a validation set, which is constructed by selecting 200 records randomly from training records, spanning the two test beds. Table 1 show the definition of the parameters which is obtained through this tuning.

Using novel CLAF method to detect certain HDs, the training and testing data are separately organized from site measured data of RAZAVI Hospital. There are totally 450 CHD, 150 hypertension (HT), 94 hyperlipaemia (HL) and 206 normal records. From them, 120 records with any kind of HD or combinational HDs, and 330 normal records are selected as the training set. The remaining records are used to verify the performance of trained CLAF. The testing results are shown in table 3 and recall rate of this test are depicted in Fig 3.

Fig. 3 shows that when the noise level (F1 measure) reaches 15%, the success rate of perfect recall using CLAF is 91.3%, even though those of the other methods are less than 70%. When the noise level reaches 20%, the perfect recall rate of CLAF is 85.8%, although those of other methods are less than 49%.

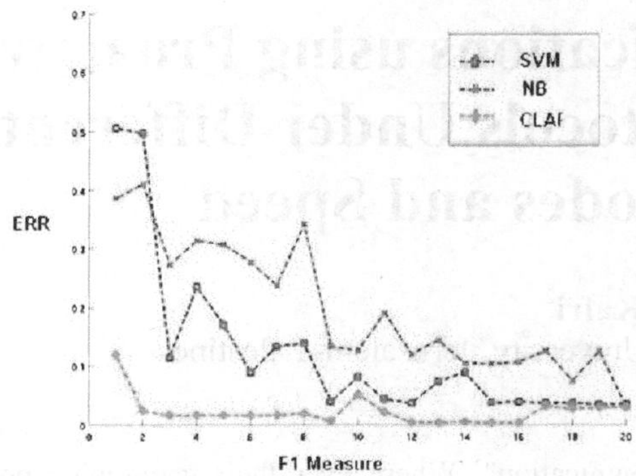

Figure 3. Error rate in HD risk detection

TABLE II. ACCURACY RATE RESULT

Algorithm	Training Record (330)			Testing Record (850)		
	HT	*HL*	*CHD*	*HT*	*HL*	*CHD*
NB	67.13	52.3	89.6	63.7	45.3	80.0
SVM	66.03	84.00	84.01	45.6	62.0	80.01
CLAF	68.13	84.01	92.03	68.1	68.3	81.2

The conventional NNs, SCM and CLAF are compared in detecting certain HDs. Table II shows that when using training data set the CLAF accuracy rate are higher than SVM, but approximately equal; while use testing data set the all methods are reduced and conventional method are still the worst.

Generally, the accuracy of detecting CHD and HT is higher than that of HL. From the testing results it can be concluded that in most situations CLAF are better than NNs with higher sensitivity in discriminating HDs.

5 Conclusion

In this research, we propose a new adaptive competitive neural network (CLAF) for heart disease risk detection. The CLAF, which provide explanation of inference procedure are applied to discriminating certain HDs. All membership functions are adjusted according to the statistical analysis. Features are also reduced so that an optimized feature set is provided for CLAF inference. This approach is tested by using site-measured data sets. Simulation result show that it promising to be applied in HDs risk detection in e-home healthcare usage. Also experiment results prove that the CLAF method has a great accuracy for heart disease risk detection. We plan to estimate the CLAF to detect another medicine risk.

6 References

[1] World Health Organization; "Prevention of heart disease: Pocket guidelines for assessment and management of heart risk," http://www.who.int/heart_disease.

[2] A. M. Sharif, Z. Irani, "Exploring Fuzzy Cognitive Mapping for IS evaluation," European Journal of Operational Research, vol. 173, pp. 1175-1187, April 2006.

[3] D. L. Hudson, Medical Expert Systems, Encyclopedia of Biomedical Engineering. John Wiley & Sons, 2012.

[4] B. Kosko, Neural Networks and Fuzzy Systems. Prentice-Hall, 1992.

[5] R. Jang, "Self-learning fuzzy controllers based on temporal back propagation," IEEE Trans. Neural Netw, vol. 3, pp. 714–723, 1992.

[6] C. K. Iftekharuddin, R. Kozma, "Automated Brain Tumor segmentation and pattern recognition using ANN," Computational Intelligence Robotics and Autonomous Systems, vol. 2, pp. 148-165, August 2001.

[7] R. Marqui, A. Pascual, "Smoothly distributed fuzzy new self organizing map," Pattern Recognition, vol. 34, pp. 2395–2402, February 2002.

[8] K. Thangavel, M. Karnan, "CAD for Preprocessingand Enhancement of Digital Mammograms," GVIP Journal, Vol. 5, 2013.

[9] J. S. Jang, "ANFIS: adaptive network-based fuzzy inference system," IEEE Trans. Sys. Man. Cybern, vol. 23, pp. 665–685,1993.

[10] I. T. Jolliffe, Principal Component Analysis. Springer, 2002.

[11] F. Forster, D. Turney, "Oscillometric determination of diastolic, mean and systolic blood pressure–a numerical model," IEEE Trans. Sys. Man. Cybern, pp. 359-364, 2010.

[12] J. Corchado, J. Bajo, and A. Abraham, "GerAmi: Improving healthcare delivery in geriatric residences," IEEE Intell. Syst, vol. 23, no. 2, pp. 19–25, March 2013.

[13] J. Bezdek, S. Pal, Fuzzy Models for Pattern Recognition. IEEE Press, New York, 2011.

[14] Hannan E. L, et al., The New York Risk Score for In-Hospital and 30-Day Mortality for Coronary Artery Bypass Graft Surgery. The Annals of Thoracic Surgery, vol. 95, pp. 45-90, 2012.

Comparison of Different Applications using Proactive, Reactive Manet Routing Protocols Under Different Application Modes, Nodes and Speed

S. Nijem[1] and N. Kafri[2]
[1]Department of Computer Science, Alquds University, Jerusalem, Palestine

Abstract *- Mobile adhoc network (Manet) is a collection of devices that work together to send and receive information in a wireless network, without using any centralized management; every device acts as a router, by sending and receiving packets while the node moves freely and can set itself in any adhoc network. Adhoc uses routing protocol to move packets from the source to the destination. The quality of service of routing in ad hoc networks is an important and complicated issue with a changing topology. In this work we have measured the performance of routing protocols, proactive, reactive using different applications such as ftp, http and database and determined the best protocol to be used with the application, under various network size, speed and modes .*

Keywords: AODV, DSR, OLSR, OPNET, MANET.

1. Introduction

Last decade has witnessed a huge growth in technology in an unpredictable, fast way, especially in wireless communications. These days a user can check his email, get to the internet using smart phone, laptops and tablet's. Devices that contains wireless technology are becoming more available to user because of their reduced cost. Moreover, they are getting smaller in size and cheaper in cost. Since each device contains wireless capability , this will make them more readily available to connect to a wireless network .This revolution in technology has made manet an important method to be studied , enhanced , especially in its performance [1].

An important requirment for a wireless node to be able to connect and communicate with a network in a dynamic way, it also must be able to transfer data to other wireless nodes, these nodes uses radio channels therefore, they must be within each other's range.

An advantage of Manet is that it doesn't depend on infrastructure meanings it doesn't need wires or cables it only needs air for a connection to be established, This feature, lowers the cost for deployment, with no obstacles to establish the network anywhere any time, "Ad hoc networks promise[2] "anytime, anywhere" operation, pervasive and ubiquitous computing environments, and Independent, free communication". Where ever their geographic position is , nodes can leave or enter the networks whenever they demand , making its topology change dynamically, this what makes manet special and unique.

Routing is needed whenever a packet needs to be sent to the destination by the temporally wireless network, ad hoc network. [3].Routing is the act of moving information from the source to the destination through intermediate nodes Each node in a wireless network moves according to a model called mobility model.

Manet uses different types of routing protocols, these protocols can be categorized into three categories:, Reactive, Proactive and Hybird.

The Reactive Protocol is also called on demand routing protocol, nodes use these protocols only when required; they don't save a predefined route to the destination, when a node needs to send data it sends it based on flooding algorithm by starting a discovery process. On the hand Proactive protocol is also called table driven protocol, nodes that uses these protocols (all participating nodes) update their routing table every period of time (discover the network) even if there is no any request, when a node needs to send a data packet, it sends it through a predefined route that was discovered before, this protocols reduces traffic load because all routes are predefined all the time.
In this paper, we have analyzed the performance of Manet routing protocol, ADOV, DSR, OLSR under FTP, HTTP, Database applications by measuring different metrics delay and throughput.

The paper is divided into the following sections: Section 2 below gives a brief description of routing protocols that has been used in our simulation, Section3 reviews different applications Section4 presents the parameters and setup of simulation environment section5 gives a summary of the work section 6 gives the conclusion

2. Manet Routing Protocols

Routing protocols discussed here and proposed here ADOV, DSR, and OLSR, below are description of each

2.1 Dynamic Source Routing protocol (DSR)

Dynamic Source Routing Protocol is an on-demand routing protocols, it was developed by Johnson, Maltz, and Broch to enable users to communicate over wireless links. It works by the concept of source routing and does not depend on a routing table [4].This Protocol consists of two mechanisms, route discovery and route maintenance that work together to allow nodes to discover and maintain routes. The optimal route from the source to the destination is found by a discovery process, Each source node add's a complete path from the source to the destination to its header packet. Hence every node in the path just forwards the packet to its next hop that exists in the header without having to check its routing table.

2.1.1 Route Discovery

The source node fetches its route cache for a valid route, if it didn't find any, it sends a Route Request Message (RREQ) to the entire network, using flooding process, each node maintains a table that contains all RREQ messages that is recently received. Each new RREQs message will be entered in the table on a pair of (initiator, request id) , when the packet is received ,first it checks if TTL (Time To Live) counter in the packet is greater than zero if not it discards the RREQ message if yes then it checks if this node is the destination as shown in fig(1).

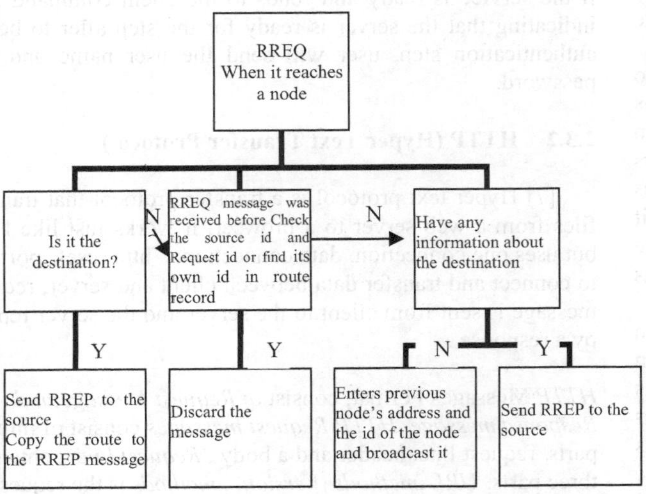

Fig 1- DSR Manet routing protocols discovery process

2.1.2 Route Maintenance

When there is a broken link between two nodes, a route error packet (RERR) is sent by the participating node back to the source node. The source node first removes any route entries in its cache to that node then initiates the route discovery process to find it.

2.1.3 Ad-hoc On demand Distance Vector Routing protocol (ADOV)

[3][4][5] ADOV protocol is a hop-by-hop protocol, it's also called reactive protocol, in this protocol routes will be created and updated only when needed, For example, a hello messages will be broadcasted every period of time to keep track of its neighbors, each node only keeps its next hop not the entire path

There are three types of messages in AODV routing algorithm Route Requests (RREQs), Route Replies (RREPs) and Route Errors (RERRs)) .

When a node requires communicating with a specific node which is not its neighbor, it broadcasts a RREQ message to the entire network Every node in the network must contain the most recent sequence number for other nodes these entries are updated whenever RREQ or RREP RRER messages are received. To discover the network all nodes sends a hello message and receive hello messages from its neighbors. First it checks its route cache (route table) for a route to the destination called "valid route" .If it didn't find any valid route it starts the route discovery process.

2.1.4 Route Discovery

The node broadcasts a RREQ message to its neighbors to find out a valid route to the destination, all RREQ message will be identified by the source id and the request id . Every time the source sends a new RREQ message the request id will change and will be incremented, neighbors that receives this message checks if the message has reached the destination if not, then it checks if this RREQ message was received before if it was received before this message will be discarded , otherwise the node will rebroadcast the RREQ message to the neighbors and the hop count will be incremented.

The node can only know that it reached the destination or an intermediate node by finding a route that is fresh enough, this is the sequence number in the table is close to the seq number in the RREQ. In AODV the seq numbers are used and updated at the destination node , to be sure of the freshness of routing Each participating node when receives a RREQ enters the previous node's address, then the id of the node that broadcast the RREQ to the previous node.

If a neighbor does have information about the destination, it will rebroadcast the message to all of its neighbors and so on. If it reaches the destination or an intermediate node that has a route to destination, it will send a RREP to the source that sent the RREQ by sending the RREP to the neighbor that send the RREQ message and the neighbor will do the same till reaches the source this is called reverse path. When the RREP Message reaches the source this route can be called acomplete route and source can begin sending packets. When a receives a RREP, information of the previous node is stored in it, to forward the packet to it the next hop of the destination.

2.2 OLSR (Optimized Link State Routing)

OLSR is the optimization of link-state routing algorithm In the link state concept every node in manet creates a plan or a map that contains complete information about the network ,in other words, every node in the network is known to which node it is connected. This process is done every period of time to update topology information at each node

OLSR works on three main concepts: neighbor sensing mechanism, efficient flooding mechanism and how to select optimal routes [6].

OLSR is also a table driven proactive protocol where routes are always available when needed. Before any source node intends to send a message routes are built by sending each node in the network HELLO messages to their neighbors to be sure of connectivity between nodes, this process is called neighbor sensing.

Three types of messages is used in OLSR: Hello messages, TC messages, MID messages *Hello messages* are used for gathering information about the link status and neighbors', they help in choosing MPRS, this kind of messages are sent up two hops away. *Topology control messages*, which are broadcast to the entire network, are used to advertise set of neighbors for each node *Multiple Interface Declaration (MID) messages*, these messages are broadcast to the entire network , only broadcasted by MPRs, this kind of messages are used to advertise nodes this node can have multiple interface address.

Every node will send a hello messages to its neighbors to check the link status and to select its one and two hops neighbors' .Each node saves the information that hello messages gathered in a table called neighbors 'table ,it enters a holding time to each neighbor, when holding time expires they are removed . It also decides based on Hello messages it sets of Multi point relay (MPR) and enters a sequence number to each MPR to specify the most recent MPR in its MPR table that is created .

MPR is an optimization of flooding standard , it is as an intermediate node or an interface in which all other nodes can communicate with a specific node through MPR, MPR is selected by one hop neighbors, after electing each node its MPR is set , it will advertise to all nodes which MPR set was elected through the next hello messages that will be broadcasted .Each node will broadcast and forward TC messages only through MPR nodes .Based on MPR selectors and TC messages the node will update topology tables to record the MPR of other nodes, route tables will be created at this stage based on the topology table and the neighbors table.

2.3 Applications

Three types of applications will be used FTP, HTTP and Database server

2.3.1 FTP (File Transfer Protocol)

[7] FTP is a two way protocol that helps in transferring data between two nodes over a network. When a user requests to transfer a file between two computers, the user will use FTP to transfer a file from a client to a server this process is called uploading .To transfer a file from a server to a client the process is called downloading.

FTP uses two types of connections the first type is for commands and is called command or control connection. The other is for sending and receiving data and is called data connection.

Data connection is opened and closed each time a file is transferred. On the other hand a control connection is opened only for one time and closed when the session ends. Session may contains more than one file to be transferred.

FTP uses a logical connection point called a port for communicating. Two ports are used in FTP, one for commands and is called command port and the second is for sending and receiving data and is called data port, the standard port number that is used for commands is 21 and the one used for data is 20. The port used for sending and receiving data depends on the mode connection, mode connection dictates who will connect the server or the client.

When a client demands to connect to a server a control connection will be created on port 21, server will check to see if the service is ready and sends to the client command 220 indicating that the server is ready for the step after to be an authentication step, user will send the user name and the password.

2.3.2 HTTP (Hyper Text Transfer Protocol)

[7] Hyper text protocol is a transfer protocol that transfer files from a web server to a browser, it works just like FTP, but uses one connection, data connection, http uses port 80 to connect and transfer data between client and server, request message is sent from client to the server and the server replies by a response .

HTTP Messages Format, consist *of Request Message and Response message ,HTTP Request messages* consist of three parts, request line, header and a body , *Request line*, contains three parts, *URL ,methods , Version*, , *methods* is the request type ,*Version* is the version of the http protocol ,http 1.1.,*Header line* ,sends extra information from the client to server ,each header consist of header name , a header value and a *Body* that contains some comment sent from the client to the server.

HTTP response messages consist of four parts, *status line, header lines, blank line and body. Status line*, consist of three fields the first is for the version of http, the second is status code as a result to the request message. *Header,* Header line sends extra information from the server to client, there may be more than header in the response message, and each header has a header name and a header value.

3. Related Work

Many researcher worked on analyzing manet routing protocol using different kinds of simulators, different kind of data traffic ,since even before 2000 and till now research field is still studying manet protocols.

[8].In 2011 they measured packet delivery ratio, end to end delay, routing overhead and throughput for reactive and proactive protocols , DSR , DSDV and ADOV for CBR traffic , different number of nodes using NS2.,results shows reactive protocol has a performance higher than proactive protocol.[9] 2010 ,Thesis has studied performance of reactive , proactive and hybrid under realistic network scenarios ADOV, DSR,OLSR and ZPR ,scenarios was made on a real live network ,mobility of nodes was simulated using GPS, traffic that has been created by a generation tool ,using 19 mobile node and a base station for 4 hours on the other hand another simulation is carried out by Qualnet simulator, through put results shows ADOV performed the best between protocols , delay shows ADOV has the lowest results between protocols , each live simulation and QUALNET simulator has exactly the same results.

In 2009 S.Dhulipala,RM.Chandrasekaran and R.Prabakaran [10] has measured time analysis, the scalability of various types of applications , CBR , FTP , TELNET , VBR using different number of nodes(10, 120, 250, 275,375, 475 and 575 nodes) , on ADOV protocol ,Qualnet simulator ,results shows the execution time for CBR was the highest on the other hand VBR was the lowest when comparing with different type of applications ,other applications showed consistent results, a year after that [11] V.Tafti, A.Gandomi used OPNET to measure Quality of service of ADOV,DSR and OLSR protocols using different metrics ,delay , throughput , packet drop rate using FTP traffic ,throughput results shows that OLSR protocol has performed in a perfect way when comparing it with other protocols in large network scale on the other hand ADOV performed better than DSR in small network scale , delay results shows that DSR has scored the worst result between protocols.

[12] S.Parulpreet , B.Ekta, W.Gurleen in 2102 has measured traffic load(HTTP , Email , Video conference) on DSR routing protocol on40 node heavy load ,speed 10m/sec,800*80 to find out that DSR scored delay when using it with video conference while HTTP scored the lowest in delay ,throughput results showed highest in Video conf and lowest in HTTP.

4. Performance Metrics

4.1 Throughput

Throughput is the ratio of all numbers of bits a destination receives from a source over a communication network. Throughput is considered an accurate choice to measure performance of a network. It is measured in bits per second (bits/sec).Mathematically, throughput can be defined by the following formula.

Throughput= (number of delivered packet * packet size)/ simulation time.

4.2 Delay

Delay is a performance tool, that measures the efficiency of a communication network by measuring the average time a packet takes to begin and end its trip from the source to the destination and called end to end delay it can be called also latency in many cases, delay can be expressed in to three kinds of delays, transmission delay, propagation delay and processing delays [10], delay is a very important metric and it can be considered as a critical parameter to be studied.

End to end delay = transmission delay + propagation delay + processing delay.

5. Simulation

5.1 Simulation Enviroment

The simulations were performed using opnet simulator, Optimized Network Engineering Tool. FTP ,HTTP ,Database servers were used with various types of loads ,three different network size were chosen , small ,10 node , medium ,50 node and big network size ,100 node in 1000*1000 meter as shown in Table1.

Table 1 Parameters chosen for the simulation

Scenario size	1000*1000 m
Scenario time	10 Min
802.11 data rate	11 Mbps
Number of nodes	10, 50,100
Nodes speed	10 m/s, 30 m/s
Pause time	of 0 sec
Services	. FTP, HTTP and Database
Different routing protocols	AODV, DSR and OLSR
Mobility Model	Random Waypoint Mobility model
Applications modes	high load , low load

Simulation has been executed for 10 minutes, the node speed was 10 meter/sec for all network size and 30 meter/sec was executed for medium network size in each scenario.

Mobility model ,represents the movement of the nodes from the beginning of the simulation. Random Waypoint Model [11] is a way a node moves according to it, in which it assumes that each node is placed initially at a random position within the area of the simulation.

When simulation begins, each node chooses a destination and then sends packets to it with a constant speed that is randomly selected from the interval [vmin, vmax]. After that it pauses for period called the pause time.

Table 2 FTP Loads used in the simulation

FTP Load Types	FTP High Load	FTP Low Load
Command Mix	50%	50%
File size	constant(5000)	constant(1000)
InterRequest time	exponential(360)	exponential(3600)

Two FTP loads were used as shown in Table2. The first is high load of file size 5000 byte and total get commands to total commands is 50%, inter request time is the time between file transfers. The start time for a file transfer is computed by adding the inter-request time to the time that the previous file

Table 3 DB Loads used in the simulations

Database Load Types	Database high Load	Database Low Load
Transaction Mix (Queries/Total transaction)	100%	100%
Transaction Interval time	exponential(12)	exponential(30)
Transaction Size	constant(32768)	constant(16)
Type of service	Best effort	Best effort

transfer started.
The second ftp load is the low load, the file size is 1000 byte. Two other types of loads were used as shown in Table3. Table The heavy browsing consist of 1000 byte page size, for images of medium size and an inter request time of 60 sec. The second type is light browsing that consist of 500 bytes

Table 4 HTTP Loads used in the simulations

HTTP Load Types	Heavy Browsing		Light Browsing	
HTTP Version	HTTP1.1			
Page Interval time	exponential(60)		exponential(720)	
Page property Object Size Object per page	Constant(1000)	Medium Image	Constant(500)	Small Image
	Constant(1)	Constant(5)	Constant(1)	Constant(5)
Initial Repeat Pages Per Server	Browse Exponential (10)		Browse Exponential (10)	

page size, small images and inter request time 720 seconds.

Two types of loads were used as shown in Table 4.The database high load consists of 100% of the total transactions and the transaction size is 32768 byte . The transaction size is the size in bytes of the database transaction request .The second type of loads is a low load which consists of 100% of the total transactions and a 16 byte size of database transaction request .The transaction interval time, defines when the next database transaction will start.

5.2 Simulation Results

We have evaluated the key performance metrics for three different applications using reactive and proactive protocols. These parameters are delay and throughput used for protocols evaluation and these parameters which considered as an important factors that affects the behavior of network communication.

First we measured number of control packets that has been sent by the source to the destination and how much time it took to reach the destination, to give an indication how the protocol efficiency acts. This parameter is called end to end delay.

For example number of packets that reach's the destination in 3 secs is not like packets that reach's the destination in 10 secs, if we considered millions and millions of packets sent and received in simulation scenario.

Table 5 FTP high Load for 10 m/s

	10 nodes		50 nodes		100 nodes	
	Delay	Th.put	Delay	Th.put	Delay	Th.put
DSR	0.0071	18287	0.0100	97075	0.0317	282203
AODV	0.0011	18982	0.0035	581853	0.0173	3273905
OLSR	0.0006	62612	0.0010	2684747	0.0014	16001374

Secondly we checked the numbers of packets that has been sent and the numbers of packets that has been received, throughput, is considered an accurate choice to measure performance of a network.

To measure and examine protocol performance, 54 scenarios has been created using different number of nodes, applications and traffic loads .Each scenario has been executed for 10 min (simulation time). In each simulation we checked the behavior of AODV, DSR and OLSR. We collected DES (global discrete event statistics) on the Wireless LAN, mobile nodes move at a constant speed of 10 m/s and 30 m/s.

5.2.1 Simulation Part One

The simulations which was measured in this part of study used the following parameters, speed 10 m/s, FTP, HTTP and Database applications, type of loads is high and low loads and a network size of 10, 50 and 100 node.

Table 5 shows the results of ftp high load using ADOV, DSR and OLSR protocols at 588 sec. When a node demands to transfer file using an ftp server with a high load., the nodes in the network will try to find the shortest path between the source and the ftp server because FTP is considered as a wireless node that gives services. After finding the shortest path, control connection will be established for sending and receiving data .Reactive routing protocols DSR and AODV have more delay when comparing them to proactive routing protocol OLSR. The source node will broadcast RREQ message to the whole network and wait till a response arrives which causes a higher delay than the OLSR when using reactive protocols.

In small , medium and large network size, high delay is noticed in DSR routing protocol compared to AODV and OLSR, due to the nature of DSR in carrying the whole path along the network ,which makes DSR routing packet larger than other's, on the other hand large routing overhead packet in the payload of the packets. OLSR was the best between other protocols. In small and medium size of networks ADOV gained not a high end to end delay but a good throughput.

When measuring protocols using FTP Low Load as shown in Table 6, we found out that DSR has the worst results in all sizes of network, on the other hand ADOV was not far away from OLSR in small size of network, but in medium and large size of the network ADOV didn't have a good results as like OLSR. When comparing results of ftp high and low load Adov protocol behaves better with Ftp low load than Ftp high load in all number of nodes, delay shows continuous increasing when using ftp high load than low load, on the other hand throughput shows better results when using ftp low load than high load

In small networks, DSR protocol shows a higher delay when using FTP low load than FTP high load. OLSR protocol has better results when using low load, on the other hand throughput has gained better results when using high load. In general OLSR has gained the best results between other results when using FTP high and low load.

In Table 8 shows results for HTTP heavy load using different simulations of ADOV, DSR and OLSR protocols at 588 sec. When a node demands an http page, first the source node will find the shortest path from the source to the destination, the http server, secondly one control connection will be opened between the source and the http server .

When measuring results in small size of network ADOV protocol shows the lowest results in end to end delay between other protocols, but its not the best throughput result in small network size, in medium and large networks, OLSR has the best results and DSR has the worst results between all protocols.

Table 6 FTP low Load for 10 m/s

	10 node		50 node		100 node	
	Delay	Th.put	Delay	Th.put	Delay	Th.put
DSR	0.0070	18286	0.0030	91419	0.0046	13341
ADOV	0.0011	565.6	0.0021	2698547	0.0071	1109631
OLSR	0.0003	42617	0.0004	3973	0.0005	15861611

Table7 HTTP light Load for 10 m/s

	10 nodes		50 nodes		100 nodes	
	Delay	Th.put	Delay	Th.put	Delay	Th.put
DSR	0.0020	966	0.0021	8563	0.0036	26336
ADOV	0.0006	1864	0.0006	245009	0.0094	1834181
OLSR	0.0004	43319	0.0004	2616318	0.0006	18400631

Table 7 shows results of HTTP light load .In all network size OLSR showed the best results between other protocols , ADOV performed in a very good way in medium and large networks size and ADOV results were very close to OLSR results .

When comparing results of HTTP high and low load , Adov protocol shows a higher delay when using heavy pages but a good throughput results. In small networks, we can observe ADOV performance that showed the highest throughput when using HTTP heavy load.DSR Protocol have an increasing delay with Heavy pages due to DSR nature of carrying all path .OLSR Protocol is better with low load than high load when measuring delay on the other hand throughput has showed better result with high load.

Table8 HTTP heavy Load for 10 m/ s

	10 nodes		50 nodes		100 node	
	Delay	Th.put	Delay	Th.put	Delay	Th.put
DSR	0.0061	15449	0.0069	76536	0.008707	158691
ADOV	0.0007	33168	0.0041	2079665	0.0195	1066485
OLSR	0.0008	57889	0.0007	2675287	0.0011	1845626

Table 9 and Table 10 identical results was shown when using light and high Database loads with different simulations for ADOV, DSR and OLSR protocols at 588 sec. OLSR performed the best between other protocols. ADOV has a good results,when comparing them with high and low database loads .Adov Protocol have a higher delay when using high load bit a good throughput. In small networks, we can observe ADOV have the highest throughput when using DB heavy load

DSR Protocol has an increasing delay with DB transactions. OLSR Protocol is better with DB low load than high load when measuring delay .On the other hand throughput has better result when using high load.

Table9 DB low Load for 10 m/s

	10 nodes		50 nodes		100 nodes	
	Delay	Th.put	Delay	Th.put	Delay	Th.put
DSR	0.0145	233812	0.0390	1157217	0.1078	1441630
ADOV	0.0022	92881	0.0044	1584772	0.0221	6513085
OLSR	0.0023	36664	0.0109	3693489	0.0149	1859211

5.2.2 Simulation Part Two

The simulations which was measured in this part of study used the following parameters, speed 30 m/s, FTP, HTTP and Database applications, type of loads is high and low loads and a network size of 50 node.Identical results were observed even when nodes speed increases to 30 m/s .OLSR has the best results of all while DSR has the worst results .However, ADOV shows an intermediate results of all.

Table10 DB high Load for 10 m/s

	10 nodes		50 nodes		100 nodes	
	Delay	Th.put	Delay	Th.put	Delay	Th.put
DSR	0.0005	2081	0.0010	23381	0.1078	1441630
ADOV	0.001	22554	0.0005	92881	0.0175	6565914
OLSR	0.0003	44174	0.0003	36664	0.0149	18592119

6. Conclusion

In this Paper we have analyzed delay and throughput for Proactive and reactive protocols with different number of nodes, speed and modes, results shows OlSR performed ina best way compared to other protocols, ADOV didn't show the best performance in throughput but it didn't show the worst performance in delay. DSR has the worst performance in throughput and delay.As a conclusion ADOV can be used in

	ADOV			DSR			OLSR		
	S	M	L	S	M	L	S	M	L
FTP High	Good	Good	Can	Bad			Best		
FTP Low	Good	Can	Can	Bad			Best		
HTTP heavy	Best	Good	Good	Bad			Good		Best
HTTP light	Can	Good	Good	Bad			Best		
DB high load	Good	Good	Good	Bad			Best		
DB low load	Good	Good	Good	Bad			Best		

small and medium network size while Olsr is best to be used in large network size.

7. References

[1] Samir R. Das, Charles E. Perkins, Elizabeth M. Royer. "Performance Comparison of Two On-demand Routing Protocols for Ad Hoc Networks". Proceedings IEEE Infocom page 3-12, March 2000.

[2] L. M. Feeney, B. Ahlgren, A. Westerlund, and A. Dunkels. "Spontnet:Experiences in Configuring and Securing Small Ad Hoc Networks," in Proceedings of the 5th Internation Workshop on Network Appliances,.

[3] Sabina Baraković, Suad Kasapović, and Jasmina Baraković,"Comparison of MANET Routing Protocols in Different Traffic and Mobility Models",2010

[4] S.J. Lee, "Routing and Multicasting Strategies in Wireless Mobile Ad hoc Networks" ,University of California, Los Angeles,2000

[5] Sabina Baraković, Suad Kasapović, and Jasmina Baraković."Comparison of MANET Routing Protocols inDifferent Traffic and Mobility Models",2010

[6] T.H. Clausen et al. "The optimized link state routing protocol evaluating through experiments and simulation, mindpass center for distributed system",,Aalborg university ,Denmark

[7] Behrouz A. Forouzan. "TCP/IP Protocol Suites"Book ,Fourth edition

[8] Qasim Nadia, Said Fatin , Aghvami Hamid ."Mobile Ad Hoc Networking Protocol's Evaluation through Simulation for Quality ofService." , IAENG International Journal of Computer Science, 36:1,IJCS_36_1_10, 17 February, 2009.

[9] Hsu,S.Bhatia , M.Takai and R.Bagrodia . "Performance of Mobile ad hoc networking routing protocols in realistic scenarios", 2010

[10] Sarma Dhulipala,RM.Chandrasekaran and R.Prabakaran "Timing Analysis and Repeatability Issues of Mobile Ad-Hoc Networking Application traffics in Large Scale Scenarios", 2009.

[11] V.Tafti, A.Gandomi." Performance of QoS Parameters in MANET Application Traffics in Large Scale Scenarios", World Academy of Science, Engineering and Technology,2010.

[12] S.Parulpreet , B.Ekta, W.Gurleen."Evaluation of various traffic loads in MANET with DSR routing protocol through use of OPNET Simulator" ,International Journal of Distributed and Parallel Systems (IJDPS), Vol.3, No.3, May 2012.

Simulation of a Remote Sensing System for Fire Detection

Carsten Paproth and Anko Börner
Optical Information Systems, German Aerospace Center (DLR), Berlin, Germany

Abstract— *We want to create a simulation of a remote fire detection sensor. The simulated sensor data could help to improve the fire retrieval algorithm. The simulation will be built by using a more general tool for simulations of remote sensing systems. The simulation tool consists of a geometric, a radiometric, and a sensory component. Artificial fire maps will serve as input to the simulation and will be created by using fractional Brownian motion.*

Keywords: sensor simulation, remote sensing, fire detection, fractional Brownian motion

1. Introduction

Simulated sensor output can often be used to support the development procedure of a remote sensing system. For example, estimations of the sensor performance or testing of retrieval algorithms could be made with simulated data before real sensor data is available. We want to adapt a simulation concept for remote sensing systems [1], [2] to a remote fire detection system [3]. The goal is to study the influence of the atmosphere on the already existing fire detection algorithm and maybe to improve this algorithm or the fire sensor parameters. The scope of this paper is the description of the main steps necessary to create the simulation of the remote fire detection sensor.

2. Simulation of remote sensing systems

The simulation of a remote sensing system consists of three main components [1]. The first component is the simulation of the geometry. With a ray tracing approach, this component calculates what every sensor pixel can see and what is shadowed or not. The second component is the simulation of the radiometry. This is the radiative transfer from the observed surface to the sensor which results in the at-sensor radiance. The final component is the sensor component which converts the at-sensor radiance into a digital output in dependence on the sensor optics and detector.

SENSOR++ [2] is an enhancement of this simulation concept. One of the improvements is the extension of the spectral range to the thermal infrared which is also needed to simulate the fire sensor. According to [4], the at-sensor radiance can be calculated with

$$L = E_{\text{sun}}\rho\tau s \text{BRDF}(\omega_i,\omega_o)(\omega_i\cdot n) + B(T)(1-\rho)\tau + L_{\text{atm}}. \quad (1)$$

Eq. (1) uses the following definitions:

$$\begin{aligned} E_{\text{sun}} &= \text{irradiance of the sun below atmosphere}\\ \rho &= \text{reflectance of the surface, } 0\le\rho\le 1\\ \tau &= \text{transmittance of the atmosphere, } 0\le\tau\le 1\\ s &= 0 \quad \text{if surface is shadowed}\\ s &= 1 \quad \text{if surface is not shadowed}\\ \text{BRDF} &= \text{bidirectional reflectance distribution function}\\ \omega_i &= \text{unit vector from the surface to the sun}\\ \omega_o &= \text{unit vector from the surface to the sensor}\\ n &= \text{surface normal vector}\\ B(T) &= \text{radiance of a blackbody at temperature } T\\ L_{\text{atm}} &= \text{atmospheric radiance.} \end{aligned}$$

The values of E_{sun}, τ, and L_{atm} are calculated with MODTRAN [5] which calculates the radiative transfer through the atmosphere of the earth. The atmospheric radiance L_{atm} includes the indirect reflected, solar scattered, and thermal path radiances. The values of s, ω_i, ω_o, and n are gotten from the geometry simulation. Only physically reasonable BRDFs are used by SENSOR++. Except for the geometric quantities, all terms of Eq. (1) depend on the wavelength. To get the digital output of the sensor, one has to calculate the electron number or radiant flux according to the used detector. Both calculations are mainly the integral of the at-sensor radiance over the bandwidth. An example output of the sensor simulation is shown in Fig. 1.

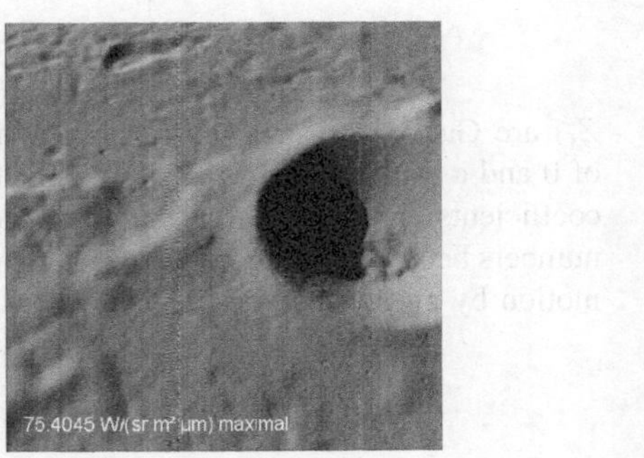

Fig. 1: Simulated camera image with the maximum occurring at-sensor radiance. This camera simulation was created with SENSOR++ and is part of a simulation of a moon lander [2]. The thin atmosphere of the moon is ignored in this simulation, thus $\tau = 1$ and $L_{\text{atm}} = 0$.

3. Simulation of the fire detection sensor

For the simulation, we have to consider the following characteristics of the fire detection sensor [3]. The sensor is a multispectral sensor with near (790 nm to 930 nm), mid L_m (3.4 µm to 4.2 µm), and thermal L_t (8.5 µm to 9.3 µm) infrared channels. It consists of line cameras with two staggered lines. The scanning is done according to the pushbroom principle. The fire detection algorithm is sensitive to sub-pixel fires, so we have to sample the fire scene with appropriate high resolution and model the point spread function accordingly.

At first, the algorithm searches for potential fire pixels by interpreting the information of the different spectral channels. The final step of the fire detection algorithm determines the fire temperature T_F, fire area A_F, and finally the fire radiative power FRP by solving

$$L_m = A_F B_m(T_F) + (1 - A_F) L_{m,bg} \tag{2}$$
$$L_t = A_F B_t(T_F) + (1 - A_F) L_{t,bg} \tag{3}$$
$$\mathrm{FRP} = \sigma T_F^4 A_F \mathrm{GSD}^2, \tag{4}$$

with the Stefan-Boltzmann constant σ and the ground sampling distance GSD. The quantities $L_{m,bg}$ and $L_{t,bg}$ are estimations of the background radiances, i.e. the non-fire part of the pixels, in the mid and thermal infrared respectively.

4. Creating artificial fires

One problem is to get input data for the simulation. We want to use artificial data which we can control but which also has some natural features. For this purpose, we want to exploit the self-similarity of a Gaussian process called fractional Brownian motion fBm [6] to create fire maps. With the Fourier filter method, we can create d-dimensional fractional Brownian motion corresponding to noise with a power spectrum of $1/f^\beta$. For it, the absolute value of the Fourier coefficients is set to

$$|C_f| = \frac{1}{|f|^{\frac{\beta+d-1}{2}}} \cdot Z_G, \tag{5}$$

Z_G are Gaussian distributed random numbers with a mean of 0 and a standard deviation of 1. The phase of the Fourier coefficients $\arg(C_f)$ is set to uniformly distributed random numbers between 0 and 2π. One gets the fractional Brownian motion by an inverse discrete Fourier transform

$$\mathrm{fBm}(x) = \sum_f e^{\frac{2\pi i}{N} x \cdot f} C_f \tag{6}$$

Furthermore, the coefficients have to fulfill $C_{-f} = \overline{C_f}$ to create only real values with the Fourier filter method. In Fig. 2, a 1-dimensional example of such a random fractal is shown. By additionally applying a threshold, we can create a 2-dimensional fire temperature distribution, see Fig. 3.

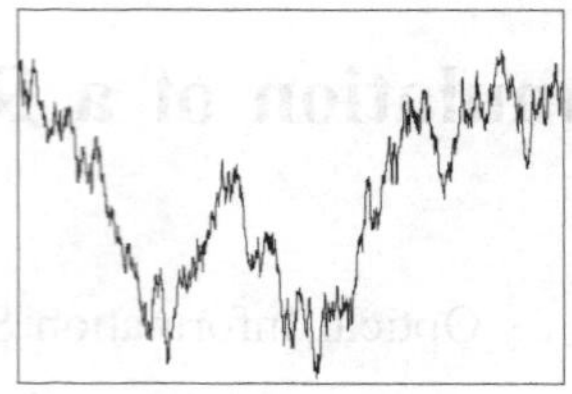

Fig. 2: Fractional Brownian motion also contains usual Brownian motion and accordingly Brownian noise. These $N = 1000$ samples were created with the Fourier filter method with $d = 1$ and $\beta = 2$.

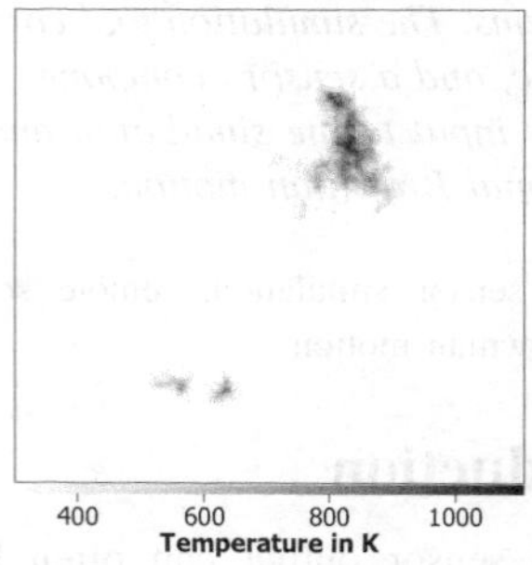

Fig. 3: An artificial fire map ($N \times N = 500 \times 500$ samples) created with the Fourier filter method with $d = 2$ and $\beta = 2.5$ and applying a threshold.

5. Conclusion

With SENSOR++ and fractional Brownian motion, we have all tools to build the simulation of the remote fire detection sensor. By using simulated sensor data to test the fire detection algorithm, one can ignore calibration problems, non-uniformity problems, and the misalignment between the different spectral channels of the real sensor. This helps us to concentrate on the atmospheric effects we want to study.

References

[1] A. Börner, L. Wiest, P. Keller, R. Reulke, R. Richter, M. Schaepman, and D. Schläpfer, "SENSOR: a tool for the simulation of hyperspectral remote sensing systems," *ISPRS Journal of Photogrammetry & Remote Sensing*, vol. 55, pp. 299–312, 2001.

[2] C. Paproth, E. Schlüßler, P. Scherbaum, and A. Börner, "SENSOR++: simulation of remote sensing systems from visible to thermal infrared," in *International Archives of the Photogrammetry, Remote Sensing and Spatial Information Sciences*, ser. XXII ISPRS Congress, vol. XXXIX-B1, 2012, pp. 257–260.

[3] B. Zhukov, E. Lorenz, D. Oertel, M. Wooster, and G. Roberts, "Spaceborne detection and characterization of fires during the bi-spectral infrared detection (BIRD) experimental small satellite mission (2001-2004)," *Remote Sensing of Environment*, vol. 100, pp. 29–51, 2006.

[4] L. Wiest, "Radiometriesimulation hyperspektraler Sensoren in der Fernerkundung," Ph.D. dissertation, Technische Universität Berlin, 2001.

[5] A. Berk, L. S. Bernstein, and D. C. Robertson, "MODTRAN: A Moderate Resolution Model for LOWTRAN," Air Force Geophysics Laboratory, Tech. Rep., 1987.

[6] B. B. Mandelbrot and J. W. van Ness, "Fractional Brownian Motions, Fractional Noises and Applications," *SIAM Review*, vol. 10, no. 4, pp. 422–437, 1968.

SESSION

LATE BREAKING PAPERS - SIMULATION, MODELING, AND VISUALIZATION

Chair(s)

Prof. Hamid Arabnia
University of Georgia

Procedural Generation of Terrain within Highly Customizable JavaScript Graphics Utilities for WebGL

T.H.McMullen and K.A. Hawick
Computer Science, Massey University, North Shore 102-904, Auckland, New Zealand
email: timmy361@gmail.com k.a.hawick@massey.ac.nz
Tel: +64 9 414 0800 Fax: +64 9 441 8181

June 2013

ABSTRACT

Modelling realistic scenes and rendering them appropriately are two key aspects of modern computer games. Scenes need to be detailed, realistically non-repetitive and computationally feasible. Procedural generation involves encoding a game scene as a recipe or procedure that can be generated and regenerated at run time, rather than just loaded from file or network server. Procedural generation in the context of web games and systems is particularly powerful in reducing bandwidth transfer requirements. We describe experiments to implement a framework for procedural generation using JavaScript and modern web client software systems such as WebGL and OpenGL shader language. Our system is able to exploit available Graphical Processing Units(GPU) and is aimed at supporting existing web based graphics engines. We present some graphical results and discuss future performance and scalability issues.

KEY WORDS

computer games; scene generation; procedural generation; spatial structure; fractals.

1 Introduction

Computer games [20] make heavy use of scene modelling [19], generation and rendering. While OpenGL [4, 6, 26] software has become the *de facto* industry standard for rendering scene, a modern generation of network and mobile games make use of web clients to run and render the system. WebGL [1, 3, 16] is an excellent bridging technology, because it allows many sophisticated scene and game rendering tasks to work within a web client context and supports game interface design [24] in a platform independent manner [18].

The advent of WebGL means that many web-based graphics utilities have been created to support simple graphical functions. We aim to improve upon the current graphic engines by allowing for a more customizable utility to be used, with functionality focused on procedural generation [7, 10]. It is the aim of this research to maximise the use of procedural generation to create different landscapes in different levels of detail. Implementation plays a large role in these tools, and so we use the Require.js module loader. With the created library it is hoped that the resulting programs, and applications will run on a range of devices. This means that several optimizations need to be researched to achieve this.

Figure 1: **Terrain Generation:** Landscape produced using the Diamond Square algorithm in WebGL. Map size is 257x257

Procedural generation is a method of using algorithms to create content. Taking this approach to creating content allows for unique areas, models and other objects to be produced. The idea behind this research is simplifying the process of creating content by utilising procedural generation. This means that if an object is created several times, they will differ slightly each time they are rendered. Procedural generation fundamentally changes the way in which a model is created. The model is generated at run time and with unique customisations that are made possible, rather than loaded from a static set of pre-generated options from a server.

Procedural generation has been used for a variety of scene aspects including village [5] or urban [25] architectural components, interior architectures [9], and organic materials such as trees [11, 13, 21]. Terrain and organic materials the generated patterns are often not simple geometric ones but are fractal in nature. This requires a more complex approach using fractal algorithms [15] such as L-Systems [23]. Various approaches to procedural generation software are possible, including the use of domain specific languages [8] to support customization. Some work using procedural generation for mobile systems has been reported on [14] but little work is available on its use in web based systems where data compression and minimizing data transfer [17] is important.

WebGL is an implementation of OpenGL designed to be run in the a web browser, using a JavaScript API [22]. It uses OpenGL Shader Language (GLSL) [2] to create and compile shaders to be run on a graphics processing unit(GPU) [12], to allow for highly dynamic and customizable graphical programming to be completed. As WebGL is web based it does come with some limitations. The limitations include restrictions imposed by bandwidth restraints, and JavaScript being interpreted code as opposed to compiled code. These limitations can be improved upon by minimising the amount of data which will need to be transferred, as well as improving the processing of data with the use of GLSL. The use of shader language means an application is able to offload some parts of the program to the GPU to be computed rather than the CPU.

As this research aims to create a highly customizable set of utilities, implementation needs to be as simplistic as possible. To help achieve this the Require.js script is used. This allows a web based application to be spread across multiple files, with each part accessible. By doing this, it helps to greatly simplify the process of creating and including code, into an web based environment.

This technology can be used to help improve upon some limitations of web based graphic engines by allowing for large landscapes to be generated, as opposed to being loaded as a file. The file is then created locally rather than being transferred from a server, which saves on bandwidth. This does create the need to generate the content rather than reading in a file, the benefits of which are discussed later on in this paper.

There are other implementations of procedural generation used within many graphical system, however ours has focused on the use of platform independence. This means that various limitations impact the design of the set of utilities. One such limitation is the maximum number of vertices which are able to be drawn in one draw call. This in turn creates the need to split up the scene and make multiple draw calls for one frame if necessary. Additional limitations are discussed throughout this paper.

Figure 1 shows a procedurally generated scene of a landscape, which was generated using the framework and utilities we report in this paper. The remainder of our article is structured as follows: In Section 2 we discuss to use of procedural generation, with a focus on the Diamond Square algorithm. Section 3 covers results from this research, while Section 4 talks about what we found, and problems were encountered. The final section, talks about what we have completed and where this research will lead to in the future.

2 Procedural Generation

Procedural generation of a landscape allows for a created environment to be based on a set of pseudo random numbers. Creating content in this manner allows for a developer to simply create unique or predefined content. The significant advantage of generating content this way, is that it allows for additional data to be assigned to each point. An example of this would be what kind of terrain it is, or if you want to have something else spawn at that location. The Diamond Square method combined with our created utilities means the Z value is the only one affected in our mesh, leaving the original environment dimensions with a minimum amount of change.

The Diamond Square implementation is a method of creating and changing the height value of a location in a square map. This method works by taking two steps, the diamond and square steps. For the Diamond step four points of a square are use to find the center point, this point has its elevation changed, in our case the Y value. The change in value is based on an offset from a random number, followed by using the average of the original four corner points. The square step involves taking the center point and using that to allow for the subdivision of the main map area, each segment being a quarter of the original size. This process is repeated till the map is unable to be divided anymore. Using the Diamond Square algorithm allows for a set of predefined pseudo random numbers to be provided to recreate a previously created environment.

Within the process of creating a procedurally generated terrain we take in the information of an area surrounding a point within the mesh, and based on that are able to define certain aspects for that point. Creating additional properties within a generated terrain like this allows for areas to have more details applied to them, and to influence surrounding areas. An example of this would be to have a tree spawn if a set condition was met, then having that tree at that location would increase the chances of the neighbouring tiles also having a tree or some other previously specified object.

To create a mesh which is able to store these details normally we would need to use a 2D array. As JavaScript does not currently have native support for 2D arrays this left two options for storing the data. The first option was to use a single array, and manipulate that to work as it would if it was a 2D array. This is done by adding supplementary information to the index when searching for a data point, such as line size, and height. The other option for creating a 2D array was to create an array, then append another array to each element within the original array. This latter method did create some unique problems when trying to access an element, but proved to be simpler in the conceptual stages of this research.

The utility uses pseudo random numbers to allow for a created scene to be reproduced. Pseudo random numbers, as the name suggests are random numbers which are not truly random. While the process of generation allows for seemingly random numbers to be produced, they are all based upon the originally selected numbers (seeds). Using this method allows for a scene which has been produced to be recreated by reusing the same base numbers. These utilities allow for the passing of predefined seeds, but if none are passed then a seed based on time is produced.

Additionally as these utilities aim at being platform independent the GPU on the device is able to help improve performance in several key ways. Firstly we are able to have the GPU colour parts of the environment based on height and location information which is passed in as the x, y, and z coordinates of a point. Using the GPU to do these calculations reduces the quantity of data that needs to be passed from the CPU to the GPU at any given time, as well as freeing up the CPU for other calculations. Another advantage of using the GLSL with the GPU is that the utilities designed allow for data which has been processed on the GPU to then be returned and worked on again. This in turn allows for a cyclic flow of information.

Algorithm 1 Diamond Square Algorithm, Square Step.

```
declare x, y, size, half, offset, avg, vertices[]
half = size/2
point1 = vertexes[x - half][y - half]
point2 = vertexes[x + half][y - half]
point3 = vertexes[x - half][y + half]
point4 = vertexes[x + half][y + half]
avg = (point1 + point2 + point3 + point4)/4
vertices[x][y] = avg + offset
```

Algorithm 1 shows the Square step in the Diamond Square algorithm, which is taking the four surrounding corners of a point, and their corresponding value to find an average value. Then an offset is added to find average, and it is applied to our central point.

Algorithm 1 shows the Diamond step in the Diamond Square algorithm which is taking the top, bottom, left and right points surrounding a central point, and their corresponding values to find an average value. Then an offset is added to find average, and it is applied to our central point.t.

Algorithm 2 Diamond Square Algorithm, Diamond Step.

```
declare x, y, size, half, offset, avg, vertices[]
half = size/2
point1 = vertexes[x - half][y]
point2 = vertexes[x + half][y]
point3 = vertexes[x][y + half]
point4 = vertexes[x][y + half]
avg = (point1 + point2 + point3 + point4)/4
vertices[x][y] = avg + offset
```

The algorithms above are the key steps within this procedural generation implementation. The overall system works using a 2D array that is recursively subdividing itself by taking a point and initially using the Diamond step to assign a value to the center point. The Square step used next involves initialising the points above, below and to the left and right of the center point. Once this is done, the area is split into quarters, and the steps repeat, but now in a smaller section using a reduced size value. This process will repeat until all the points within the 2D array have become initialized.

Figure 2 shows the process of moving through a 2D mesh, using the Diamond Square algorithm. We can see in the first image the selection of the four corners, from this we move on to initialize the center point shown in tile to the right - this part was the Diamond step. Next we apply the Square step to the mesh, filling in the data for the center of each edge. Once we have completed both steps the area which we work in is reduced, and then the steps are repeated. The last part of figure 2 shows the final step; the Square step. Once applied, the whole grid has been initialized with a value which can then be used for the height of a location in the mesh.

3 Experimental Results

The system created is built up of several key parts; firstly the implementation of the Diamond Square algorithm to build the procedural generation for the utilities. This included simplifying the process of creating a scene, by using created functions. The optimization of code, and utilisation of GPUs have played a role in improving the system in speed and in bandwidth consumed. Finally the limitation of vertices able to be rendered in one draw call needed to be addressed to allow for larger terrains. Each of these parts played a vital role in creating this system, and will be expanded upon below. A performance review is also included so as to see the resulting improvements over other methods.

Implementing the Diamond Square algorithm required the use of several steps as explained in figure 2. This research aimed at producing a simplified method of implementing

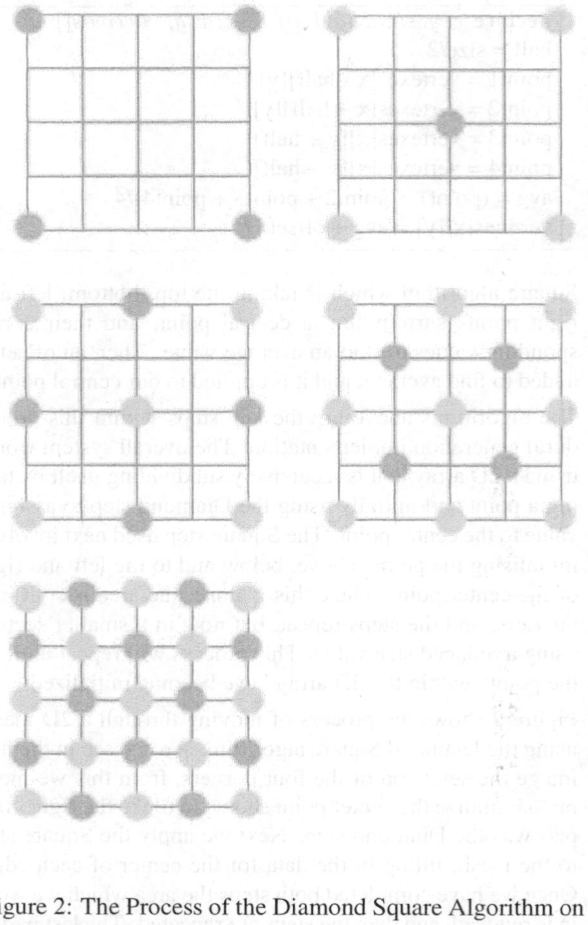

Figure 2: The Process of the Diamond Square Algorithm on a 5x5 grid

these, along with allowing for customisation of additional data points. This was achieved by creating several functions which would set up the scene, and create the terrain. The produced environments can be based on various map sizes, and heights, along with various colors or textures if required. This resulted in allowing for a scene to be set up and rendered using fewer lines of code, as well as allowing for more complex environments to be produced if required.

For optimizing the algorithms and effects applied much of the work was passed to the GPU of the device. When a scene is created, based on the required setup, the GPU will use different shader code, producing different effects. The simplest and greatest improvement was achieved by having the coloring of an environment based on the x, y and z coordinates of the vertex. The result of this style of processing helped to minimise the data which needed to be passed between the CPU and GPU, along with reducing the work carried out on the CPU. By comparison, other implementations require that additional texture information be passed to the GPU, including imaging and coordinate data. These techniques, though they can lead to some visually creative effects, do not fit well with the idea of procedural generation.

With WebGL we are limited by the number of vertices that are able to be drawn in a single GL.DrawElements function, some steps are needed to overcome this. The limitation occurs due to the indices using 16 bit for each data point, causing wrap around and other ill effects when trying to render over the limit of 65000 points. To work around this requires the use of multiple draw calls, based on multiple index arrays. This method splits up meshes which are over this limit into several smaller ones, and creates relating indices for each, along with using a repetitive draw function which will loop through each draw call and thus mesh.

The performance of this research plays a large role. To check this, an obj file was produced using the Diamond Square algorithm. For a mesh the size of 256 x 256, a file of 3.5 mb was produced. This would take several minutes to load in the file and set up the arrays in order to be rendered. Comparatively, a landscape created in JavaScript using the same algorithm was able to be loaded and set up within a matter of milliseconds. This is because when loading in the file it would need to be read, and parsed from a string to float. As seen in figure 3, it can be seen that a mesh of 256x256 would only take 34.8 ms to generate and load. This shows that a landscape which is generated is able to have a much larger scope, due to improved performance. Another upside of this method is that it saves in bandwidth as a large file does not need to be passed as only a small set of numbers are used to produce the area.

With these results it is clear to see the improvements made to generating terrain with WebGL for three reasons. Firstly, the speed in which a scene can be set up and rendered has been improved upon. Secondly, the limitations in the maximum numbers of vertices able to be rendered in one draw call have been worked around. Finally, we include optimizing the use of the GPU within this area of study.

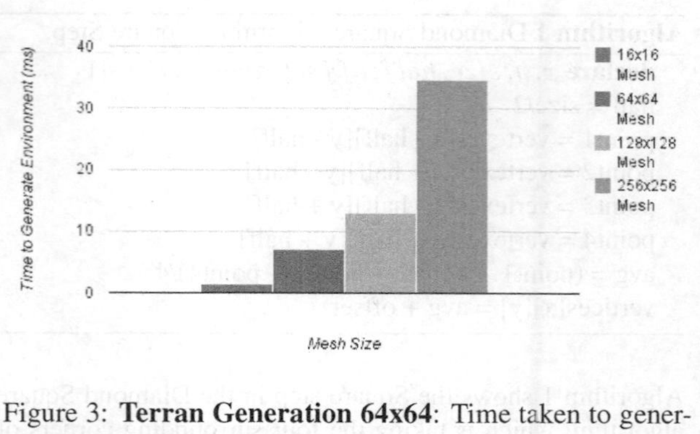

Figure 3: **Terran Generation 64x64**: Time taken to generate environments in various sizes

Figure 3 Shows the time taken for meshes of various sizes to be rendered. A mesh of 16 x 16 takes on average 1.5 milliseconds, while one of 64 x 64 takes 7.1 milliseconds.

A larger area such as 256 will still only take part of a second to create, with a timing of 34.7 milliseconds to generate the terrain.

4 Discussion

This research has resulted in various improvements in generating unique scenes in web based applications using WebGL. These include; the improved performance of producing unique terrain within a WebGL application, the ability to reuse these improvements by using a created set of utilities in future areas of research, scaling an area based on a the performance of a device, and the required level of detail has being addressed, along with created applications being support across a range of devices. Various landscapes have being produced, and have created challenges rendering.

The ability to create dynamic and various environments simply by using different random numbers allows for a larger and more immersive scene. This has been achieved through the use of the Diamond Square algorithm, as seen in figures 4, 5 and 6. Figure 4 displays a smaller mesh which is 16 x 16, this was generated in 1.5 milliseconds, but evidently it is very jagged as it has a low polygon count. In Figure 5 it is clear that by increasing the size the mesh produces a more fluid landscape, and this can be seen improving across all the meshes produced, such as in figure 6 and figure 1. This allows for a more unique terrain to be created with WebGL.

As research is able to be integrated into other projects, it is necessary to allow for it to be built upon and customised. One feature is that each data point of the mesh can have additional associated values assigned to it. This allows for a graphic engine to know when and how to produce another object within a scene. To produce a project using these utilities helps remove the need to manually set up a WebGL environment as this has been replaced with smaller functions to work with the other functions within the utility.

As a range of devices are able to run applications based on this research it is necessary to allow for the environment to be generated based on the device. The range in support hardware lead to the need to scale an area based on the processing power available. Conventional PCs and laptops ran the application smoothly across all ranges tested, but the larger terrains were slower to render on tablets and smart-phones, due to the limitations within the GPU. With the rendering side being affected it is necessary to, in this case, optimise the application to maximise the use of the CPU rather than the GPU. The process of creating the environment was slightly slower, but did not affect the performance of the application as greatly as the rendering. To overcome this we used smaller meshes with a smaller height limitation. This meant larger areas needed to be covered by each produced triangle, but with a smaller rise, which produced a smoother effect, and allowed for lower end devices

Figure 4: **Terrain Generation 16x16**: Landscape produced using the Diamond Square algorithm in WebGL. Map size is 16x16, this does correctly create a environment, but the edges are sharp, and could easily be improved on.

to run with noticeably improved performance.

With many of the produced landscapes exceeding the limitations of a single draw call within WebGL, this issue needed to be addressed. The cause was found to be the use of a 16 bit short to store the indices. This is intended to allow for applications to be cross platform, and work on a range of hardware. To overcome this, when necessary, once the mesh is created it will be split up, and each part draw in a different draw call. This is completed by creating a class which stores the numbers of meshes, along with each mesh within it. When the draw cycle begins, it is looped through using a different set of indices each time, for each mesh.

5 Conclusions

This research has produced a set of utilities to improve upon the limitations of WebGL and platform independent based graphics. The use of procedural generation enables the process of creating unique environments. Optimizations were made to maximise the use of the GPU, along with minimising bandwidth. The speed at which an environment is created has greatly increased, as the scene can be created without the need to load in a new file. The ability to run applications using this is also taken into consideration with the use of various techniques to create a smooth environment for the user.

While undertaking this research various problems were found with the current methods of achieving much of our

Figure 5: **Terrain Generation 64x64**: Landscape produced using the Diamond Square algorithm in WebGL. Map size is 64x64, here we see that the edges have become smaller, and smoother, helping to create more realistic environments.

Figure 6: **Terrain Generation 128x128**: Landscape produced using the Diamond Square algorithm in WebGL. Map size is 128x128, another improvement in creating a realistic scene within WebGL with noticeably fewer sharp edges, and a greater range in terrain created.

aim. These issues were comprised of the limit in elements able to be drawn at a single time, the size of a created mesh when loaded from a file, and the methods used to help smooth jagged edges.

In future this set of utilities will be added to, improving the creation of procedurally generated environments, with the addition of trees and water flow. It is hoped that with additional features such as these, creating a fully interactive and high quality environment will become simple and effective. We hope that once these future goals are complete, the use of procedural generation will make a substantial effect on how 3D applications are created and used in the Web.

In summary, procedural generation implemented with JavaScript has been shown to achieve significant reduction in bandwidth requirements and this is particularly useful in web-oriented scene generation applications.

References

[1] Anttonen, M., Salminen, A.: Building 3d webgl applications. Tech. Rep. Report 16, Tamperer University of Technology, Finland, Department of Software Systems (2011)

[2] Bailey, M., Cunningham, S.: Graphics Shaders - Theory and Practice. CRC Press, second edn. (2012), iSBN 978-1-56881-434-6

[3] Cantor, D., Jones, B. (eds.): WebGL Beginner's Guide. PACKT (2012), iSBN 978-1-84969-172-7

[4] Cozzi, P., Riccio, C. (eds.): OpenGL Insights. CRC Press (2012), iSBN 978-1-4398-9376-0

[5] Emilien, A., Bernhardt, A., Peytavie, A., Cant, M.P., Galin, E.: Procedural generation of villages on arbitrary terrains. Vis. Comput. 28, 809–818 (18 April 2012)

[6] Hearn, D., Baker, M.P.: Computer Graphics with OpenGL. No. ISBN 0-13-015390-7, Pearson Prentice Hall, third edition edn. (2004)

[7] Hendrikx, M., Meijer, S., Velden, J.V.D., Iosup, A.: Procedural content generation for games: A survey. ACM Trans. on Multimedia Computing, Communications and Applications 9(1), 1–22 (February 2013)

[8] Huisman, P.: Procedural content generation with use of a domain-specific language - Nature's recursive nature and other natural phenomena. Master's thesis, Centrum Wiskunde and Informatica, Universiteit van Amsterdam, Netherlands (15 August 2012)

[9] Ilcik, M., Wimmer, M.: Challenges and ideas in procedural modeling of interiors. In: Proc. Eurographics Workshop on Urban Data Modelling and Visualisation. pp. 29–30 (2013)

[10] Khaled, R., Nelson, M.J., Barr, P.: Design metaphors for procedural content generation in games. In: Proc. ACM CHI'13. Paris, France (27 April 2013)

[11] Kim, J., Kim, D., Cho, H.: Procedural modeling of trees based on convolution sums of divisor functions

for real-time virtual ecosystems. Computer Animation and Virtual Worlds 24, 237–246 (2013)

[12] Leist, A., Playne, D.P., Hawick, K.A.: Exploiting Graphical Processing Units for Data-Parallel Scientific Applications. Concurrency and Computation: Practice and Experience 21(18), 2400–2437 (25 December 2009), CSTN-065

[13] Longay, S., Runions, A., Boudon, F., Prusinkiewicz, P.: Treesketch: Interactive procedural modeling of trees on a tablet. In: Proc. Eurographics Symp. on Sketch-Based Interfaces and Modeling (2012)

[14] Lopes, R., Hill, K., Jayapalan, L., Bidarra, R.: Mobile adaptive procedural content generation (2013), delft University of technology, Netherlands

[15] Mandelbrot, B.B.: The Fractal Geometry of Nature. W.H. Freeman (1982)

[16] McMullen, T.H., Hawick, K.A.: Webgl for platform independent graphics. Tech. Rep. CSTN-185, Computer Science, Massey University, Auckland, New Zealand (October 2012), in 8th IIMS Postgraduate Conference

[17] McMullen, T.H., Hawick, K.A.: Improving platform independent graphical performance by compressing information transfer using json. In: Proc. 12th Int. Conf. on Semantic Web and Web Services (SWW'13). p. SWW4052. No. CSTN-174, WorldComp, Las Vegas, USA (22-25 July 2013)

[18] McMullen, T.H., Hawick, K.A., Preez, V.D., Pearce, B.: Graphics on web platforms for complex systems modelling and simulation. In: Proc. International Conference on Computer Graphics and Virtual Reality (CGVR'12). pp. 83–89. WorldComp, Las Vegas, USA (16-19 July 2012), cSTN-157

[19] Muehl, W., Novak, J.: Game Development Essentials - Game Simulation Development. Delmar (2008), iSBn 978-1-4180-6439-6

[20] Novak, J.: Game Development Essentials - An Introduction. Delmar, 3rd edn. (2012)

[21] Pirk, S., Stava, O., Kratt, J., Said, M.A.M., Neubert, B., Mech, R., Benes, B., Deussen, O.: Plastic trees: interactive self-adapting botanical tree models. ACM Trans. Graph. 31(4), 50:1–10 (Jul 2012)

[22] Powell, T.A., Schneider, F.: JavaScript: the complete reference. McGraw-Hill (2012), iSBN 9780071741200

[23] Prusinkiewicz, P., Lindenmayer, A.: The Algorithmic Beauty of Plants. No. ISBN 978-0387972978, Springer (1990)

[24] Saunders, K.D., Novak, J.: Game Development Essentials - Game Interface Design. Delmar, 2nd edn. (2013), iSBN 978-1-111-64288-4

[25] Vanegas, C.A., Kelly, T., Weber, B., Halatsch, J., Aliaga, D.G., Muller, P.: Procedural generation of parcels in urban modeling. Eurographics 31, 681–690 (2012)

[26] Wright, R.S., Haemel, N., Sellers, G., Lipchak, B.: OpenGL Superbible. No. ISBN 978-0-321-71261-5, Pearson, fifth edn. (2011)

HumMod-Golem Edition: large scale model of integrative physiology for virtual patient simulators

Jiří Kofránek[1,2], Marek Mateják[1], Pavol Privitzer[1], Martin Tribula[1], Tomáš Kulhánek[1,2], Jan Šilar[1,2], Rudolf Pecinovský[2]

[1]Charles University in Prague, Laboratory of Biocybernetics, Prague, Czech Republic

[2]Creative Connections, Ltd., Czech Republic

Abstract - *In teaching medical decision-making, comprehensive training simulators are of great importance. These must include models of various physiological subsystems, and also integrate them into a comprehensive whole. Medical simulators have recently become a highly sought-after commercial commodity. Like an airline pilot simulator, a medical simulator is controlled by a remote operator, who manipulates the simulated patient and chooses between various scenarios to simulate different maladies. The core of a medical training simulator is a complex model of the human body's internal physiological regulators, connected with a hardware simulator. Its detailed structure (the system of equations and the parameter values that feed into them) is usually not published, becoming a carefully-protected piece of trade secrets There are also open source models of integrated physiological systems. One is a large model by Coleman et al. called HumMod (http://hummod.org) implemented by thousands of XML files. Our implementation of this model in the Modelica language has brought a much easier description of the simulated complex physiological relationships than XML implementation. We uncovered several mistakes in the original model, and we have modified and expanded the original model (particularly in modelling acid-base homeostasis). Our new model is called HumMod – Golem Edition (http://physiome.cz/hummod), and will provide a new theoretical basis for medical training simulator. In its implementation we will use our web simulator creation technology.*

Keywords: Education, Modelica, Simulator, Virtual Patient

1 Introduction

"Tell me, I'll forget; show me and I may remember; involve me and I'll understand"—this ancient Chinese wisdom is also confirmed by modern learning approaches, where training simulators are widely applied.

Simulators make it possible to test the behavior of the simulated object without any risk—trying to land a virtual airplane, or provide diagnostic and therapeutic interventions for a virtual patient. Or in another medical example, monitoring the behavior of individual physiological systems in response to various pathological states and therapeutic interventions.

The connection the Internet allows between interactive multimedia environment and simulation models provides quite new pedagogical opportunities, particularly when it comes to explaining complex relationships, actively exercising practical skills, and verifying theoretical knowledge. The old credo of the pioneering 17th century pedgagoue John Amos Comenius—Schola Ludus, i.e. "school as a play" [4]—finds its application in incorporating multimedia educational play into training courses.

2 Virtual patient simulation

One of the most exciting innovations in the field of medical education is these virtual patient simulators [6]. Like an aircraft simulator, virtual patient simulation allows for implementing a quite new way of teaching where the student may practice diagnostic and therapeutic tasks in virtual reality, with no risk to the patient. Like an airline pilot simulator, a medical simulator is controlled by a remote operator, who maniuplates the simulated patient and chooses between various scenarios to simulate different maladies All the student's actions are monitored, and the simulator provides material for later debriefing the diagnostic and therapeutic performance of the students [7].

New opportunities for medical education are found in virtual 3-D worlds delivered over the internet. These can include a virtual patient—a programmed avatar linked to a simulation model—and there may also be an avatar controlled by the teacher [2].

The interface of educational simulators need not be merely a computer screen. The development of haptic scanning technology and virtual reality imaging has brought a new class of simulators. These simulators are designed for training practical performance of some medical tasks (cardio-pulmonary resuscitation, catheterization, endoscopy, patient intubation, etc.) on a patient mannequin. However, hardware virtual patient simulators have also been offered in increasing complexity designed for training medical decision-making. For example, the Norwegian company Laerdal (http://www.laerdal.com/) manufactures robotic virtual patient mannequins for the training of doctors and nurses. The American company CAE Healthcare (https://caehealthcare.com) is another successful manufacturer whose robotic virtual patient simulators provide a highly efficient (although costly) educational aid for the training of health care profesionals.

3 Scenario-driven and model-driven simulators

There are basically two approaches to managing the parameters in a virtual patient simulator.

1. ***Scenario-driven simulators.*** The behavior of these simulators is controlled by simulated disease scenarios. These scenarios are branched or statechart algorithms that respond to inputs (therapy, testing requirements, etc.), altering the parameters and showing the result. These simulators demand very complex scripts, which must be prepared by an experienced clinician. These scenarios can implement realistic results based on real patients, however, user inputs to these simulators usually consists of selecting from preset options. In these simulators it is difficult to program responses to fine-grained or quantity-based inputs (such as medication dosage, artificial ventilation settings, etc.).
2. ***Model-driven simulators.*** The behavior of these simulators is based on mathematical modeling of the physiological systems. Diseases and their treatment are simulated mainly by changing the parameters and some inputs of the model. The simulator reacts to user inputs and new values for the variables are calculated as the outputs of a mathematical model. The script requires correctly setting the model parameters for the simulated disease, which demands proper scenario debugging. On the other hand, these simulators allow entering quantified inputs (different doses of drugs, etc.). The effectiveness of this type of simulators is highly dependent on how realistic the model is. The detailed structure of these models—the system of equations and parameter values—is usually not published for commercial simulators, and becomes carefully guarded technological know-how.

4 Large-scale integrative physiology models for virtual patient simulators

Just as the theoretical foundation of an aircraft simulator is based on an airplane model, model-driven medical simulators are based on accurate models of the physiological systems in the human body. Models used as the theoretical foundation of virtual patient simulators include mathematical *models not only of individual physiological subsystems, but also their interconnections, thus forming a more complex unit.* The field of ***integrative physiology*** deals with the study of these connections. It seeks to describe physical reality and explain the results of experimental research, and also to create a formalized description of the how these physiological regulations are interconnected, and to explain their function in a healthy human and their misfunction in the presence of various diseases.

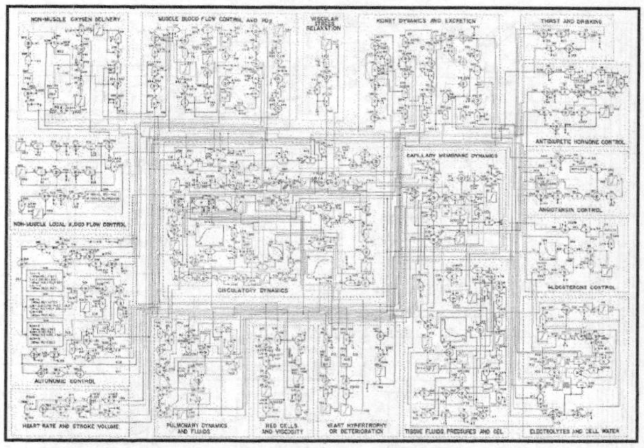

Figure 1: Guyton's 1972 blood circulation regulation diagram .

One of the first extensive mathematical descriptions of these interconnected subsystems was published in 1972, by A. C. Guyton and two other authors [9]. From the start, the article went far beyond the scope of the physiological articles of its time. Its heart was an extensive diagram pasted in as an appendix, resembling a drawing of some electronic device. However, instead of electronic components, the diagram showed interconnected computational blocks (multipliers, dividers, summators, integrators, functional blocks, and so on that symbolized mathematical operations performed with physiological variables. Instead of writing out a system of mathematical equations, Guyton et al. used a graphical representation of mathematical relationships (Figure 1). The whole diagram was a formalized description of how the circulatory system self-regulates and its context within the body, using a graphically expressed mathematical model.

This method was quite new then. Yet the comments and reasons given for assigning the various mathematical relationships were very brief. In 1973 and 1975, further monographs [10, 11] were published providing a more detailed explanation of a number of the approaches applied.

Guyton implemented this model in Fortran. Today, designing simulation models is facilitated by specialized software environments. Matlab/Simulink by Mathworks is one. It includes a graphical simulation language, Simulink, that can be used to set up a simulation model from individual components using the mouse—providing a model of software-based simulation parts that are connected to form simulation networks. Simulink blocks highly resemble the elements used by Guyton et al. in their formalized expression of the physiological relationships; indeed, their graphic design is the only difference (Figure 2).

This similarity inspired us to resurrect the classic Guyton diagram and transform it into a functional simulation model. We tried to preserve the same external appearance of the Simulink model as in the original graphic diagram—the layout, placement of wires, variable names , and even block numbers are the same (see Figure 3).

However, simulation-based visualization of the old

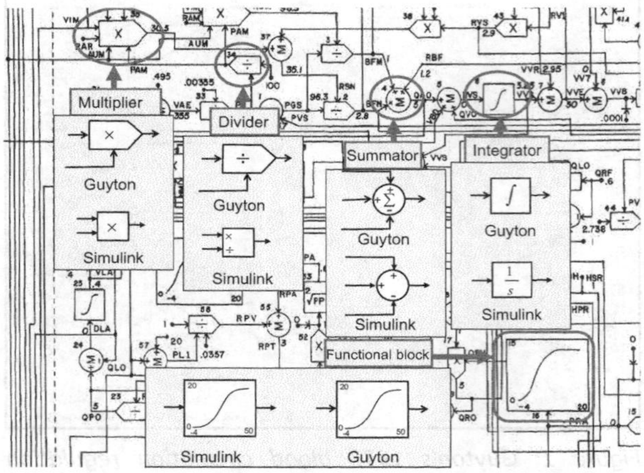

Figure 2: Blocks in the original Guyton notation, and the same blocks in Simulink.

diagram was not easy—namely, because there are errors in the original diagram! This is not a problem in a printed picture, but if we try to liven it up in Simulink, the model collapses immediately. For a detailed description of the errors and their corrections see [19]. Our Simulink implementation of the (corrected) Guyton model is available for download at http://www.physiome.cz/guyton. A Simulink implementation of a much more complex later Guyton model is available on this website as well. At the same time, a very detailed description is provided of all the included mathematical relationships, together with reasons for them.

In 1982 Thomas Coleman, one of Guyton's collaborators, created a model named ***Human***, designed primarily for educational purposes [5]. The model allowed for simulating a number of pathological conditions (cardiac and renal failure, hemorrhagic shock, etc.), and the impact of some therapeutic interventions (infusion therapy, effect of some drugs, blood transfusion, artificial pulmonary venti-

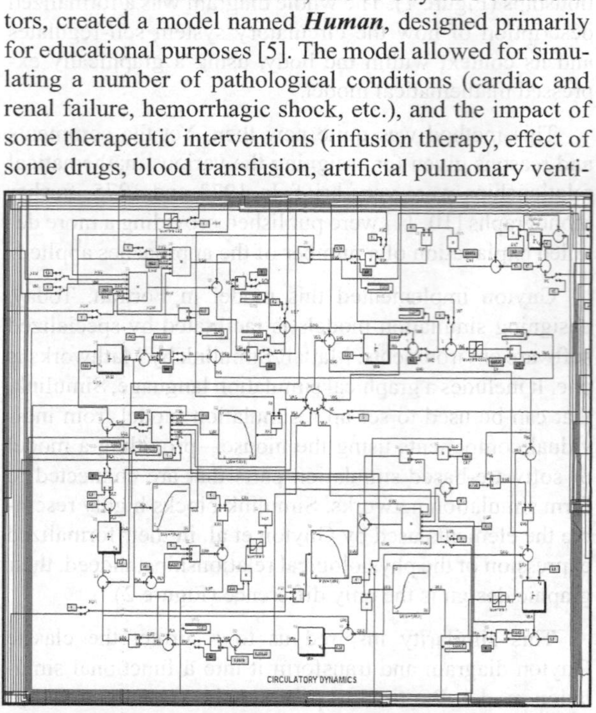

Figure 3: Circulatory dynamics – detail view of the central part of the Guyton's model implemented in Simulink, which shows blood flowing through aggregated parts of the circulatory system, and the pumping action of the heart.

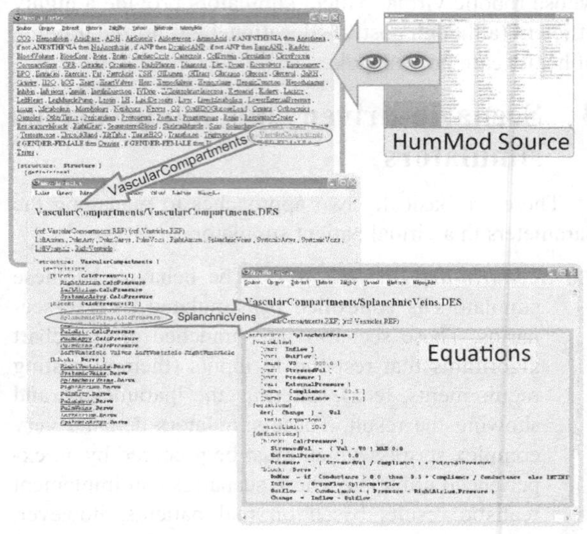

Figure 4: The visualization tool we created, which simplifies viewing of the HumMod simulator structure. This structure contains thousands of XML files, scattered across hundreds of directories, where relationships and links between them may not be apparent.

lation, dialysis, etc.).

Coleman's model was elaborated on in the large educational simulator ***Quantitative Circulatory Physiology (QCP)***. ***QCP*** can be downloaded and installed on a Windows computer. It includes a high number of variables (several thousand). The simulator allows for changing the values of approximately 750 parameters that modify physiological functions. The values of these parameters can be saved or read from an external file, which enables the user to prepare a number of scenarios for various pathological conditions. The authors of ***QCP*** have prepared many scenarios (as input files) for educational needs, and, together with appropriate comments, have made them available for free download from the ***QCP*** website. This simulator has proved useful in teaching [1].

The successor to the ***QCP*** simulator is ***Quantitative Human Physiology (QHP)***, renamed to ***HumMod***. This simulator supports the simulation of numerous pathological conditions, including the effect of the therapy. With more than 5000 variables, ***HumMod*** seems to provide the most extensive integrated model of physiological regulations available today. Unlike ***QCP***, whose mathematical background is hidden from the user in the C++ source code, HumMod's [12] authors decided to separate the simulator implementation from the description of the model equations, in order to make the model structure clear for a wider scientific community.

Unlike commercial virtual patient simulators, where the structure of mathematical model is hidden, ***HumMod*** is available as open source code (the model and the simulator are available to the public at http://hummod.org).

5 HumMod Golem Edition

HumMod's mathematical model is written in a

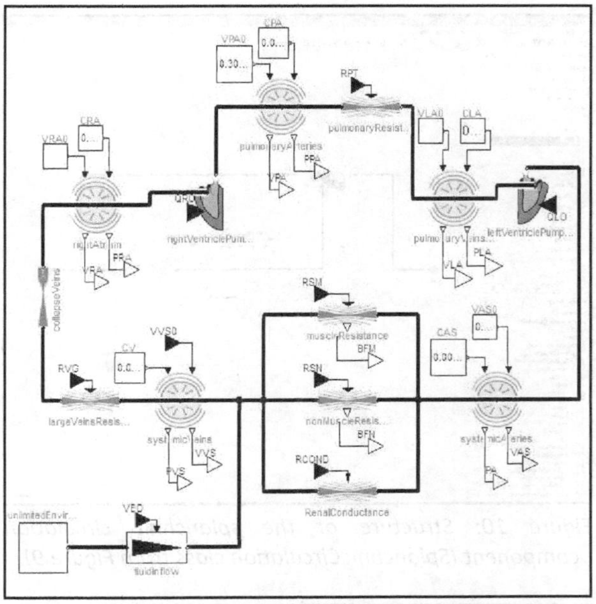

Figure 5: The same part of the model as in Figure 3, but implemented in Modelica. The model contains two connected pumps (the right and left ventricles of the heart), elastic vascular compartments, and resistances. In comparison with Figure 3, it can be seen that the model structure in Simulink resembles to a computational algorithm, while the model structure in Modelica shows more of the underlying structure of the modelled reality.

special XML language. The last version of HumMod (version 1.6) incorporates 4352 files spread across 1071 directories. Thanks to this fact, the model equations and their relationships are comprehensible only with difficulty, and many research teams developing medical simulators prefer to use older models as a basis for their own expansions—for example, the Guyton model of 1972 [9], or Ikeda's models from 1979 [13]. This is the path taken, for example, by the SAPHIR (System Approach for Physiological Integration of Renal, cardiac and respiratory control) international research team, as they found the source text of the ***QHP/HumMod*** model very difficult to read and understand for the project participants [21]. Similarly, Mangourova et al. [20] recently implemented a 1992 Guyton model [3] in Simulink, rather than the more recent (but poorly legible for them) version of ***HumMod*** created by Guyton's collaborators and students.

We were not discouraged by this difficulty, however, and have cooperated with the American authors of ***HumMod*** to improve ***HumMod***. We have designed a special software tool [16] that creates a clear graphic representation of the mathematical relationships used, visually representing the thousands of files of source texts used by the model (Figure 4). Besides other benefits, this has also been helpful in discovering some errors in the ***HumMod*** model.

Together with American authors of ***HumMod*** we are of the opinion that source texts for the models that are the foundation of medical simulators should be publicly available, given that they are the result of freely-available theoretical studies of physiological regulations—then it becomes easy to find out to what extent the model corresponds to physiological reality. The structure of our model, which is called ***HumMod-Golem Edition***, is published on our project website (http://physiome.cz/Hummod) in its source form, together with the definitions of all variables and equations. Unlike our American colleagues' implementation, our model is implemented in ***Modelica***, which makes it possible to provide a very clear expression of the model structure.

Modelica [8] is a modern simulation language. It is a non-proprietary, object-oriented, equation based language to conveniently model complex physical systems. It is often used to model mechanical, electrical, electronic, hydraulic, thermal, control, electric power or process-oriented subcomponents. Unlike other object-oriented languages, classes in Modelica may contain equations. Each class in Modelica can be externally represented by user defined icon. A component in Modelica therefore represents an instance of class for which equations or parameters are defined. Components (represented as icons) can be linked through connectors. The user graphically links these icons to create a system of equations. The structure of the model in Modelica therefore reflects the structure of the modeled system, unlike the model in Simulink, which expresses the structure of the calculation procedure rather than the structure of the modeled reality.

Unlike the block-oriented simulation environment in Simulink, the structure of Modelica models corresponds to the physical essence of the modeled reality (the compiler takes care of the "dirty work" of solving the resulting system of algebraic differential equations). Models in Modelica are, compared to those in Simulink, clearer and more self-documenting. This advantage can be demonstrated, for example, by comparing an implementation of the classic

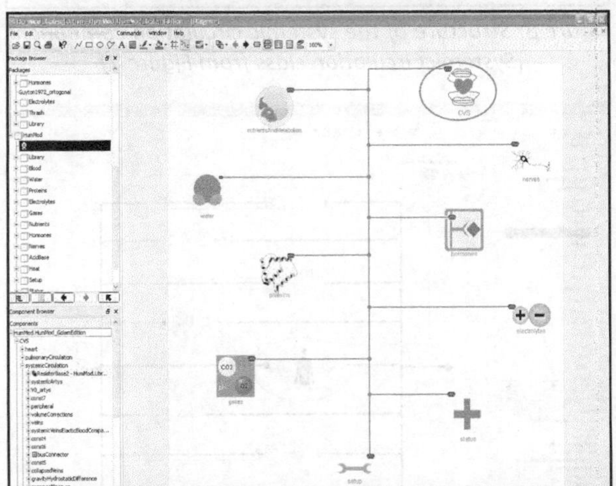

Figure 6: Structure of the HumMod model in Modelica. The model consist of the following components: cardiovascular (CVS class); nutritient and metabolism; water and osmolarity; proteins; O2, CO2 and acid-base regulation; electrolyte; nervous system regulation; hormone regulation; virtual patient status; and setup. All components are connected wtih bus connectors.

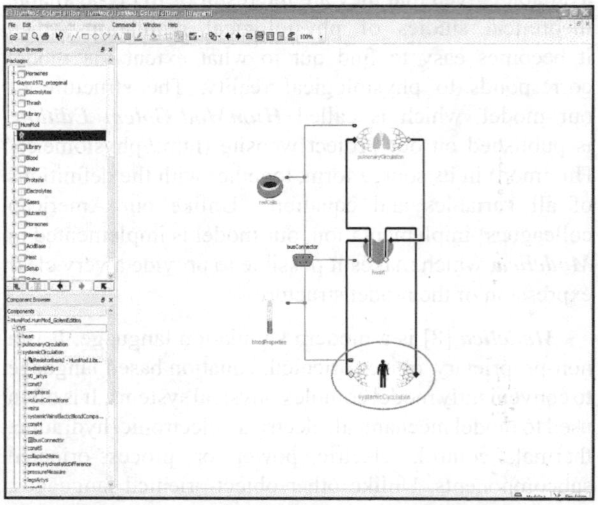

Figure 7: Structure of the cardiovascular component (CVS class from Fig. 6).

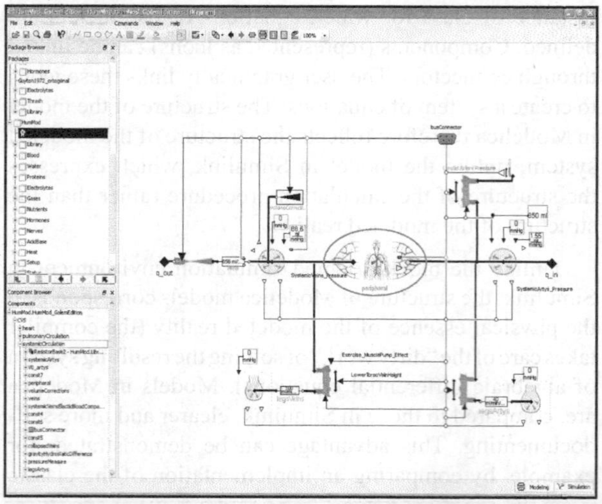

Figure 8: Structure of the systemic circulation component (SystemicCirculation class from Figure 7).

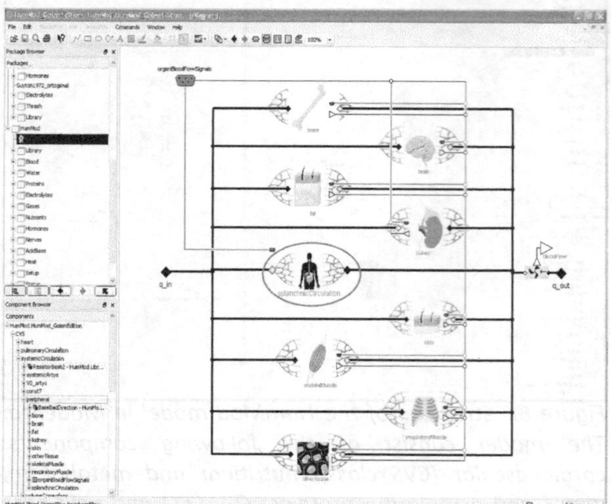

Figure 9: Structure of the systemic peripheral circulation component (Peripheral class from Figure 8).

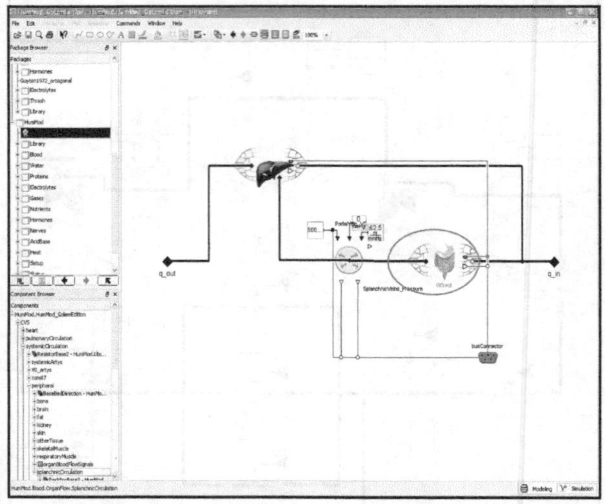

Figure 10: Structure of the splanchnic circulation component (SplanchnicCirculation class from Figure 9).

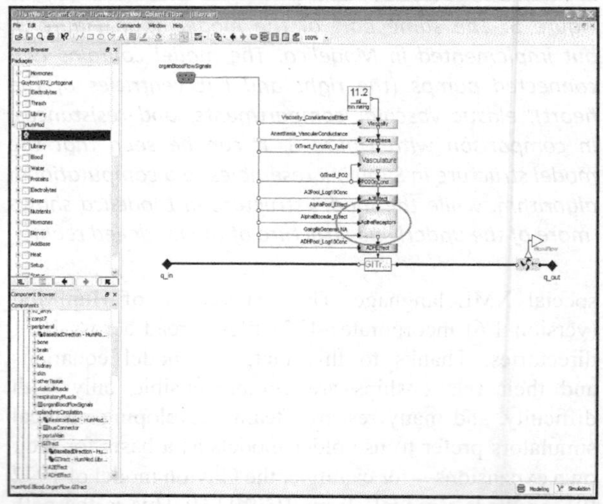

Figure 11: Structure of the gastrointestinal vascular resistance component (GITract class from Figure 10).

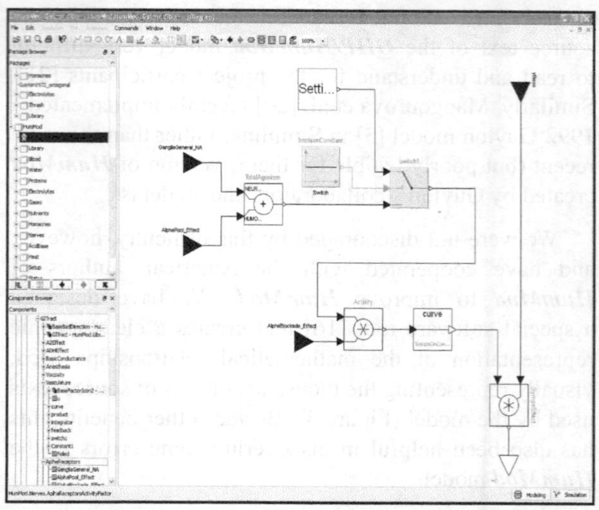

Figure 12: Structure of a component calculating the influence of alpha receptor stimulation on gatrointestinal vascular resistance (AlphaReceptors class from Figure 11).

Guyton model [9] in Simulink (Figure 3) and in Modelica (Figure 5)

The ***HumMod*** model has been modified and expanded, particularly in the field of blood gas transfer and regulation of acid-base homeostasis. Our goal is to create an educational simulator designed primarily for teaching emergency medicine, in which disorders of blood-gases and acid-base homeostasis occur frequently. Among other sources, our modifications stemmed from our earlier complex model of physiological regulations, the core of the educational simulator ***Golem*** [14].

See Figures 6–12 for illustrations of the hierarchic structure used by ***Hummod-Golem Edition***.

The model allows a user to simulate a number of physiological and pathophysiological actions—for instance, the failure of individual organs and organ systems, and the body's subsequent adaptation; the effect of any chosen therapy; response to physical load; and the body's response to a change of some external condition (for example, a rise in temperature). ***Hummod-Golem Edition*** provides a theoretical foundation, and is used by the medical educational simulator ***BodyLight***. However, its further development and identification are only the first challenges that must be faced. Another problem consists in programming the simulator itself as an educational aid. Our aim is to make the simulator available as a teaching aid through the Internet. Our web simulator design technology [15] (which is described in Figure 13) will be used in its design.

Instruction models (and apparently not only complex ones with hundreds of variables) in themselves therefore are not enough for efficient use in teaching. They must be accompanied by explanation of their application – using interactive educational applications at best. The possibility of using all advantages of virtual reality to explain complex pathophysiological processes arises only upon establishing connection between explanation and interactive simulation. In order to link the possibilities offered by interactive multimedia and simulation models in medical teaching, we have designed the concept of an Internet computer project, the ***Atlas of Physiology and Pathophysiology*** [17, 18], conceived as a multimedia instruction aid that should help to explain, in a visual way using the Internet and simulation models, the function of individual physiological subsystems, the causes and manifestations of their disorders – see http://physiome.cz/atlas. The Atlas thus combines explanation (using audio and animation) with interactive simulation play with physiological subsystems models, all available for free from the Internet.

6 From art to industry in designing of virtual patient simulators

Individual enthusiasts created the first educational programs at the turn of the 80s, excited by the potential of personal computers. Their time is long gone. Today, high-quality educational software must utilize the potential

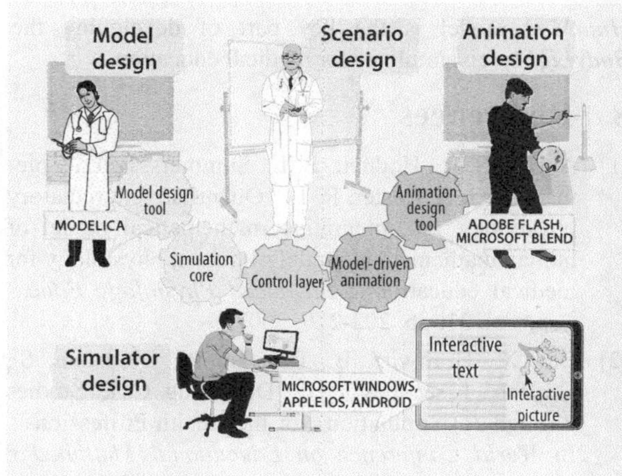

Figure 13: Our approach to designing interactive textbooks with model-driven animations.

of new information and communication technologies. This means it must be built on more than the diligence and enthusiasm of individuals. It is a demanding and complicated process, requiring a creative team of specialists across various professions: Experienced teachers whose scenarios provide the foundation of a good-quality educational application; system analysts who create the simulation models themselves; artists and UI designers who create the external form and software interface; and finally, information science specialists (programmers) who "stitch up" the whole application into its final form [15].

For such interdisciplinary cooperation to be efficient, numerous development tools and methodologies are needed for every stage of development; such tools and methodologies make the work of individual team members easier and help them to overcome interdisciplinary barriers. Considerable efforts must be devoted to the process of creating and mastering the tools, but it pays off in the end. With ***Golem/BodyLight***, just such a cross-disciplinary team was able to unify excellent underlying code (from ***HumMod***) with new visual and analytical clarity inspired by the Guyton model, to create a system which is more than the sum of its parts.

7 Conclusions

Complex hierarchical models of human integrative physiology are the key to model-driven virtual patient simulators. Such simulators include models of not only individual physiological subsystems, but also of their connection into more complex units. Modelica is a very convenient developing tool for designing these models.

The ***HumMod*** model clearly shows the benefits using the Modelica language. If we compare the complex structure of the original ***HumMod*** model written in XML [11] with implementations done in Modelica (Figures 6–12), we can clearly see that the implementation done in Modelica creates a transparent and legible model structure and therefore offers easier model modifications. Our Modelica implementetation of a modified and extended

HumMod model is the key part of developing the ***BodyLight*** web simulator for medical education.

8 References

[1] Abram, S. R., Hodnett, B. L., Summers, R. L., Coleman, T. G. & Hester, R. L. "Quantitative circulatory physiology. An integrative mathematical model of human mathematical model of human physiology for medical education."; *Advanced Physiology Education*, Vol. 31, pp. 202-210, 2007.

[2] Bai, X., Horowitz, B., Duncan, R., Glodstein, S., Graffeo, J., & Lavin, J. "Designing Case Studies through 3D Simulations for the Health Professions". In *World Conference on Educational Multimedia*; Hypermedia and Telecommunications, Vol. 2011, No. 1, pp. 907-910, 2011.

[3] cellML. "*Description of Guyton 1992 Full cardiovascular circulationmodel*"[Online]http://models.cellml.org/exposure/cd10322c000e6ff64441464f8773ed83/Guyton_Model_1-0.cellml/view

[4] Comenius, J. A. "*Schola Ludus, seu Encyclopaedea Viva*". Sarospatak, 1656.

[5] Coleman, T. G., Randall, J. E. "HUMAN. A comprehensive physiological model"; *The Physiologist*, Vol. 26, pp. 15-21, 1983.

[6] Cook, D. A., Erwin, P. J., Triola, M. M. „Computerized virtual patients in health professions education: a systematic review and meta-analysis"; *Academic Medicine* Vol. 85, No. 10, pp. 1589-1602, 2010.

[7] Cooper, D. D., Wilson, A. B., Huffman, G. N., Humbert, A. J. „Medical Students' Perception of Residents as Teachers: Comparing Effectiveness of Residents and Faculty During Simulation Debriefings"; Journal of Graduate Medical Education Vol. 4, No. 4, pp. 486-489, 2012.

[8] Fritzon, P. „*Principles of object-oriented modeling and simulation with Modelica 2.1*". Wiley-IEE Press, 2003

[9] Guyton, A. C., Coleman, T. G., & Grander, H. J. (1972). „Circulation: Overall Regulation" ; *Ann. Rev. Physiol.*, Vol. 41, pp. 13-41.

[10] Guyton, A. C., Jones, C. E., & Coleman, T. G. „*Circulatory Physiology: Cardiac Output and Its Regulation*". Philadelphia, London, Toronto: WB Saunders Company, 1973

[11] Guyton, A. C., Taylor, A. E., & Grander, H. J. „*Circulatory physiology II. Dynamics and control of the body fluids*". Phildelphia, London, Toronto: W. B. Saunders, 1975.

[12] Hester, R., Brown, A., Husband, L., Iliescu, R., Pruett, W. A., Summers, R. L., Coleman, T. "HumMod: a modeling environment for the simulation of integrative human physiology." *Frontiers in physiology*, Vol. 2, Article 12, pp. 1-12, doi: 10.3389/fphys.2011.00012, 2011.

[13] Ikeda, N., Marumo, F., Shirsataka, M. „A Model of Overall Regulation of Body Fluids"; *Ann. Biomed. Eng.* , Vol. 7, pp. 135-166, 1979.

[14] Kofránek, J., Anh Vu, L. D., Snášelová, H., Kerekeš, R., Velan, T. (2001). „GOLEM – Multimedia simulator for medical education"; *Studies in Health Technology and Informatics*, Vol. 84, pp. 1042-1046, 2001.

[15] Kofránek, J., Mateják, M., Privitzer, P. „Web simulator creation technology"; *MEFANET report*, Vol. 3, pp. 52-97, 2010.

[16] Kofránek, J., Mateják, M., Privitzer, P.: „HumMod - large scale physiological model in Modelica"; *Proceedings of 8th. International Modelica conference*, Dresden, Germany, March 20-22, 2011, Dresden, Linköping Electronic Conference Proceedings, pp. 713-724, 2011.

[17] Kofránek, J., Matoušek, S., Rusz, J., Stodulka, P., Privitzer, P., Mateják, M., Tribula, M. „The Atlas of Physiology and Pathophysiology: Web-based multimedia enabled interactive simulations"; *Computer methods and programs in biomedicine*, Vol. 104, No 2, pp. 143-153, 2011.

[18] Kofránek, J., Privitzer, P., Mateják, M., Matoušek, S. "Use of web multimedia simulation in biomedical teaching"; *Proceedings of the 2011 International Conference on Frontiers in Education: Computer Science & Computer Engineering, WorldComp 2011*, Las Vegas, Nevada, pp. 282-288, 2011.

[19] Kofránek, J & Rusz, J. „Restoration of Guyton diagram for regulation of the circulation as a basis for quantitative physiological model development"; *Physiological Research*, 59, pp. 897-908, 2010.

[20] Mangourova, V., Ringwood, J., Van Vliet, B. „Graphical simulation environments for modelling and simulation of integrative physiology"; *Computer Methods and Programs in Biomedicine*, Vol. 102, No. 3, pp. 295–304, 2011.

[21] Thomas, R. S., Baconnier, P., Fontecave, J., Francoise, J., Guillaud, F., Hannaert, P., Hernándes, P., Hernándes,A., La Rolle, V., Maziere, P., Tahi, F., White, R. J. „SAPHIR: a physiome core model of body fluid homeostasis and blood pressure regulation." *Philosophical Transactions of the Royal Society*, Vol. 366, pp. 3175-3197, 2008.

Acknowledgement

This paper describes the outcome of research that has been accomplished as part of research program funded by the Ministry of Industry and Trade of the Czech Republic by the grant FR—TI3/869 and by The Ministry of Education, Youth and Sports by the grant SVV-2013-266509.

email to corresponding author: kofranek@gmail.com

Predicting Hysteresis Loss in Hip Joint Implants

M. Hodaei, K. Farhang and N. Maani
Department of Mechanical Engineering and Energy Processes
Southern Illinois University Carbondale

Abstract : *Wear is an important issue in hip implants. Excessive wear can lead to toxicity and other implant associated medical issues such as patient discomfort and decreased mobility. Since implant wear is result of contact between surfaces of femoral head and acetabulum implant, it is important to establish a model that can address implant surface roughness interaction.*

A statistical contact model is developed for the interaction of femoral head and acetabulum implant in which surface roughness effects are included. The model accounts for the elastic-plastic interaction of the implant surface roughness. For this purpose femoral head and acetabulum implants are considered as macroscopically spherical surfaces containing micron-scale roughness. Approximate equations are obtained that relate the contact force to the mean surface separation explicitly. Closed form equations are obtained for hysteretic energy loss in implant using the approximate equations.

Keywords: Contact Mechanics – Roughness – Hip Implant – Wear – Energy Loss - Toxicity

1 Introduction

Hip joint serves as one of the most important load bearing joints in human body. Studies have shown that up to 5.5 times the bodyweight is tolerated by femur and pelvis during daily activities [1-3]. These include normal activities such as walking, going up or down a set of stairs, getting up or sitting down, carrying groceries or other loads. A hip joint provides, in addition to its load bearing ability, the needed mobility that includes extension, rotation, and flexion. Most importantly hip joints provide smooth articulation of limbs necessary for bi-pedal gait.

Hip joint malfunction may occur as a result of many factors. The most prevalent cause of hip joint surgical operation and hip joint replacement is osteoarthritis (OA). OA occurs when the cartilage fissuring is severe enough to a point where bone contact is initiated at the hip joint. OA is attributed to many causes [1] that include age, overuse, excessive loading, or flaw in the hip joint geometry referred to hip dysplasia. It is estimated that about 200,000 hip replacements occur in the United States due to hip joint OA. Other hip joint problems include osteolysis, avascular necrosis, neck fracture of femur [4-5-6]. The purpose of the present paper is not to address the causes of hip replacement, rather it is to address the performance of a hip joint after surgery.

Hip joint implant is designed to provide the same mobility and stability of the original functioning hip joint. Certainly, the design of hip joint implant needs to investigate all parameters such as wear, roughness, erosion, tribology, materials, and also many problems caused by surgical procedure including bone replacement. Some of these factors have been studied since about 50 years ago. About 50 years ago, McLaurin [7] investigated the manufacturing of hip prostheses. At that time, the design encountered wear problems because of metal on metal contact. Smith and Nephew [8] made an experimental model of hip joint using oxidized zirconium alloy technology in femoral head of hip joint to reduce wear and improve longevity in comparison with using ceramics for femoral head. In the last two decades, advances in imaging technology has allowed better preoperative data generation and improve preparation and planning of surgery [9-12]. A more recent work by Shapi et al. [13] allows preoperative measurement of the size of acetabular implant in total hip replacement.

Hiroyuki et al. [14] evaluated the effect of RF heating on hip joint implant during MRI examinations. They used two types of different implants in material and shapes. They found that the electrical characteristics of metallic implants have influence on RF heating. Maximum temperature was found to occur at the tip of the implants, location of large curvature. Zhang et al. [15] compared stress distributions between silicon nitride and cobalt-chromium-alloy in hip prostheses. The results related to stress distributions with the implanted silicon nitride hip resurfacing prostheses are very close to the corresponding stresses for health, intact femur bone. Scifert et al. [16] developed a new design to reduce the tendency of dislocation in Hip implants in patients. The authors claim that their proposed design increases stability of total hip joint and decreases by fifty percent stress distributions around impingement zone of polyethylene. Phillips et al. [17] used an elasto-plastic material model to show constitutive behavior of morsellised cortico-cancellous bone graft. Three 3D load scenarios related to walking, sitting, and standing were applied at the center of femoral head to check migration and rotation of the acetabular cup. Walking cause superior migration and rotation in abduction of the acetabular cup while sitting down and standing up cause posterior migration and rotation of the acetabular cup. Jonathon et al. [18] investigated dangerous effects of metal release from hip prostheses on patients.

Metal-on-metal hip prostheses failed in some patients due to the release of metal debris resulting in revision surgery.

Symptoms such as neurological impairment, cardiomyopathy, and hypothyroidism were reported in their study. Steens et al. [19] showed the effect of ceramic-on- ceramic toxicity in the blood can lead to impairment of hearing, sight, numbness in feet, and dermatitis in head and neck. Tower [20] also showed that the dangerous effects of metal debris in human blood pain such as onset of anxiety, major depression, tinnitus, high frequency hearing. loss, peripheral neuropathy, and cognitive decline. Alan and Swarts [21] investigated the effect of modularity on tapered cone of Margron hip prosthesis. Their study found that increased modularity can cause corrosion and crack, debris of particles, and metal ion generation. Brodner et al. [22] investigated the levels of serum cobalt in patients before and after implantation of non-cemented total hip arthroplasties. As a result, they show that the metal-on-metal prostheses produce detectable levels of serum cobalt in comparison with the ceramic-polyethylene prostheses as metal-on-metal prostheses generate some systemic release of cobalt.

This paper develops a contact mechanics model of hip joint taking into account the effect the surface finish property and surface roughness geometry of the implant. An elastic-plastic model of the spheres in contact representing the femoral and acetabular implants is developed.

The specific contribution of this paper includes:

- Inclusion of implant surface roughness in hip implant contact model
- Approximate equations relating the contact force to minimum mean plane separation in an explicit form
- Energy loss per cycle that include macro and micro geometry of the implant surfaces
- Characterization of hip implant natural contact frequency and contact damping

The results agree with the recent issues with hip implant failures when metal-on-metal is employed. The model presented is, therefore, a necessary first step in the prediction of possible wear in hip implants and issues related to wear borne toxicity in implant recipients.

2 Hip Contact Model:

The schematic diagram of a hip joint is shown in Fig 1. Figure 1 shows that force transfer to hip gives rise to contact force between the femoral head and acétabulés, whose shapes are approximated using spheres. Let R_1 and R_2 be the radii of curvature of the femoral head and acetabulum, respectively. Figure 2 details the contact between two spheres of radii R_1 and R_2. When roughness of the surfaces is incorporated into the contact model, it is expected that the load-carrying zone be defined by a minimum separation with symmetrically distributed pressure about the minimum separation. Since the number of contact points and their respective pressure depend on the mean surface separation of the two spheres, it is necessary to develop the expression for mean separation as a function of minimum separation and the geometries of the two spheres. In contact of femoral head with acetabulum, we confront a conformal contact. This is represented by the sphere contact in Fig. 1.

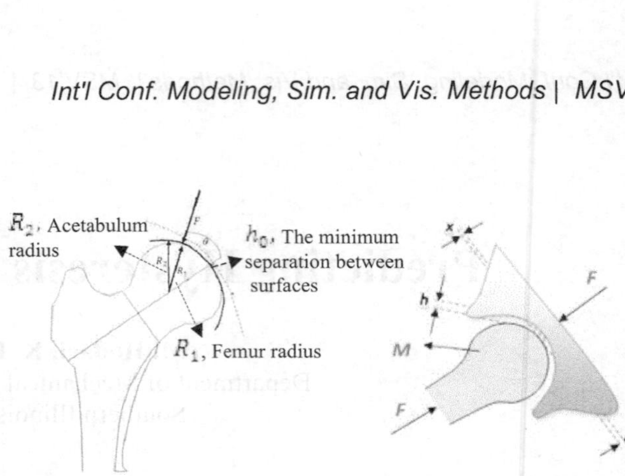

Figure 1. Schematic depiction of contact force in hip joint

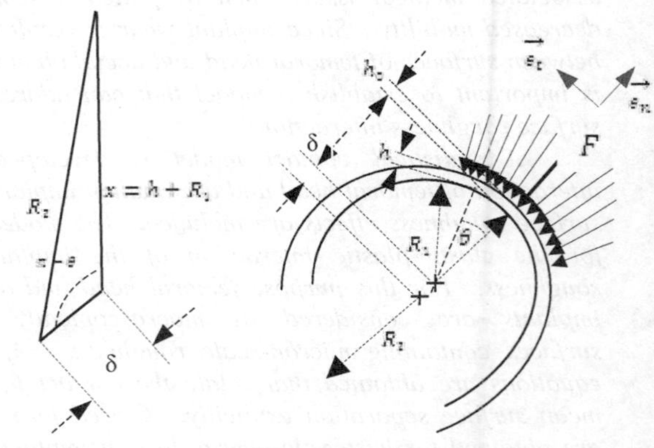

Figure 2. Spheres in internal contact

The schematic drawing of the mean spheres of the femoral head and the acetabulum surface in Fig. 2 shows that for a mean surface separation h_0, the offset between sphere centers, δ, can be expressed in terms of h_0.

$$\delta = R_2 - R_1 - h_0 \quad (1)$$

$$R_1 + h = x \quad (2)$$

Where, the triangle shown in Fig 2, clearly shows that the mean plane separation, h, can be found in terms of minimum separation, h_0, radii of the two spheres, R_1 and R_2, and the angular location measured with respect to the inner (smaller) sphere.

$$x = -\delta\cos\theta \pm \sqrt{\delta^2\cos^2\theta + R_2^{\,2} - \delta^2} \quad (3)$$

An acceptable solution in Eq. (3) must yield a positive x. Therefore,

$$x = -\delta\cos\theta + \sqrt{\delta^2\sin^2\theta + R_2^{\,2} - \delta^2} \quad (4)$$

Substitute for x in terms of R_1 and h and solve the resulting equation for h, the separation at location θ. We find from eq. (2) and (4),

$$h = R_2\left(\left(-\frac{\delta}{R_2}\right)\cos\theta + \sqrt{1 - \left(\frac{\delta}{R_2}\right)^2 \sin^2\theta}\right) - R_1 \quad (5)$$

Substitute for δ from eq. (1) to find

$$h = R_2\left(\left(-\frac{R_2-R_1-h_0}{R_2}\right)\cos\theta + \sqrt{1-\left(\frac{R_2-R_1-h_0}{R_2}\right)^2 \sin^2\theta}\right) - R_1 \quad (6)$$

Since the mean surface separation is defined, we can proceed to derive the contact force per unit nominal area due to elastic-plastic interaction of the roughness of the femoral and acetabulum surfaces. The contact force per unit nominal area can be expressed as follows [23],

$$P(h) = P_{ec}(h) + P_p(h) \quad (7)$$

Where, $P_e(h)$ is the elastic force per unit nominal area given by the following equation,[23],

$$P_e(h) = C\left(\int_h^{\infty}(s-h)^{\frac{3}{2}}e^{-\frac{s^2}{2}}ds - \int_{w_c+h}^{\infty}(s-h)^{\frac{3}{2}}e^{-\frac{s^2}{2}}ds\right) \quad (8)$$

Where,

$$C = \frac{4}{3\sqrt{2\pi}}E\eta\beta^{\frac{1}{2}}\sigma^2 \quad (9)$$

s and *h* are both dimensionless. s is the ratio of an asperity height over the standard deviation of asperity summit distribution, σ, and *h* is the ratio of the mean surface separation over σ. When the surfaces are pressed together, there may be locations within the contact zone where asperity interference results in onset of plastic deformation. Greenwood and Williamson [24] defines asperity critical interference to be the onset of plastic deformation. In following the CEB model [25], the authors employed the definition of the critical interference to formulate the elastic-plastic model of contact. In eq. (8) w_c represents the dimensionless critical interference. Greenwood and Williamson [24] defines plasticity index and critical interference for a surface as follows:

$$\psi = \frac{E}{H}\sqrt{\frac{\sigma}{R}} \qquad \omega_c = \left(\frac{H}{E}\right)^2 R$$

Where, *R* is the average asperity summit radius of curvature, *E* is the equivalent modulus and *H* is the hardness of the softer material. Letting $w_c = \frac{\omega_c}{\sigma}$ be the dimensionless critical interference, the plasticity index, ψ, is related to the w_c as follows

$$\psi = \frac{1}{\sqrt{w_c}} \quad (10)$$

Equation (8) uses a constant *C* and the dimensionless force expression in integral form for the elastic part of the surface interaction. *C* is defined as given by eq. (9), in which *E* is the reduced modulus of elasticity of the two surfaces, β is the dimensionless equivalent average asperity radius of curvature. The reduced modulus of elasticity is derived from the properties of the material used in the implant. It is given by the following equation

$$\frac{1}{E} = \frac{1-\nu_1^2}{E_1} + \frac{1-\nu_2^2}{E_2} \quad (11)$$

Where, E_1 and ν_1 are the modulus of elasticity and Poisson ratio of the femoral implant material and E_2 and ν_2 are those of the acetabulum implant. The equivalent asperity radius is found using

$$\frac{1}{\beta} = \frac{1}{\beta_1} + \frac{1}{\beta_2} \quad (12)$$

Where, β_1 and β_2 are the average asperity radius of curvature of the femoral and acetabulum implants, respectively. η is the asperity density per unit area. The force per unit normal area due to plastic interaction in an elastic-plastic contact is [58, 60].

$$P_p(h) = C\left(\frac{3}{2}\sqrt{w_c}\int_{w_c+h}^{\infty}[2(s-h)-w_c]e^{-\frac{s^2}{2}}ds\right) \quad (13)$$

To obtain the contact force along a particular direction, one must sum the force components along that direction due to infinitesimal contact forces that occur over an infinitesimal area. Sum of the contact infinitesimal contact forces along the line of symmetry will be result in the total contact force, whereas those along the normal to the line symmetry vanish. Sum the force components parallel to the radial line of symmetry with respect to the nominal contact area to find

$$F = \int_0^{2\pi}\int_{-\frac{\pi}{2}}^{\frac{\pi}{2}} P(h)R^2 \sin\theta \cos\theta \, d\theta d\phi \quad (14)$$

Where, *R* is the equivalent macro radius of curvature of the spheres representing femoral and acetabulum implants

$$\frac{1}{R} = \frac{1}{R_1} + \frac{1}{R_2} \quad (15)$$

The integral in eq (14) can be reduced to the following

$$F_n = 4\pi\sigma^2\int_0^{\frac{\pi}{2}} P(h)R^2 \sin\theta \cos\theta \, d\theta \quad (16)$$

It will prove beneficial to express eq (16) as an explicit function of the minimum separation, h_0. Since *h* is a function of integration variable Θ, eq (6), the integral in eq (16) can only be found numerically. As a result, we set out to find an approximate relation between contact force *F* and the minimum separation h_0. It will be shown in the next section that the contact force may be estimated using a function of the form $\aleph e^{-ch_0^{b_1}}$.

2.1 Dependence of Coefficients on Hip Radii

In this section acetabulum and femoral radii are used as parameters in the approximate expression relating contact force to minimum mean surface separation. It can be shown that the approximate equation is of the following form

$$F_{na}(h_0, R_1, R_2) = \aleph(\psi, R_1, R_2)e^{-ch_0^{1.2}} \quad (17)$$

The values are generated for various femoral head radii, ranging from 5 mm to 25 mm. Where, the coefficients $\aleph$ and *c* are expected to depend on the geometry of the hip and the plasticity index.

$$F_n(h_0, R_1, R_2) = 4\pi\sigma^2\int_0^{\frac{\pi}{2}} P(h)R^2 \sin\theta \cos\theta \, d\theta \quad (18)$$

In obtaining the approximate equation, the femoral radius is varied, and the acetabulum radius is assumed to be 0.2 mm larger than the femoral radius. Femoral radius is varied from 5 mm to 25 mm [61] while in each case acetabulum radius is kept 0.2 mm larger.

2.2 Dependence of Coefficients on Plasticity Index ψ

In this section, approximate functional relationships between the coefficients and plasticity index are established for plasticity index ranging 0.3 to 1.3. Keep in mind that for surfaces characterized by $\psi < 0.6$ the surface is considered predominantly elastic, while for $0.6 < \psi < 1$ the surface is viewed as elastic-plastic.

$$N(\psi, R_1, R_2) = a(\psi)R_1^2 + b(\psi)R_1 \quad (19)$$

$$a(\psi) = a_3\psi^3 + a_2\psi^2 + a_1\psi + a_0 \quad (20)$$

$$a_3 = -6.179 \times 10^{-5}, a_2 = 1.65 \times 10^{-4},$$
$$a_1 = -1.237 \times 10^{-4}, a_0 = 7.132 \times 10^{-5} \quad (21)$$

Likewise, the fitted function for b is

$$b(\psi) = b_3\psi^3 + b_2\psi^2 + b_1\psi + b_0 \quad (22)$$

with coefficients

$$b_3 = -0.012313, b_2 = 0.032885,$$
$$b_1 = -0.024663, b_0 = 0.010218 \quad (23)$$

The function $c(\psi)$ is defined as follows

$$c(\psi) = c_0 + c_1\psi + c_2\psi^2 + c_3\psi^3 \quad (24)$$

Where,

$$c_3 = -0.118687, c_2 = -0.069481,$$
$$c_1 = 0.513741, c_0 = 1.7366 \quad (25)$$

Finally, plasticity function with low percent error for $a, b,$ and c is

$$F_{na}(h_0, R, \psi) = [a(\psi)R_1^2 + b(\psi)R_1]e^{-c(\psi)h_0^{1.2}} \quad (26)$$

The max error between the approximate and original elastic-plastic contact force is less than 5% over the entire range of parameters considered.

2.3 Energy Loss in Hip Implant

The contact between femoral and acetabulum implant surfaces consists of asperities experiencing elastic and plastic deformation. A close look at the loading and unloading process reveals that both energy loss and elastic recovery are involved in the process. During the increase in contact load both elastic and plastic deformations can occur at asperity deformation level. However, during unloading asperities undergo only elastic recovery. Therefore, the load and unload process will follow different paths, resulting in hysteresis type energy loss in the hip joint contact.

We can employ the approximate equations for elastic-plastic contact and purely elastic contact to represent the loading and unloading process mathematically. The force during loading is denoted $F_{nL} = \alpha_{1L}e^{\alpha_{2L}h_0^{\alpha_{3L}}}$ and that during unloading, $F_{nU} = \alpha_{1U}e^{\alpha_{2U}h_0^{\alpha_{3U}}}$. Based on the results of the previous section, the respective coefficients of contact force during load and unload are as follows:

$$\alpha_{1L} = a_L(\psi)R_1^2 + b_L(\psi)R_1 \quad (27)$$

$$\alpha_{2L} = -c_L(\psi) \quad (28)$$

$$\alpha_{3L} = \alpha_{3U} = 1.2 \quad (29)$$

$$\alpha_{1U} = a_U(\psi)R_1^2 + b_U(\psi)R_1 \quad (30)$$

$$\alpha_{2U} = -c_U(\psi) \quad (31)$$

To study energy loss and storage in a hip joint, we consider an equilibrium contact force. For example this may correspond to an individual standing still and a contact force equal to the equilibrium force exists between femoral head and acetabulum. The equilibrium contact force is associated with an equilibrium minimum mean plane separation, h_0. A disturbance from equilibrium is denoted x. Therefore, to study the behavior of the contact near an equilibrium state, we can use the contact force equations above. Depending on the nature of the disturbance, the load may increase from equilibrium or decrease from it. If the load is increasing from equilibrium then both elastic and plastic contacts must be included in the calculation of contact force. If the load is decreasing from the equilibrium state, then only elastic contacts contribute, since this is a load recovery process. The following expressions will be adequate to account for either load change scenarios.

$$F_{nL}(h_0, x) = \alpha_{1L}e^{\alpha_{2L}(h_0-x)^{\alpha_{3L}}} \quad (32)$$

$$F_{nU}(h_0, x) = \alpha_{1U}e^{\alpha_{2U}(h_0-x)^{\alpha_{3U}}} \quad (33)$$

Here F_{nL} denotes the normal contact load due to both elastic and plastic interaction of surface roughness, and F_{nU} is the normal contact force due to only elastic interaction of the roughness. When the disturbance is small, the above force equations can be written in linear form using truncated Taylor series expansion of F_{nL} and F_{nU} about the equilibrium minimum separation.

$$FL_{nL}(h_0, x) = -\left(\frac{h_0^{\alpha_{3L}-1}\alpha_{1L}\alpha_{2L}\alpha_{3L}e^{h_0^{\alpha_{3L}}\alpha_{2L}}}{1!}\right)x + \alpha_{1L}e^{\alpha_{2L}h_0^{\alpha_{3L}}} \quad (34)$$

$$FL_{nU}(h_0, x) = -\left(\frac{h_0^{\alpha_{3U}-1}\alpha_{1U}\alpha_{2U}\alpha_{3U}e^{h_0^{\alpha_{3U}}\alpha_{2U}}}{1!}\right)x + \alpha_{1U}e^{\alpha_{2U}h_0^{\alpha_{3U}}} \quad (35)$$

Figure 3 illustrated the contact forces along with their linear estimates about an equilibrium position for a relatively high plasticity index. The area between the load and unload forces represents energy loss per cycle. Figure 4, shows a similar force history corresponding to a lower value of the plasticity index. As expected the area between the load and unload phases are reduced to zero for a plasticity index of 0.5, since it corresponds to elastic behavior of contact. It is a simple task to estimate the energy loss per cycle.

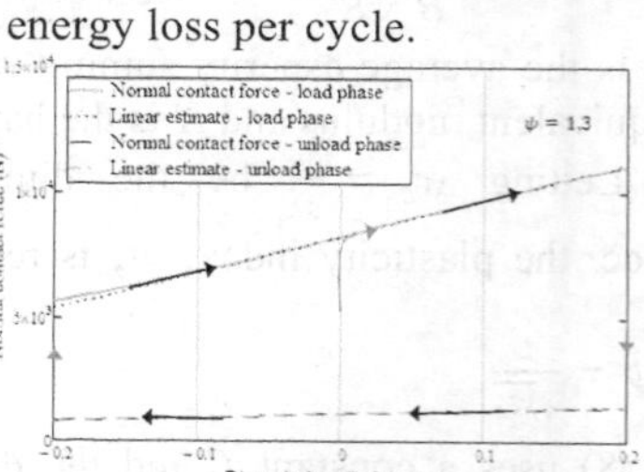

Figure 3. The schematic of load – unload phases in high plastic zone

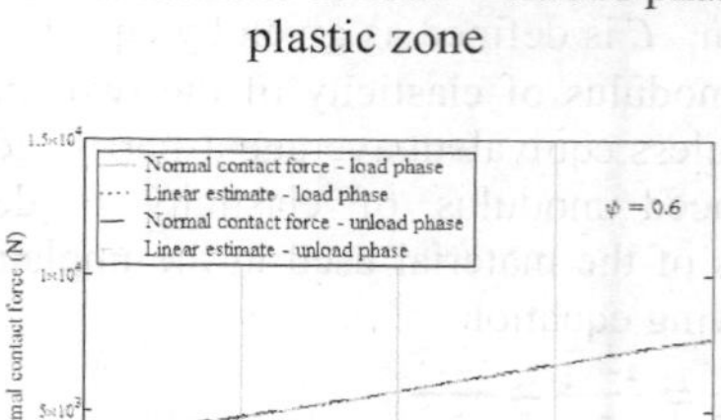

Figure 4. The schematic of load – unload phases in low plastic zone

We can perform integration of force over displacement in the load and unload phases and obtain the energy loss in a single cycle. For amplitude of oscillation of x_a from equilibrium, we can express the energy loss per cycle as follows.

$$E = \int_{-x_a}^{x_a} F_{nL}\, dx - \int_{-x_a}^{x_a} F_{nU}\, dx \quad (36)$$

That can be simplified by using the linear approximation of each load function in eqs (34) and (35). We find

$$E_L = 2Cx_a\left(\alpha_{1L}\, e^{\alpha_{2L} h_0^{\alpha_{3L}}} - \alpha_{1U}\, e^{\alpha_{2U} h_0^{\alpha_{3U}}}\right) \quad (37)$$

E_L is the energy loss per cycle. The energy per cycle can be expressed in dimensionless form by dividing eq. (37) by C x_a. So the dimensionless energy loss per cycle is

$$E_L = 2\left(\alpha_{1L}\, e^{\alpha_{2L} h_0^{\alpha_{3L}}} - \alpha_{1U}\, e^{\alpha_{2U} h_0^{\alpha_{3U}}}\right) \quad (38)$$

Figure 5 illustrates dimensionless energy per cycle and plasticity index as functions of dimensionless critical interference. When critical interference is low (high plasticity index), the interference enters the plastic regime for less contact load. Therefore, energy loss per cycle is higher for low critical interference. As critical interference increase, the number of asperities experiencing plastic interference decrease, thereby, reducing the energy per cycle. This is clearly shown to be the case in Fig. 5.

A similar plot, which directly relates energy loss per cycle to surface roughness, is shown in Fig. 6. In this case the abscissa represents the dimensionless average radius of curvature. It is observed that as dimensionless asperity summit radius of curvature is increased (surface is made more smooth) the energy loss per cycle decreases.

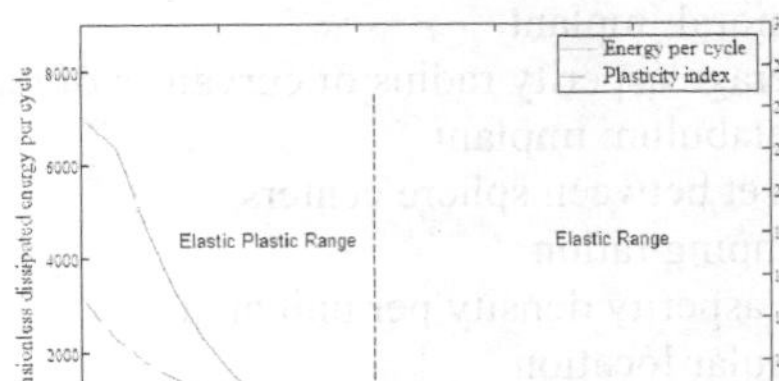

Figure 5. Dimensionless energy loss per and surface plasticity index versus critical asperity interference.

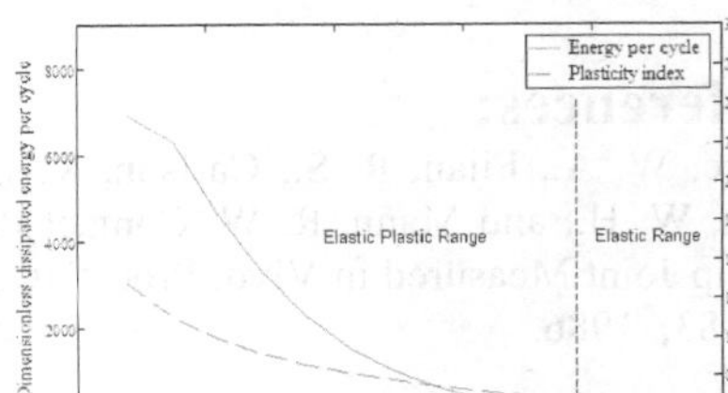

Figure 6. Dimensionless energy loss per cycle and surface plasticity index versus dimensionless average asperity summit radius of curvature

Recent legal litigation regarding the use of similar implant material shed light on the difficulty faced in using similar material in hip implant replacement. Cobalt-Cobalt implant was alleged to result in excessive degradation of implant material, generating unacceptable amount of wear debris to the level of presenting toxicity in the patient. Based on the present study, use of Cobalt-Cobalt implant would require a very high level of surface finish to reduce plastic deformation. Consider, for example, the equation for plasticity index given by Greenwood and Williamson [59]

$$\psi = \frac{E}{H}\sqrt{\frac{\sigma}{R}}$$

Table 1. Material and surface properties used

Parts	*Materials*	*Young's Modulus*	*Poisson's Ratio*	*Geometry (mm)*
Femoral Head	*Cobalt-Chromium-Alloy*	*200 Gpa*	*0.3*	*Sphere Radius 5-25 mm*
Acetabulum	*Polyethylene*	*0.64 Gpa*	*0.4*	*Sphere Radius 6-26 mm*
Surface Properties				
property	*values*			
η *(asperity/area density)*	$11 \times 10^{10} \frac{1}{m^2}$			
σ *Standard deviation*	0.5×10^{-6} m			
β *Mean asperity rad (R/σ)*	*200*			
E equiv. elasticity modulus	7.572×10^{5} Gpa			

For Cobalt-on-Cobalt implant we can use the properties in Table 1 to find E = 62 GPa and H = 700 MPa. For average dimensionless asperity summit radius of curvature $\beta = R/\sigma$ = 4600, we obtain a surface plasticity index of ψ= 1.3 which puts deformation in the plastic range. In fact to ensure that contact is in the elastic range, the surface finish must be enhanced to a degree that would result in β = 21,600, an unrealistically high number. This result is consistent with the latest news regarding the failure of many implants involving metal-on-metal material.

Figure 6 corresponds to typical ranges when dissimilar materials are used in hip implant. For Cobalt-Polyethylene, we use E = 0.75 GPa, and H = 120 MPa (Table 1) for the Polyethylene, the softer material, and β = 25, the surface plasticity index ψ = 0.953, putting the contact in the elastic-plastic range, whereas for β = 112, the plasticity index reduces to ψ = 0.586, yielding elastic contact. The plot in Fig. 6 well represents this range. The advantage of using dissimilar material is clearly shown in the above discussion. It is easy to obtain surface finish that would yield an elastic interaction at the contact of femoral head and acetabulum implant if one employs dissimilar material, while using similar material, such as Cobalt-Cobalt, is quite problematic since to guarantee elastic contact the surface finish requirement are not attainable.

3 Closing Remarks

This paper has developed an elastic-plastic contact model of hip joint implant. The model treats femoral and acetabulum implants as spherical solids in internal conformal contact and accounts for the roughness effects of both surfaces. An equation relating force to minimum mean surface separation was derived using statistical integral over contact region of effective interaction. Approximate equation describing force explicitly in terms of minimum separation was obtained and used to find closed-form equation for contact energy loss per cycle. It is shown that energy loss per cycle varies with plasticity index of the surface of the weaker implant. For an assumed lump mass representation at contact of implant, the utility of the approximate equations were exemplified by deriving expressions for contact natural frequency and damping ratio.

The specific contribution of this paper includes:

- Inclusion of implant surface roughness in hip implant contact model
- Explicit function for hip implant for a considerable range of hip implant joint sizes
- Energy loss per cycle related to macro and micro geometry of the implant surfaces
  - Closed-form equation for hysteristic energy loss per cycle was obtained using load/unload process at the hip implant surfaces. The energy per cycle was related explicitly to the material properties and surface statistics of the implant.

Simulation of load/unload process on hip implant using similar material, Cobalt-Cobalt, and dissimilar material, Cobalt-Polyethylene, for the femoral head and acetabulum showed that:

- Similar implant material was more prone to plastic deformation, thereby suggesting the increased possibility of wear. Cobalt-Cobalt contact required an unreasonably high surface finish to minimize plastic energy loss. Such high requirement of surface finish is impractical and even if possible would be highly costly.
- Dissimilar implant material was shown to be superior in that it is easier to guarantee elastic contact so that the plastic energy loss is minimized for a practical range of surface roughness.

The above result is consistent with recent issues related to the use of similar material in hip implant. Recent litigation won by an implant patient in California against Johnson and Johnson related to failed implant due to the generation of excessive wear and the resulting toxicity. According to the news, the reason was primarily due to the use of metal-on-metal in the hip implant. Many more lawsuits relating to the metal-on-metal contact in hip implants against Johnson and Johnson are being submitted to the courts.

The potential usefulness of the results on estimation of hip implant contact frequency and damping can involve the issue of potential vibration and noise generation. These not only can result in accelerated fatigue wear of implant surfaces but also can relate to implant recipient's comfort level.

4 Nomenclature

C	a surface constant
E	equivalent modulus of elasticity of the two surfaces
E_1	modulus of elasticity of the femoral implant
E_2	modulus of elasticity of the acetabulum implant
E_L	energy loss per cycle
F	total contact force
F_{nL}	normal contact load due to elastic-plastic interaction of roughness
F_{nU}	normal contact load due to elastic interaction of roughness
h	mean plan separation
h_0	minimum separation
m_0	mass of femoral head
$Pe(h)$	elastic force per unit nominal area
$Pp(h)$	plastic force per unit nominal area
$P(h)$	contact force per unit nominal area
R_1	radius of femoral head
R_2	radius of acetabulum
s	ratio of an asperity height over the standard deviation
w_c	critical interference
x	a disturbance from equilibrium
x_a	amplitude of oscillation
α_{1L}, α_{2L}, and α_{3L}	coefficients in the approximate function for loading phase
α_{1U}, α_{2U}, and α_{3U}	coefficients in the approximate function for unloading phase
β	dimensionless equivalent average asperity radius of curvature
β_1	average asperity radius of curvature of the femoral implant
β_2	average asperity radius of curvature of the acetabulum implant
δ	offset between sphere centers
ζ	damping ration
η	the asperity density per unit area
θ	angular location
υ_1	Poisson ratio of the femoral implant
υ_2	Poisson ratio of the acetabulum implant
σ	standard deviation of asperity height
ψ	plasticity index
ω_n	natural frequency

5 References:

[1] Hodge, W. A., Fijan, R. S., Carlson, K. L., Burgess, R. G., Harris, W. H., and Mann, R. W. Contact Pressures in the Human Hip Joint Measured in Vivo. Proc Natl Acad Sci USA 83,. 2879-83,. 1986.

[2] Bergmann,G.,Deuretzbacher, G., Heller, M., Graichen, F., Rohlmann, A.,Strauss, J., and Duda, G. N. Hip Contact Forces and Gait Patterns from Routine Activities. J Biomech 34,. 859-71,.2001.

[3] Bergmann, G., Hip98: Data Collection of Hip Joint Loading on CD-Rom. Free University and Humboldt University, Berlin, 1998.

[4] Pramanik, S., Agarwal, A., K., and Rai, K., N. Chronology of Total Hip Joint Replacement and Materials Development. Trends Biomater. Artif. Organs,19,.1,.15-26,.2005.

[5] Charbonnier, C., Schmid, J., Kolo-Christophe, F., Magnenat-Thalmann, N., Becker, C., and Hoffmeyer, P. Virtual Hip Joint: from Computer Graphics to Computer-Assisted Diagnosis. Eurographics, 2009.

[6] Montecucchi P. C., "Total Anatomic Hip Prosthesis. Montegen,540 Beverly Court, Suite1- Tallahassee FL 32301 – USA, Via G. Dezza n. 24 - 20144 Milan – Italy; 2002.

[7] Mc Laurin, C. A. Hip disarticulation prosthesis. Report 15, Prosthetic Services Centre, Department of Veterans Affairs, Toronto, 1954.

[8] Richards, S., and Richards, N. Artificial Hip Joints: Applying Weapons Expertise to Medical Technology, E&TR 1994.

[9] Klein, M. Using Data in Making Orthopedic Imaging Diagnoses. Advances in Experimental Medicine and Biology 44,.104-111,.2005.

[10] Yusoff, S. F. Knee Joint Replacement Automation Templates. M.sc Thesis, UniversitiKebangsaan Malaysia, Bangi, Malaysia 2009.

[11] Arora, J., Sharma, S., and Blyth, M. The Role of Pre-operative Templating in Primary Total knee Replacement. Knee Surgery, Sports Traumatology, Arthroscopy, 13,.3,.187-189, 2005.

[12] Kosashvili, Y., Shasha, N., Olschewski, E., Safir, O., White, L., Gross A., and Backstein, D. Digital Versus Conventional Templating Techniques in Preoperative Planning for Total Hip Arthroplasty. Can J Surg. 52,.1,. 6–11,.2005.

[13] Shapi, A., Sulaiman, R., Hasan, M. K., and Kassim, A.Y. M. An Automated Size Recognition Teqnique For Acetabular Implant In Total Hip Replacement. International Journal of Computer Science & Information Technology (IJCSIT) 3,.2,.2011.

[14] Hiroyuki, M., Takayoshi, H., Yoshitake, U., Shuji, U., Nobuyoshi, T., and Osamu, N. Evaluation of RF Heating on Hip Joint Implant in Phantom during MRI Examinations. Japanese Journal of Radiological Technology, 66,.7,.25-733,. 2010.

[15] Zhang, W., Titze, M., Cappi, B., and Writz, D. C. Improved Mechanical Long-Permrealiability of Hip Resurfacing Prostheses by Using Silicon Nitride. J Mater Sci: Mater Med , 21,.3049-3057,. 2010.

[16] Scifert, C. F., Brown, T. D., and Lipman, J. D. Finite Element Analysis of a Novel Design Approach to Resisting Total Hip Dislocation. Clinical Biomechanics ,14,. 697-703,.1999.

[17] Phillps, A. T. M., Pankaj, P., Howie, C. R., Usmani, A. S., and Simpson, A. H. R. W. 3D Non-linear Analysis of the Acetabular Construct Following Impaction Grafting. Computer Methods in Biomechanics and Biomedical Engineering. 9,.3,.125-33,.2006.

[18] Jonathon, R. Campbell, P., and Mathew, P. E. Metal Release from Hip Prostheses: Cobaltand Chromium Toxicity and the Role of the Clinical Laboratory. Clinical Chemistry & Laboratory Medicine. 51,.1,.213-220,. 2013.

[19] Steens, W., Foerster, G. V., and Katzer, A. Severe Cobalt Poisoning with Loss of Sight after Ceramicmetal Pairing in a Hip—a Case Report. Acta Orthopaedica, 77., 5., 830–832. 2006.

[20] Tower, S. S. Arthroprosthetic Cobaltism Associated with Metal on Metal Hip Implants. BMJ, 344:430., 2012.

[21] Alan, M. K., and Swarts, E. Corrosion of a Hip Stem With a Modular Neck Taper Junction.The Journal of Arthroplasty, 24,.7,. 2009.

[22] Brodner, W., Bitzan, P., Meisinger, V., and Kaider, A. Elevated Serum Cobalt with Metal-on-Metal Articulating Surfaces. The Journal of Bone and Surgery, 79-B,.316-21,. 1997.

[23] Sepehri, A. and Farhang, K. An Extension of CEB Elastic-Plastic Contact Model. Proceedings of the STLE/ASME International Joint Tribology Conference, San Diego, California, 22-24,. 10., 2007.

[24] Greenwood, J. A., and Williamsom, J. B. P. Contact of Nominally Flat Surfaces. Proceeding of the Royal Society of London. Series A, Mathematical and Physical Sciences, 295., 1442., 1966.

[25] Chang, W. R., Etsion, I., and Bogy, D. B. An Elastic-Plastic Model for the Contact of Rough Surfaces. ASME J. Tribal, 109,2., 257-263., 1987.

[26] Walker, J. M., and Goldsmith, C. H. Morphometric Study of the Fetal Development of the Human Hip Joint: Significance for Congenital Hip Disease. The Yale Journal of Biology and Medicine, 54.,411-437., 1981.